MEMBERSHIP OF THE BOARD OF DIRECTORS

The Job Top Executives Want No More

Also by Dimitris N. Chorafas

STRATEGIC PLANNING FOR ELECTRONIC BANKING
ELECTRONIC FUNDS TRANSFER
APPLYING EXPERT SYSTEMS IN BUSINESS
ENGINEERING PRODUCTIVITY THROUGH CAD/CAM
THE ENGINEERING DATABASE
FOURTH GENERATION PROGRAMMING LANGUAGES
INTERACTIVE WORKSTATIONS
PERSONAL COMPUTERS AND DATA COMMUNICATIONS
MANAGEMENT WORKSTATIONS FOR GREATER PRODUCTIVITY
HANDBOOK OF DATA COMMUNICATIONS AND COMPUTER NETWORKS
SOFTWARE HANDBOOK: ANALYSIS, DESIGN, PROGRAMMING
INTERACTIVE MESSAGE SERVICES
BANKING AUTOMATION
TELEPHONY: TODAY AND TOMORROW
LOCAL AREA NETWORKS
DBMS FOR DISTRIBUTED COMPUTERS AND NETWORKS
INFORMATION SYSTEMS IN FINANCIAL INSTITUTIONS: A Guide to Strategic
    Planning Based on the Japanese Experience
MICROPROCESSORS FOR MANAGEMENT: CAD, CAM, AND ROBOTICS
OFFICE AUTOMATION – THE PRODUCTIVITY CHALLENGE
DATABASES FOR NETWORKS AND MINICOMPUTERS
INTERACTIVE VIDEOTEX – THE DOMESTICATED COMPUTER
MONEY: THE BANKS OF THE 80s
COMPUTER NETWORKS FOR DISTRIBUTED INFORMATION SYSTEMS
IMPLEMENTING NETWORKS IN BANKING AND FINANCIAL SERVICES
(with Heinrich Steinmann)

Membership of the Board of Directors

The Job Top Executives Want No More

Dimitris N. Chorafas

MACMILLAN
PRESS

First published 1988

Published by
THE MACMILLAN PRESS LTD
Houndmills, Basingstoke, Hampshire RG21 2XS
and London
Companies and representatives
throughout the world

Filmsetting by Vantage Photosetting Co. Ltd
Eastleigh and London

Printed in Hong Kong

British Library Cataloguing in Publication Data
Chorafas, Dimitris N.
Membership of the board of directors: the
job top executives want no more.
1. Directors of corporations — Great
Britain
I. Title
658.4'22   HD2745
ISBN 0–333–46366–8

To Konrad D. Fuchs and Alan J. Rowe for their contributions to the art of management

Contents

Foreword

Konrad D. Fuchs

'Structure follows strategy', one of the fundamental principles of general management, is equally valid for the top of the organisational structure of any business organisation. In connection with the Board of Directors, however, this includes the question of the role of the latter in developing, enhancing and supporting corporate strategy.

The changing economic, technical, international, social, cultural, legal and political corporate environment creates the changing framework of growing challenges and risks at the same time. It requires new and changing corporate strategies which impact heavily on the structure and function of one of the very important assets of any economy: the way entrepreneurial, managerial and financial elements are integrated for the benefit of the corporation and the economy.

Various developments, which are not new at all, such as corporate failure or crises or takeovers, economic or legal pressures from various sides, occasionally lead to the notion of the institution of the Board of Directors being in crisis.

The reader of Professor Chorafas's newest book will more clearly than before see that there was and is no crisis. However, more demands from the environment and strategy of corporations place more demands on the Board of Directors, the top of the corporations. Long-term corporate success is also the result of a successful synchronisation process, and vice versa – as many cases in this book demonstrate.

Corporate history started with the corporate ownership and entrepreneurial role in one person or family enterprises. The trend of the separation of ownership – which culminates in millions of direct or indirect stockholders – and the delegation of the entrepreneurial function to professional managers has resulted in the dual role of the board: its role as corporate management, and its role in supervising corporate management. The great strength in the broad legal framework of American corporate constitutions is the flexibility for individual company solutions as to the balance between both roles (management v. supervisory role), the balance of executive to non-executive members, its substructures such as committees, etc.

The question of checks and balances of management and supervision started with the institutional point of view (what is best for the corporation and its owners?). In more recent times there has been a certain trend to include additional 'external interests' such as employees, customers, minorities, consumer groups in the Board of Directors. This trend, which – in the case of employee representation – is quite advanced in some European countries, has several dimensions in respect of the board's respective functions to manage and to control. In general this trend favours the emphasis on more control and a certain tendency to a separation of the management function from the control function, which coincides with the distinction between non-executive and executive directors.

Corporate law, for example in Germany, where the unified Board of Directors of Anglo-Saxon origin already has for more than half a century been separated into the external 'supervisory board' (where for more than three decades employee representatives have accounted for half of the board members with almost full voting rights) and the internal 'management board', and an individual can be a member of only one of them. Nevertheless many companies are bringing more and more questions on corporate policy and strategy to the supervisory boards if only for deliberation and major corporate decisions are often subject to supervisory board approval.

The EEC plans concerning a harmonisation of European corporate law allow both the unified or the dual board system. Summarising this short historical and continental tour one can see there is a trend of convergence in the basic structure and function of the Board of Directors. Considering global economic challenges, integration and competition this is not a surprising trend.

Professor Chorafas's book addresses most of the issues to improve effectiveness and efficiency of the Board of Directors to manage and control modern corporations: its role in developing and enhancing corporate policy, strategic planning and control, its role in corporate consolidation, mergers and acquisitions, its role in making better decisions for planning and control by training programmes and better management information for board members, its role in executive management recruitment, etc. He also addresses the quantitative and qualitative composition of boards which match future corporate demands and ways to reduce corporation and directors' risk, board recruitment, etc.

This book, which combines the knowledge and experience of a long and diversified academic and management consulting life with hundreds of organisations will serve for most present or future members of Board of Directors as a very useful reflection of common issues and possible directions for improvement.

In addition I hope that many non-members of boards, both inside and outside corporations, will improve their understanding of one of the most important and responsible institutions in modern society: the Board of Directors.

DR KONRAD D. FUCHS
Professor in Banking,
Vice-Chairman of the Board of Management,
and Executive Vice President,
First Austrian Bank, Vienna

Alan J. Rowe

Dr Chorafas clearly shows that the crucial role of the corporate director is dealing with the major changes confronting today's organisations as a consequence of restructuring, take-overs, mergers, etc., the unrelenting competition, and a turbulent economic environment fired by fluctuating oil prices, constantly shifting exchange rates, disarmament talks and possible flare-ups in regional wars. The corporate director can bring to bear an objective perspective on how best to cope with this treacherous environment while at the same time ensuring appropriate performance and profitability. Without this perspective, management can too easily respond in a manner that can prove disastrous to the organisation and to the shareholders.

The author has recognised a salient problem confronting today's organisation: How to attract and retain board members in order to focus more effectively on satisfying the information needs that reflect the requirements of a knowledge society. Precisely because of the complexity confronting managers and board members, we have to look beyond the normal measures used to determine effective performance. Decision styles – the ways in which individuals perceive information, solve problems, reason about consequences and make choices – have a significant relationship to managerial performance.

Chorafas has shown the relationship between decision styles and the traits desired in the board members. In addition to the normal professional expertise that is expected, board members will have to have the ability to recognise future requirements and consequences of decisions that are made. This style is described as the 'Conceptual' in the Rowe decision style model. It reflects both high cognitive complexity and orientation to future opportunities using creative, inductive reasoning and judgement based on beliefs and values. Research on presidents and chairmen of the board in 80 major US corporations highlighted the fact that over 90 per cent of the persons interviewed had a Conceptual style, in addition to other styles.

A major issue confronting organisations is the question of who to attract and how best to utilise the talents of board members. Because of the excessive amount of litigation in the US, many otherwise qualified board members have not accepted positions on boards that would benefit from their knowledge, skills and perspective. It appears that legislation will be required to protect the rights of board members so that they, in turn, can protect the rights of shareholders. Board members will increasingly be required to be involved with operational information using computer-based systems to supply them with the requisite knowledge. They will utilise more sophisticated tools such as simulation models and expert systems to augment their reasoning power when considering future alternatives.

This combination of human expertise with computer power portends the direction in which organisations will have to move to utilise board members appropriately and to assure survival in an extremely hostile, competitive environment.

DR ALAN J. ROWE,
Professor of Organisation and Management,
University of Southern California, Los Angeles, California

Prologue

The indispensable man, the man who commands the enterprise, is not a mere technician. He is the animator, the promoter, the planner, the organiser, the person who values above all the character qualities of hard work, of creative imagination, of internal drive, and of unbiased judgement. Perfection in the preparation, daring in the execution, submission to the facts and impartiality in regard to his own interests will be found in varying degrees in all great industrial leaders. There exist people who do things well and accomplish their distant objectives; there exist people who bring, wherever they go, order, clarity and success. There exist others who bring confusion and unhappiness.

The *gifted* executive prepares himself over long, tedious periods of time to become the man at the centre of industrial destinies. For destiny cannot be left to chance. More failures, more alibis, less constructive accomplishments are often the results of applying the fallacious idea that not men but the nasty notion of chance and of supernatural forces run the affairs of the world.

In no company, large or small, local, national or international, whether in manufacturing, distribution or finance, can the members of the board of directors afford to be less than gifted executives. Therefore, whatever has been stated in the preceding paragraphs is applicable to the members of the board.

This means preparation. Industrial leaders who advance do so because, other things being equal, they obtain more results than others. Yet few people ever realise how hard such men have to work to obtain results: it is hard and often lonely work. In business, in industry, in finance, in religion, in war or in the affairs of the state, time has honoured the ancient axiom of command: 'To try, to fail, to struggle, to win, and to know how to be alone.' It takes effort to achieve it.

We live in a time of breathtaking scientific and technological developments, but the true pace of advance is not in the soul-less matter of science. It is inside the human mind. Evolution and progress, the way we make it, require a new infrastructure. This in turn implies original forms of industrial leadership. At every moment the executive needs to depart from the 'old reality' because of new developments, concepts, and tools. He cannot afford to waste his time and power in vain speculation about what might have been, and he knows that no system is good for ever, that the moment a policy or a means is inefficient, inadequate or obsolete he must have the courage to abandon it.

Here exactly the need for physical and moral courage starts; and with it the need for insight, for creative imagination, for speculation, intuition, calculation and foresight. One of the principal justifications for the job the executive holds is the assumed capacity of its holder to complete the exploration of a given course of action in simulation before he undertakes it in fact. It is precisely at this point that incompetence most frequently reveals itself. The executive fails in his job because he did not expect the unexpected, not because he did not do his best to avoid the rocks as soon as he saw them, but because he should have been aware of their existence without the need to see them.

In practice the whole problem is far more complex, since every executive has to deal with human beings and so does the organisation as a whole. Ideally the executive seeks to induce his subordinates to work in a co-ordinated fashion towards common objectives, and to do so with enthusiasm and imagination. The trouble is that enthusiasm and imagination conflict with co-ordination; individualism is the negation of conformity.

This text is written for members of the boards of directors and for the senior management of corporations. It brings together facts and theory in a pragmatic, comprehensive form. The book starts with a hot subject on which Chapter 1 focuses: *Why is board membership the job top executives want no more?* The exodus from the board is considered from different angles – from the the long lists of litigations to personal accountability and the impact of a changing environment.

Chapter 2 discusses objectives: what they are, why they are necessary, how they can be clarified, explained, tested and set. Chapter 3 focuses on how a strategic plan can be made. The emphasis is placed on a winning mentality, but also on the formalisation of corporate planning. The separation of ownership and management promotes this basic notion of strategic perspectives. This provides the background for strategic planning, which is explained in Chapter 4.

Duties of the members of the board of directors, as well as the distinction between inside and outside directors, are discussed in Chapter 5. Chapter 6 focuses on the business of the board: choosing the top executives, deciding on policy matters, making the important deliberations for the survival of the firm. Several Japanese examples are referred to. They are the result of a research project conducted in Japan in September 1986, where policy making and strategic planning – by industrial firms, financial institutions, and state organisations – could be appreciated.

Chapter 7 elaborates on the strategic role of corporate policy; Chapter

8 on the qualities a board member needs and the salient problems he is facing; Chapter 9 on the lifelong learning necessary to keep up the skills and know-how of corporate directors. How to satisfy the information needs of the board is the subject of Chapter 10.

Louis Sorel, my Professor of Business Strategy at UCLA (University of California at Los Angeles), used to say that more companies fail because their products and services are out of tune with the market than for any other reason. This is the subject of Chapter 11. The risk of product obsolescence and of the failure to respond to market drives can be magnified both with national and with international operations. The distance between decision-makers and the domain where the action takes place adds more to the challenge – and to the risk, as documented in the discussion on *Zaitech*. Chapters 12 and 13 address the problem of organising for international operations, and suggest structural solutions.

Whether local, national, or multinational, the modern firm has another fear: litigation. Chapter 14 treats its social impact, reflects on the Sherman Act in the United States, then focuses on information technology which is one of the most foggy fields when it comes to the law of the land.

Products can be acquired, if not developed in-house. The theme of Chapters 15, 16 and 17 is mergers, acquisitions, disinvestments, risk capital and corporate raiding. Through practical, everyday examples success and failure are demonstrated, the whole subject culminating in the question: 'How profitable can a consolidation policy be?'

Chapter 18 is rich with reflections and examples on partnership and conflict, particularly the relationship which exists (or in other cases should exist) between government and industry. Hence again, Japan is taken as a positive case study.

The text concludes with an Epilogue. It focuses on individual decision styles, discusses qualifications for board membership, emphasises the importance of staying involved as well as elaborating one's homework in a detailed manner, and challenges the reader with the idea of establishing metrics and measurements at board level.

This book is practical and for good reason. Theories span the gap between what an executive seeks to accomplish and the means he selects to attain these ends.

But practical examples are the bridges that relate a director's personal philosophy to the management policies he follows; these policies to particular programmes; these programmes to specific practices; these practices to his own decisions.

Let me close by expressing my thanks to everyone who contributed to making this book successful: to my colleagues for their advice, to the organisations I visited in my research for the insight, to Keith Povey for his editorial work, and to Eva-Maria Binder for the drawings, typing and index.

PROF. DR DIMITRIS N. CHORAFAS
Valmer and Vitznau

1 Risks, Challenges and Benefits from Board Membership

Concerned about increasing legal problems and faced with unprecedented time demands, many directors are quietly stepping down from board memberships. Prominent executives confide that when their current terms expire they will not stand for re-election to the boards of directors they now serve. An increasing number of cognisant and well-known executives are turning away all invitations to serve as board members. This has a heavy toll on a number of troubled companies, which need strong directors. Though unthinkable some ten or even five years ago, some companies are forced to employ professional recruiters to search for top executives willing to do board duty. Even the headhunters are having a tough time.

The result is a trend toward smaller boards, fewer meetings, and more inside directors. Board composition is shifting toward senior managers who are dependent on the chief executive officer (CEO) for their livelihood and less likely to challenge him. And there is a compound effect. This shift comes just as many boards face proposals for takeovers, divestitures, stock repurchases, and management buyouts. Some fear that the changing landscape of board membership will result in increasing stiffness, that is, a condition affecting the arteries of companies, resulting in loss of function. Though symptoms differ, others think that the desertion of board membership by the most able people might be a contagious disorder that can prove fatal.

Confronted with demanding issues relating to new product policies, buyouts, financial crises, and marketing challenges, boards are increasingly in need of careful scrutiny by strong directors. Membership of the board has taken on new dimensions. Directors today are expected to study ever more complicated strategic and financial issues, with *increased likelihood of being sued*. If a crisis surfaces, such as an unwanted takeover offer, board members can suddenly face weeks or months of constant meetings and phone calls.

There is also a challenge in terms of policy. Outside directors can be strongly independent overseers who ask tough questions and go around the entrenched power structure to find out what is wrong. The deterrent to this approach is that one does not make friends and influence people in the boardroom or elsewhere by raising hard questions that create embarrassment or discomfort for management.

As a cover story was to suggest,[1] Charles R. Schwab was not an outside director at BankAmerica Corp. Yet neither was he part of the inner circle. Having sold in 1983 his brokerage firm to the bank holding company for stock, he stayed on to run Charles Schwab and Co. taking a seat on the board.

Like Ross Perot at General Motors, Schwab emerged as an outspoken critic of the management's handling of operations and problem loans at the Bank of America. As a result he ran into a problem common among board members who assert independent views. This is the other side of the coin in the change characterising board membership.

The alternative for an outside director is to operate as a rubber-stamp for management, thus acting as a club member and also reducing the workload an activist policy brings up. Either way, the position is a hot seat. Activist directors run the risk of being labelled troublemakers and of losing a vital network of business contacts. Rubber-stamp directors take an even bigger gamble. The probability has vastly increased that they will be sued for not properly looking after shareholder interests. Some statistics tend to suggest that from 1986 onwards board members have a 20 per cent chance of being party to a shareholder suit. Directorships are no longer the cosy existence they once were. And there are the symptoms of a wasting disease.

American boards spend too much time protecting their members from personal liability and their companies against takeovers – even if the latter might sometimes be desirable. British boards stubbornly retain the characteristics of clubs, while worrying about being the next victims of the ailments afflicting the United States. German boards have found no magic solutions in their experiment with worker directors which started in the Hitler years. They more or less ignore the worker representatives. Japanese boards are big and slow – which may be all right for small, insulated firms, but not for global corporations.

THE EXODUS FROM BOARD MEMBERSHIP

There are large differences between the business cultures of different countries. Furthermore, statistics about boards and their behavioural aspects are scant outside the United States. It is simply not possible to make generalisations with confidence, but some specific examples can help.

The first boards were formed in the United States in the eighteenth century. They were largely gentlemanly forums made up almost entirely of the company's owners. Outsiders did not join boards until the nineteenth century. This typically started with the company's auditors and legal counsels. Though many people fail to realise it, it was only in the early 1960s that US companies began to emphasise the election of outsiders, under pressure from Washington and Wall Street. By the 1970s outsiders had become a majority on the boards of many large corporations. This has been the situation until last year.

Yet, while in the background of the government's and Wall Street's drive for outside directors was *independence of opinion*, there are a lot of so-called outside directors who are not all that independent. They are close friends of the chief executive officer, the company's banker, lawyer, or top management consultant.

In spite of this apparent contradiction, many management scholars and financial analysts tend to think that the rise of outsider directors has had an impact. It has helped to make boards less insular and more conscientious. Others, however, disagree. Theirs is the opinion that members of the board everywhere tend too often to underplay the interests of those they are elected to serve: the shareholders.

The basic thought behind this last opinion is that non-executive directors are not necessarily effective watchdogs. At the same time, and at an increasing pace, mergers and takeovers have given many companies an opportunity to restructure their boards. While this may be good for the firm, it has added a different dimension to the classical notion of the director's job security. Some directors also allow their concerns about liability and job instability to impede their work as members of the board. Rather than take a risk and vote *yes* for a merger, they may vote *no* because of what it will mean to them personally. And, in connection with the question of liability, it has been known for a director to transfer his wealth to his wife. This ensures that he will not have deep pockets in the event of being sued – but may lose his wealth if the wife leaves him and sues for divorce.

Liability has become important in many industries including banking. Increased director responsibility also increases potential director liability. It is estimated that about 60 per cent of American banks now have director and officer liability insurance. No wonder qualified people would not become directors without the bank having that coverage. The legal costs alone for defending a suit can quickly run into substantial six figures.

There is an increasing number of cases where directors who discontinued vital insurance coverage on an economy kick suddenly found themselves defendants in a large lawsuit that plagued them individually for years. A well-considered, frequently re-evaluated, all-risks policy should be an absolute necessity in any director's plans. Protection from most liability situations can be provided by a properly selected policy, but fail-safe solutions really do not exist.

Members of the board of an increasing number of firms are frightened today:

- First, that the company's insurance policy will not cover them fully against personal liability;
- Second, that raiders will sack them.

This is true of bureaucratically inclined directors, whose main interest in board membership is to protect their perks.

But court litigation is a deterrent. As a recent survey indicates, court decisions make it harder for companies to attract new board members. One example is the 1985 ruling in *Smith* v. *Van Gorkum* by the Supreme Court of Delaware in the United States. Jerome Van Gorkum was chief executive of Trans Union. At a two-hour meeting in 1980 Mr Van Gorkum and his fellow directors decided to sell the company to Chicago's Pritzker family for $55 a share, $15 above the stock market price at that time. A shareholder subsequently sued the directors for acting too quickly on too little information. He alleged that if they had consulted more widely they would have found that the company could have got more money. The shareholder won. The court held the directors personally liable for 23.5 million dollars, of which only 10 million dollars was covered by their insurance policy. The case seemed to change the rules. Insurance companies raised their premiums for members of boards; and top executives thought more than twice prior to accepting directorships.

In early 1986 Cincinnati Gas and Electric reached a 14-million-dollar settlement in a shareholder suit that charged directors and officers with improper disclosure concerning a nuclear power plant. News like that is a cold shower for board members.

These 1985 and 1986 rulings have been followed by several others. The rising tide of shareholder litigation and the fear of liability judgments is driving many directors away. Insurance companies raised their premiums for liability insurance, not by 10 per cent but by 1,000 per cent, a tenfold increase in the past two years. At the same time, coverage has been sharply reduced and in some cases cancelled outright. Insurance companies have come to wield an important behind-the-scenes influence on the longevity of a board, and hence the subsistence of a company.

When a firm loses its liability coverage, directors flee. Their departure robs the enterprise of:

- continuity;
- stability;
- valuable outside expertise.

Control Data Corporation lost its directors' insurance in December 1985. The company's 568-million-dollar loss in 1985 prompted Pittsburgh's National Union Fire Insurance to decrease coverage to one-fifth of the previous year's, while substantially raising the premium. As a result of this move, Control Data suspended its policy. Subsequently three directors resigned and three retired. Of the six who left, four were outsiders.

Eight of the ten directors on the Board of Armada Corporation, a steel company, resigned in early 1986 because the company suspended its liability insurance. The premiums had been increased from 22,500 dollars a year to 750,000 dollars a year, a result of Armada's losses, which began to mushroom a year earlier.

The move away from boardrooms is likely to continue, as more outside directors avoid service altogether or significantly cut down their board memberships. However, not everybody sees the impact of these changes on the classical board structure in a negative light. A number of management scholars think that this shake-up of the old standards can have salutary effects as it increases the expectations of what directors should be doing: 'That's why we are seeing increased litigation against directors. The public is holding them to a higher standard of expertise and moral government' was suggested in a financial meeting in New York (April 1987). A few directors tend to take a similar view, on the premise that the more rapid and dynamic is the rate of change, the more help they get from chief executive officers who are exposed to the same problems on a daily basis and therefore the more comfortable they feel.

Typically the directors who are most likely to take a strong position in board meetings and persist more in spite of adversity are those with big ownership positions. H. Ross Perot won a seat on General Motors (GM)'s Board after he sold his company, Electronic Data Systems, to GM and became the motor manufacturer's biggest stockholder. After Laurence A. Tisch acquired a 21.5 per cent share of CBS stock, be began taking a prominent role in the financial management of that company.

Ross Perot hit hard at the GM Board to enact the changes which he believed necessary. As a result in late 1986 GM bought back his interests, granting him a significant profit. But typically directors find subtler

ways to reveal their opinions. If they have a problem with a recommendation of management, they will see the chief executive officer privately.
If they are opposed, they may not vote. While this often makes good
sense in terms of company politics, it is one of the reasons for rising
litigation. Active questioning and scrutiny is the exception, not the rule,
in today's boards. This is also the Achilles' heel of management.

A SENSE OF PERSONAL ACCOUNTABILITY

Management is accountable to the board, but to whom is the board
accountable? The most universal answer is: to the shareholders. But if
shareholders ask no critical questions, boards are answerable to nobody.
Shareholders cannot pose significant questions unless they have detailed
information on company operations – which they usually lack. It is
precisely for reasons of responsibility that a corporate director's primary
job is watching over the shareholders' interests. But is that what the
company books say? In practice most boards interpret the job to mean
active support of management. This is precisely what many shareholders
object to.

There are plenty of ideas for reform. T. Boone Pickens, Jr., contends
that directors with a stake in a company are usually conscientious, so he
suggests that directors be required to own company stock. The
American Law Institute believes that:

(1)   New board members should be chosen by a nominating committee
      entirely composed of outsiders.
(2)   More qualified candidates would emerge if directors' liability were
      held to the amount of their board renumeration.

Other opinions suggest that outside board members have independent
staffs to help them monitor corporate management or, that boards
should more broadly reflect a company's various constituencies. Still
others recommend a steady training programme for members of the
board, including *computer literacy* and appreciation of *high technology*.
Industrial organisations send their managers and professionals to
seminars, meetings and courses at which new viewpoints are being
stressed. Many conduct their own development programmes to teach
the skills which should be possessed. Why not to extend this programme
to include the company's directors?

But do there exist any universal traits for successful management? If so, how many directors and managers truly possess them? How many corporations realise their fundamental importance? And do organisations really care for men with poise?

As quoted by *Business Week*, T. Boone Pickens blames the post-war advent of the professional manager for divorcing managerial and shareholder interests: 'The only real stake many company managers have is their jobs.'

● The 200 members of the Business Roundtable, a group of chief executives of the largest US companies, own less than three-tenths of 1 per cent of their companies.

● A May 1986 survey by *Fortune Magazine* showed that 9 per cent of *Fortune* 500 Chief Executive Officers (CEOs) own no stock in their companies.

Fortune 500 refers to the 500 larger American companies. Though this list is no yardstick, it constitutes a good frame of reference. The marked separation between ownership and management is, in itself, significant.

The premise that managers sometimes put other interests (including their own) above those of shareholders has support from detached analysts. One of the most recent comes from a Twentieth Century Fund paper written by Edward Jay Epstein, a respected investigative journalist. Entitled 'Who Owns the Corporation? Management vs. Shareholders', it asserts that the cause of economic efficiency would be served by freeing up the market for corporate control. But isn't it also true that in the large majority of cases decision-makers are not going to take sensible measures until they are forced by crisis? A serious crisis obliges leaders to tell the facts, face the challenge and act before the damage is overwhelming.

Companies don't die because their directors make an occasional mistake. They die when the board, and top management generally, loses touch with the world it is supposed to reach. That is where accountability should start.

The issue of accountability is real and of growing importance. In late 1986 Touche Ross, the accounting firm, warned Britain's 50,000 board directors to look sharp as a series of new laws was to take full effect in December that same year. The rule changes put a greater burden of responsibility on directors. Those who fall short could face disqualification for up to fifteen years, liability for company debts and even imprisonment.

The rule changes also had an impact on public accountants. When liquidating a British company, the latter must now report to the Department of Trade and Industry on directors who have

- failed to keep proper accounts,
- omitted to file annual returns,
- removed assets beyond the reach of creditors or
- diverted them to their benefit.

One of the partners in Touche Ross's London office says his firm has already turned in dozens of directors for infractions.

The sense of accountability should be strengthened, rather than weakened, by the fact of the significant length of time it takes to get to trial – thus increasing the share of uncertainty. 'Sometimes you just have to advise your client to settle for what is less than justice,' says a top lawyer. And getting to trial means only the first date: after that it takes another three to five years to get through the appelate court. In all you have got ten to fifteen years to determine the case.

With the overburdened judicial system in some countries it is a hard thing to get a verdict. In the United States, for example, the judicial system is overburdened because the name of the game is to sue. It is a national pastime feeding on uncertainty.

Better accountability is based on more informed and properly equilibrated decisions. This often goes contrary to a prevailing practice where board members, corporate executives and accountants may at times be acting at cross-purposes.

- The executive might, for instance, be making business decisions without thought to tax ramifications flowing from those decisions.
- The accountant might be making tax decisions without knowledge of the underlying business facts supporting the tax position taken.

Problems such as this can be avoided by the establishment of a strict corporate policy, enhanced by a direct line of communication between the operational and policy-making arms of a corporation.

This is particularly valid for the multinational corporation. A major problem for foreign corporations is that there are often practices in their home countries which lead to contempt problems. For instance, many countries have secrecy or confidentiality laws which US courts on occasion do not fully respect. The sense of accountability must be so much greater in an international business landscape, as foreign corporations may be led into conflicts between the laws of their own countries and the laws of countries where they transact business. This explains why on occasion foreign nationals have been reluctant to testify in the United States for fear of personal contempt and detention. As an example, a case before the Temporary Emergency Court of Appeals, Washington, could have a far-reaching effect. It could subject corporate officers and directors to personal liability for any failure of a corporation to comply with a regulatory standard. That is the belief of the US Chamber of Commerce, which has filed an *amicus curiae* brief supporting Citronelle-Mobile Gathering Incorporated, Mobile, Alabama. The small petroleum pipeline firm argues that its corporate officers should not be held personally liable for the corporation's non-wilful violation of a petroleum price-control regulation.

These are cases bad enough in a national environment, but much worse when international operations come under scrutiny. No wonder IBM spends a rumoured 2 per cent of its income annually on legal fees and settlements to protect itself from court actions.

The importance of personal accountability and legal caution should not be misinterpreted as a call for *corpocracy*, which Richard G. Darman defines as 'large-scale corporate American's tendency to be like the government bureaucracy that corporate executives love to malign: bloated, risk-averse, inefficient and unimaginative.' Greater accountability is based on the director's *individuality*. That is where the frame of reference should start and end.

THE BOARD TURNS ON ITS CHAIRMAN

Thirty-four years ago, as a postgraduate student at the University of California, I had a professor who used to say: 'Becoming a member of the board is less a process of learning to do something than one of learning *not* to do something.' Decades of experience have proved the wisdom of this observation. We learn not to do something through two main avenues which are complementary rather than exclusive of one another:

(1) *Research*, more precisely competitive forces analysis. *Figure* 1.1 outlines the key components of this approach. The kernel is a competitive strategy with major contributions made through such factors as: *our* current products and services, new products *we* have under development, *our* client base and projected clientele, *our* direct rivals, the new entrants to the market(s) to which *we* appeal, and *our* suppliers.

(2) *Past experience*, our own as much as that of our competitors, suppliers and other parties.

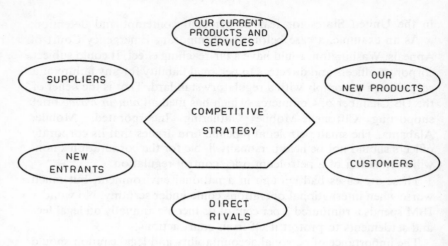

A COMPETITIVE STRATEGY MUST ALSO INCLUDE SUBSTITUTES

Figure 1.1   Strategy formulation presupposes the analysis of competitive forces as well as identification of key factors.

This, common sense says, should have been obvious and applicable. But common sense is a widely distributed quality: that's why each one of us has so little.

The recent top management shake-up at United Airlines (Allegis Corporation) offers a good example. Richard J. Ferris stubbornly clung to the notion that he could turn United Airlines into a full-service travel company, though other experiences – TWA (Trans World Airlines), Pan American – clearly documented the wisdom of avoiding this road. Ferris resorted to the ploys of entrenched managers. He courted the confidence of his Board of Directors, lined up a prospective white knight, and planned a huge dividend to placate stockholders. But in mid-June 1987 these efforts ended in failure. The board of Allegis Corp. turned on him. After a seven-hour meeting in New York, the Board forced the CEP to resign.

The troubles began in 1985. That year United bought Hertz and started praising the virtues of a one-stop travel service – a concept few others in the industry or on Wall Street agreed with. Part and parcel of this concept was the acquisition of the two leading hotel chains: Hilton International and Westin. Compounding the effects of over-expansion outside the airline's mainstream business – thus spreading management too thin – Richard Ferris confronted a 29-day pilots' strike. He forced the union to accept a two-tier wage system and permanently alienated the strikers. In early April 1987 the pilots made a $4.5 billion bid for the airline. The offer was short on specifics but it suggested that the company might be worth more divided than united, and Allegis became a takeover candidate.

Then the Board entered the scene. In June 1987, as the senior Board member of Allegis Corp., Charles Luce led the charge to quash Richard J. Ferris' grand plan for a unified travel-services company.

Allegis is not a case of impatient shareholders unwilling to wait for a future pay-off, but rather an attack on the long-term strategy itself. Since the issue at Allegis is not long-term versus short-term gains, the Board's action sets a positive precedent. 'The financial community may no longer wait till the policy causes bad performance. It may move faster to get it corrected than before,' suggests Paul W. MacAvoy, Dean of the Graduate Business School at the University of Rochester. 'Board effectiveness may be higher in the future.'[2]

With Richard Ferris gone, the directors could do what the company's unions and most of Wall Street wanted to do for some time: break up the company. Most significantly, the Board showed that it is not afraid to change its mind in the face of pressure. Boardroom battles may not come naturally, but they do come. Allegis said it would sell its Westin and Hilton International hotels and Hertz car-rental operations. It would then restructure the airline to allow for employee ownership. 'Somebody had to figure out how to calm the pilots down, keep the unions happy and carry out a plan that would make the shareholders happy,' said one insider. The company also said it would change its name back to United Airlines Incorporated.

What happened at Allegis may mean the start of a less disruptive era in the restructuring of corporate America. Proxy fights and bear hugs (unsolicited but too-good-to-pass-up offers) may be used more often. However reluctantly, directors may start to show how a board can play its part. The members of the board should set an example and that example should make CEOs more accountable. Investors would wait for a long-term pay-off if they had confidence in the company, its products and its management. By contrast, investors will not wait for a long-term payoff when such confidence is missing and short term profits are at hand.

There are also other lessons to be learned from the United Airlines case. Morgan Stanley's defence tactics proved fruitless. Or is it rather that when Ferris and his investment adviser, Morgan Stanley, began to devise a defensive strategy, the embattled CEO was already being undercut by some of his outside directors?

Whatever the case, the financing side itself did not make much sense.

At the April 1987 board meeting, Richard Ferris proposed recapitalising the company and paying shareholders a $60 cash dividend with $3 billion of borrowed money (!). The Board rejected this plan as being too risky, and the CEO, in an ultimately fatal move, went along with them. He then suggested enlisting support from Boeing. As a partial payment for an order of 747s, Ferris persuaded the Boeing Company to take $700 million in notes that could be converted into roughly 16 per cent of Allegis's stock, eventually returning to United Airlines to its origin in the Boeing fold. That agreement ensured that Boeing would not vote against him in a hostile takeover. That move, too, had been ill conceived.

Short of breaking up Allegis, the Board concluded that the only way out was to leverage the company and do the recapitalisation, valued at $85 a share. This also was too little too late. The value of the stock had climbed too high to entice Coniston and the other shareholders with such a deal (A New York investment group called Coniston Partners was quietly buying the company's shares for some time). The pilots then increased their offer for United by $500 million; analysts estimated their new offer was worth $90 a share.

While the outside directors began to push openly for Ferris's ousting, the CEO apparently did not get wind of the Board's decision until almost the end. The weekend before the final board meeting, Ferris spent hours with the union's representatives seeking a compromise. Two days later he was out.

Allegis director Charles F. Luce suggested that the Board assumed its role reluctantly. The members of the Board repeatedly backed Ferris and his full-service travel company strategy, even though outsiders often questioned its wisdom. More recently they had approved two management entrenchment plans, including one that would have severely burdened the company with debt. Yet, when the market spoke, directors had to act. One of the triggers for action was what happened to the market price of the stock. Wall Street pushed Allegis's stock price above the value of the company's recapitalisation plan, thus declaring its preference for a breakup – or at least a major change in course.

In early December 1987, Stephen M. Wolf, the new head of Allegis Corp., put forward two goals: cut costs and improve labour relations at the company's United Airlines unit. The appointment of an executive known for his ability to rescue failing carriers ended months of uncertainty that began when Richard J. Ferris was fired as Allegis's chairman in June 1987. However, without the earnings of the non-airline units to smooth the ups and downs of the airline business, the reborn United Airlines may experience high earnings volatility, especially if

Wall Street's collapse brings a severe recession.[3]
Not all corporate affairs which go sour end in the ousting of the CEO. At times both the market and the board may also over-react. As an article[4] suggested: 'Who would have predicted that Digital Equipment would rise from its sickbed and put its CEO on the cover of *Fortune*? Who would have predicted that General Motors would post losses as Chrysler became profitable or that Larry Holmes would lose his heavyweight title to a man who did wind sprints and followed a computerized training regimen? Nobody could have predicted these things – nobody but Ken Olson, Lee Iacocca, and Michael Spinks.'

GOOD NEWS FOR CEOs AND BOARD MEMBERS: GOLDEN PARACHUTES

In the case of Allegis Corp., Richard J. Ferris wins despite losing. A golden-parachute arrangement approved in April 1987 guarantees him his $578,981 annual salary until 1992. When the day came for his expulsion from the company he had been with for seventeen years, he floated quietly away with $3 million.

This is not a unique case, nor is the $3 million a reward for outstanding performance. For one thing, corporate chiefs are held more accountable than ever these days. In recent months, for one reason or another, several of them have been forced out. Here is a recently published list:[5]

● J. David Barnes, Mellon Bank: Bad loans, a big dividend cut and the bank's first loss in history greased the way.
● Samuel H. Armacost, BankAmerica: Huge foreign and domestic loan losses.
● Ralph D. DeNunzio, Kidder, Peabody: After the insider-trading scandal, parent General Electric installed its own man.
● Michel Vaillaud, Schlumberger: Confronting a tough marketplace, he couldn't please the company's controlling family.
● William H. Bricker, Diamond Shamrock: Bungled acquisitions made him expendable when a raider attacked.
● Thomas J. Rattigan, Commodore International: Even a mild turnaround couldn't save his job once he clashed with the company's biggest stockholder.
● John Schmidt, Santa Fe Southern Pacific: His dogged railroad merger policy helped alienate directors.

But today it is common practice for top executives in big and well-known US corporations to fall from grace, cushioned by generous severance payments. Former Bendix chairman, William M. Agee, got one of the first highly publicised golden parachutes in 1983. Such payments are rewards for leaving, and they are way out of line with individual worth or contributions to the company.

Companies that provide parachutes for their executives say the payments are a recruiting tool in the fierce world of mergers and acquisitions. In the merger fever of the last few years, some of the most secure jobs at US corporations have been eliminated. Written agreements, providing a healthy multiple of salary and a variety of benefits, were installed to cushion a drop from the corporate hierarchy after a takeover, but also many of them could be triggered by loss of a job for any reason. The size of these contracts and their growing number have made them the centre of a debate over the proper pay for a chief executive. 'From the beginning of time and forever the question will be how much is a good man worth and how little should a bad one be paid,' said Agee, who got a $4 million severance payment after he sold Bendix to Allied Corporation.

When he retired in May 1987, E. F. Hutton's former chairman, Robert M. Fomon, who headed the brokerage firm during the worst scandal in history, got $4 million in cash, a subsequent reward of $465,000 annually in additional pension benefits, and a consulting contract with Hutton that could be worth $3.5 million. His salary was $1.25 million a year.

When General Electric Company replaced the top management of its Kidder, Peabody Group subsidiary in the sping of 1986 – after an internal investigation of the firm's role in insider trading – the company said it would honour the employment contract of its former chief executive officer, Ralph D. DeNunzio. Yet Kidder, Peabody agreed this month to pay the federal government $25.3 million to settle allegations that it made millions in illegal trading during DeNunzio's tenure. (Nevertheless, the latter has not been formally accused of wrong-doing.)

Not everyone is happy. As revealed in a recent article by the *International Herald Tribune*,[6] the union leadership at *Time Incorporated* is unhappy with a $4 million severance package a former Time Inc. chairman, Ralph P. Davidson, is collecting now and after his retirement from the Board at the end of January 1988. Similarly, employees at CBS who have lost their jobs criticise Mr Wyman's (the Chief Executive's) settlement and that of Van Gordon Sauter, who was President of the troubled CBS News Division.

Still, the payment that really raises eyebrows in the corporate world is the diamond-lined parachute of $35 million that Michel C. Bergerac – my former co-student at UCLA and Revlon's former Chairman – took with him when Ronald O. Perelman deposed him. Robert B. Reich, Professor of Political Economy at Harvard University's John F. Kennedy School of Government, views parachutes as a form of bribery that suggests that managers would not act in the interests of shareholders otherwise.

Some shareholders and critics of parachutes in general are also irate over how they are installed. Although such packages have to be disclosed in companies' proxy statements, many are nearly impossible for the average shareholder to understand. Just as unclear is when parachutes are approved. Many come with a last-minute approval by a sympathetic board. Last-minute approvals of that type are no reward for professional merit. They do not originate from commitments made in the recruiting process, but are brought about by one of two causes: one is a *club-driven* principle that awards way in excess of what might be due to a former colleague; the other is an expedient way of getting rid of a no-longer-wanted personality.

CLUB-DRIVEN AND MARKET-DRIVEN PERSONALITIES

Nelson Bunker Hunt of the Texas Hunt family used to say that 'people who know how much they are worth generally are not worth much.' It is a saying that applies to corporate directors and distinguishes the entrepreneurial from the bureaucratic species.

The late David Sarnoff is a good example of a chief executive officer and board member whose strategy embodied the long-term view of the future, the refusal to be discouraged by setbacks, the almost mystical faith in problem-solving ability. This is an example of what can be obtained by *intelligence* and *willpower* put together. To a very large extent, Sarnoff's success story has been market-driven – and this contrasts with the club-driven executive personality.

Figure 1.2 makes this point by comparing four quarter spaces. The axes of reference are:

●   amount of available information;
●   time available to reach a decision.

When the former is large but there is little time to decide, we have a market-driven environment. By contrast, when the amount of available

AMOUNT OF AVAILABLE INFORMATION

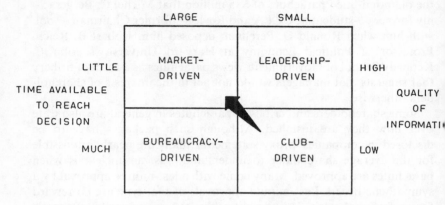

Figure 1.2   There are market-driven and club-driven types of decisions. In the
long run the one may lead to the other as personalities change and
the environment evolves.

information is small – as applies to several boards of directors because of
the time constraints of their members – and at the same time decision-
making is not pressing, the conditions are ideal for a club-driven
solution. Eventually, the latter lands the company in trouble.

This is not to say that the more the information the better it is. Despite
the money invested to date in office automation, management decision
support and information systems generally, many boards are in fact not
much more efficient than those 100 years ago. Nonetheless, the rapid
changes brought about by the use of computers and communications
has been prompting much speculation and more than a few misconcep-
tions about what is done or should be done. On the one hand is the fact
that 70 to 75 per cent of essential managerial functions have not been
automated – and cannot be automated without fifth-generation computers and artificial intelligence. On the other is the consciousness that
much more information is not necessarily better.

We refer of course to information which helps enlarge and clarify the
directors' comprehension of the issue under decision. Is there a basic
information background the members of the board are expected to have
as a matter of course? The answer is negative. G. William Miller, the
former President of the US Federal Reserve Board liked to tell the story
of a mythical poll in which the American people were asked to define
what the Federal Reserve actually was. According to Miller, 23 per
cent of them said it was an Indian reservation, 26 per cent thought it a

wildlife preserve and 51 per cent identified it as a brand of whisky.

Because of its size, a bureaucracy may possess in the cumulative large amounts of information – often the wrong sort. But the real characteristic of the bureaucracy is the vast amount of time it takes to reach decision if it ever makes one.

The underlying factor of successful market-driven and leadership-driven situations is the time available to reach decisions. In both cases it is small. Information is truly communicated and serves a purpose only when it is received and acted upon. Peter Drucker, the Austrian-born expert, who is one of the fathers of American management theory, observed once that 'communication is the act of the recipient.' In fact, information overload indicates failures in communication, not a successful system. Such overload often leads to communication blackout.

When directors know how to explore market data, they invariably find that markets, in effect, process two kinds of information:

(1)   Information about what people want;
(2)   Information about the economic costs of meeting those wants.

Markets send out signals which guide producers in deciding what and how much to make, and consumers in concluding what and how much to buy. All this happens simultaneously for thousands of producers and billions of different transactions.

We can review the director's work habits based on these premises, taking in the process a better look at his responsibilities. As Figure 1.3 suggests, *intelligence* can be *cumulative* or *individual*. A competitive environment has cumulative intelligence but reacts fast. Bureaucracy might also exhibit cumulative characteristics, but it is too slow in its work habits, thus destroying any intelligence there might have been.

In a competitive environment the directors, who have more to fear of mergers, takeovers and also of litigation, are the sitting ducks. Those who have linked their fortunes to bureaucracy are the most vulnerable. They are cogs in a chain, workers in an ant society.

Individualists are of a different breed. 'Only the strong can be productive and only the productive can be free,' John Foster Dulles once said. Fast work habits coupled with the characteristics of individual intelligence and high initiative are what makes a tycoon. Great entrepreneurs take this road.

Boards are more constrained. Club membership sees to it that work habits are slow. Committee-type arrangements reduce the level of

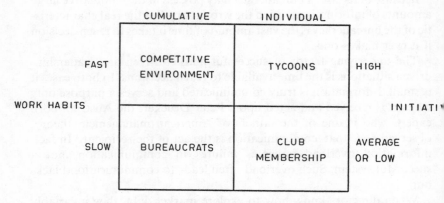

Figure 1.3   At varying degrees, the intelligence applied to the job, the work habits and individual initiative help identify the type of the individual decision maker.

initiative. Mr Urwich, the British management, organisation and productivity expert of the 1920s and 1930s was to suggest that 'A committee has neither a soul to blame nor a body to kick.' Some of the legal liability problems faced by members of the board come from this very fact: their belonging to a committee. They may work hard and prepare themselves both mentally and financially for adversity. But this they do in an individual sense – often forgetting there is also the committee sense to account for.

Given the realities board members have to face, it is not surprising that in several cases security is based on understanding the answer to two questions: 'If I were fired today, what would be my defence policy? My monetary worth in the free market?' Not everybody prepares himself in this manner. I have seen senior executives devastated both emotionally and financially when adversity hit. Happily, I have also seen many others who were always prepared just in case and who have benefited markedly from facing adverse conditions in an able manner.

Dr Lawrence Koltonow was to suggest in a recent meeting that during the Second World War the American military taught its officers how to survive if they had to land in the desert or in the jungle, at sea, or crash land on snow. But nobody, no university or corporate programme teaches senior and junior executives *how to survive in the corporate world*. This lack of training leads to frequent, fast and unwanted *burn-out*.

What is important for survival is *personal identity*. 'Whenever you have a stress-to-crisis cycle you may have regression', psychiatrist Koltonow advises. 'The best defense is a strong sense of identity. Corporate health will usually depend on the health of its executives.' Board membership is like any other job. It is a *prestigious assignment*, but it is *not void of the risks, challenges and benefits* other human activities involve. To do it in an able manner, board members must have imagination. They should also master very clear ideas on objectives – both corporate and their own. We will return to this subject of decision styles in the Epilogue.

NOTES

1. *Business Week*, 8 September 1986.
2. *Business Week*, 29 June 1987.
3. *Business Week*, 9 November 1987.
4. *Information Center Magazine*, May 1987.
5. *Newsweek*, 22 June 1987.
6. 19 June 1987.

2 Imagination and Corporate Objectives

Imagination is one of our most precious assets. It permits us to develop exciting new ideas, ways to improve our business and to make a positive impact on our society. Imagination lets us travel into the future to plan the world we are creating, to look back into the past for guidance, to ask the question 'what happens next if we take the course we propose?'

Just as important as imagination is another characteristic: the sense of vision. Vision harnesses imagination, focusing on a clear perspective. It gives us the knowledge that there is no end-point in human development, only a series of way stations on the road to tomorrow. The realisation that the road is open, that we can look ahead rather than bumping backwards into tomorrow is a cornerstone in creating a new world, a better world for the people our company is serving. To that task we must bring our commitment. To be valid such commitment can only start at one point: at the board of directors.

Establishing corporate objectives is a creative act. It involves the conceptual elaboration of goals, testing them against the reality of consistency with market drives; growing internal resources to meet them, affecting environmental conditions; ways and means for accomplishing the broader corporate plan. In this effort we see the familiar concept of creativity, involving exposure to strategic objectives, accounting for internal and environmental constraints, facing challenges, going through gestation, testing against reality, and finally in implementing the objectives.

Imagination is necessary in order to adjust swiftly to a changing environment yet still think and act in terms of long-range goals. A general direction should dominate our thoughts, integrating all key functions under our control, as suggested by Figure 2.1. But within this perspective we should maintain a great deal of flexibility. Borrowing from studies of creativity, we can see that when we are creative on the practical level we can not only establish goals but also devise ways to reach them – provided we have appropriate exposure to the company situation and market drives. We must always be aware of situations where objectives are set without adequate exposure to environmental conditions. Then even the most elaborate plan will fail. Likewise, we

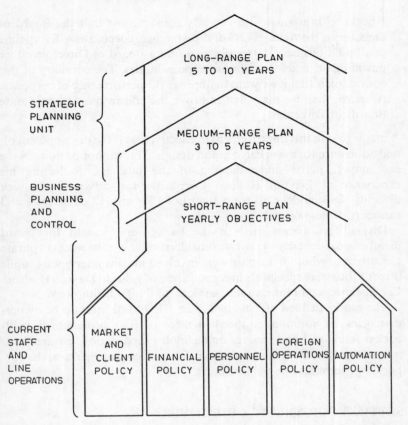

Figure 2.1   The general direction of corporate development is set by the long-range plan which itself is composed of shorter range, individual plans.

must beware of situations where objectives are set without adequate study and analysis.

A workable grand design thus emerges as an especially creative act. There are no broader objectives to be guided by than those set by a strategic plan. The creators of such grand design have as tools market needs, values, and drives, and the company's resources: human, financial, technological – as well as the main challenges.

Are these qualities to be found in the board? In his article: 'From the Board Room,'[1] Kenneth N. Dayton answers this question:

I begin with a conviction . . . My conviction is that the Board of Directors is the Achilles heel of the American corporation. Every time you find a business in trouble, you find a Board of Directors either unwilling or unable to fulfil its responsibilities. The corollary of this conviction is that if we want to improve the performance of corporate America, then we must first improve the effectiveness of corporate Boards of Directors.

A major part in this improvement in effectiveness is the development of, and adherence to, a workable grand design. This cannot be done in the abstract. It needs understanding of the business. Reflecting his experience at Dayton Hudson Corp., Dayton advises: 'We seek diversity. Our model calls for a Board of 15 – with 12 outsiders and 3 members of management.'

Diversity is documented in the background sought for board members, particularly the twelve outsiders: eight or nine were corporate executives of whom five or six were involved in consumer goods, while three or four were specialists in certain areas of value to Dayton Hudson. For instance, communications, services, and high technology.

The model defined at least five to be CEOs and three to be owner-managers. In addition, it specified three or four professionals with backgrounds and perspectives on technology, education, government, international affairs, economics and finance, consumer research, corporate governance, or public affairs.

SETTING CORPORATE OBJECTIVES

The better use of the term 'objective' is in the relatively broad sense it commonly has in everyday business language. An objective is an aim or end of action: it is a goal or guide to intermediate decisions and actions taken to see these decisions through.

Yet while objectives should be clearly understood by everybody, in many organisations, if we asked a number of managers to write down their principal objectives, we would most likely get strongly conflicting answers. As a result, money is sometimes spent on programmes and projects which are later abandoned as inconsistent with broader corporate objectives and strategic plans. Corporate objectives should be set by the board of directors, but in business and industry policies and practices don't always go by the book. Many boards and their members spend countless hours thrashing over problems unrelated to the overall purposes of their organisation.

In corporate life, crises come and go. The worst part of a crisis is being unprepared. But crisis can be managed if seen coming, ahead of time. By removing the unexpected aspect, we are removing that which is most unnerving. Positioning the firm against the forces of the future is a valid approach in managing crisis. A study by Kodak demonstrated that it takes six years for a strong company to run down, if nothing is done to avert the trend. The changes which took place in the automobile industry in the late 1970s to early 1980s help document the Kodak hypothesis.

If crisis can be managed, normal operating conditions can be better planned and controlled – even in times of rapid technological change. Aggressive pricing, for instance, has become a normal condition in business life. Felt industry-wide, its impact should be accounted for in setting objectives and in developing plans to meet them.

Corporate planning, but also planning for financial resources, personnel, research and development (R&D), manufacturing, and marketing, organisation and structure, properly begin with the question, 'What are our overall objectives?' Siemens has been ingeniously shifting its business orientation for two decades. Figure 2.2 presents the product mix in industrial activities by Siemens with three milestones: 1975, 1985 and (est.) 1995.

Objectives at the board of directors level primarily focus on corporate survival. But this can be done successfully only when the organisation's objectives are really known and understood. Objectives should aim at creating constancy of purpose for improvements of products and services, with a plan to become competitive and to stay in business. In turn, this calls for a new philosophy. We are in a new economic age and can no longer live with commonly accepted levels of delays, mistakes, high costs, and defects.

Paine Webber's *Automobile Monthly* once commented on the US car manufacturers: 'As the low-cost U.S. producer, Chrysler should enjoy surprisingly good earnings even in the inevitable auto sales downturn which we predict will occur sometime after 1986.' Major quality improvements and becoming a low-cost producer were the two topmost objectives set by Iacocca as he took over as CEO of Chrysler.

Not only cost and capacity position, earning power, valuation, cost/performance and liquidity measures, but also research projects, marketing thrust and innovation are key areas where objectives must be set. While the maturing of the sales force has important implications for future growth, marketing perspectives encompass much more than sales results. Such perspectives should be set at board level.

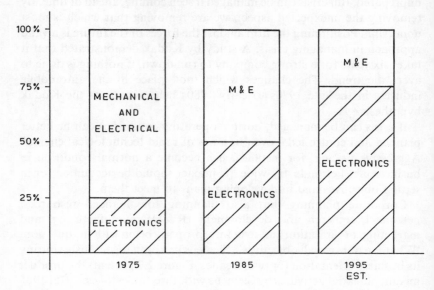

EVOLUTION IN YEARLY BUSINESS OF SIEMENS AG

Figure 2.2   The evolution in type of business of Siemens AG dramatises the shift which is taking place in the mechanical, electrical and electronic engineering industry.

Diffusion of advanced technology into products and processes throughout the economy is a market process. It cannot be defined, understood and pursued in a manner independent of market drives and the direction such drives are taking. A strong technology industry is the result of planning, but it is also the result, not the cause, of a strong, healthy economic and technical climate.

Though they are not synonymous, a strong technical company and a strong marketing company have much in common. Among other things, they exemplify flexibility in tailoring the product line to changing market tastes, while avoiding the risks of obsolete equipment or facilities. Today's markets are worldwide and their exploitation calls for radically new approaches, different from those we were accustomed to in the past. Objectives should be set accordingly. Products must be extensively test-marketed at prices that incorporate a generous profit margin before production commitments are made, limiting the risk of a major mistake.

Protected markets are no answer to strategic survival – in fact, they may be a liability rather than an asset. The French electronics industry, for example, does profitable business with the state-run phone company or the Ministry of Defence, where competition can be halted by government order. But the same French manufacturers are weak in selling consumer electronics that require agile adjustments of products and technology to respond to a quickly shifting international market.

Goals set by the board to induce successful new approaches should start at the innovation level, with imaginative product definition and R&D projects. Unfortunately in most European countries the educational and research communities are separate, self-regulating and often inward-looking bodies. Their corporatist nature both perpetuates separations between and within the two structures and contributes to the isolation of each from industry. Approaches which might have worked with the technology of the 1960s and 1970s will not work with microelectronics, biotechnology, the new communications and the other advanced technologies of the 1980s. The problem now is to spot tomorrow's winning technologies, and the market will outperform the lagging imagination of bureaucrats every time. The nuclear, aerospace and early telecommunications programmes that have been success stories involved essentially mature technologies. In other words, European engineers could see what Japan and the United States had accomplished. They could concentrate on finding their own paths to similar solutions. But what is happening to Europe today may be the American fate tomorrow.

Objectives are set both by the corporations and by states. In July 1985 Saudi Oil Minister Sheikh Ahmad Zaki Yamani warned that his country had borne too much of the burden of sustaining prices. He threatened to boost production to over Saudi Arabia's 4.35-million-barrel-a-day quota and push prices down. Yamani proved true to his goals. During the second half of 1985 Saudi production climbed to between 4 million and 6 million barrels a day, and the country looked capable of waging a war of attrition against any and all other producers. At recent prices the Saudis get less per barrel, but they are selling about twice as many barrels as they did during much of 1985, so their revenues are jumping by 40 per cent.

In the broader sense of tariffs and trade, within a market which is becoming increasingly international, the real debate between trading partners has nothing to do with co-ordination versus non-coordination. It has to do with who takes the losses when the exchange rates change. That is very important from the standpoint of governments and major central banks. The real exchange rate is the exchange rate adjusted for inflation in different countries and it is one of the instruments in setting trading goals.

LONG-TERM OR NEAR-TERM NEEDS?

Clear objectives are a prerequisite to technological improvement, and such improvement is necessary for corporate profit growth. Another prerequisite to corporate survival is executive flexibility and productivity. The power equation has been subtly reshaped by technology and training. Quite vital, besides technology and training, is the psychological contract, one of the basic issues of change management. The psychological contract describes an agreement in the mind or, more precisely, an agreement between the minds. Psychological contracts are never in writing, and yet they govern virtually all aspects of organisational lives. They are an often complex web of expectations and understandings that underlie and surround all of our relationships.

Our on-the-job behaviour is governed largely by the contracts in force at any particular time. When we introduce change we disturb these contracts, maybe even violate them in ways of which we sometimes are unaware. Yet change is vital to corporate survivial, particularly so when we think of the longer term.

There is another basic issue affecting the longer term and this is market valuation. Dayton says:

> My first dream is that the [stock] market is beginning to look beyond this year's [or next quarter's] estimate of earnings. If that day ever does come, it will bring recognition that corporate governance is every bit as important as corporate management to ensuring the future of corporate America.

It is simply not possible to reach far-out decisions with both eyes on last quarter's balance sheet. To survive and prosper, a company must be focusing more attention, capital, and people resources on high-growth and greater-added-value products and markets, rather than on those which represented its strengths yesterday. For a computer company, for example, this means workstations, office automation, communications. Most importantly, it means the ability to offer solutions to its clients (Figure 2.3).

Fundamental objectives and long-range, strategic plans should never be compromised to meet the company's near-term tactical needs. Neither should the board be surrounded by an old guard who tells the board's member what they want to hear. Critical analyses and warnings

FOUR SOURCES OF INCOME

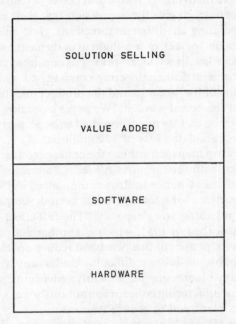

SOLUTION SELLING

VALUE ADDED

SOFTWARE

HARDWARE

Figure 2.3   The best sources of income in the coming years will be derived from solution selling, followed by a value-added offering, with pure hardware becoming the junior partner as an income source.

should be welcome; they must not be filtered out. Near-term needs are the wrong guide for survival. While some of the objectives to be set should reflect the near term, the pivot points must be anchored in the future. As most industries have found, long-range strategic planning is vital in a business. A big ship cannot change course fast enough *after* the reef has been spotted: a long-range view is required. An anticipatory management to be exercised by the board must be based on a worst-case scenario. It takes a well-trained organisation to make this approach effective.

While precise goals and the plan to reach them should be there, the skill to improvise is also important. As a matter of principle, nothing really works out just the way the president and the members of the board want. Industrial history bears good witness to the fact that successful chief executive officers gained their stature not so much by doing what they promised as by improvising wisely when they faced the inevitable

surprises. And the same is true of members of the board.
One of the board's main tasks should be to raise important problems or a least to make them highly visible and better perceived. Yet the way some board meetings go give the impression that their members are on roller skates pointing in different directions. Too many companies expand and then die for lack of top-flight management and this ability to make tough decisions. I was once working as consultant to the board of a major German electrical engineering company to which I suggested closing down one of the factories and the product line that went with it. The response of the board was flat: 'We never close down or give away our factory.' Yet the factory operations had to be phased out three years later, with an accumulated loss of $200 million.

In other cases top management has the courage to take radical action when confronted with the facts. As AT&T (American Telephone and Telegraph) Chairman Charles L. Brown announced in 1983 with regard to Western Electric, 'a long term plan has been developed to downsize the company's manufacturing capacity.' The full effect of the costs of doing so was absorbed in 1982, which is another act of courage. The AT&T decision to phase out one plant and reduce operations at others was as inescapable as it was difficult. Under any conditions, but especially in today's increasingly competitive environment, it is essential that a leading manufacturing concern continuously seeks to improve the utilisation of its plant and to reduce its costs.

Slow response often indicates that a traditionalist board of directors is not positioning itself for the type of industry in which it operates. Policy-makers often fail to appreciate that one of the big reasons companies falter is that they lose sight of what is important within the steadily developed environment. This does not mean that board members should be involved in day-to-day operations. Far from it. The directors of a firm are policy-makers and they have to *manage by exception, not inspection.* But to do so they have first to define what constitutes the right course.

The role of a strategic planning function is to be always aware that something extraordinary is happening to our entire way of life. 'Business as usual' is very dangerous in an environment which is, for all practical purposes, in steady change. The company's key assets must be protected and strengthened. These are:

●   people (our customers);
●   people (our own, source of firm's know-how);
●   other key assets (technological infrastructure, products, production/distribution system, money).

In setting objectives, focusing on the longer term, and asking for thoroughly thought-out plans, the board should encourage 'descent' – provided it is done in a documented manner. Asking for descending opinions till the final decision is taken helps in training the company executive and also produces alternative options. Some of the most successful managers I know are the ones that are good at challenging upward. The policy-setting directors establish target zones. The details are elaborated by the company managers and professionals. For a target zone to succeed, certain preconditions must be met. Meeting them is a good training ground. Even if abundant, lip service to this principle of creative descend is not enough. The board must establish a more tolerant way, one that rewards freedom of expression and open-mindedness. This way, as many corporate ladder-climbing executives have painfully learned, it will be shown that gaping discrepancies exist between rhetoric and reality. Every strategy, even the best thought-out; every report, even the most clearly written; every idea, including the most valid; can be broken down by emphasising its weakest elements. That is what the board should be doing after granting the freedom of descent.

An equally challenging task for the board of directors, pointing toward the longer-term perspective, is to command confidence in its own decisions and in the company as a whole. This is fundamental for survival. Convincing travel agents and prospective customers that the airline will keep flying has become a priority task for many carriers. Typically, airlines sell 80 per cent of tickets through travel agents. Agents hate the problems involved with tickets written on a carrier that stops flying. A trade survey showed that about two weeks before Braniff International stopped flying, 42 per cent of the travel agents polled avoided providing Braniff tickets. From Eastern to Pan Am, several US airlines had to assure worried agents that they would keep flying.

At the same time, the board should be busy reassuring employees about the same facts. Even a belt-tightening plan can provide such needed assurance, provided management really means to stick to it. Eastern Airlines' acceptance of a $600-million takeover bid from Texas Air emphasises how the aggressive, low-cost operating strategy of Texas Air's chairman, Frank A. Lorenzo, is contributing to the transformation of the US airline industry. The fear of that strategy has had its impact. Unions were successful in opposing his bids in 1984 for Trans World Airlines (TWA) and Frontier, citing his wage cuts at Continental Airlines. But they nonetheless had to agree to some pay cuts with other acquirers.

Eastern Airlines' agreement to be taken over by Texas Air brings more pressure to bear on the air transport industry to reduce its overall operating costs. Lorenzo increased profits while keeping Continental's fares among the lowest in the United States. This has been the result of carefully trimming the airline's average cost per seat mile – a key measure of efficiency in the industry.

The future belongs to those who can cut costs, the more so in an environment which is slashing the prices of products and services – from computers to air fares. There is much to be gained through rationalisation and a sharp fat-cutting knife. As Fritz Philips once suggested, when he asked the CEO of a company 'How many people do you have working?' he got the answer: 'About half of them.'

THE CHIEF EXECUTIVE'S INITIATIVE

To accelerate Nestlé's growth and raise profit margins to the target of 4 to 5 per cent, Managing Director Arthur Fürer decided he must spend his time in strategic planning instead of supervising day-to-day operations as he and prior chief executives did in the past. A big part of the strategic decisions to be made is what he calls one of Nestlé's key goals: finding ways to 'reduce our dependence on developing countries, which are often not so stable.' These areas accounted for 33 per cent of the company's sales.

Able chief executive officers manage change within their own system. Before General Douglas MacArthur's masterstroke, the landing at Inchon, his advisors, and emissaries sent from Washington said it could not be done. The harbour, the weather, the ships, the tides – everything was wrong. After all the sceptics had spoken, MacArthur rose. In his memoirs he wrote, 'I could almost hear my father's voice telling me as he had so many years before, "Doug, councils of war breed timidity and defeatism".' All councils do. There never was a bold committee. Boldness is individual.

Can Nestlé do more than just respond to changes in the world? Yes it can, because its Chief Executive is involved himself with the new directions. He does not delegate his topmost mission to third rates. He knows that if Nestlé cannot get ahead of the action, it will leave opportunities for smaller companies that are more willing to adapt – and there goes the market.

More than any post-war President, Reagan is interested in economics. Kennedy once said he had difficulty remembering the difference between fiscal and monetary policy unless he thought: William McChesney Martin is head of the Fed, and his name begins with 'M', so monetary policy is the Fed's business. But Reagan knew that as President it was his responsibility to give the Federal and State governments the tools to control costs, and the directives necessary to reach this goal. To meet a nation's economic challenges it is not sufficient for the government simply to 'get off the back' of business. The US economy, like all major corporations, must practice strategic planning. A new national consensus among business, labour and government becomes a partner in the creation of new wealth. And the same is true of any business.

The chief executive's initiative starts with imagination and ends with involvement. Any president's orders have a way of disappearing into the bureaucratic morass without real impact. 'He will sit right here,' said Harry Truman of his elected successor, 'and he will say "Do this, do that", and nothing will happen. Poor Ike. It won't be a bit like the Army. He will find it very frustrating.' And so it happened, if history books tell the truth.

Other Presidents since Dwight Eisenhower have learned that same lesson. When Richard Nixon wanted the Washington, DC, Mall cleared of unsightly temporary buildings erected fifty years earlier, it took months of his personal involvement to prod the bureaucrats into relocating. When the day came, almost a year later, for the demolition to begin, Nixon called several aides to exclaim, 'We have finally gotten something done.'

Abraham Lincoln felt that it was right to reserve to himself the final decision. He was the President. When the votes were cast regarding acceptance of a certain proposition, the story goes, Lincoln responded: 'Seven nays and one aye; the one aye has it.' But what about the implementation?

The late Clinton Rossiter of Cornell took a sweeping view of presidential power. He saw the President as 'a kind of magnificent lion who can roam widely and do great deeds so long as he does not try to break loose from his broad reservation.'

Lyndon Johnson has had a sense of timing and a reading of the innermost thoughts of other senators. 'It was uncanny how (Johnson) could predict votes other senators did not even know were going to be cast,' says Reedy.[2] 'He could sense the impact of events upon political individuals, and he invariably knew the right time to vote and the right time to decline battle.'

Remember the immediate months after President Reagan's inauguration? Some media were euphoric about his transition plan for taking over as 'chairman of the board.' It has the resonance of men seated around a big table, each clutching his corporate fiefdom, dispatching their feudal affairs in a hard-nosed way. But other media descended on the characterisation. They pointed out this was a dubious hallo since many corporate managers are not very effective. That is true – it was written at the time – of the motor and steel industries and a number of others. Some signalled another fact: no one has yet figured out how to run a sprawling leviathan like the US Federal Government. A good deal depends on what you think the Government is: a business firm? a bureaucratic machine? an army?

ARE THERE MODELS TO FOLLOW?

Dwight Eisenhower as President used the army model. He wanted a decentralised government where everyone on the domestic side would report to Sherman Adams and everyone on the foreign side to John Foster Dulles, and he himself would make only the big decisions presented by his two chiefs of staff. But the politically intense government model is different from the army. It stresses autonomy, fighting parties, old-chap clubs and intrigue.

What about the corporation? As far as the modern large business entity is concerned, an often overlooked fact is that the executive office, including the board of directors, hardly seems to have been designed at all. It just grew. Many companies, particularly the larger ones, look like bloated, rather disorderly staffs, units, departments, subsidiaries and groups with strikingly different histories, purposes and problems. As offices sprawl, staffers often spend time creating nuisance work for lower-level managers, inventing then fathering projects and hatching intrigues sometimes related to presidential objectives in a negative sense.

As a result – in a way not unlike what happened in ancient empires, in Byzantium and in the Florentine city-state – to gain control a new chief executive must reorganise. He must:

● move out units not related to his concerns;
● evict managers with single-interest connections;
● establish clear lines of authority throughout;
● restore communication with the corporate divisions and departments – no matter where they may be.

The chief executive must use his imagination to create the proper climate for innovation. 'Board members coming up with solutions are like taxicabs, plentiful when the sun is shining, but scarce on a rainy day,' said a disgusted CEO. There has been some recent thinking in managerial theory which puts emphasis on internal professional standards, weighting individual contributions and recognising that any business executive worth his salt reaches far beyond the organisation chart.

The trouble with the army model is that a corporation is not an army, with fixed lines of authority over life-and-death situations. It is a business: designing, manufacturing and distributing products with a bottom-line profit and loss criterion of success and failure. A corporation is like a vast organism on the model of the human organism, with all the human frailties but also with potential human strengths and creativeness. Reduced to its essentials, the organisation is a cluster of minds, commanding bundles of energy and experience. A small group of minds at the centre, including the CEO, the members of the board and their closest advisers, must somehow communicate their energy, experience and vision to a cluster of other minds in larger and larger circles around them. What counts is whether new ideas and energies get developed and exchanged through the whole vast organism, to and from people composing the organisation – as well as the other entities in the market interaction.

Asked which of his achievements he cherished the most, the late Marcel Dassault was to answer: the innovative aircraft propeller which he designed in the First World War. Yet at his death in 1986 Dassault also controlled and directed financial, real-estate, publishing, wine-making and film interests. His aircraft company, Dassault-Breguet, employed 16,000 people and sold thousands of civil and military planes, notably the delta-winged Mirage fighter jet that is in service throughout the world. The Dassault of the first World War (whose name at birth was Marcel Bloch) was a *promoter*. There are other promoters who became famed captains of industry.

In the first stage of the development of the modern great corporation there was always an innovative and dominant personality: Rockefeller at Standard Oil, Ford at Ford, Sloan at General Motors, Firestone at Firestone, Watson at IBM (International Business Machines), Dupont at Dupont, Sewell Avery at Montgomery Ward, Julius Rosenwald at Sears, Juan Trippe at Pan Am, Amadeo Peter Giannini at the Bank of America. Such an originator, the imaginative driver, can be identified with nearly every one of the *Fortune* 500 or the companion corporations in merchandising, transportation or finance.

Then some of the originators got old and lost contact with the evolving reality. In the 1940s, under Henry Ford, the founder, Ford

Motor Company landed third in the big league. As head of Montgomery Ward, Sewell Avery became an ultraconservative manager who decided not to allocate any money for future development after the Second World War. He was sure the world was coming to an end and America was doomed. His decision proved to be a disaster for Montgomery Ward, overtaken by Sears. In 1950 at IBM, Thomas Watson, Sr, refused the opportunity offered by Dr Eckert and Dr Maughly to buy Univac, saying this was a University professor's toy and its market limited to a two-digit number of units.

There comes a limit with the promoter. At a second stage (sometimes strongly resisted by the original entrepreneur, as in the case of Henry Ford) the organisation takes over. One of the challenges the organisation man should be answering is setting goals in the choice between two different business philosophies: Shall we be 'first' or 'second'? The answer is often situational. Sometimes accidents can strike gold. IBM's refusal to buy Univac led to an educational strategy, intensive management attention to internal development, and a change of management philosophy. The principle is: 'we can't be first in every field, but we must have a good basis to sustain ourselves in the market.'

Keeping a low profile while demonstrating a first-class know-how can be of help in shaping a successful strategy and in obtaining acceptance. A good example is the Olympus case with optical discs, where the Japanese company became the basic supplier of practically every optical disc vendor.

But the greatest challenge when the organisation takes over is sharing responsibility. This must be done in a way the system can still work in an exemplary manner. Sharing responsibility is up to a certain point prompted by the fact that the requirements for decision are now too diverse for one man. Any important action calls for a large range of specialised knowledge. Formal organisational structures are developed – the Sloan legacy at General Motors, for example.

But at a third stage, formal organisations get rusty. The system no longer functions as it used to. This may lead to decline – the case of Chrysler in the 1970s – or to restructuring. Restructuring is done through the management of change. And this is the better way to go.

THE MANAGEMENT OF CHANGE

In the last analysis, it all boils down to whether we want to take control of our destiny or prefer to let the events overtake us. This is not just a problem facing one or two companies – or even confined to corporations. Whole countries are subjected to it. We live in a time of turbulence where the only sure thing is *change*. Shall we manage change or let it run over us?

The industrial prospect ahead for rich countries is that the old, big, trade-unionised, brown-power industries: steel plants, car plants, chemicals and oil are moving out of the mainstream of basic resources, substituted by knowledge-intense industries. In all developed countries there is under way a sharp shift to skilled jobs requiring higher capital investment – in new and growth lines of business. The fast-growing need is being felt to *manage the development* of the new key resources:

- knowledge;
- time;
- capital.

It is becoming apparent that capital investment has become inseparable from the need for more knowledge work. But we also experience a not-yet-conscious realisation that the productivity of people requires lifelong, continuous learning.

The basic if not yet fully appreciated reality is that knowledge has to be applied to all resources: time, capital, key physical elements and knowledge itself. This has to be done within a properly projected and well-coordinated extensive plan. In a knowledge society we must back up our hunches by calling upon all our objective knowledge – our experience, our reading, our listening – before making a final decision. The knowledge environment calls for preparation. Events develop so fast we simply must do our planning.

'The secret of performance is motivation,' as the GE (General Electric) chairman aptly commented. Strategy is not a lengthy action plan but the evolution of a central idea through continually changing circumstances. Both the imagination and adaptation are prime qualities for survival.

We cannot match the longer-range vision of our competitors through piecemeal, uncoordinated programmes. To benefit from the new technologies we must place a great importance on human resources. An advancing technology increasingly implies a change in education itself:

(1) Overall, a change from the now passive education to active education because results are so much more visible.
(2) In retraining for the new technologies, a conversion from collective instruction to individual hands-on experience and interactive computer devices.

(3) The realisation that education is a logical infrastructure and modern tools, efficient media, as well as management goals, require that we change the way we look at things.

In short, we must not only improve our human resources but also change our way of thinking. We have always thought that development is strictly economic. Now we come to recognise that this is erroneous: development is above all human. Once again: shall we miss the opportunity?

In moving ahead toward new, largely unknown fields of endeavour, there will be accidents – but accidents help the prepared mind. Like all innovators we should be willing to make mistakes, recognise them, correct them, and learn from them. We cannot stay still, behind ill-fated, obsolete barriers, while others erode our markets and take away our opportunities. We must feed our opportunities and starve our problems. And we have to strip the problems to their core, in order to find valid solutions. We must plan for the ongoing microprocessor revolution, and foresee the resulting operational and managerial problems, rather than leave them to blind forces. And we should be keen to make sense out of conflicting elements.

More than anything, our problem is a human problem. Our people are not trained to look ahead. They are too defensive. *People-oriented drawbacks can only be overcome with imaginative approaches, steady training, and people-orientated applications.* The strength of a company hinges on its ability to shape sound industrial strategies which target economic winners.

Our transition from an agricultural to an industrial society was aided by accumulated experience: more than three centuries were required to transform the society in a way that ultimately allowed industrialisation to take hold. But the transition to a *knowledge society* in which we are now involved is without precedent. No nation has as yet developed the wealth and the goods-producing capacity to afford dedicating more than half of its workforce to occupations from which no tangible output flows. Yet that's what is shown by statistics on this colossal ongoing change.

● If we can understand how an information-rich society can function effectively, we will provide ourselves with a useful model to approach the transition to a post-industrial era.

● If not, the transformation from the business of today – in industry, banking and government services – to the more efficient business of the future will be elusive, and the projected results by no means assured.

A transition towards new knowledge-intense goals turns out to be more difficult and complex than the changes that were necessary for industrialisation. It is therefore of no surprise that companies unable or unwilling to adapt to the new information technology will lose their competitiveness and face a high rate of bankruptcies.

Furthermore, our appreciation of the financial resources themselves is in the middle of change. In high inflation periods, as those we experienced for a dozen years up till 1984, the assets of a company are no more a reference base. They have been developed and valued under different economic conditions. Under inflation it is no longer possible to balance equities, assets and liabilities in the absence of a yearly re-evaluation of the fixed assets. With disinflation different rules must be applied, providing for discontinuities to one of the oldest and most classical processes known to business – the accounting books.

As markets become increasingly demanding, no company should try to exclude the microprocessor-based technology from products and manufacturing processes in order to preserve jobs. That would merely make our products (and banking services) uncompetitive against products from other, more far-sighted competitors of ours. If anybody tries to obstruct change, we should ask: Are we too old or insufficiently flexible to acquire new skills or, more simply, to exploit our opportunities?

Experience teaches that in a deflationary environment competition is more ferocious than ever. There is simply no room for the mediocre suppliers of products and services. Managements that hand on to weakness for whatever reason – tradition, sentiment, their own lack of management skill – will not be around in 1990.

NOTES

1. *Harvard Business Review*, January–February 1984.
2. George Reedy, *Lyndon B. Johnson. A Memoir*, Andrews and McNeel, New York, 1982.

3 Making a Strategic Plan

The concept of management strategy as a formal discipline is considered an achievement of comparatively recent years, but the military has had formalised theories on strategy for a long time. Von Clausewitz in 1818 described the principles of war in his book, '*Vom Kriege*' and these principles still guide the teaching at military academies today. These principles are: the objective; simplicity; unity of command; the offensive; manoeuvre; mass; economy of force; surprise; and security. Business and industrial strategy might well use the same terms, modifying the fine print according to the situation.

We all use or misuse strategies, and we are subject to strategies used against us. However, independently of where it is put into action, strategy is not just planning, although a good deal of planning is involved in strategy. The definition of long-term policy decisions, the administration of research and development, financial planning, the evolution of product lines, and decisions as to timing and technological obsolescence, are indicative of why strategic decisions for industrial management are quite different in scope and perspective from those of the military.

A strategic plan is fundamental but just because a company has such a plan doesn't mean it knows where it is going. Many organisations are deluding themselves; they get into trouble because they have not developed a vision of the future. Most long-range plans that now guide business are visionless: they only measure performance against the previous year. They do not focus on the future, nor position the company and its people against the forces of the coming years. Such positioning is fundamental in setting goals, and in attaining them. What it is that makes man an intelligent being is his reaching out for involvements beyond himself. What it is that ultimately makes him happy is having those involvements. And since business is made up of human beings, what we just said is valid both for persons and for organisations.

It should be the role of the board of directors to set strategy and define goals, as, it is the board's role to control conforming to policies and plans. The same is true of a nation's political leadership. To govern does not simply mean to give orders,' Napoleon once said: 'The chief must also assure his orders are executed.' Whether or not this controlling role is executed, is a different question. Quite often it is not. The reason two chapters of this book focus on strategic planning can be precisely found in this very fact.

Some of the strategic decisions business and industrial management are faced with can be phrased in the following terms: set the initial and continuing scope or objective of the business; determine what products or services it will have for sale; elect what markets will be served; select the channels which will be used to reach these markets; decide how much direct and how much supporting work to do on the company payroll, or how much to purchase from outside suppliers; determine the exact timing of each new product or service; set priorities on research and development investments and determine the direction of corporate research activities. The stimulus for these strategic decisions is an opportunity for profitable expansion that stems from basic environmental changes. The response is management's planning and programming actions, committing resources and setting timetables which ultimately find expression in the products or services being sold. The stimulus must be translated into a result of growth and survival.

Expansion policies, decisions on inside or outside financing, the establishment of an optimal level of financial reserves, the determination of personnel characteristics, the evaluation of performance and promotion, decisions on business and industrial coalitions: these are examples of the ingredients of a successful strategic plan. The same can be said of acquisitions. Their timing is critical to long-term success, and though it is easier to view timing in retrospect than through the crystal ball the life cycle of a dynamic enterprise does not allow even the thought of facing the fast-pacing world of tomorrow through the rear-view mirror.

THE WINNING MENTALITY

Winners will be determined primarily by two factors: the resources and capabilities inherent in their persons, and the degree of skill, planning, judgement and energy which they apply to their jobs. Leadership is the art of influencing others to co-operate in the achievement of a common goal (authoritative or persuasive in nature, or both). And, in retreat, it is through the distraction of the commander's mind that the distraction of his forces follows. The loss of his freedom of action is the sequel to his freedom of conception.

Industrial and military strategies demand at least one thing alike on behalf of those who formulate them. They must first prove their ability in facing opponents, the most formidable of them being resistance to change. In a time of accelerated evolution of concepts and media, the board of directors needs all the support it can muster to alter the images prevailing in the organisation, which might have answered the past in a perfect way but have become unfit for the future. This can be credited as being the foremost aim of a strategic plan and it lays most emphasis on the human resources.

Within this broader perspective of positioning ourselves and our company against the forces of the future, the choice of a type of strategy depends upon the operation of the rules of the game which prevail in the fields of human endeavour – such as rules governing the conduct of war, business, parliamentary practices, court procedures, all games of varying types – as well as upon the variety of risks that inhere in the several fields or that are created and accepted therein, and the conditioning of minds that is the prime factor of strategy. The types of strategy are difficult to differentiate and identify; phrases chosen for the purpose may include two or more phases; even when a type can be pinned down and identified, it may operate differently at one time than at another, and in one field than in another. Nevertheless, though these difficulties do stand in the way of a systematic classification of strategy (and tactics), in the following section we will list those most often encountered, simply to convey an idea of the number and variety that we do obtain.

Reference has been made to tactics. In the military, strategy and tactics are very well distinguished from each other. In business, it is a little more difficult to differentiate. The master plan and the execution of it is *strategical*; the specific detailed operations and their follow-up are *tactical*. Thus in industrial practice tactics can be thought of as 'minor strategies'. In principle, the plan and execution of the major lines of a campaign are strategical; the conduct of each separate unit on the march, their deployment, the final manoeuvre and the subsequent operations are tactical in nature.

Yet, in general, one may even be at pains to differentiate policy from strategy, grand strategy from lesser strategy, tactics from strategy, strategy from objectives, and so on. From a concept originally confined to the physical force phase, business strategy has branched out into the psychology of the mass, with propaganda strategy (advertising) first, and direct attack on the markets only after the former has done its work.

Strategy formulation, as conceived today in business and industry, falls into categories which together form a whole for the development of an intelligent and successful plan:

- Analysis of strategic moves, including market research and business opportunity studies.
- Innovation plans at large, and new product planning in particular.
- Financial strategy ranging from cash flow forecasting to cost/benefit evaluation.
- Marketing strategies, including critical analysis of moves against competition.
- Retrieval and reactivation of historical strategems:
- The operational studies, including means of mathematical programming and simulation, and study of *what if*.

The preparatory phase of strategems, in business or war, dictates the need to analyse the possible courses of action of the 'opponent'. Furthermore, the reactions of the opposition must be studied in the light of our own established strategies, or those which are under development. In regard to planning against corporate opponents, strategy should be viewed as a matter of dealing with the rules of the game. A company, of necessity, has to behave within rules and constraints. In entrepreneurial activity there exist certain things that cannot be undertaken because they are unfair. Yet there also exist many leeways. The rules of the game are usually set by laws, international agreements, governmental regulation, inter-industry agreements, and so on. Part of the strategy is to recognise when and where you can bypass such rules. Strategic planning should provide for a certain share of bluffing. Bluffing, in itself, is not foreign to either individual, industrial or military moves. Executives plan their action with a view to winning by outwitting their opponents, choosing the best courses of action under all circumstances. This is equivalent to the old chess adage that a good player always plays the board and not the opposing player.

EVALUATING STRATEGIC APPROACHES

Strategy requires months and years in the making. It extends beyond the areas of planning and of execution: some say, 'it is the adroitness to combine theories throughout time . . .' Strategy is not something one could get from a balance sheet or the income statement of an enterprise. In some respects strategy is an intangible, but its application rests on concrete, well-established steps.

Strategic planning should co-ordinate and combine the individual operating unit plans into an integrated whole. The latter has several components:

- An outline of the broad objectives for the time period under consideration;
- A summary of key problems and opportunities facing management;
- Targets for the coming year's operations;
- Activities planned to achieve targets;
- Measurements needed to assure conformity to plans;
- Co-ordination of the different entities into a coherent system.

For the purpose of controlling managerial action the board must look at the morale of the people, in the organization. By contrast, controllers and auditors look at accounting data, profits and losses, the volume of operation, expenses *vs* budgets, and so on. Both the board and the controllership need to look over a long period of time, analyse changes and evaluate consistency, in order to be able to assure conformity to policies and strategy – if any.

Strategy does not have to be presented in its real terms, if ever there is a need for communicating some of its aspects. For example, if one discriminates against people, the usual statement is: 'I do not discriminate'. Often 'artifice' and 'strategy' are considered to be synonymous both in the military and in business.

Some strategems employed since the beginning of time appear to be of limited use to some people since moral principles would preclude them. Thus a ruthless opponent has the advantage of a wider choice of strategies. For this reason, in judging what strategems an opponent may use, knowledge of his character is important. Furthermore, a careful look should be given below the surface for hidden motives, since the moves of opponents may mask the true intent of those involved.

One of the strategems which found considerable applicability in business and industry is the indirect approach. Its objective is to mystify, mislead, and surprise. This has its analogy in military strategy in the form of the 'envelopment', defined as an attack on an enemy's flank or rear. Just as industrial executives sometimes praise the indirect approach as a superior strategem, army doctrines state the envelopment to be a preferred method of attack. Army manuals discuss the element of surprise and point out that it is often achieved by variation in the means and methods employed in combat. The same variation can be effectively used in modern industrial warfare. The indirect approach presents a comparative advantage over the direct approach because the opponent is not on guard. The element of surprise has proved its comparative advantages both in the military and in industry. The concerns who employ it can pick the time and place, thus avoiding unfavourable conditions, while the corporate opponent is kept in the dark about the company moves, and has less information to use in his decision making. Experiences in war have proved the advantages of the indirect over the direct approach. In some cases, both approaches have shown properties of fundamental worth. They have also demonstrated that they are both applicable to broad spheres. Comparing the direct to the indirect approach one could say that a common fault of both military and industrial leaders is that of sacrificing truth to expediency without any ultimate advantage.

Both psychological and physical factors must be considered in an indirect strategy, but when all pertinent factors are established and evaluated against the objective, management should not hesitate before using the strategic approach which has been chosen: the purpose of management is to look after the interests of the corporation. There are many points which could be mentioned linking military and management strategy, but perhaps an enumeration of the fundamental strategems themselves would best help to illustrate this subject. In politics, in industry and in any type of human conflict men have used:

- strategies (or tactics) that accept the principle but . . .;
- strategies of relying upon the status quo, letting well enough alone, negation, the veto;
- strategies of multiplying objectives, to consolidate the proponents and to divide the opposition;
- strategies of killing the impact of the adversary by admissions and frankness;
- strategies of camouflage, of apparently striving for the opposite objective
- strategies of the 'red herring', or assertion that is all there is in opposition.

This strategy is most popular with politicians, but it is also used in business. Mr Perot says:

'I thought one of Roger's [General Motor's Chairman, Roger Smith] major reasons for acquiring EDS was that I had certain strengths that he did not have. My long suit is execution. Roger is a great financial guy. But he did not spend his career down in the trenches cracking the whip, getting it done. I thought he felt I could work with him, with me getting down there, to get it humming. He got me convinced that there was nothing better for me to do with the rest of my life than help GM build the finest cars in the world.[1]

An often practised strategy is that of challenging the opponent's credibility. In the same reference Ross Perot is quoted summing up GM's management as 'that whole big amorphous featherbed up there.' 'I would get so frustrated,' he recalled. 'Roger would shout an order, saying absolutely the right things, and nothing would happen.'

One of the most widely used strategies is that of divide and conquer. It is fed by the fact that there were never in the world two opinions alike, any more than two hairs or two grains; the universal quality is diversity. An enterprise can effectively mask its real aims through means of commercial propaganda and by a well-timed leakage of information. This is essentially a strategy of creating confusion about aims and objectives. To break the morale and use up the resources of the opponent one can employ the strategy of continuous pressure, without let up. Political and military men have often applied the strategy of claiming the credit and never letting their opponents get any.

History shows that in war, politics, law and business there exist distinct strategies of the weak as opposed to the strategies of the strong. Strategies of the weak are usually those of compromise, of providing something for everyone, of employing a whipping boy, of emphasising the interests of minorities, or suppresed groups, etc., to achieve own objectives. The strategy of not attacking the other fellow's interests but simply seeking your own, that of escapism ('we are so humble'), that of waiting upon time to soften the situation, avoiding conflict and progressing little-by-little, belong to this same category.

The strategy of the big lie, misrepresentation, advertising puff or insinuations has been used to advantage both in industry and in military warfare. The strategy of the lone operator versus the wolf pack has been shown to have its merits. The strategy of slogans has served many an enterprise, the strategy of rule or ruin has made several nations and corporations big, and by the same token it has ruined several others.

Many a corporation has successfully used the strategy of introducing new products under old forms, and that of preserving the appeal of old products and trademarks under new forms. In politics one of the favoured strategies is the one that turns the tables on an opponent. An example can be taken from a debate in the House of Commons on British overseas policies:

'MacLead's trouble,' Salisbury suggested, 'might lie in his fondness for bridge', a past-time at which he earned his living for two years as a bridge expert on the London *Sunday Times*. 'He understood,' said the Marquess of Salisbury, that 'it's not considered immoral, or even bad form, to outwit one's opponent at bridge. The completely outwitted white settlers could only conclude that it was the (revolutionary) nationalist leaders whom the Colonial Secretary regarded as his partners and the white community, and loyal natives, that he regarded as his opponents.'

Another strategic approach is one which has brought straying husbands to heel since the dawn of time: embarking on a new flirtation. In the course of the post-war years, a favoured industrial strategy was that of hastening the obsolescence of a product in order to keep the demand curve from shifting unfavourably due to saturation of the market. Advertising plays a very large part in this strategy.

Substantially used in industry is the strategy of manufacturing products sufficiently similar to the products of competitors, so that the firm can take advantage of the demand created by the others' products – yet make them different enough so that careful advertising can use these differences to present the product as superior to that of the competitors.

ELABORATING PRODUCT STRATEGIES

In his book *The World-Wide Industrial Enterprise*[2] Frederic G. Donner, former chairman of the board of General Motors, describes the GM strategy: 'A Car for Every Purse and Purpose.' He also underlines how the board realised that with the growth in the size of the market, customer preferences would become increasingly diverse, reflecting a greater variety in the use of cars as well as differences in individual tastes and incomes.

This is a good example of a decision which may be elaborated by the management of the company but should be finally reached at the board level. A product line orientation based on the diversity in customer preferences is not a matter to be left for final decision down the line. It greatly impacts on product policy and, by consequence, on product design. It affects its flexibility and functionality of the product line – from where the company's future income will come – but it also interlocks with the officers' objectives and so on down the organisational pyramid, as Figure 3.1 demonstrates.

Significantly, Mr Donner's reference to the American market regards General Motors' policies in the 1920s, not in the 1960s when he was chairman of the board. He speaks of Alfred Sloan's strategies which made GM great, overtaking the Ford Motor Company as market leader.

'The growth in motor-vehicle ownership and use in Europe in the 1950s closely tracked the rate of growth in the United States in the 1920s,' Frederic Donner suggests. 'Therefore, it did not come as a surprise that in the 50s, as in the United States thirty years earlier, our attention was directed toward evaluating the manufacturing economies and marketing efficiencies of full-line operations overseas. However, the GM motto of the early 1920s "A Car for Every Purse and Purpose" was not achieved in England and in Germany until the early 1960s'. Therefore, one of the outstanding qualities of board-level strategies is *timing*. This is as true with automobiles and other manufactured products as it is with investments in stocks. Investment specialists advise that if you wish to make a profit in the stock market by far the No. 1 is *when* you enter and exit the market. Which stock you select is less important.

Exploiting the diversity in customer preferences has been a strategem on many companies capitalised to reach eminence, but then they forgot the lesson. Their competitors resurrected the strategy and profited from it. Bringing computer-aided design (CAD) to the showroom, Toyota permits its customers to design their own car for custom-made production.

Product strategies are among the most complex the board is faced with. First, able product strategies require a valid knowledge of the market and its drives – as well as of competition. Underestimating and overestimating competitors are among the common pitfalls which, in many occasions, proved to be disastrous.

Second, inside the organisation product strategies are multifunctional. They require co-ordination with research and development, finance, production, marketing, and distribution. That is with all key line departments. The board needs the contribution of these departments to be able to establish the major strategic moves for the year to come.

The primary risk of reaching decisions at the individual officer's or senior manager's level is that while the individual executive may be setting objectives which are compatible with the projected work of other

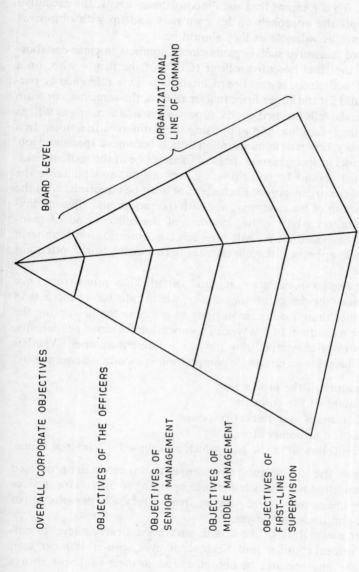

Figure 3.1 Strategic planning is based on overall corporate objectives. These should be established at board level and followed by the line of command.

departments, there is no assurance that these other departments will be pursuing activities which are compatible with the needs of the company as a whole. To the extent that such inconsistency exists, the executive who attempts the approach on his own may end up with objectives which are not as valuable as they should be.

The board can solve such organisational conflicts in close collaboration with the chief executive officer (CEO) of the firm – who, on a number of occasions, is the board chairman. This reference is particularly valid for the larger firm. In a small firm, the same man or team buys materials, sells finished goods, supervises manufacturing as well as co-ordinating, planning, and appraising these different functions. In a large company, however, administration usually becomes a specialised job. There are risks in specialisation. Loss of focus is one of the greatest risks.

The board should be co-ordinating, appraising, and planning the activities of the organisation. Each director must be concerned with the long-run health of his company, not with its smooth and efficient day-to-day operation which is the business of the officers and of management. The board duties call for such concentration on long-term planning and appraisal, though in real life this distinction is often not clear cut.

Product line strategies are many and varied. They range from *price competition* to the design of *sales ability*, which calls for an increase in quality rather than a decrease in price as a means for promoting the demand for a product. In this type of competition the customer benefits, as he does in price competition, only in a different manner. Whether there is to be price or non-price competition is mostly determined by:

● The nature of the product.
● The image of the company.
● Market drives and market response.
● The action of competitors.
● Policies followed in the past which established a reference frame.

For instance, the idea of non-price competition is especially promoted by merchandising firms which compete by trying to offer extra services to the consumers, such as free parking, free delivery, a larger selection of products, and trade-in allowances.

Another major duty of the board, within the strategic level orientation, is resource utilisation. Seldom, if ever, can a 100 per cent utilisation of any resource be obtained, and so there is almost always some capacity (in R & D, manufacturing, sales or even finance) that cannot be used. Ironically, the amount of unused capacity often may be increased through higher efficiency. In this context, overall strategy, investments, and streamlining is the board's business, not the non-essential details.

The most important resource in an organisation being its people and its customers, personnel planning – specifically at the management level – is an undisputed board responsibility. At Siemens, one of the members of the board dedicates all his time and attention to preselection and development of the *next* top management team. Clear-eyed companies are very keen in assuring that the right management will be in place, not only today and tomorrow, but also further out in the future.

In 1912 Andrew Carnegie, the king of the steel business in America, was asked by some of his friends if he were to lose all of his factories or all of his people which one he would rather let go. Without hesitation Carnegie answered: 'My factories. Because if I have all of my people, I can recreate the steel empire.'

It is a sound strategy (both for industry and for the military) to move always faster than the opposition, to carry the battle to the field of the competitors. Other frequently used approaches are injury by deputy and benefit by person; asking for far more than you expect to get; fighting a last battle for saving face; and the strategy of silence, of ambush, and sabotage.

As opposed to the strategies of the weak, the strong have often used strategies of humiliation, the strategy of keeping the principle out of negotiations, of holding the initiative, of being the first, and of creating reputation by word of mouth or press agent's accounts. In the same class can be added those approaches directed towards weakening morale, perversion, and corruption; blasting the diseases of the social structure; the brainwash; the strategem 'costs little to us, much to the opponent'; confusion and uncertainty; 'smile' and anger; and mass power: military, economic, industrial.

Favoured one in politics is the debate strategy: suggest that there is evil only on the opponent's side; if the opponent presents a remedy, show that this is no remedy, then demonstrate that your own side has better to offer. Guilt by association is often used in debates. Use of statistics, data, and testimonies to show the superiority of your side and the inferiority of the opponents is an often-favoured approach.

Both industry and the military have used the strategy of multiplicity of objectives to fool the opponent about where one is going to strike. Writers, inventors and social reformers have employed the resurrection strategy: resurrecting something that another generation knew, capitalising on what was known already and has been forgotten. Industries have used the strategy of converting propaganda into news items; military men applied the strategy 'in reverse': 'by indirection find directions out'.

History shows that human action has favoured the strategy of conceding everything possible but standing firm on the essential point, as opposed to that of fighting every issue or contesting every step of the way. Politicians utilised the strategy of getting rid of 'poor laws' by working them to death; companies got rid of many poor executives in a similar manner. Often, in practice, business and the military use a strategy of risks; the man to succeed must take a risk, the good strategist takes risks which have a calculated return rather than an uncertain one.

Executives have tried, to advantage, what is known as the 'trial balloon' strategy, where something is manipulated and presented just to see the reaction, without having the intention of doing it at the time. Nations, corporations and individuals have applied to a substantial extent the strategy of 'secrecy', not letting the left hand know what the right hand is doing. Governments and company managements have many times used the strategy of preserving the competition to camouflage their own strong position.

Owing to failure to elaborate a simple structure that could provide the principles for strategy formulation we are often obliged to refer to historical examples. The following is a brief summary of the major strategems used in war, law, politics and business:

● divide and conquer;
● test opposition for weak spots;
● diversionary action, divert attention from the real objective;
● Fabianism, delay or avoid decisive engagements;
● surprise, use an unguarded gate, or make an unexpected manoeuvre;
● employment of a series of connected actions whose impact is not evident until completed;
● bi-partisan strategy, be prepared to spring either way, have an excuse for not springing at all;
● neutralism, let them kill each other off;
● burrowing from within, penetration to weaken opponents with their own elements;
● security strategy, preserve your lines of communication, conserve adequate reserves;
● manifestos, stating exactly your aims and what you mean to do, on the rationale that they are so fantastic that no one will believe them.

Tough strategies involve draconian measures, procedures and policies which are usually getting harder or stiffen all at once. Then, through an apparently soft move, they give something up to create the impression of a change. Soft strategies rest on collective approaches to decision making as a means of arriving at an end. They also attempt to avoid decisive conflicts.

IMPLEMENTING A STRATEGIC PLAN

Within the broader framework of the strategic approaches which we have considered, strategic planning defines the longer-term objectives and establishes the broad strategies for achieving these objectives. In contrast, operational planning and control define the specific steps to be taken in the coming year (or two years) in order to implement established strategies. They provide a framework for monitoring and controlling performance against plan (Figure 3.2).

Successful strategic planning systems include five key features in terms of their development and organisation:

(1) *Objectives* are established by the board of directors and senior management.
(2) The *overall* strategic plan is divided into *component* plans for each individual operating unit (division, department, geographic areas, major functional area).
(3) Strategic planning *procedures* follow a regular cycle, phased in with the operational planning and control process, co-ordinated from a central planning department.
(4) Periodic *reviews* are made (regular and by exception) to assure plan/actual performance and correct deviations.
(5) The strategic plan itself is periodically *re-evaluated* to assure that it remains valid and dynamic.

The following critical phases will characterise the establishment and upkeep of a strategic plan: building the information base; identifying planning gaps and analysing ways of closing the planning gaps; setting or revising long-term objectives; exploding into component parts, elaborating each plan individually, then assembling them into a unified, coherent strategic plan (Figure 3.3).

The development of strategic plans calls for information relating to

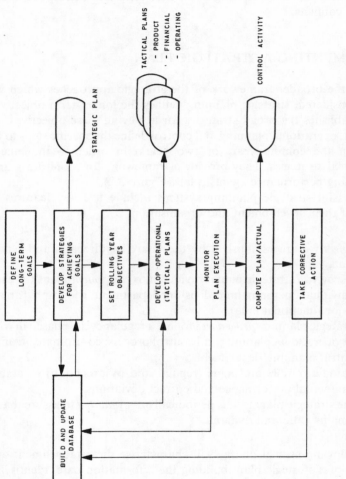

Figure 3.2 The definition of long-term goals can be made in an interactive manner through computer support. The same is true of strategic planning, tactical plans, and control action.

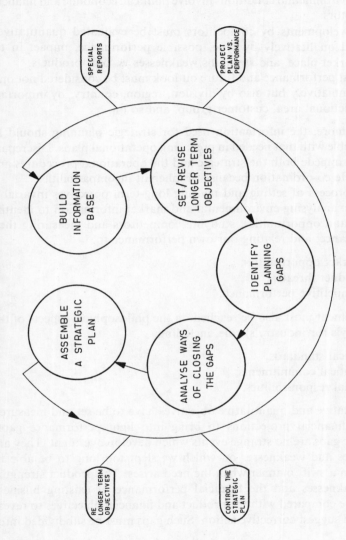

PHASES OF STRATEGIC PLANNING

SPECIAL REPORTS

PROJECT PLAN VS. PERFORMANCE

BUILD INFORMATION BASE

SET/REVISE LONGER TERM OBJECTIVES

IDENTIFY PLANNING GAPS

ASSEMBLE A STRATEGIC PLAN

ANALYSE WAYS OF CLOSING THE GAPS

RE LONGER TERM OBJECTIVES

CONTROL THE STRATEGIC PLAN

Figure 3.3 All five phases of strategic planning can be supported interactively through computers and communications. Expert systems are very helpful in obtaining results.

environmental conditions, developments by competitors, and the organisation's own past performance and future outlook.

● Environmental conditions involve political, economic and financial factors.
● Developments by competitors must be evaluated quantitatively and qualitatively by type, possible performance, impact in the market-place, and strengths/weaknesses *vs* 'our' products.
● Past performance and future outlook must be considered not only cumulatively but also by division, region, country; by important functional area, customer group, and so on.

Furthermore, the information used for strategic planning should be compatible with that needed in preparing operational plans. Discrepancies will impede both the strategic and the operational procedures and invalidate co-ordination because of inherent incompatibilities.

The process of setting and revising long-term objectives invariably involves: analysing environmental and market information to identify threats and opportunities; studying competitors and measuring their performance; and relating our own performance to:

● market opportunities;
● product threats;
● competitive performance.

Agreement must also be reached on the philosophical aspects of the company's (or industry's) role, including:

● ethical standards;
● political commitments;
● social responsibilities.

Qualitative and quantitative objectives have to be set and measured against financial projections to bring into light performance gaps. Strategic gaps are no strange events which develop overnight. They are exposures and weaknesses on which we slept too long to be able to handle in a swift manner when the need arises. The product strengths and weaknesses and the financial performance of existing business should be compared with the product and financial objectives to reveal gaps and suggest corrective action. Such gaps must be subdivided into:

● *Performance* issues which indicate the extent to which the total planning gap can be bridged by improving existing business.
● *Strategic* matters underlining the most serious aspects to be bridged by new activities and crash programmes.

In this sense, developing a strategic plan will practically involve co-ordinating and combining the distinct plans for countries, divisions and departments into an overall framework; reviewing and amending this framework through integration of the operating perspectives and the definition of gaps to be closed; improving activities by:

● identifying areas of potential improvement;
● estimating levels of return on investments;
● evaluating financial projections;
● identifying threats and opportunities;
● estimating their impact;
● introducing new activities in order to close possible gaps and move forward.

Strategic plans must be developed covering these areas for all business opportunities, cutting across the organisational divisions and integrating product, market, client base and financial information.

FORMALISING CORPORATE PLANNING

The task of defining corporate planning is both challenging and complex because there are no universally accepted definitions of the concepts with which we are dealing. Companies look at strategic planning at different levels of generality. Even people in the same organisation may define planning differently. Corporate planning is meaningful, but its concepts may take a range of meanings depending upon company culture. It would change colour and dimension according to the time, place and people involved. Furthermore, planning structures vary widely, and organisations often define planning in terms of a part of the whole. This approach fails to appreciate that the failures in human decisions concerning even departmental issues often have implications for the life of the whole enterprise. Strategic planning is handicapped.

Global planning involves the search for alternative courses of action affecting every sector of the business, the expression of the criteria to be used in the evaluation of such alternatives, the acid test of the alternatives themselves, and the selection of a course of action. All these steps demand executive decisions which are far reaching and cannot be confined in one focus. In addition, an important subject in strategic planning is the focus on the future: future markets, future trends, innovation, competition, growth, and so on. Inability of management to forecast the future with a reasonable degree of accuracy is one of the reasons why some firms fail. Sometimes this inability is traceable to the tendency to avoid thinking, which in turn results in poor decision-making.

There are, for example, two ways of looking at the acquisition of Electronic Data Systems (EDS) by General Motors. A limited one is to consider the contribution the acquired company (an acknowledged leader in data processing) can bring in revamping GM's information systems operations. The broader (and true) one is to make General Motors a premier technology company. Some analysts do not even rule out the possibility that GM eventually might offer an array of financial services with EDS, which has been a major supplier of data processing services to financial concerns. One person who thought this possibility could exist was none other than H. Ross Perot, the energetic EDS chairman who, for some time continued to head the Dallas-based concern after its absorption by GM, and who was also appointed to the motor manufacturer's board. 'You have raised a valid question, and described a capability, that exists at EDS,' he said in an interview, but hastened to add that whether such venture would carry 'a high, low or medium priority is up to GM.' The primary purpose of the acquisition has however been to make GM more competitive with its Japanese adversaries.

Terence Quinn, a technology analyst at Dean Witter Reynolds said at the time: 'GM's immediate problems won't be remedied at once. It will be quite a task to make GM lean.' Other GM watchers were to comment that when those few years have passed the question will arise of 'What to do with EDS next'. They note that:

- The motor vehicle market is essentially finite.
- Given sharp competition throughout the world, a motor manufacturer can hope to improve market penetration by only so much.
- Further, GM has indicated it hopes by 1990 to derive as much as 30 per cent of revenue from non-motor-vehicle sources, compared with 5 per cent at the time of the EDS acquisition.

Could there come a day when GM might acquire a Merrill Lynch, Hutton or Paine Webber? 'They should do it now, when the industry is on its rear end', and while a major securities firm could be bought relatively cheaply, suggested a financial analyst. In fact, a major GM asset in any move into financial services would be its General Motors Acceptance Corporation unit (GMAC), with its huge bank of credit information on 6.5 million retail customers to whom it lends money to buy cars at favourable terms. This is a potential customer base for financial services. If marketed correctly, it could sell them any number of other services and products. Lending money to such large customer base is a hand-holding operation. It is also a clear example where optimising one unit's business in a king-size organisation does not provide the best solution for the whole. A corporate-wide view has to be taken.

A similar case can be made about products coming out of research and development and the effort of marketing them. Not only close co-ordination but also a corporate-wide view is necessary. Strategically, being the 'technology first' is not really the best idea. What's best in terms of strategy is to be first in satisfying market needs. Jack Tramiel, the man who made Commodore and then gobbled Atari, not only got this message but also applied it. His adage is: 'Business is war.'

Just because company life and the underlying business philosophy varies so much from one firm to the other, the only way to find the potential giants of tomorrow is to get on the road and meet the companies. You must also understand their mentality, asking compan-ies about their competitors and discovering which they feel are doing interesting things.

In business research one can find quite a few companies growing from $20 million to maybe $100 million in revenues this year, but which are one-product companies facing the looming threat of new competition. How do we realistically value those companies? To do so you have to study their corporate planning – if there is any. Can the company continue to be successful? Besides excellent management, there should be a proprietary product for a large, fast-growing market and a clear strategy for future products. A sense of realism by management as to the possible competitive threat is also important.

'You also have to study trends,' suggests Mr Soderberg, the chief executive of a Swedish investment firm. 'Sweden used to be the world's largest steel producer, then the British and Germans overtook us, the Americans followed, then the Japanese and Koreans and so on. Investment in these old industry sectors is stagnating in Europe. That is why there must be a strategy change.'

In formalising corporate planning it is wise to start from the fundamentals. This means the conceptual method of evaluating the future and its consequences. That is why the introduction to logical thinking was so important. Formalisation helps bring into perspective the need for an examination of evolving chains of cause, effect, and decision based upon choice. The period involved should be at least that which terminates in the liquidation of commitments – because that is what planning is all about: the commitments which we have made or are planning to make.

The planning period will extend at or beyond that time, leading to a conscious choosing from among alternative courses of action. As it is conceived in the business world, long-range planning is not long-range because it covers a future time-span. It is long-range because it attacks in a systematic way the opportunities and problems important to the future of the organisation. Hence, formal planning should begin with the specification of basic purposes, then develop objectives, aims, targets, goals to form a network of milestones. This helps define strategies and policies needed to attain these goals with least unexpected cost. It also helps elaborate subordinate goals and plans to reach basic purposes.

The cost often involved in meticulous planning, and the decisions regarding the wisdom of this cost, is one of the reasons for planning failures. Some companies do not realise the importance of strategic planning, and even if they can afford the respective cost, they are not willing to invest in it. Other firms may be willing to do long-term planning but, management thinks, their financial position does not allow them to secure the services of analysts, researchers, system engineers and other specialists, and the tools they need to do their work in an able manner. In either case, a management decision is behind the resulting failure.

Yet the future is uncertain – and therefore rewarding. If an analyst makes an estimate of a future situation it is inevitable that he will make certain assumptions as to what 'might happen'. The less skilled the analyst, the more these assumptions may turn out to be wrong. But also, the less skilled the analyst the less he would be paid. Sometimes management decides that the less the company pays for services, the better. The opposite is true. I remember in a meeting of IBM stockholders one of the delegates asked a corporate executive why IBM pays its people so much. The man to whom the query was addressed replied, 'Because if you pay peanuts, you get only monkeys.'

Often the failure in planning lies in the ability of management to identify the target factors. Many times management is utterly wrong in its diagnosis. Diagnostic work is one of the most difficult types in making decisions.

Another reason for failure lies in the unwillingness to accept the fact that, in this modern age of technical progress, obsolescence, product risk, and the time factor are three major risks with which we are faced continuously in business. Consequently these risks are not taken into consideration when a plan is being made and the plan is simply not realistic.

No link between the planning section and the operating departments is one more reason that accounts for the failure of some firms in their planning premises. Plans become superficial if they are not related to the real conditions of the enterprise. They lose contact with the happenings in the operating divisions, concentrating on what the staff departments think about them.

Some organisations are better than others at establishing formal planning processes and in making realistic forecasts. A couple of years ago Soviet officials were sniffing around the Department of Agriculture in Washington. Their mission: obtain up-to-date American projections of Russian crop production, based on satellite runs over the Soviet Union. Soviet agricultural officials in Moscow indeed admitted that US information on the country's farm outlook is better than that available to the Kremlin. This can be the result of better experience, but also of a planning methodology based on properly elaborated formal steps.

As an example from the business side, one known construction-industry supplier routinely performs analyses of its cost structure and develops simple five-year projections based on known, or extremely likely, changes from current circumstances. These evaluations take account of recent trends in materials costs and uncontrollable wage increases dictated by union contracts, cost-of-living escalations, anticipated requirements for statutory and contracted pension contributions, and a variety of other bases for projecting the future. The aim is to analyse those cost changes through current known factors, rather than to assess the future by the seat of the pants. The results of this simple, routinely produced analysis are often illuminating.

NOTES

1. *International Herald Tribune*, 19 November 1987.
2. New York: McGraw Hill, 1967.

4 Reasons for Strategic Planning

As we look to the future, with its challenges and opportunities, we are faced with the urgent need to develop an increasingly competent plan of action. The opportunities which we have can go by default to competitors who are planning today for their needs tomorrow. We must do the same and do it better.

To secure our future, we must build a management group which is second to none. These managers have an essential role in helping our organisation to meet its objectives. To the extent that they do their job in an able manner, they would plan for the future on a solid foundation. Our immediate future and the organisational efforts we have been making depend on sound management – now and in the future. As managers we have a major responsibility to develop strategic plans, keep them dynamic and implement them.

A simple definition of management is that it is the direction of an organisation of people towards its goals. Forecasting, planning, organising, staffing, directing (co-ordinating, motivating) and controlling are its functions, as we will see in the appropriate chapter. Management can fail by weakness in any of these areas, and a company is obviously no stronger than its managers.

As Figure 4.1 properly underlines, a company's strength can be assessed in a layered fashion, starting with strategic planning at the top, and with financial staying power on the bottom line. To survive, a firm needs management able to reconceptualise products, revamp procedures, revitalise programmes – before crises make drastic changes unavoidable or reach the point of no return.

In line with our growing needs, our strategies and our polices, we must develop plans. Such plans should be properly prepared to direct our resources. They should be supported by people of professional performance and potential. We must search for management in depth. This is one of our most important responsibilities. Its able execution calls for:

(1) Management philosophy;
(2) Skill and know-how;
(3) Management principles;
(4) Decision-making potential;

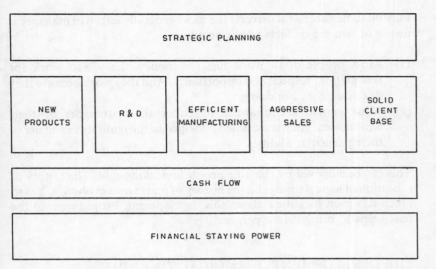

Figure 4.1　New product development, research activities, efficient manufacturing, aggressive sales, a solid client base, are the pillars on which a strategic plan rests. The financial staying power is the foundation.

(5)　A steadily improving management inventory;
(6)　Guidelines for management development.

Sound decision making helps achieve a reasonable profit through a valid organisation. We must not only hold but also improve our position in our industry. Decision making is a trust. Each of us merits that trust to the extent that we assist our organisation to achieve its goals. Competition is useful. We can thrive on it or succumb to it. We should choose to meet and surpass our competition. Excellence, with commensurate rewards, should be our company's and our personal objectives. We must be builders for the future as well as performers in the present.

Management is a challenge attained by awareness that we manage men first, then money, products, markets, methods and machines. For every management position there should be authority commensurate with responsibility. It should be used in harmony with other managers and departments to achieve organisational goals.

There is of course no magic formula for effective management. As people differ, so do managers. One thing, however, seems certain: the best managers are leaders who command respect, enthusiasm, and collaboration. But whether a manager is a leader or a driver (and there may be some successful drivers) the most generally effective manager is aware of two major facts about people.

(1) Most people don't work just for money. They also work for recognition, respect, and opportunity. And they work because they like what they are doing.
(2) Most people are unaware of either their strengths or their weaknesses. They must be led or helped to the realisation and use of their particular abilities.

This can be achieved by teaching people logical thought. The history of evolution of logical thought is the history of man's own evolution. Yet so much has been forgotten about this development. Projecting into the past helps to bring it into perspective.

THE DEVELOPMENT OF LOGICAL THOUGHT

There is always rationality and irrationality in management decisions. Often it depends on civilisations. What is rational for one civilisation may be irrational for another, and this makes quite a difference to the future course of events. Each major culture of the past – the Babylonians, the Chinese, the Greeks, the Romans – had its own definition of rationality. Such a definition permitted the men who lived under a specific culture to advance in a certain domain, but also checked their advance in other fields.

It is not often appreciated that within each culture and epoch the prevailing definition of rationality tends to block out certain domains and to forbid a number of hypotheses. Thinkers who break the barriers which the prevailing thoughts establish are often labelled heretics. Whether they will become pace-setters or odd-men-out depends on their ability to overcome these barriers and bring their ideas into perspective.

A comprehensive, self-explanatory approach, able to lead an organisation toward the fulfilment of its goals is one of the foremost aims of strategic planning. As Figure 4.2 suggests, it integrates know-how and timing, but also investment perspectives and cash flow, as well as a range of other issues which are key to survival. Technological breakthroughs, deregulation, volatile interest rates and widely fluctuating currency exchanges make such forward-looking, co-ordinating effort, necessary.

Strategic planners are people who break the barriers established by

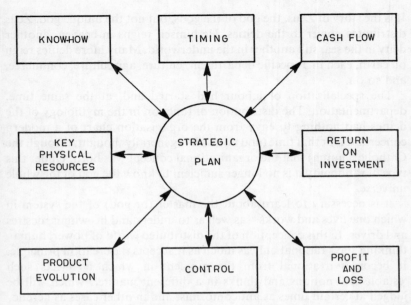

Figure 4.2 Know-how, timing, cash flow, are key components of a strategic plan. Another basic element is the research activity.

the past. They are by no means a homogeneous lot. By abiding by a different type of rationality, different people have been able to analyse, then integrate, a different concept of the world. This is just as true of individuals as of companies, nations, and whole continents. It constitutes a first milestone in examining human thought.

Other milestones must be brought under perspective. For many reasons, the next most critical in terms of rational thought is relative to the concept of power, namely, the mythology which surrounds the impact of power on human affairs and the implementation of power itself. Whether in ancient mythology the supreme being was called Bel Marduk or Kronos, it marked the beginning of a single all-mighty source of power. But slowly, as humanity developed in terms of rational thought, the unipolar idea of power was replaced by a plural world of roughly equal power sources. In a corporate context, this comes close to the institution of the board of directors.

Back to mythology again, in this restructured world of the intellect, each newly-defined 'supreme being' had its domain; it opposed its will to that of others, and disputed the course of events. Only at crucial moments, in the event of conflict, did a sovereign higher impose his will.

It is the story of Zeus, the god of the gods, but not the unique god. Zeus distributes power to the deities. He himself reigns in heaven, another deity in the sea, still another in the underworld. Many more deities reign on earth, each in a specific department: culture, agriculture, commerce, and so on.

The specialisation of labour had started and, at the same time, departmentation. The distribution of function in the mythology of the deities had nothing to envy from the organisation chart of a modern concern. It is at that time (and not, as it is generally thought, through the Catholic Church) that the organisational concept was born. Under this type of rationality it is no longer sufficient to know the god of the whole universe.

It is necessary to learn about the master (or god) of the system in which one lives and works – as well as to understand his whims, desires and drives. In this conception of the distributed world of power, human thinking stays rational only as much as it accepts the creation principle. It becomes irrational from the moment in which it rejects such 'established' notions and thinks in a different manner, which will be judged at certain times as anticonformist and in other cases as heretic.

While this is a limiting sense of looking at rationality and irrationality, it has had in itself a favourable outcome leading to another milestone. The very existence of such a dividing line channelled the thinking of men towards research on the guiding principles. In other terms, confronted with rational thought, the kingdom of the heavens carried within itself the seeds of its own destruction. With time and effort, open-eyed researchers and philosophers were able to penetrate beyond appearances.

- They were capable of explaining the sense of things and their origins.
- They were no longer governed by a deity which was established and fixed.
- They tried to find and define the principle on which power was established.

This is the third milestone in rational thinking and, as well, in human society. It made feasible the development of laws to regulate the affairs of men. It also brought a new structure of society.

Laws are rules. The legacy of the development of laws has been that the principle is no longer a force bigger than other forces and therefore determining the state of things, as Zeus used to do. The principle is part of a system of laws aiming to establish an equilibrium among elements. As is well known, this system of laws started with Solon (640–

558 BC). He was a world-travelled historian and writer before becoming a legislator. Solon's major contribution was a vast political and social reform precisely formulated in a system of laws.

Laws are the infrastructure of a process which largely rests on description of 'do' and 'don't' as well as on qualification. Next to qualification came the need for quantification. As a result, metrics was invented. Our desire to know things led us to the requirement of measuring them.

The development of qualifiable and quantifiable expressions, as well as their multiplication has been a rewarding experience. In line of rational thought, the next requirement was that of abstraction. Though in early human culture the process of abstract thinking was not flawless, it did open a new horizon in terms of our world conception. On its foundation, more exact approaches have been built. Even mistakes played a large part on the events which became the landmarks of mankind.

Qualification, quantification, idealisation, concretisation have been milestones in the development of rational thought. They are also to be found in the background of the process through which we reach decisions, though today we consider it to be a kind of second nature. From its exhaustive review of pertinent factors, management for instance concludes that overall objectives should include a policy stating the following goals:

(1) New product policy.
(2) Pricing targets.
(3) Return on capital employed not less than 'X' per cent.
(4) A defined amount of appreciation in earnings per share.

In addition, management may set other specific targets for itself: computer literacy, product and market diversification, growth through acquisition or company-wide cost reduction.

Considerable mental stress must be undergone when setting these objectives. For instance, an exhaustive analysis might leave management with two long-range objectives – to return the present business to a satisfactory earnings level or sell out to a better diversified corporation.

If the board reaches this *a priori* decision, strategic planning will come into play in rounding out the picture by contributing important facts and integrating divergent views. If the members of the planning team have different backgrounds, they can provide valuable criticism of proposed activities including:

- Initial conception.
- Painstaking analysis.
- Details of a possible technical implementation.

The latter must be the work of an individual who can devote much time and thought to the project. Forecasting, for example, requires care in collecting, analysing, checking, and weighing facts. It calls for intuition and imagination in drawing and presenting conclusions, qualities more likely to be shown by an individual than a group. Table 4.1 suggests planning cycle responsibilities by power centre in an enterprise. The reference also includes control level perspectives. The purpose of control is to determine whether objectives and policies have been carried out. Techniques of reporting include accounting, costing, statistics, decision support systems and graphic presentation.

As a policy-making body, the Board will concern itself with one or more major aspects of management: planning, control, formulation of objectives, organization, and senior management selection. Also with juristic questions. All these references require a significant amount of rational thought.

MILESTONES IN MANAGERIAL AWARENESS

Abstract thinking led to the appearance of conceptual categories which were then generalised, starting from the point they represent in a physical sense. When this approach reached its limits, thinkers found it necessary to reorganise the system of thought in order to improve their own conceptual capabilities.

Here comes the other milestone: that of the conversion from mainly oral to predominantly written word. Abstract thinking can be handled only so far in an oral dialectic form, but as experience accumulates we must have the possibility of recording it. In fact, if we carefully look into the process of the development of humanity, we should notice the passage from the oral to the written word. The same is true if we examine the way in which our thinking, plans and decisions are made.

It is not often appreciated that this passage from oral to written communications has been a fundamental change in the cultural efforts of man as well as in his decision-making abilities. Writing establishes:

- a new method for the exchange of ideas;
- a structured logic to guide our thinking;
- a more comprehensive type of communication between people.

Table 4.1 Management's responsibility for planning and control

Board of directors	General management	Departments
1. Establishing goals and objectives ● Earnings ● Growth ● Share of market ● Products and services ● Financial performance 2. Reviewing, revising, appraising results, approving 3. Promoting, changing, taking corrective action	1. Providing leadership and co-ordination 2. Elaborating plans 3. Committing available resources 4. Making investments 5. Assuring proper operations 6. Consolidating responsibility 7. Providing feedback 8. Developing income plan 9. Acquiring actual results 10. Comparing actual results with plan, controlling	1. Following-up on specific goals 2. Performing day-to-day operations 3. Obtaining results as per plans 4. Evaluating revenues and expenses 5. Assuring performance by line of business: ● R & D ● Manufacturing ● Marketing ● Finance ● Personnel ● Services 6. Using plan as basis for control operations

Notes:
1. Strategic planning works both for the board and for general management.
2. Plans must be reviewed on predetermined periodic basis with revised projections being developed.

Writing is much more of a critical form than oral discourse. And for good reason. This was duly appreciated in antiquity. Since the beginning of the fourth century BC, Platon made repeated attacks against the established pedagogical system which, at the time, was based on oral poetry. The alternative which he offered was the philosophical dialogue which itself evolved from oral to written form. A written text is a text to which we can return; it is one which can be subjected to a critical evaluation. A written text also permits the definition rather than simply the description of things – thus helping to eleminate incomprehensions and inconsistencies.

Robert McNamara, formerly President of Ford, Minister of Defense and President of the World Bank, gives the following advice on the discipline of writing:

(1) The discipline of *writing* something down is the first step towards making it happen.
(2) Put your idea on paper. If you cannot do that, you have not thought it out.
(3) Write down the ten things you absolutely have to do. Concentrate on them. As for the rest: forget it.
(4) Never make major decisions without having a choice of at least vanilla and chocolate.

The steady inquisition into the nature of things led to another aftermath which eventually became the seventh milestone of logic. This is the process of questioning the origin, nature, substance, sense and intent of things. This inquisitory logic (of which Socrates is the patriarch) is different from those preceding it: not only does it define the problems, it also allows (indeed implies) searches for their solution. Part of the solution is the connection which exists between the component parts of a given system. It will be appreciated that historical dates do not always follow the chronological order of the outlined milestones. A principle (logical or physical) maybe discovered, but some time may elapse before its implementation.

Centuries passed by before this inquisitory process – and the system thinking to which it leads – was put into effect. Searching for astronomical laws, Johannes Kepler (AD 1571–1630) tried to establish the relations which exist between planets and their orbits. To achieve this he conceived a planetarium in which the orbits of five planets were described and a sun placed at the centre of the system, which was revolutionary for his time. The then-established notions were challenged not by another new mythology, but through a logical system of thought.

The great discoveries of the post-medieval time are due not only to the talent of great mathematicians, astronomers and physicists, but also to the methodology of observation and of classification of experience. These discoveries also required a prodigious scientific imagination leading to hypotheses which were almost heritical at the time.

But scientific thought had a prerequisite which in terms of human accomplishments is best described by the evolutionary concept established through the practice of history, namely, the elaboration of case studies. The development of historical thought which preceded scientific thought by many centuries was instrumental in creating the methodology of coherent and consistent observations and the collection of references, thus creating the eighth milestone. Historical thought preceded scientific thought in the establishment of a concept of non-contradiction – even if the case studies history books describe have often been manipulated. This was in itself a mainstream development with a far-reaching impact. Granted, as far as Western thought is concerned, the concept of non-contradiction has its origins in the laws of Solon, the geometry of Pythagoras and Euclid, the logical process of Thales. But it is one thing to deal with a closed system, another with an open one which features many unknowns. Here we are talking about the coherence and comprehensiveness of a discourse – and therefore of logic.

Having established a rigorous methodology, scientific thought laid the grounds for another human accomplishment: management thought and decision making, that is, the ninth milestone.

Prior to having a methodology of appraisal, we had no sense of reaching conclusions. We were, therefore, incapable of making decisions which could stand logical tests. Many things escaped our attention: above all, the ability to make a correct evaluation of circumstances and to apply measure; and also the ability to be factual and able to document our decisions. We were lacking effective intelligence, or more precisely, the ability to mobilise intelligence for a practical end in an actual situation. As practised in business and industry, effective intelligence is distinct from academic intelligence which is the possession of knowledge. Effective intelligence implies the ability to arrange facts and queries into a decision-making sequence.

Paraphrasing Winston Churchill, managerial courage is no whore to be picked up on the street by a man with a tommy-gun. To manage effectively the resources at our disposal we must have the courage to stick our necks out – lose or win.

Managerial courage is one of the vital ingredients in decision making, but it is not the only one. The how-to-do of the manager owes a great deal to:

- the technical concepts of the profession;
- the logic of physics and of mathematics (which developed earlier);
- the order of operations which the slowly established analytical logic made feasible.

We have plenty of reasons today to ensure that the development of rationality is no revelation in itself but follows a historic character. We have reviewed nine milestones in the evolution of logical thought; now comes the tenth.

Goethe (1769–1832) once wrote in a correspondence: 'Dear friend: Sorry to write you such a long letter – but I don't have the time to write a short one.' The sense of *time* as a basic human resource established itself a mere two centuries ago. The orderly, punctual life which first took place in monasteries is not native to mankind, though by now the West is so thoroughly regimented by the clock that it is second nature. The measurement and observance of time is no fact of nature, but it is the basis of our civilisation and culture. 'Time is money.' The clock, not the steam engine, is the key machine of the modern industrial age. During the last forty years, the computer has become the electronics/information extension of the clock. Time has now become a second human nature and, as such, it influences and affects rational thought. Time has become as precious as any other resource at our disposal: managerial know-how, technical skills, money, the physical assets, appealing products and market standing.

These ten milestones characterise the evolution of managerial thinking. Strategic planning did not come out of the blue. It developed as a matter of course because of competitive pressure, but in so doing it capitalised on the work of giants and, sometimes, on outcomes from pure chance.

Strategic planning does, however, require a methodology. Such a methodology is analytic. The road to every manager's success is paved with a solid understanding of strategy, analysis and culture. Combining the underlying ideas can provide the necessary foundation. There exist, of course, different approaches to methodological analysis. In our Western civilisation, one of them is the Harvard type. It contrasts managerial goals, the means available to an enterprise to meet such goals, and exogenous variables.

Another is thorough planning, albeit with uncertainty a major ingredient. More specifically, planning is the process which permits an organisation to study, analyse, formulate and explain its strategy, after having asked itself about the dominant alternatives.

A third is corporate management of the Zeus conception. It uses the privileges of the top executive level in establishing overall goals, channelling resources and assuring corrective action relative to interruption or discontinuities created by an unstable environment and/or internal resources which have run out of control.

A fourth, recently on the increase, is the dialogue method. It puts senior executives in a logical conflict with one another, each maintaining and defending a thesis:

● One person (or team) follows the organisation's own strategy to reach its goals.
● Another person (or team) follows the anti-strategy, or that of the opponents.

From this can result a most valuable methodology which is becoming known as gap analysis.

GAP ANALYSIS AND PRODUCT PLANNING

At board meetings of General Motors, Alfred P. Sloan, Jr, used to provoke disagreement and had no time for 'yes men'. Once he said to the other members of the board of directors: 'Gentlemen, I take it we are all in complete agreement on the decision here.' Everyone nodded assent, and Sloan concluded: 'Then, I suggest we postpone further discussion of this matter until our next meeting to give ourselves time to develop disagreement and perhaps gain some understanding of what the decision is all about.' The aim was to challenge the issue and, by so doing, flush out its weak spots.

The Japanese excel in encouraging such disagreement and even more so in reaching a consensus, termed by them *nemawashi* or root binding. Everyone involved in implementing the decision also takes part in helping reach the decision. This is an essential part of Japanese society. No matter how large the group, from the smallest enterprise to the multibillion-dollar multinational, nothing gets done until the people involved first disagree, then reach a group consensus. The term *root binding* is very apt for, as a gardener carefully wraps the roots of a tree together before transplanting it, senior executives in Japan involve all the concerned people in the decision-making process. This approach, does at first sight seem to be tedious and rather slow. But the challenge is what counts.

Back in 1953, Louis Sorel used to say that the greatest gap companies

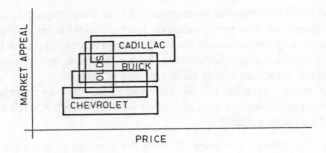

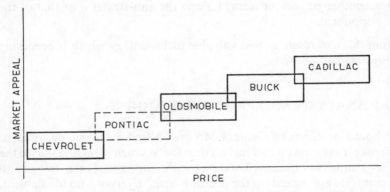

Figure 4.3   In the 1920s, Alfred Sloan reorganised an overlapping line of
            products at General Motors and streamlined them for better
            market appeal.

experience – as well as the No. 1 reason for their downfall – is in their
product line. Quite often the products overlap. In other cases, they leave
uncovered a wide market range.

Sorel was taking as an example General Motors. Plot in function of
price *vs* market appeal, the upper part of Figure 4.3 shows the GM
product lines prior to the Sloan restructuring of the late 1920s. The lower
part exhibits the restructuring Alfred Sloan has done.

But not all companies are as careful with their product lines. When, in
the early 1960s, General Electric acquired the French Compagnie de
Machines Bull, and Olivetti Elettronica in Italy, it found itself with five
different product lines largely overlapping one another – all being in
internal competition for technical/financial resources and management
attention, rather than presenting a dynamic product range able to
conquer the computer market.

No gap analysis was done. The conflict remained. Gamma 10 and

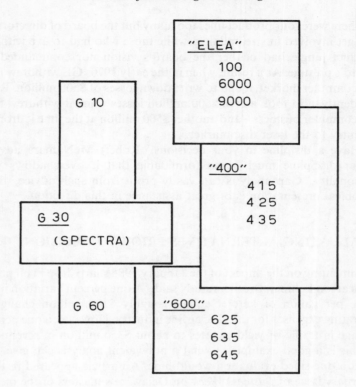

"ELEA"
100
6000
9000

G 10

"400"
415
425
435

G 30
(SPECTRA)

G 60

"600"
625
635
645

- DIFFERENT PRODUCT LINES
- DIFFERENT BASIC TECHNOLOGIES
- DIFFERENT BASIC SOFTWARE
- NO AP PORTABILITY
- DIFFERENT SUPPORT REQUIREMENTS

Figure 4.4   In the 1960s, the computer line at General Electric/Bull/Olivetti
Elettronica did not undergo the necessary streamlining. The
aftermath was disastrous.

Gamma 60 came from Bull; G30 was another name for Spectra, an RCA
computer; Elea 100, 6000, 9000 was the Olivetti Elettronica line. GE had
three 400 models. GE also had three 600 models (Figure 4.4). The latter
was the outgrowth of a Department of Defense computer designed by
GE. The former was the follow-up of a contract GE had landed in the
late 1950s with Bank of America.

There were four product lines too many but the board of directors did not get involved in streamlining, while those who had to live with this product jungle had neither the board's vision nor commanded the board's prestige. As a result, when in the early 1970s GE withdrew from the computer market, it had to write down losses of $500 million. RCA, incidently, also took a cool $500 million losses when it withdrew from the computer business – and another $500 million at the time it dropped its entry to the laser disc market.

'Have a disipline in your decisions,' Robert McNamara advises. 'Your discipline must be so formidable that it overshadows your personality.' Gap analysis can vastly profit from such advice, and a graphical presentation is of great assistance in this direction.

EVALUATING ALTERNATIVES PRIOR TO DECISION

Commenting on the impact of the January 1985 sharp drop in oil prices, a Shearson Lehman Brothers study said: 'A one percent variation in the price per gallon of kerojet equals roughly $100 million change in operating expenses for the U.S. airline industry. However, a one percent change in traffic or yield equates to about $350 million in revenues.'

This is a good example of what a polyvalent analysis can give, and what a one-sided evaluation would hide. An article appeared in the 3 February issue of *Business Week* on Delaware's masters of the merger game, and made the following comment: 'The two attorneys skillfully played both sides of the merger game – representing raiders or defending companies under attack.'

In the long run, the debate and consensus process saves time. Having arrived at a decision themselves, the decision-makers feel committed to it.

● It is their decision, hence
● they implement it with great zeal and speed.

They have a moral commitment to the consensus decision and feel bound to put it into action quickly. There are no reservations, as is always the case when executives are simply ordered to implement a decision taken at the top. 'Flat orders,' Sloan once remarked, 'destablize the base.'

But there is more to it when using analytic, dialectic approaches able to identify gaps and pin-point weak spots. Firstly, indecision is expensive – sometimes very expensive. Apart from its high cost, indecision can harm both the organisation and the individual executive.

It is a habit, a bad one, and unless it is broken it can break the corporate standing.

Secondly, the lack of an analytic approach leaves too many dark areas. Decisions are not reached with a full view, much less understanding, of the relevant facts.

The appropriate examination of alternatives seeks to ascertain how large a gap will exist between corporate objectives and probable reality, if we rely wholly on current information. It should be done by professionals with sufficient familiarity with their company and its place in its industry, to make a rough first estimate of the gap between aims and reality. There is no need for precision at this stage. The first question is: 'Which are my alternatives?' After the apparently best is selected, the question is not exactly how big the gap may be between goals and solution but, rather, *where* it is. An order of magnitude evaluation will be satisfactory at this stage.

First, the board needs to consider the corporate plans. Then it should evaluate whether the plans, available resources and going procedures can realistically be expected to fill the gap(s). If the answer is *yes*, it is one thing. If *no*, corrective action must start rolling.

Sometimes solutions which, from a distance, look clear and favourable may turn out to be quite the opposite. In September 1987 an arbitration decision in a dispute between IBM and its largest mainframe rival Fujitsu, opened the lid of Pandora's box – to IBM.

The arbitrators upheld Fujitsu's claims of access to critical IBM information, albeit for a very substantial fee and for a limited time. The IBM-Fujitsu fight centered on *operating systems* (OS) that guide the basic operations of computers and control their communications with the outside world.

The arbitration result is a binding decision that lets either company, for a fee, inspect the other's software and try to emulate it. It is also a good example of gap analysis in action (inspecting the OS for evaluation of gap and emulation reasons), as well as a telling sequel to the choice of an alternative.

Prior to the arbitration ruling, Fujitsu's very future as a maker of IBM mainframe clones was in doubt. It looked as if IBM might pursue it in court for years to come for its mainframe OS clone. That made many customers jittery about Fujitsu and is rumoured to be the reason why Siemens severed the Fujitsu link. After the ruling, Fujitsu will be able to keep its operating system compatible with IBM's over an estimated five to ten years timeframe.

So sweeping policy issues are handled by the board. When detail is necessary professionals are called into play. Their assistance is often vital as many situations are obscure and require deeper study than a given board member (or even line manager) can provide from his experience and judgement alone. Rough estimates of situations and implications might yeild and appropriate decision. If they do not, further analysis and planning is required.

Corporations go broke in good times when they become overextended and undermanaged – which are usually the same thing. The troubles of Penn Central and the Chrysler of the mid-to-late 1970s reflected decisions to finance ambitious growth projects via ever more expensive (and less available) credit passing on higher costs through higher product prices, while repaying debt with cheaper dollars. In the good old inflationary times, the game might have been worth the candle so long as product demand extrapolations were reasonably near the mark. If they were not, trouble came thick and fast. Braniffs, International Harvesters, Wickers and so many others reflected the side effects of declining rates of inflation: lower profits and cash flows, the need to refinance debt with dearer dollars, overextended inventories that could be reduced only at a loss and, above all, the need for a management to adjust its planning and budgeting to financial and economic trends, which they did not have the guts to do.

Even if a gap analysis is made largely on the basis of the chief executive's judgement and personal knowledge, it can be refined by providing assessment of where the present momentum of the firm will carry it, five, ten or fifteen years hence. Such assessments often have to take account of external issues such as industry trends, raw material supplies, competition, the influences of economic, technological, social and political factors, as well as a variety of others. Each of these can represent a threat or opportunity that could upset tradition and modify, upward or downward, the present momentum of the company.

A similar examination has to be made of an organisation's internal strengths and limitations of the potential for improvement. Of considerable importance is gauging the hidden cost of non-formal planning, that is, the cost in terms of lost opportunities, undetected threats, and such intangibles as corporate morale and standing in the financial community. What would it have meant to our company had we foreseen seven years ago the development that today is at the root of our problems?

Appropriate charts will help executive vision. In general the following comparisons of projected performance might be of worth.

(1)   Our firm's sales growth v. the growth of the economy as a whole.
(2)   Our firm's sales v. the growth of industry sales.

(3) Competitors' share of market and our share of market.
(4) Our firm's return on equity v. the average return on equity in the industry.
(5) The average profit after taxes as a percentage of sales in the industry and our firm's projected performance.
(6) Our own profit performance v. that of industry leaders.
(7) Direct labour and direct material cost as a percentage of the market price of the finished product.

Gap analysis is critical in identifying business opportunities, both potential and lost. Therefore it plays a major role in formal long-range strategic planning and marketing.

Japanese companies are a good example. Their marketing starts long before their goods are produced and continues long after sales are made.

● Firms first search for attractive opportunities.
● Then they develop appropriate products that represent a value to the customer.
● They evaluate strengths and weaknesses – and only then.
● They choose market-entry points and times.

This is done carefully with the purpose of gaining a strong initial foothold. Then, by capitalising on their strengths and starving their weaknesses, they shift into market-penetration planning aimed at broadening their customer base and expanding their market shares.

When Japanese companies finally achieve substantial market leadership, they adopt strategies to maintain and defend their market position. As this process builds momentum, it grows beyond the logical boundaries of gap analysis, and becomes a process of target industry identification – then of target products. A *target industry* is an industry worthy of whatever support is deemed necessary to make it strong domestically and to help it become and remain competitive in the international arena.

The adoption of a target-industry approach capitalises on strengths. Such strengths should be seen under the aspect of the *new competition*, characterised by fairly different variables from the old. When we talk of gap analysis, our reference should be towards the new competitive forces invariably identified as: a highly intelligent, disciplined and skilled workforce with co-operative labour–management relations, in sharp contrast to the adversarial pattern of old days. Emphasis is specifically placed on the medium and high technology that enables Japan (and other Asian countries) to compete in the very industries that are mainstays of the Western economy. The new competition also involves capital sources that accept a lower rate of return and a considerably longer pay-out horizon, as well as:

● Government direction and subsidies to help business;
● Home markets that are protected, often explicitly but sometimes subtly;
● A sharp, aggressive export orientation;
● Sophisticated concepts of business and marketing strategies; and
● A steady search for competitive improvements.

Some authors cite in their explanations of Japanese success character- istics such as lifetime employment, quality circles, and just-in-time inventories. yet, in contrast to single-factor explanations, the japanese success story must be understood as the result of a complex interplay of several important issues, a steady gap analysis and correction being one of the pillars.

A WINNING STRATEGY

A winning strategy has to have a vision and a message. The preferred approach must be one which examines each risk carefully and assesses the balance of benefits which may be achieved. If every development can be seen to pay for itself, the second-order effects will contribute to corporate well-being. This presupposes the ability to pass from planning to implementation without the loss of time or resources. Unless we can implement plans, they have no value whatsoever.

Military strategy was reflected in battlefield performance by General Patton. He appreciated what it meant to be offensive: 'Wars are won by killing people, not by defending land. Let the enemy have any land he wants if we can get him into a position where we can kill him.'

The implementation message which should accompany a strategic plan must be clear and comprehensive. As Alfred Sloan was to remark with reference to General Motors: 'The primary object of the corpora- tion, we declared, was to make money. Not just to make cars. Positive elements like this have a flavor that has gone out of fashion. But I think the ABC of business has merits for reaching policy conclusions.'[1] While profits are not the only measure of corporate success, it is the one that can be best subjected to metrics.

But if the implementation of a strategic plan is made outside the prevailing corporate culture, the odds are that it will fail. Even in the same country, and in the same industrial brance, corporate culture can differ. Such differences condition the people working for the firm and, therefore, their decision-making ability.

Among Japanese trading companies, Mitsui is known for its more individualistic, less formal style. There is a saying in Japan: 'Mitsui for people, Mitsubishi for organisation.' Mitsui is also considered more aggressive and more apt to take investment risks.

When management takes investment risks the opportunities for profits may be greater, and so is the probability that once in a while it will get clobbered. Furthermore, it is wrong to assume that size and decades of experience in business translate automatically into financial health. There is a long list of corporate giants with these qualifications that have plunged into bankruptcy or oblivion. A winning strategy must consider this evidence.

In the longer run, in the life of a corporation, what seems to matter dearly is who has the most money and the most physical endurance. Managerial talent and sophistication play their part. But on the bottom line, the contest is between top quality people. There is a saying in business: 'Don't count out a $50-billion company.' And it is true – but within limits.

On 9 April 1984, the New York Treasury-bond-futures market was stunned when Marsh and McLennan, the largest US insurance broker, said it was writing down its first-quarter earnings by $60 million because of losses in the bond market. A write-down of that size would normally indicate that the actual losses were at least twice that much. Yet it was not the size of the reported loss that shocked the bond-futures traders. Rather, it was the questions it raised, questions that some futures-market specialists say probably tell more about the losses than whatever else will surface on the subject. Typical of the questions were those posed by Richard L. Sandor, senior Vice-President of Drexel Burnham Lambert, who remarked in *Business Week*:

> Given the fact that, to our best knowledge, all the losses occurred in the cash-bond market, I'd like to know two things . . . How a top company could lose so much money in so brief a time without internal alarm bells ringing in the auditor's office. Secondly, why would any money-market professional go naked in the market in this day and age, instead of hedging all or part of the exposure with futures.

A winning strategy will profit by following the advice which can be read between the lines of Sandor's queries. Strategic planning is not a matter of laying out some beautiful-looking plans. Such plans must have a backbone and the backbone is solid business practice.

A 1982 newsletter by Prudential-Bache Securities on the then developing illiquidity problems in US industry said: 'That we have illiquidity problems is clear. Government deficits and bad loans around the world mean that less credit will be available for more normal uses as business expands. At the same time, we see signs that consumers and corporations are not financially prepared to sustain a strong recovery.' That is the case when solid business practices at board of directors level have taken the back seat.

A winning strategy will pay due tribute to the management of change. Organisational change does not come as a matter of course. Mr Scott's attempt to revitalise the A & P stores' management ran into stiff resistance from company veterans. 'Changing this company is harder than reforming the civil service,' groaned one senior A & P executive at the time.

Revitalising can be done internally with a sharp knife or, when product problems prevail, through partnership. As the chief executive officer of a computer manufacturer asked himself on one occasion: 'Are we willing to set aside our egos and find companies that have complementary strengths to ours? Technology and low-cost manufacturing; hardware and software; PBX and computers; systems and components; a valid distribution network; entries to the office market to extend the reach of our scientific market operation?' (*Business Week*)

George B. Merrick, an engineering Vice-President at Rockwell said:

> 'There used to be head-scratching out in Cedar Rapids, where we build that inertial equipment, wondering what the hell Rockwell was doing building a satellite that will negate its other equipment. But believing you can't hold back technology, Rockwell concluded that since technology is going to wipe us out in some areas, we would better be at the front end of it in others. (*Business Week*)

Even well-intentioned internal barriers to innovation stifle the creative process which exists. They strangle the effort to develop products and processes that meet or anticipate customer requirements, hence keeping the company profitable and prosperous. I know at least one major firm which started its long decline by filling much of the giant facility with obsolete equipment from factories it was closing down elsewhere.

And there is precisely the opposite, winning posture. In 1981 Iowa Beef earned $58 million on sales of $5.2 billion. Company officials have consistently pumped profits back into upgraded facilities. Said spokesman Charles Harness: 'We have a philosophy that if we can still recognise a plant after ten years, we must have done something wrong.'

An integral part of the strategy of an enterprise is the plan of allocation and utilisation of available resources, including the future resources and the commitments we have made in terms of the future. The object of a strategic plan should be to modify, or adjust, the competitive equilibrium which exists between resources and requirements. This helps stabilise the operational base in an organisation. Overall strategies drive functional strategies, which in turn guide resource allocation. This means tactical decisions.

Take the steel industry as an example. In late 1985 it was estimated that the West's producing capacity stood about 20 per cent above need. But then it was stated by Thomas C. Graham, President of Jones and Laughlin, that the US steel industry was the most economically efficient in the world. True, the Japanese produce a lot more cheaply than the Americans, while Koreans still expand steel output because they are obviously confident of their ability to compete. By economically efficient, however, Graham explained that he doesn't mean cost of production. He means profits.

Steel is capital-intensive, and it takes healthy profits to raise the new money to modernise plants and thus to lower production costs. The Japanese, Graham said, almost make never more profit than 1 per cent of sales, far too little to induce investment on the US capital market. Japanese firms operate with as much as 80 per cent debt, whereas a steel firm in the United States with 50 per cent borrowed capital would be considered heavily overloaded and would be unable to attract further financing.

Evidently strategic planning and cultural differences tend to merge: the one is embedded in the other. The cultural difference often leads to a reshaping of the organisational structure. Compared to European and American firms, Japanese companies are distinguished by a fairly flat organisation: between the President and the foreman, Toyota features five layers; Ford has ten. The fewer layers of authority, the more efficient the organisation. An operating executive trying to get something done for a client should not have to go through more than two levels to get a resolution. This is a strategic consideration in terms of organisation which does not very often get appreciated – yet it counts a lot in terms of operating efficiency. (See Figure 4.5.)

Another important criterion is flexibility. Like good sailors, good managers are those mentally fit to take whatever comes to them. They can accept a bad environment to make themselves better managers. And enthusiasm also matters.

A winning strategy would focus on areas where there is no end to

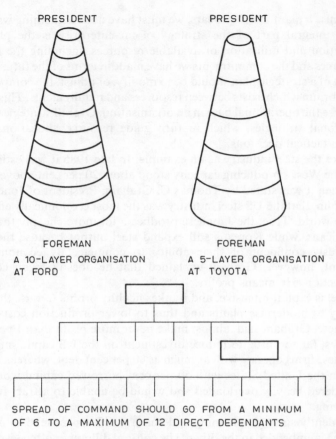

Figure 4.5   Our goal should be to reduce the management layers in the organisation and expand the span of control. High technology is instrumental only when management decides that the organisation must change and sticks to its decision.

proficiency, where products are always being introduced and techniques are always changing. Able management would ask itself whether an area is intensive enough – and whether there are enough ingredients for competitive products. This creates market leadership.

NOTE

1. *My Years with General Motors* (New York: Doubleday, early 1960s).

5 The Board of Directors

The last two chapters focused on strategic planning, on the decisions taken by the board of directors cannot be made independently of corporate strategy, and they are often conditioned by the latter. Similarly, government policy not only shapes the economic future, but it can both promote and inhibit the development of national and multinational enterprises – as discussed in the concluding chapter of this book.

It is therefore no surprise that today a growing number of US, British, German, French, Italian, Japanese and other firms employ full-time analysts to study the political climate at home and abroad. They examine the government decisions being made, the impact these will have on their operations, as well as the political, economic and social climate at large.

Virtually all major multinational companies are seeking ways to improve their in-house political analysis skills, as turmoil in the Middle East and revolution in Africa, Asia or Latin America underscore the need for better information product demand, market growth, political stability, and at home – from employment patterns, to taxation. Political stability, labour-strife, foreign-investment opportunities, associated risks, new legislation affecting taxes, currency exchange rates and profit remittances, are highlighting specific areas of interest. These issues are taken up (more precisely, should be taken up) in a critical manner by the corporation's board of directors, where policy decisions are (or should be) made.

The study of literature relating to corporate life, however, reveals that in relation to its importance the board of directors has probably undergone less study than any other critical organism of industrial operations. This lack of study may arise from the fact that few men combine a practical experience in board activities with the urge and skill to analyse and write about their experiences, but most likely the primary reason is that there is nothing standard about board activities and the deliberations which take place in board meetings.

There is, as well, a major difference in board function between American and central European practices. The real authority in a German, Swiss or Austrian company is what might be called in the US an *internal company board* which, to differentiate, I call the *board of management*. Correspondingly the equivalent to an Anglo-Saxon board of directors is referred to in Continental Europe as a *supervisory board*. In the United States, too, the board of directors may be internal, while the more widely practised external board is not always the real authority running the firm. Quite often the real authority is concentrated in an executive committee. Figure 5.1 gives an example of possible functions.

With these reservations being made, it must be underlined that the corporate board of directors is an important nerve centre in our industrial society. For this reason it should become a subject of research and study to discover the most effective methods for its operation well beyond what is available or being done at present time.

Boards differ remarkably in their patterns, despite the apparent similarity of their legally defined functions. One explanation is that any board is an organism undergoing a continuing process of development. This takes place in response to company needs which are themselves steadily evolving. As a result, not only are there differences in board patterns of activity, but there is also the opportunity to use this concept

● to identify the state of development of the firm and
● to shape the board activity to meet the needs of the evolving perspectives

By and large, there are two main patterns of action and decision at the board of directors level. One is those which want an active part in company management decisions. The other is those which prefers to keep a supervisory role. The two cannot be reconciled.

Decisions reached by the board typically fall in one or more of the following classes: financial appropriations, new business prospects, corporate policies (long and short term), current operations, competition, evaluation of personnel and bonuses, employee relations, distribution of profits and other stockholder matters; also public relations, advertising, the corporate image and, of course, government relations. The larger firms, and those with government contracts, tend to give this last topic more consideration. The greatest agreement boards come to in terms of topics being treated is voting dividends and bonuses. In many companies, surprisingly enough, long-range perspectives come up only occasionally.

THE SHORT AND THE LONG RANGE

One of the key questions I have been asking board members is whether they spend more time on immediate issues or concentrate on long-range goals. The answers to this question are sharply divided.

85

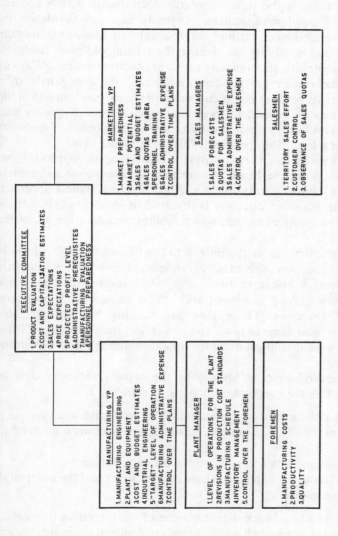

Figure 5.1 Functional chart outlining the specific responsibilities of the executive committee including the co-ordination of manufacturing and marketing for better performance in the marketplace.

EXECUTIVE COMMITTEE
1. PRODUCT EVALUATION
2. COST AND CAPITALISATION ESTIMATES
3. SALES EXPECTATIONS
4. PRICE EXPECTATIONS
5. PROJECTED PROFIT LEVEL
6. ADMINISTRATIVE PREREQUISITES
7. MANUFACTURING EVALUATION
8. PERSONNEL PREPAREDNESS

MARKETING VP
1. MARKET PREPAREDNESS
2. MARKET POTENTIAL
3. SALES AND BUDGET ESTIMATES
4. SALES QUOTAS BY AREA
5. PERSONNEL TRAINING
6. SALES ADMINISTRATIVE EXPENSE
7. CONTROL OVER TIME PLANS

SALES MANAGERS
1. SALES FORECASTS
2. QUOTAS FOR SALESMEN
3. SALES ADMINISTRATIVE EXPENSE
4. CONTROL OVER THE SALESMEN

SALESMEN
1. TERRITORY SALES EFFORT
2. CUSTOMER CONTROL
3. OBSERVANCE OF SALES QUOTAS

MANUFACTURING VP
1. MANUFACTURING ENGINEERING
2. PLANT AND EQUIPMENT
3. COST AND BUDGET ESTIMATES
4. INDUSTRIAL ENGINEERING
5. "TARGET" LEVEL OF OPERATION
6. MANUFACTURING ADMINISTRATIVE EXPENSE
7. CONTROL OVER TIME PLANS

PLANT MANAGER
1. LEVEL OF OPERATIONS FOR THE PLANT
2. REVISIONS IN PRODUCTION COST STANDARDS
3. MANUFACTURING SCHEDULE
4. INVENTORY MANAGEMENT
5. CONTROL OVER THE FOREMEN

FOREMEN
1. MANUFACTURING COSTS
2. PRODUCTIVITY
3. QUALITY

In some corporations the board concentrates on, or is even limited to, long-range rather than immediate problems. Such companies feel that because of its key role the board must focus on major policy decisions; hence long range is the right orientation. Short-term profits are not indicative of good management. Anybody can pay dividends by deferring maintenance, cutting out research, or acquiring another company – that is, adding old plant to the existing old plant facilities, rather than renewing the company's own productive capacity. Ways of doing business with government authorities, the company's own management, its vendors and its customers that were good enough in the past must now be revised to meet new requirements of quality and productivity. A drastic revision is necessary and the board of directors should take a leadership position. This is rarely the case.

In most firms (in fact, the majority) the board takes the opposite view. The practice is for the board of directors to concentrate its greatest attention on contemporary matters. And there is a hybrid approach whereby the board of directors is involved in long-range objectives, though the majority of matters which require consideration are of the current type.

At the same time, in sharp contrast to the 1950s and 1960s when the board of directors was able to muster significant appreciation, there are today dissenting voices as to its role. Carl Icahn, the New York financier, was quoted as having said:[1] 'You know how I feel about Boards of Directors. Those guys are nothing but self-interested ignoramuses who come to town and just collect their checks and leave . . . These guys should get hung for how they mismanaged this airline (TWA).'

The board of directors should be the highest authority able to reconceptualise the corporate functions. It should:

● advance the underlying assumptions of corporate strategy;
● think of the effects of innovation and diversification on the product line;
● evaluate markets and competitive product pricing;
● foretell how the ongoing change affects clients and the company's own personnel.

Figure 5.2 puts in a block diagram some of the foregoing thoughts.

As a number of research projects tends to confirm, the more classical business topics brought to the board's attention are business prospects, competition, financing, manufacturing output, inventories, distribution and some business-cycle effects. Still more time is devoted to labour

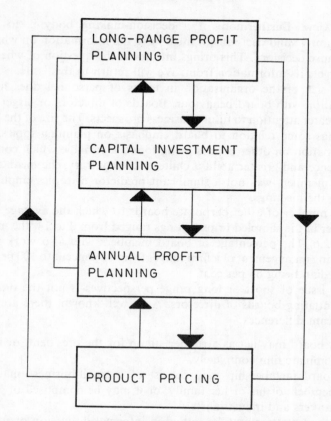

Figure 5.2   Long-range profit planning is inseparable from capital investments as well as from competitive product planning.

relations, taxes, government relations, stockholder relations, pricing and distribution of profits.

Through successive research projects I have undertaken with my graduate students while in the faculty of Washington State University and the Georgia Institute of Technology, it has been documented that most frequent attention is paid by the boards to subjects related to immediate corporate survival. The less frequently treated topics of business perspective and corporate survival are being particularly promoted by board members who serve simultaneously on other corporate boards and are better acquainted with the longer-term view. In other words, in most cases premium time is spent on immediate problems, though companies do recognise the importance of a long-range view. Furthermore, if a decision-making body is to make consistantly valid decisions, it must have the information on which to base those decisions. This brings into focus the question of where the board gets its information from. We will return to this issue.

The size of the organisation in terms of personnel does have a correlation with board behaviour. Boards of directors or larger firms give greater attention to future business prospects. The size of the board itself has some relation to board emphasis on planning topics, with participation on other boards being found a variable which connotes experience and greater ability. Quite to the contrary, the mean age of board members was not a significant predictor of topics emphasised during the meetings.

The number of other corporate boards to which the average board member in the sampled firms belongs ranged from 0 to 14, the median being 2.6. The percentage of board members who also work in the operating management of a firm ranges from 13 per cent to 100 per cent, the median being 66 per cent.

The issue of short or long range perspectives is not the only one differentiating boards of directors. As is well known, there are other significant differences:

● A board may act as a rubber stamp for the president, or it may dominate him completely.

● Board membership may consist of a small-business man plus members of his or her family, or it may be composed of known bankers and industrialists.

● Board matters may be settled in informal discussion or in long, factual and documented deliberations.

● Board meetings may extend from less than an hour to more than a day.

● The subject agenda may be restricted to key issues, or it may include all sorts of trivialities.

When we study the patterns of activity of boards of directors, it becomes evident that this range of variation is not meaningless. The task faced by a board is usually close to the situation which it confronts. Hence, differences among boards lie in the fact that they serve companies of various types, sizes, states of growth and maturity.

A line of reference could be traced between the role of the board in a large corporation and that of the Federal Reserve. Former Federal Reserve chairman William McChesney Martin used to say the job of the

Federal Reserve Board was to take away the punch bowl when the party was just getting good. And as Paul Volker was to comment: 'We are caught in the position of sometimes reminding people of the limits.'

As the making of decisions affecting the company has gravitated increasingly from owners to career managers, one of the informal roles of the board has assured is to act as a force of balance between owners and managers. To meet this need the board includes internal directors, while external directors are usually elected to represent the capital.

Historically, the original directors of the company were those who put up the money. But times have changed. While in principle the members of the board should test and check on management, asking the right questions, such questions are not always being asked. There are three key questions to which the members of the board should address a significant part of their attention:

(1) The strengths and weaknesses of their firm, both in absolute terms and against competition.
(2) The fit of the organisation to the problems facing it and within its operating environment.
(3) Planning the human inventories and training to maintain its knowhow.

All three questions are vital to the organisation's long future. How will our company stand against competition in the next ten years? How will it hold or better its market?

The answers are not self-evident. Neither is the future automatically secure. Figure 5.3 tells the story of realignment of leading telephone manufacturers within the 1978–85 time-frame, in a worldwide sense. A realistic survival analysis should be top of the list in the preoccupations of the board.

Back in the late 1950s, Professor Parkinson wrote a hilarious but valid book[2] about board meetings, advancing the axiom that the time a board spends on a given subject is inversely proportional to the importance of the subject itself. The more technology dominates new product developments, the more the vice-president for research and development and the vice-president of engineering will impress the board's members and carry the day. In a government the politicians (by majority lawyers) don't have the needed background to scrutinise. With rare exceptions, this is also the case in a corporate board of directors – particularly for the larger, publicly held firms.

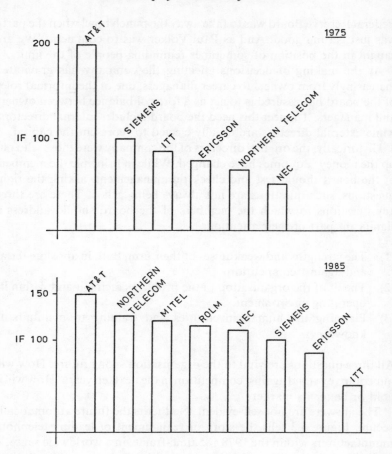

Figure 5.3   Lines shipped by leading telephone manufacturer world-wide in 1975 and 1985. These are not charts on installed value. Lines shipped is a more significant criterion in judging control of the market by a vendor.

A BOARD'S THIRST FOR INFORMATION

As with any other body, there is an evolution in a company's board, as the company itself reaches maturity. Though there has been little study of how boards evolve, industrial literature tells a lot about how companies evolve. Therefore we can use our knowledge of company development and correlate to it, by time period, the board's decisions.

But because there are so few available studies of the board's activities, on several occasions the public insight into corporate boards of directors is somewhat vague and inaccurate. This is equally true of the board's deliberations and decisions.

(1) What does the corporate board do at its meetings?
(2) What are some of the probable determinants of what it does?
(3) Are such deliberations a matter of group rather than individual behaviour?
(4) What is the most characteristic behaviour of the board members?
(5) Are the board's decisions based on research finding or on ill-prepared trial and error?
(6) Who puts up the necessary research?
(7) Who assures (and how) that board decisions reflect the company's real interests, and do not turn into irrelevance?

Are issues treated in a factual and documented manner in board meetings? To respond to this query we should determine just what kind of information a member of a board needs to enable him to make his greatest contribution to the company he serves. This question is more critical as far as the *outside directors* are concerned, that is, members of the board of a company who are not employed by that company in a line management capacity, and are typically involved with more than one corporate board. For a meaningful discussion on the amount and type of information needed by outside directors, it is worth while to reflect on the type of company involved, the composition of its board, and the primary areas of its responsibility. This will be done in more detail in a subsequent section, the following discussion having a generalised sense.

In an unpublished research project I made on this subject, both *inside and outside directors* were found to want the same information given the president, with the ability to ask for back-up support data from line management. Citing the constraints of time, outside directors preferred quantitative snapshots like summary profit and loss statements, budgetary and marketing trends – with the ability to informally and selectively circumvent management, if necessary. Neither of these two groups (inside and outside directors) appeared willing to believe that the information system at their disposal could not be improved. Nor were they willing to accept that, as it currently stood, data processing could be of service. On the contrary, corporation officials generally felt that the biggest fault with existing computer-based systems was that they gave out too much information for board members to cope with – or too little.

Prior to proceeding with the outcome of a research project I did while in the faculty of Washington State University, let me take a few paragraphs better to focus on inside and outside Board members. Harold S. Geneen, former chairman and (CEO) of ITT Corp., says in his book *Managing* that inside directors (managers) still dominate board meetings: 'Outside Board members sit there and listen. Then they go to lunch, and then they go home and open the envelope which contains their fee.' But times have changed, and the intensifying push for more accountability may go a long way toward altering the reality Greneen describes.

The opening salvo in Chapter 1 has been that a seat in the boardroom used to be corporate America's surest sinecure, a way to pick up an extra $30,000 a year and a bit of prestige. Today it is a job that nobody wants it is said. Litigation seems almost inevitable for directors these days, as raiders' attacks and boards' defensive tactics proliferate. If the outside directors do not even have the possibility of getting properly informed, the job is hardly worth the 30 kilobucks.

Lack of appropriate information to reach learned decisions and, in cases, to assimilate it, is one of the reasons why knowledgeable people are not so happy to serve on boards. Lester B. Korn, chairman of Korn/ Ferry International, an executive search firm, says the pool of people willing to serve on boards is shrinking, and he warns that the wave of litigation is only beginning.

Most courts still give company leaders broad discretion. Critics, however, question whether judges are qualified to second-guess management decisions that must often be made in a matter of hours. Suggests Joseph Auerbach, professor at the Harvard business school: 'A Board knows its own company better than any outsider could. How do the courts know what to decide? How did they get to be such experts?' Or as another expert put it; 'We will never know how many deals weren't done because the lawyer scared off the CEO.'

The chief executive officer is the typical example of an inside director. In most cases he has pertinent information on which to decide. Less well-placed on that score are outside directors. Yet, if properly informed, their experience can be a big help in company objectives, policy decisions, budgets – and most particularly strategic plans.

Outside directors being third-party viewpoints to bear in assessing the performances of managers, resolving internal disagreements and weighing the progress being achieved in reaching goals. This reference is particularly valid whenever we talk of people with experience in operations of the corporation's size, if not its exact type of business.

Another precondition to valid contributions is that outside directors should neither be expected nor expect to inject themselves personally into day-to-day company activities. They are there to guide, advise and help decide.

Also, a word of advice for individuals who have been invited to become a member of a board. Before accepting it would be well to talk to your attorney about the legal accountability the position can entail. In so doing, go beyond the broad legal aspects, which have become much more restrictive in recent years. Explore whether the company asking you to come aboard has any serious financial or legal problems or is involved in activities in which you would not wish to take part.

Walter Wriston, the retired chairman of Citicorp and an outspoken critic of the current litigation-happy business scene, however, was to suggest:

> Too many lawyers forget that corporations are risk-taking enterprises where profit accrues to those that take risks. The cumulative effects of all these lawsuits is to slow all of American business by limiting risk-taking. There is too much concern with form over substance. Don't forget that the most thoroughly researched product in America was the Edsel.[3]

The thesis *Forbes* develops is that many of the greatest decisions of this century were *bet the company* gambles in which visionary chief executives either had the backing of their boards or rode roughshod over the opposition. Would Thomas Watson Jr have been able to make a success of the company's System 360 mainframe in 1964 if he had had to justify his strategy to a board scared to take so bold an initiative? Would Lee Iacocca have been able to engineer the greatest corporate rescue act of the post-war era if his every move were second-guessed and analysed by Chrysler's Board?

William H. Whyte, Jr says:[4]

> The most misguided attempt at false collectivization is the current attempt to see the group as a creative vehicle. Can it be? *People very rarely think in groups*. They talk together, they exchange information, they adjudicate, they make compromises. *But they don't think; they do not create.*

Bishop Berkeley was to add: '*All men have opinions, but few men think.*'[5]

If Whyte and Berkeley are right, a collective body cannot think. But if it is not well informed, it cannot even have documented opinions. A Board of Directors worthy of its name and function *has to be properly informed.* In the Washington State University study we found that to the question: 'Who did the research for the board?:

● So firms replied that outside directors did some of the research.
● Others indicated that inside directors are more apt to do some of the research.
● But most responded that the greatest part of the research was done by various members of the company staff.

Some indicated that DP/MIS (data processing/management information system) was used in the process, to the extent that it was available (!), but quite often the time available to respond to board queries was limited (!!) and the responses could not be precise or even could not be given at all.

This may seem a contradiction, but it is not necessarily so. Practically all companies indicated they do not consider their present information systems the final answer to the needs of the board. But there are exceptions. The chairman of a leading bank was to comment:

> It is probable that we all would interpret the definition of computer-based management information systems in a different way, but our Bank is extremely pleased in the progress we have made in developing such a system. It requires continual refinement in its application, and continues to evolve as new services and changes in reporting requirements are introduced.

While the majority of boards of directors have not yet discovered the support well-tuned computers and communications can provide, there exists a continental divide between the smaller and the larger firms. General Motors is a company whose board is known to make extensive and ingenious use of information systems. But rather than always taking the largest corporations as examples, let me focus on two other examples.

Back in 1980 I was giving a computers and communications seminar in Chicago. On this occasion, I was invited by a member of the board of Gould Industries to visit their headquarters near O'Hare Airport. There in the boardroom was installed and operating an information centre capability accessible to all its members. A member of the board making a presentation or an inquiry could call from an online terminal and project on a wall-sized screen infopages from the information centre database. Through menu selection he could also descent a tree of detail in database search, should the board discussion call for it.

Bangor Punta of Greenwich, Connecticut, is another good example.

The chairman of the board is also member of the board of another corporation in New York. In January 1982, in a board meeting in New York City, he was exposed to microcomputer terminals which, introduced at that time, were supposed to be extensively used a year thereafter. Returning to Greenwich, the Chairman, Mr Wilson, instituted a personal computer and local area network program for the Bangor Punta Board. Every member was to be provided with an intelligent workstation with direct access to the file server. Instituted in the month of February, this system became operational in June that same year. When I visited in October 1982 there were already four months of accumulated experience.

THE MEMBERS OF THE BOARD

Rarely, if ever, are there job descriptions regarding board members, but qualifications include ingredients such as experience in business, objectivity in the evaluation of problems, independence of judgement and, most importantly, nomination to this job.

Nomination to membership of the board of directors may concern inside or outside members and is the first important reference, but professional qualifications should be present. A board manned by less experienced people starts on an awkward basis and may never develop smooth, effective operation. While this should be self-evident and lead to the exclusion of non-qualified members, it is just as true that a small, struggling company has difficulty in attracting men or women of adequate qualifications to its board. Board membership does indeed carry status, but status can be negative as well as positive.

In a number of cases, board memberships are stratified. Stratification also stems from the needs of the situation: companies of very large size logically tend to appoint directors who have experience with the problems of giant corporations. However, since people look on directorships as status symbols, they become correspondingly selective. While sophisticated outsiders have no strong urge to join the board of a small company, the not necessarily experienced insiders do. The more qualified the members of a board of directors, the better will be the decisions.

One of the key questions is: 'What is the board's composition?' In a research project of Washington State University (WSU) undertaken to answer this query, the average for the Boards returning the questionnaire was: 15.6 members, 9.6 of whom are outside directors. Of the outside members, 8.7 come from industries with products or services different from that of the responding company; 9.4 of the members also served on boards of at least one other corporation. At a typical board meeting, 95.6 per cent of the inside members will be in attendance, while only 83.6 per cent of the outside members will attend. The trend was for board meetings to be held 4, 5, 6, or 12 times a year.

In another study WSU has found that 85 per cent of the boards of directors in industry have between 7 and 15 members. Said one chairman: 'The optimum number is best expressed by a fabricator of nonferrous metals who describes the ideal size as follows: "A Board should not have so many as to make free discussion impossible, nor so few that a breadth of viewpoint is not obtainable."'

There did not seem to be any breakdown of the aforementioned statistics by corporation size. Apparently the size of a corporation has little to do with the composition of its governing board. However, it seemed clear that most firms made a special effort to enlist directors who are members of other boards and/or outstanding people from other fields. 'It is a definite advantage and experience has demonstrated the enhanced value of members who sit on the Boards of other unrelated corporations,' stated on board chairman. Others said that often the opinions of directors from unrelated fields result in a different and very valuable perspective. It also helps in reaching timely decisions.

It was generally felt that the outside board members should have a special information channel to help keep abreast of important company issues. The point made was the ability to provide more background to the issues involved and to give the outside director an inside look at matters over which he will make a decision.

There appeared to be little correlation between size and agenda. Information showed marked differences in the topics discussed by the board. Topics being listed were given different weights of frequency and importance by the responding companies.

The population of directors whose temperature was taken for this report was wide and diversified. However, it is interesting to note that 92 per cent of the large companies responded to the questionnaire, but only 50 per cent of the medium-sized companies did so.

A subject not relevant in the United States (except the Continental Illinois Bank) but very much so in Europe is that of state-owned firms. How is the board of directors composed? What are the personality profiles, the personal qualifications, the reasons for election to the board? The results of confusing ownership with the regulatory authority of the government? Generally, boards of state-owned corporations tend to be of a fairly mixed type with official and non-official representation, but weighted in favour of the former. The practice is to have a mixture of full-time and part-time members. Non-officials are normally appointed as part-time members. Directors of the Ministry will normally not be on the board, but they may be appointed after leaving the Ministry. The same is true of the ministers themselves and of retired high-ranking officers of the military.

Though the practice varies from country to country, in general, under the law of the land, members of parliament are disqualified from holding membership of boards. But some do sit on boards of public undertakings under special dispensation. There may be advantages of this to the state-owned corporation, but the disadvantages far outweigh the advantages.

The tendency on the whole has been to avoid representation of particular interests on such boards. Even where labour interests have been represented, they were not supposed to represent the claims of labour on the board. It is felt that on the board there should by only one loyalty and that is to the interests of the nationalised firm – though it does not work always that way. The oldest official Act affecting the representation of labour dates from the National Socialist Germany in the 1930s. It was subsequently taken up and implemented by socialist governments throughout Europe following the Second World War. US corporations are not immune to it.

There can be considerable argument about whether, and if so how, labour should be represented on boards of directors. The Trades Union Congress in Britain set its face against association of the trade unions with the functions and responsibilities of management. In Yugoslavia, on the other hand, trade unions have been actively associated with the management function. In other countries, there is a middle course. Such a course has been found in appointments to boards of directors of persons who have been engaged in the labour movement and have an understanding and experience of labour affairs, though not directly connected with the trade unions or workers of the enterprise itself. These Directors do not necessarily represent labour interests on the board they sit on, but some of them do.

In the United States, a well-known example is Eastern Airlines Incorporated, where employees owed 20 per cent to 25 per cent of the common stock and had four representatives on the board. Yet, despite years of extensive labour–management collaboration and productivity improvements, the company and its three unions have been embroiled in something like an old-style labour-management shoot-out.

There is the case of Continental Steel Coporation (in Kokomo, Indiana) where a director representing the United Steelworkers reluctantly resigned when the company's law firm concluded that he could not discuss or vote on labour issues without generating a potential conflict of interest. If labour is to share decision-making power, management must give up some power, and workers must accept some responsibility for the business. Tradition makes this change in roles very difficult.

These examples help document the fact that there is no unique answer to the question: 'What should be the composition of the Board?' There is much room for variety, and certainly room for trial and experiment. Certain trends have, however, crystalised. In my judgement, boards of directors should include both inside and outside members. They should be fairly small, but not too small. On a statistical analysis, and keeping in mind variations depending upon size of the company and the nature of its activities, the figure for the average board could be fixed at about seven to nine directors. Membership of the board should be on the basis of ability, experience and administrative competence. Having been selected to serve on the board, all directors must identify themselves with the interests of the firm which they serve.

EMPHASIS PLACED IN BOARD MEETINGS

The subject-matter and pace of board meetings can be limited by the perspective of those members who are least knowledgeable in top management decision making, have limited business experience, or fail to appreciate the board's mode of operation. Competence as a specialist or as a manager is by no means the same thing as competence as a board member, although these skills are not mutually exclusive.

In a number of cases, responding companies suggested that the board of directors is an almost isolated corporate body. It is quite distant from the detailed workings of the corporation in the sense that the time spent working for the company and learning about the company is usually a small percentage of the director's working time, and certainly much less than the many hours spent by the management. Outside directors, unlike management, do not have the time available to become intimately associated with the daily and weekly workings of the firm. This is quite a pity. The members of the board will only then be worth their salt if they are able to look at critical issues, in an individual as well as in a

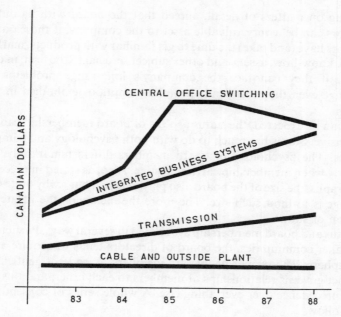

Figure 5.4 Past and future business prospects of Northern Telecom, identifying the shift in the market for telephone switching (from a financial analysis by Paine Webber, New York City).

cumulative sense. If a subject is critical it is strategic – and if it is strategic it is critical.

Strategic issues abound in any dynamic corporation. As Figure 5.4 suggests:

● some product lines may have stopped growing (cable and outside plant);
● others grow rather slowly (transmission);
● new product lines progress fast (integrated business systems);
● still others are passing their peak (central office switching).

Such differentiation in market pull and product achievement exists in all corporations. Is the board of directors taking notice? Are its decisions leading rather than following a trend?

What's the recommended level of detail necessary for the directors to make informed decisions and judgements? Can the future course of a corporation be traced without sufficient documented reference to lower-level workings? Most of the executives queried in a USA research focusing on matters of detail, agreed that the board with its outside directors can be a very valuable asset to the company, if these outside directors have (and take) the time to get familiar with products, markets, clients, know-how, assets, and other subjects crucial to the firm, in other words, if they can face the company's long-range problems and challenge even the most fundamental assumptions embodied in their mission.

As can be expected, the status aspects of board membership can also be decisive. Status has much to do with both psychology and company politics. The psychology of board members differs remarkably, particularly when membership carries prestige. Also, as stated in preceding paragraphs, the size of the board also plays a role. That's why quite often the urge is to limit such size. The more the members, the greater the dilution of status.

Status and board membership are related in several ways. Particularly in smaller communities, the board of directors tends to acquire a club atmosphere. The proper people are members. A code of gentlemanly conduct governs relationships of members to each other, and this code takes precedence over everything else. A whole series of consequences may follow.

The opposite is also true. Undue emphasis on status can reduce the usefulness of board members. Hence, a proper balance must be found. It is hardly possible to overstate the importance of objectivity as an attribute of a prospective board member; at the same time this member will look towards the contribution he makes to the board as a status symbol.

One of the top qualifications of a Board member should be independence of judgement. Lack of independence can result in serious misdirection of board activity. This is particularly visible in an inside board when most members are subordinate to the president or the principal owner of the enterprise. In such cases, board members are circumspect about opposing the position of the dominant member. He is the boss outside the board meeting and they cannot forget this fact inside the meeting. Typically, inside members are unwilling to express themselves in an open way. Such lack of independence places a burden on the outside directors and also deprives them of needed information.

Tenure is another key subject to be brought into perspective. It is well to keep in mind that membership on a board exhibits unusual tenacity. Few tenures, industrial or otherwise, are as durable. Incumbents also face the problem of appointing new directors, and they should recognise that the penalty of this year's opportunism goes on for a decade.

Particularly very large multi-billion-dollar industrial companies have been tending towards a board form in which membership is often self-perpetuating rather than mainly selected by the shareholders. Such a self-perpetuating board is basically different from a truly elective board in many respects.

The implications of such differences can be profound. This is critical in matters of qualification for board membership and of the responsibility of directors. For such companies, board members have an uncommonly high moral responsibility for seeing to it that corporate affairs are conducted in a way which balances fairly the interests of the various claimants for the income from business. They also face the problem of avoiding misuse of the great economic power of the corporation or self-aggrandisement by any members of the board itself. The best advice is that the board exercises power for which it is fitted and liable to account. Failure to do so would frustrate it and compromise its decision making.

A counterpart in state-owned enterprises is the so-called advisory board. Advisory boards have the danger that they can diffuse responsibility. Unless an agency has the specific duty to discharge responsibility under strict accounting according to law, such as accounting through audit, or as laid down by law, it would tend to become confused and would itself be a cause of diffusion of responsibility. In this as in other cases, any advice if it is to be worth something should be backed by some sanction for its adoption, otherwise the advice tends to be useless – and one the whole it seems best to be without it. Furthermore, an advisory board in the handling and management of state enterprises would tend to become an intermeddler, unless it gives advice on points on which there is no accountability – in which case it becomes meaningless.

Finally, it is proper to make reference to *ad hoc* committees, set up to deal with specific problems, reporting to the board on the conclusion of their work. Committees which are given specific tasks within a clearly defined area of functions and responsibility on behalf of the board have often done well. But not always.

INSIDE AND OUTSIDE DIRECTORS

Let's start with an extreme case. A small company forms its board of directors. The number of members is three: the owner plus two others who will sign anything. For all practical purposes this is a one-man board. The legal shell ratifies such one-man decisions that require formal board deliberation.

Now let's modify this extreme by assuming multiple owners. Though the membership may increase, domination of the company by one owner still limits the other owners to the right to express dissenting opinions, but not to see them through. With public stock offering and with the growth of the company, the professional managers become more numerous. This gets to the point where hired managers exceed owner-managers in number. Slowly the board becomes a device for power and status. Professional managers press for membership as well as owner-ship of part of the firm through participation plans and bonuses.

Inside directors would typically exhibit a mixture of strengths and weaknesses. Strengths include a detailed knowledge of the business. Weaknesses may involve a reluctance to take a strong stand, so as not to upset top management, and an avoidance of looking after weak spots so as not to spoil club membership. Also, club membership confers special privileges as to job assignment, standard of performance, pay scale, incentives, and fringe benefits.

Outside directors help balance the system and can help correct some of these weaknesses – if they don't take the attitude of a club member. The entry of able, strong and independent-minded outside directors brings extensive changes in habits for the insiders. Often the least obvious, but by far the most important, is the change in concept of what a board meeting is.

Years spent considering all problems as day-to-day operating problems, rather than in separating board problems from other problems, leave deep-rooted habits among the inside members. Their regular activities keep them informed on these matters, so there appears to be no need for special reports to be prepared for board meetings. The entry of outsiders changes this approach. Provisions must be made to bring the outside directors up to date monthly, and we will be talking of them in the appropriate chapter. But they key issue at this point is the outside directors' contribution. Conscious of the need for such contribu-tion, they not only ask that day-to-day matters be kept off the agenda, but also bring up matters to which the insiders may have given little attention in the past. As the member of the board of directors of a leading European industrial combine was to say: 'In every bottle, the bottleneck is at the top.' Often decisions which weigh heavily on the future of the enterprise were not treated because the proper attention was not paid at board level.

This brings the right focus on the query: 'Just what does an outside director do for the company?' Is it enough if he adds a great deal of prestige but spends very little of his time treating the problems? The reverse also must be examined: Why do top executives devote valuable time to the affairs of companies other than their own?

Starting with the first question: 'Why do companies reach hard for outstanding people from other fields?' we can say that precisely because a member of the board is not an employee of the company, he has a better vision beyond the day's length – and more independence in his opinion. Outside directors are the ones who can bring objectivity to bear on such sticky question as salary increases, stock options, and beyond, items one could hardly expect inside directors to approach without bias.

Another answer is that the object of the game is the same for all industry – the variation being in techniques, not in principles. Even with unrelated product lines or services, companies do have common aims to satisfy. They are in business to please the ultimate user so well, so effectively, so efficiently, that profits are earned in the doing.

As competition gets stiffer, winning this game and staying ahead is an increasingly difficult task. With teamwork, including the continuous interchange of ideas and viewpoints, a board drawn from various industries (including financial industries) permits, even increases, the chances of success. Most importantly, it focuses on the longer range rather than the day-to-day activities. Typically, insiders are emphasising their products, processes, daily sales, costs, variances, and so on. Outsiders put stress on return on investment, comparison with competitors, direction of the business, growth, share of market and future competition.

This is an argument which has often been overlooked. Yet a study commissioned in 1984 by American Airlines to identify its key competitor in 1995 did not name another airline or transport company. The number one competitor, this study documented, will be AT & T. 'Communicate, don't commute' is the motto.

In addition, outside board members often raise questions which require answers in the form of policy declarations to be made after the concepts being promoted have been cleared and it is possible to obtain a sense of the meeting. Sometimes, when views of the outsiders prevail, the agenda becomes more selective as to subject-matter and the board decisions more to the point.

Certain experiences help demonstrate that inside directors adapt well to these changes. They may undergo some disruption of their habits, but they tend to accept the constructive aspects of the new views and feel they are broadened by them. The removal of club privileges can, however, create bad feelings. The differing views of the outsider and the insider with respect to privileges may not be simply the result of greater vested interest by the inside director.

● Often, the entry of the outside director is the result of public financing, hence he regards himself as in a position of trust for the stockholders' money.
● On the contrary, the insider has a long history of dealing mainly with his own company or with the money of a small group in which he is an accepted member. Habit patterns are acquired during this history, and the inside director does not suddenly shed them when stockholders' equity comes along.

The benefits from outside directors do not stop in the boardroom. Every management can profit by exposure to the way another company does business, how another company manages for growth, how it tries to win and hold the allegiance of the consumer.

Critics, though, may add that outside directors may also turn to overprotectiveness. Some companies seem to operate a mutual protective society for presidents. They cross-exchange. They stay on each other's boards and they protect each other. They put out a ballot with one slate and you can vote yes or no, but there is a 99 per cent sure vote because there is only one slate. In other words, the view exists that outside directors, too, have problems of independence of opinion as members of the board. This view can be expressed as 'swim with the chief executive or sink'. Some people feel that all too often outside directors, especially if their presence on a particular board represents the culmination of an ambition, are unwilling to dispute active management's viewpoint. The risk of discord, this thesis maintains, is almost certain to assure that voting goes in favour of the chairman.

Other criticisms are also phrased, such as the need for greater emphasis in the responsibility assumed through proxy statements. And there is a counterweight. As a former chief executive said: 'Some managements are more interested in promoting the stock; making speeches to financial analysts; or hiring Wall Street consultants to tell them about their business. They forget that, if the business is soundly run, it will do the most for the stock of the company.'

Having said this, it is proper to add that the majority of chief executive officers are of the opinion that directors from outside the company temper the whole by providing an objective viewpoint. The outside directors have a broad background in industry and finance which is extremely valuable. They serve as a check and balance and can put the brakes on such things as nepotism in internal executive succession.

SELECTION AND DUTIES OF OUTSIDE DIRECTORS

Board chairmen who participated in the WSU research project previously mentioned, agreed unanimously that they expect their outside directors to participate actively in the board meetings. They also indicated that selection is generally made by criteria of broad business experience rather than a certain specialisation or by prestige considerations. Although nobody stated that prestige was enough, several let it be felt that it was important and was a consideration in selection. A comment by the board chairman of a small airline was: 'Outside directors serve as a valuable supplement to a company's public relation program.'

The following reference on member selection and qualifications was made by the chairman of a large aircraft company: 'I feel strongly in the importance and value of outside directors with the greatest possible variety of experience. Their broad and deep business experience is more valuable than specific knowledge of our business.' The president of a large electronics firm was to remark: 'Each outside director is an expert in his field and contributes his expertise to the company's operations. Their most important contribution is their objective evaluation of corporate matters based on their outside experience.'

It was found that most companies with outside directors chose them from firms in other fields than their own. A significant number were from subsidiary companies, however, and from companies otherwise related, holdings being an example. Generally, the opinion was expressed that the outside directors should actively participate both inside and outside of the board meetings. Most companies expect significant contributions from their outside board members. As one executive commented, 'That's what they are paid for.' Another relevant opinion was as follows: 'A director is of more use to a company through informal discussions of specific business problems with senior management than by strict attendance at formal Board meetings.'

Some companies mentioned that during the interval between board meetings the outside member may concern himself in three areas of business:

● The first is committee meetings. Many times a board member will spend more time preparing for committee meetings than for the full board meeting.
● The second is keeping abreast of current company developments.

Increasingly companies see as a duty of the board member to become aware of important issues regarding the going business. This also helps him prepare to take active part in the next board meeting.

● The third is doing research for the board.

Some boards do not require its outside members to do any research; others call for it. One company said, 'Outside directors sometimes are asked to obtain views and data from their own sources as the basis for group discussion.'

There were varied responses to the question of how much time an outside member should devote to his between meetings business'. Most said 'very little', or 'not much'. However, other statements were: Ours would vary from 20 hours down to 2 hours.' Some stated: '6 to 8 hours'. Still others said that it depended entirely on the upcoming agenda.

Quite evidently, outside directors who participate in many boards simply don't have the possibility to spend so many hours on current business subjects. The exception is full-time directors; often called professional directors. A full-time director typically is a well-known, high-power consultant. He participates in one or more boards, but no more in number than he has the ability to handle in terms of devoting a good deal of his attention to following the business. A professional director typically has more detailed information as to how the company is progressing. Company secrets are rarely secrets to him, if he is properly performing his duties. This evidently requires full access to all information concering the company and its business. To do his job in an able manner, some good advice for the full-time director is to obtain information for himself that is more detailed than the concerns of the Board will require. How much and what kind of information should be available to him depends on what functions he is supposed to serve, and it relates to the reasons for his selection to board membership.

If he is chosen for expertise in specific fields, he would function as expert in that field. In this capacity he needs all information which would permit him to give advice and provide objectivity in regard to his field(s) of specialisation.

If he is selected due to the general knowledge of the company's industry and proven success in that industry, he would require across-the-board references in order to play a prominent role in the decision process. In this latter case, objective counsel and broad guidance are more important than specific knowledge of a given field. Objective counsel would seem to come mostly from generalised expertise in the world of business and industry.

The composition of a board along lines of specialisation is also a pertinent matter. A major stockholder once commented that he was not pleased when, instead of a well-rounded board, he saw a body loaded in certain specialisations. Too many lawyers is the the most frequent case. Said he, 'Here is an occasion calling from broad interests, and lawyers are not inclined to be the best businessmen. As for too many bankers, there is some question whether they represent all of the stockholders, or just the financing end.'

Diversity of opinion as to what is best for the firm is one of the reasons why policies concerning the wisdom of using outside directors (or the lack of it) can vary significantly from one company to another. As the chairman of a science-based industry said: 'We are technically oriented and it would be virtually impossible to communicate with outsiders.' In this company, the only outside director also acts as a consultant to top management and is paid for his consulting services.

Questions of compensation and of time expended on board business complicate the subject. The root of this argument is a query we have already treated: 'How good can an outside director be if he is not studying the problems of the company whose policies and future he helps shape?'

Other questions follow: Should outside directors extend beyond their board duties? Must they attend monthly meetings? Should they serve on committees which frequently meet and study material beforehand for the meetings? Such hard-working directors can accomplish a great deal, but there are also limitations in personal time and in budgets allocated to this end.

· NOTES

1. *Fortune Magazine*, 17 February 1986, pp. 21 and 22.
2. C. Northcote Parkinson *The Law and the Profits* (London: John Murray, 1960).
3. *Forbes*, 10 February 1968.
4. *The Organization Man* (New York: Doubleday Anchor Book, 1956).
5. Jonathan Barnes, *The Presocratic Philosophers* (London and New York: Routledge & Kegan Paul, 1986).

6 The Business of the Board

The preceding chapter discussed the business of a board of directors, but not all pertinent subjects have yet been treated. It has, however, been said that boards often concentrate their greatest attention on contemporary or current matters though (as was emphasised), from an importance standpoint, the long-range issues should take the lion's share of attention. It was also stated that in the larger corporations the business is mainly long range.

In general, there are two ways that a discussion of a particular subjects commences during a board meeting. One is that the chairman or president reviews the subject in very brief form. The other is that company technicians are asked to appear before the board to give the pros or cons of the subject.

Topics to be treated during a Board meeting are determined by the agenda, but the agenda never tells a subject's relative weight and what level of attention should be given during the meeting. In the WSU research, one corporation suggested that its policy has been to examine actively only one topic per meeting, but most others indicated that several subjects are discussed each time. Normally, a detailed agenda is prepared in advance of each meeting and distributed to each member of the board. Such an agenda is accompanied by substantial documentation including technical resolutions and related material upon which board action is required. We will treat this issue in the appropriate section.

It is important to take notice that for over twenty years there has been . a changing emphasis of board time utilisation. Not too many studies are available on this subject, though a field inquiry would be useful. From the information which has been published, a couple of trends are evident: there is a reduced emphasis on current problems and increased amount of time and interest spent on long-range issues. At the same time, the total hours spent on board deliberations are shortened.

Board deliberations should exploit every opportunity the business presents. Even an old-fashioned downturn can do wonders for a company's efficiency. Belts must be tightened, inventories should shrink, and instrumental cost controls cut out waste. Then, when an upturn comes, company profit margins can widen awesomely. The board should see to it that this happens.

The board may assign its members into a number of high-level committees, some of them being the most frequently noticed. The *executive committee* exercises certain powers of the board. It approves appropriations in amounts exceeding the limits of officer authority, for:

● capital investments
● research and development
● lease expenditures

and so on. The executive committee also approves the disposition of significant capital assets. Other companies assign these functions, as well as top-level budgetary decisions and cash flow evaluations, to the *finance committee* of the board.

The *audit committee* is typically composed of directors who are neither officers nor employees of the corporation. It reviews the company's annual consolidated financial statements, registration statements and prospectuses, prior to board approval. It also checks on audit activities, and recommends changes in accounting policies for board approval.

The *management resources and compensation committee* recommends for board approval the appointment and remuneration of corporate officers. It reviews the appointment and remuneration of the officers of the principal subsidiaries and recommends new employee benefit plans and material changes to existing ones. Some companies assign to this board committee the authority of setting policy regarding recruitment and executive development programmes and planning for succession to senior management. It recommends appropriations under incentive plans, and suggests individuals for nomination to the board.

Some companies have instituted an *operations advisory committee* of the board to serve in a consultative role on international operations and key world-wide subsidiaries. Finally, the *pension fund policy committee* approves the investment policies for, and reviews the performance of, the corporation's pension funds.

CHOOSING THE TOP EXECUTIVES

The board of directors designates the chairman. The chairman may be the chief executive officer (CEO), in which case the president is the chief operating officer. But in other cases, the chief executive officer is the president. There is no fixed rule in this respect. In either case, the chief executive officer is directly responsible to the board of directors and has the overall complete management responsibility.

It might have been a pleonasm to underline that the chief executive

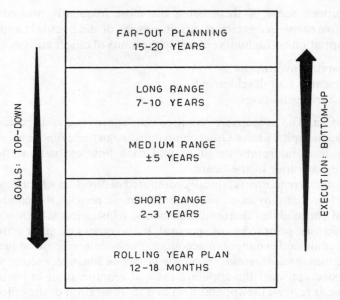

Figure 6.1   To establish lasting goals, the board should look at the far-out plan.
Control action must however be based on the rolling plan and it
should be steady.

should be the number one person in the organisation to recognise the
new necessities dictated by change, to take positive action in a planned
direction, to plan for the long term. This is a precondition for success,
but it is not always the case. Only when the chief executive's mind works
along the lines Figure 6.1 presents, can he be expected to demonstrate
coherent vision and valid strategy.

Is the choice of the chief executive and of the chief operating officer
part of the board's business? The answer is definitely 'yes'. Is an
executive's chance of heading his firm related to excellence in the field in
which he has been a specialist? Here the answer is not so clear. There has
been a variety of speculation on this point, with some observers seeing a
future in which large industrial corporations would be dominated by
engineers and other technical specialists. The opposite viewpoint senses
a trend towards experts in marketing and finance, or towards men whose
careers include experience in a variety of areas rather than concentration
on only one. In this particular case, statistics have not necessarily been a
basis for prediction. Statistics can tell if there have been changes, over
time, in the backgrounds of presidents. They can show a trend towards

one of the aforementioned. But statistics don't answer the critical question: 'What about the degree of specialisation in presidential careers?'

To obtain the answers to such questions, it is more informative to turn to career histories of men who have served as presidents. One of the projects I did focused along this line. It demonstrated that the division of presidencies among men from various occupational backgrounds has remained relatively stable over time. The typical president clearly has spent the majority of his working years in one field, with general management discounted as a specialised field. Executives from general management, marketing, and production have generally led in percentages of presidencies held. Many firms tend to switch from one type of specialist to another when a new selection of CEO or chief operating officer comes up. Boards have also a tendency to choose different profiles for the two jobs: if the one is marketing or finance, the other tends to be engineering. While Board choices don't cluster in a way to provide a good predictive mechanism, the majority of cases indicate a tendency not to repeat the same field immediately when choosing a new president. In some cases this was said to be related to balancing the corporate political structure.

The relatively stable numbers of corporate presidents coming from the various background fields conceal an underlying tendency for firms to change from one type of specialist to another; but there do exist indicators of a trend to broaden the scope of experience of corporate presidents. Here statistics are helpful as they tend to indicate:

- a definite drop in the percentage of presidents who had no experience whatsoever outside their own fields, and
- a notable increase in the percentage with experience in three or more fields.

Hence, while in the past chief executives have usually been rather highly specialised in terms of the proportion of years spent in this field, records show a change towards those with a diversification of experience. Sometimes such diversification is achieved by giving the specialist a relatively short tour of duty in areas outside his own specialty, which is not enough to build a broad background prior to heading the corporation.

The making and able maintenance of a valid management plan is a good test of the chief executive's polyvalent qualities. As Figure 6.2 outlines, at the heart of such a management plan is profitability. We need profits, not only to give the stockholders a return on their equity,

112

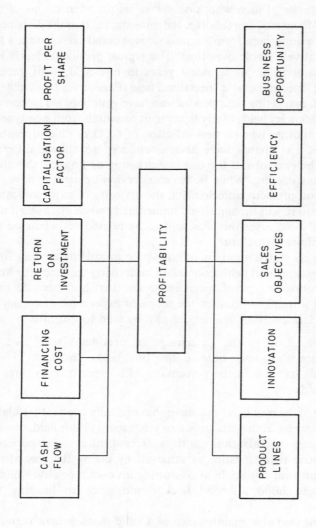

Figure 6.2 A management plan must focus on profitability. Ten critical inputs to profitability are identified in this figure.

but also to invest in the future. New technologies open fresh possibilities which will be lost unless the proper investments are made. A generalist in management can appreciate this fact much better than a rather narrow-minded specialist. By blindly defending the old order, the latter might merely succeed in castrating the company.

Looking at policies corporations tend to follow, we can see that there are also some significant changes in job routes through which various classes of specialists rise within their areas. For instance, in finance, experience in accounting declined over the years in favour of treasury duties, budgeting and controllership. Similarly, among the relatively small number of presidents who are legal specialists, the inside lawyer appears to be gaining preference over the outside lawyer. The majority of legal specialists tend to have experience both in private practice and in the legal department of some corporation, with polyvalence becoming a determining factor.

Origins in general management prior to promotion to the top corporate job constitute a special situation. In the immediate post-war years, a sizable share of this group was made up of men who were founders or co-founders of industrial companies. Thus the high proportion of total presidencies held by general management men at that time can be explained by the fact that many companies were headed by those who were instrumental in organising them.

Over the 1960s, 1970s and 1980s the number of presidents who have come up as entrepreneurs shrank. Also the ageing entrepreneurs were being replaced by men whose backgrounds were of a professional management nature. A trend toward experience as assistant to the president illustrates the increasing importance of this type of back-ground among general management specialists. At the same time, among the assistant-to-the-president group, some careers suggest a pattern which has been described as that of the *crown prince*. This is no generalised trend, if for no other reason than because the entrepreneurs continued to leave faster than the crown princes multiplied.

The references which have been made not only document that a major board of directors' responsibility is the able choice of the CEO and of the chief operating officer, but also that in order to do this work correctly it needs to have a close co-ordination with career planning. The adminis-tration of a career planning programme involves more than just able personnel choices. It calls into play:

- forward-looking organisational planning;
- selection of candidates for replacements;

● appraisals of executive abilities;
● steady training programmes to fill gaps in experience.

Particular emphasis must be placed on the preparation of replacement tables and the board will be well advised to take a keen interest in them. Opposite the names of the incumbent for each position must be listed the names of one or more persons who can be considered candidates to fill it in case of a vacancy – as they now stand, or after the appropriate experience and training which should be specified.

In order to work, this system requires the submission each year of the following formal information by the director of personnel to the board of directors: first, the evaluation of managers and professionals who have been identified as having high executive potential; second, information on how the corporate executive development programme affected the progress and the activities of each high potential candidate; third, a formal 'executive manpower plan' for the new year, and for the next five to ten years.

The board of directors has to make sure that not only the current but also the future operating executives are of the proper timbre. Equally, provision must be made that at the firm's top management level there is enough interest in the longer term and not all thoughts (and worries) taken up by day-to-day business. A good example of this is given by Nestlé. In the mid-1960s there were two managing directors: the one addressed himself to day-to-day business, the other to long-range planning. Significantly, every three years they switched jobs. He who led the long-range studies took over the day-to-day operations, and vice versa.

At about the same time, General Electric ran a far out planning department in Santa Barbara, California, with a similar objective. It emphasised the next ten, fifteen, twenty years – hence a much longer span in projections than the now classical long-range planning. This operation was staffed with former general managers of operating GE departments, whose mission was to answer the question: 'What will GE be making in fifteen years? in twenty years? From where will the income and the profits come?'

THE AGENDA AND THE DELIBERATIONS

We have already said that the composition of boards of directors are as intricate and diverse as are the means whereby individuals obtain success and the accomplishments of their goals in life. But we have not yet discussed how often boards meet, how a meeting's agenda is structured, and how the deliberations are done.

In answer to the question 'How frequently does the board meet?' a financial institution responded as follows:

> Our organization is a multiple corporation structure and the members of the Board of Directors also serve three or four of the major wholly-owned subsidiary entities. The members of these Boards will meet almost every month in attendance at one or more of the major corporation Boards. Each of these Boards meet not less frequently than 6 times per year.

A leading manufacturing firm responded in the following manner:

> The Board of Directors meets regularly each month of the year with the exception of the months of December and January and may have additional special meetings. A detailed agenda is prepared in advance of each meeting and distributed to each member of the Board of Directors.

It was further explained that the agenda is accompanied by substantial documentation including:

● detailed current financial analysis of the corporation;
● detailed management reports by the executives in charge of the major operations of the corporation;
● technical resolutions and related material upon which board action is required.

During the course of the meeting, this corporation said, all of the documentation furnished in advance is reviewed to the extent desired. Supplemental reporting pursuant to the agenda is made by the chairman of the board and by the president, along with other management personnel as necessary. Any additional documentation or information requested by the board of directors in connection with any matter involving the corporation is made readily available.

During the course of the meetings, the board of directors establishes the broad management policies and makes the top management decisions, which guide the chief executive officer in carrying out his responsibilities. One of the companies participating in the study advised as follows on the main classes of topics and the time they consume. These were on average:

(1)   Current problems: 53%
(2)   Future operations: 20%
(3)   Policy formulation: 19%
(4)   Other issues, including the mechanics of the board itself: 8%

It was also indicated that over the years effort in policy making had gone down after much of the policy had been determined. Time devoted to planning had increased, in terms of proportion. However, the total length of the meeting dropped from six hours to three and a quarter. The bulk of this drop took place in the time devoted to current problems and policy issues.

There are many boards which dispatch their business with great speed in meetings that consume less than two hours. Typically, in these high-speed cases, the president presents a summary of company operations for the last month and for the year to date. He also elaborates on the data with verbal comments. Specific resolutions on major expenditures are put to the board, as well as routine resolutions on formalities. A vote is taken and the meeting ends.

There is a management proverb which says that a job that does not deserve to be done well does not deserve to be done at all. If the board's deliberations have to be cut short because time is of essence more than quality, they should not be held in the first place. I personally favour afternoon meetings for the board, so that the time can be extended into evening hours for which there is (or at least should be) no commitment. Subjects have to be treated well, and this means that:

● They first have to be cleared and become fully comprehensive.
● They must then be thoroughly discussed – with dissent playing a key role – until a consensus of the meeting emerges.

Management should expect each director to articulate his judgements and viewpoints. His expressions must contribute something of value to the decisions made. The *sense of the meeting* is a good rule to follow. The sense of the meeting is not necessarily consensus, but it is the nearest thing to subject clarification and agreement.

In answer to the question: 'What do you principally discuss at your board meetings?' one of the members of the boards participating in the survey suggested that the directors should:

(1)   concern themselves with a review of the operating reports submitted by the officers;
(2)   consider and pass on all recommendations of management in the

important areas of policy determination (such as the establishment of new branches);
(3)   evaluate the acquisition by cash purchase, mergers or exchanges of stock of other institutions engaged in businesses similar to theirs;
(4)   treat various elements of working capital structures (such as lines of bank credit);
(5)   study long-term debt, both senior and subordinate, and additional equity capital marketing.

Reports are also made and considered by the board in establishing such policies as employee relationships, administrative salaries and related compensation, evaluation of advertising and business acquisition programmes, proper responsibilities of a community and social nature. Management also keeps the board informed concerning state and national legislation affecting the business, tax problems, and developments within the industry that influence the trends and the competition.

To the question: 'How far in advance are the topics of the discussion known?' the answer was given that on all major matters concerning direct action of the board, advance information is mailed to each board member 'sufficiently prior' to the time of the meeting. This enables the member to generally familiarise himself with the subject.

The information given to members of the board is as detailed as is deemed essential by management to acquaint each member fully with the matter. In the presentations at the meeting an additional effort is made to fully inform directors. Such information is not compiled to withhold any major factors, or coloured in order to conceal or to slant the facts. Every effort is made to inform the outside directors fully but it is not expected that they will be able to develop the same 'feel' in these matters as the inside directors possess, who have the direct responsibility of operations. The main guiding factors in the decisions reached by the board are governed by the evaluation of the information provided and the judgements of the directors which flow from their knowledge, experience and executive expertise.

Another bank was to comment that, in its view, the basic function of the board of directors is to carry out its responsibilities to the stockholders of the corporation by reviewing regularly the corporation's policies. Also, most importantly, to observe management on a continuing basis both as to incumbents and proper individuals in succession. Let me emphasise this point. Most of the companies participating in the study felt that the directors had a large and direct responsibility to the stockholders. This is only natural, as they do represent the stockholders. What was a little unusual about the responses was how they felt they should carry out this responsibility and what emphasis should be placed on their activities.

Some companies felt that their board members should spend most of their time on future prospects and long-range policies with a secondary view on profits and losses – even if long-term policies and strategic issues were not at the top of the list. Others suggested that the board should above all be a watchdog on management, leaving management to make the decisions.

Many companies felt that there was a major distinction between board functions and executive functions and that these functions needed different data. Said the chairman of the board of a major publishing firm:

> We made a clear distinction between policy matters which are properly determined by the Board of Directors, and administrative procedures which are properly left to corporation management. As the president of a company is an executive officer, he should have at his disposal considerably more detailed information than outside board members need to reach policy decisions.

At what point does management become policy-making information? This is one of those grey areas which can only be defined by each corporation, and each will define it differently. Such a definition will even vary as a function of time.

To the question: 'Are Board deliberations a matter of group rather than individual participation and behaviour?' each board questioned stated that all its directors have equal voting privileges and outside members take an active part. 'Their advice, counsel, and guidance is sought at each meeting,' says one president. However, a Board chairman had an interesting comment on the relative weight given to the opinions of outside directors. He stated:

> So far as the reaction of the Management to the opinions of the outside directors is concerned, this would depend upon the fresh viewpoints contributed by the outside directors, the relevance and intrinsic value of the contributions made in the past by each outside director, and the opinion of management of the professional competence of an outside director in the areas of the matters under discussion.

Another CEO was to suggest: 'Through experience our management has learned that even our most valued and highly regarded directors are not, per se, possessed of infallible competence and judgement in all areas of the corporation's activities.' Only a few chairmen admitted that many times an outside member may be a member in name only; that he adds a great deal of prestige but spends little of his time dealing with company problems.

There are also numerous situations in which informal, casual boards have been found to be a simple, practical means for dealing with problems. This is typically the case of a single-owner firm, but even when there are several owners, informality may provide a practical form of board. In closely owned small companies, the owners are also the directors, the officers and the top managers. Informality has, however, no place when the company reaches a state which requires clearer separation of ownership from management, or when several owners find themselves in a quandary over equality of their rights as owners – which they have pretty clearly spelled out in law – or over their rights as managers, which they can assert only by violating a cardinal rule of management: the single chain of command.

CAN THE EFFICIENCY OF THE BOARD BE INCREASED?

A necessary element for board efficiency is strong leadership. Work begins when one is elected, as the director must grow with the organisation he serves and must challenge it. Efficiency is important but efficiency brings under perspective many considerations. One of them is planning.

Boards demand of management three to five-year plans but seldom demand them of themselves. When proper planning premises are established, at the end of each fiscal year, the board meeting dates for the next year should be selected and approved. All committee meetings, whether monthly, quarterly or semi-annually, depending on their purpose and necessity, should also be approved, with all dates listed in a board of directors' handbook.

Planning does not stop at determining dates. Boards must clearly establish what general areas they wish to explore in the three to five years to come and prepare master plans at the beginning of each fiscal year. This is in addition to their regular responsibilities in evaluating company performance on an ongoing basis.

Boards should challenge management and themselves to determine the appropriate future course of their industry and of their firm. The function of planning at the board level is charged to the chairman of the board. Something similar can be stated regarding the effective use of time. Board meetings should not last longer than necessary. This requires leadership of the chairman.

The preceding section brought to the reader's attention that preparation, dissemination, and adherence to an agenda is important for efficiency. The agenda permits the members of the board to know exactly what will be discussed, the priority of each item and the actions to be requested by management.

It is advisable to have the agendas standardised. They can be sent by electronic mail to computer literate directors. In the agenda's structure, recurring items should appear with approximately the same priority for each meeting.

Periodic reports, such as those of the finance committee, planning committee, technology committee, audit committee and other *ad hoc* committees, should be entered at regular meeting dates. They must always be included when they are to be discussed. Resolutions should also be included as part of the agenda, with summaries of reports that require action attached to it. Only in the case of an emergency should something be discussed that is not on the agenda, and even emergencies should be screened as to their importance.

Since the best board meetings are those which are interactive, a question-and-answer period should be included on the agenda. During it, questions can be directed by board members to management, other board members, or the chairman. No decisions should be reached during this time, and even relevant matters brought up during the question-and-answer period should be channelled by the chairman to be placed on the agenda for a future meeting.

All agenda items demanding decisions at the meeting should have resolutions reviewed by legal counsel and should be submitted to the directors before the meeting. This reduces the time necessary to pass resolutions, since it is easier to modify a working draft than to attempt free-hand a resolution during the meeting.

Advance preparation of a proposed board resolution is better than having the secretary attempt to draft such resolution after the meeting. Such draft might deviate from actual decision, the resolution may not cover everything the board passed, or it might not reflect the entire sense of the meeting.

A board meeting is so much more effective when the board members are properly informed in advance of issues relating to the company's business to be discussed (see also Chapter 10 – Satisfying the Information Needs of the Board). It is imperative to disseminate financial, technical and managerial information with sufficient time to encourage, and even demand, that directors read it.

Optimally, board meeting materials should reach directors approximately one week before meetings. In case some information should never leave the organisation, it is a good idea to produce two board of directors' books, the first being a compilation of nonconfidential material, the other containing confidential information. Directors should be made aware that it is available to them at the organisation before the board meeting.

Furthermore, information at the disposition of the directors should cover not only the current fiscal year but also at least two years of comparative monthly statistics as well as at least five years of quarterly, semi-annual and annual statistics. The best system is to make available such information in the corporate database, for instance, the Infocenter, accessible to authorised users. This suggestion presupposes computer literacy on behalf of board members.

Graphic presentation can greatly enhance the comprehensive picture the directors need to have, with details available on request. Furthermore, all reports submitted to the board, whether voluminous or simply memoranda, should be summarised. In principle, voluminous reports should not be given to the directors.

There are other issues influencing the efficiency of the board. For instance, the directors' compensation. It has been nearly a tradition to pay directors by the meeting. There is a presumption that if one pays the board members by the meeting, they will attend more meetings to get more compensation. But meeting-by-meeting compensation also promotes additional meetings in order to gain compensation rather than to solve problems.

Remuneration by the year, based on the overall responsibilities of board members is a more sound alternative. Board members should be paid well and, as Chapter 1 underlined, they should be provided with liability insurance.

Finally, the performance of the board, as a strategic planning and policy-making body – whether through its meetings or other functions – must be monitored. At the same time the board itself should be given a factual and documented feedback to be sure all decisions are carried out on behalf of the organisation – and that such decisions were well taken, having had favourable effects.

DECIDING ON POLICY MATTERS

A valid discussion on the elaboration of policy issues by the board of directors has to differentiate between the aforementioned two different patterns of operations: in the one (class A) the board is concerned with establishing long-term goals and broad policies which represent the stockholder's interests; in the other (class B), the board addresses itself mainly to day-to-day activities. Even within the B class, a differentiation should be made in terms of the mission given to the board, and ownership's appreciation of such mission. Let's call the case of lesser appreciation, B1.

An example of B1 is offered by a statement made by one of the respondents:

> Within our company, there is a strong, capable management and therefore the Board of Directors is not given enormous amounts of information. Otherwise the Board of Directors is only second-guessing management and could be put in the position of usurping the powers and responsibilities of management, thus taking away the vital ingredient of management initiative and entrepreneurship.

In B2 the board is relatively dominant, concerned with establishing company policies instead of accepting those of management. An example is described in the following statement:

> The articles of incorporation provide 'the business of the corporation shall be managed by the Board of Directors.' In addition to selecting and electing the management, the Board of Directors actively directs by appropriate action or by specific delegation the operations of the company including the adopting of financial and management policy, approval of capital expenditures, purchases, disposition and leasing of properties, and so on.

Evidently a discussion on the board's contribution to policy matters is relevant only in classes A and B2. The elaboration of policy has as a basic objective to avoid repetitive decisions on matters which have been settled once for a certain period of time. Clear board polices are beneficial to management as they:

● help guide its hand in daily business;
● give direction in developments regarding the longer term.

A vital issue to corporate survival is the evaluation of risk by cognisant board members. High technology companies are particularly sensitive to this subject. As *Business Week* recently suggested:[4] over the next ten years about 200 commercial communications satellites must be put into orbit, either to replace elder ones, or to offer expanded services. That amounts to a $1 billion-a-year launch-service market. Just as impressive is the risk.

General Dynamics is gambling a rumoured $1 billion to build 18 Atlas-Centaur rockets. Martin Marietta's marketing teams visit Australia, Japan, and European countries. Pushing its new Delta II rocket, McDonnell Douglas claims seven contracts and thirteen options. All entrants must now assume an awesome financial liability for the damages that might result if a rocket crashes. That burden used to be carried by the government. And insurance premiums for private companies are steep. The industry is being asked to buy $500 million of coverage per launch.

These are decisions of such magnitude that only the board of directors could or should decide. The problem is that, though they may be competent in their area of activity, most board members lack the technological background necessary to evaluate both *opportunity* and *risk*. yet, since technology is so much embedded in operations, the longer term cannot be successfully evaluated today without technological background. This is precisely the reason why I advise the wisdom of having a competent board member as *Chief Technology Officer* (CTO) giving him the mission of being an innovator and integrator, as well as a consultant to his peers.[2]

In the coming decade the chief technology officer will play an important part in business, industry and finance. He will deal with the chaotic state of many computer and communications installations, healing the wounds that result from unplanned integration of incompatible systems, devices and services. Most importantly, he will be the board's member dedicated full-time to looking into the technological future. Another board member should take a similar look into the international world of finance and economics.

This top-level financial function is today much more of a top management practice than that of the CTO which is just starting. Capitalising on some current practices – particularly those reflecting Du Pont and General Motors organisational principles – Figure 6.3 explains the relation between:

● Strategic planning function.
● Executive committee responsibilities.
● The area covered by the forward-looking, world-wide financial executive.

124

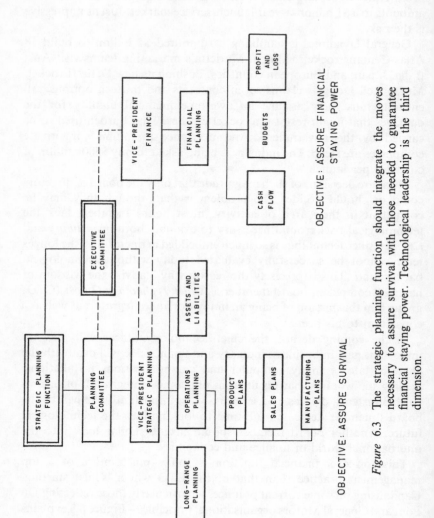

Figure 6.3 The strategic planning function should integrate the moves necessary to assure survival with those needed to guarantee financial staying power. Technological leadership is the third dimension.

As John Maynard Keynes once suggested: 'The energies and skill of the professional investor and speculator are devoted to anticipating what average opinion expects the average opinion to be.' But expectations based on extraneous factors and on guesses about the behaviour of others can become self-fulfilling and not necessarily for the best. The chief financial officer must be a leader in forecasting – as well as being in a position to follow shorter-term operations

Two key charts from daily business which can have an impact on the longer term are projected divisional profit and return on investment (ROI). Suggested procedures are outlined in Figures 6.4 and 6.5. The information necessary should be computer-based, brought to the senior executive's attention in graphical form, with ample detail available for further documentation if necessary.

When the company is small, intended action can be predicted through personal knowledge. The personality of the owner-manager is decisive in what the company does or intends to do. As the company grows, executives who need these predictions can no longer secure them through personal acquaintance with one owner. Ownership and management start being different spheres of action. If there is to be prediction, it must be through knowledge of corporate policies.

Policies are key ingredients of corporate personality. As they are thought through, deliberated, written, published, and lived up to, they become reliable references. Policies are a statement of a company's intent, goal(s) and course(s) of action. Deliberated and elaborated at the board level, policies tend to reflect the corporate philosophy and serve to guide executive action. Typically, policies deal with broad matters, not detail – and they should be enforced fully. Polices may be concerned with the philosophical, ethical and moral principles, not solely with business matters. But contrast, procedures generally regard how actions are to be taken. They reflect the habits of actual action – whether written or not.

Policies can be applied to the business of the board itself, not just to line management. A valid policy, for instance, is not to appropriate money for new equipment unless management can demonstrate by statistical evidence that they are using their present equipment to full realisable capacity, or equipment renewal provides a fast track towards becoming a low-cost producer. Another valid policy at the board of directors level is the exercise of an acid test over the decisions and acts of management. Practice shows that this is rarely done. The don't-rock-the-boat policies threatened nobody except, in the longer run, the company.

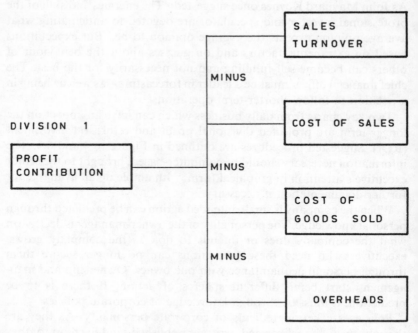

Figure 6.4   Financial control and cost/benefit evaluation must be based on established policies. This figure shows a typical breakdown of projected divisional profit.

Policy formulation should require profound study, with alternatives taken into consideration and possible aftermaths brought into the picture. Policies tend to extend over a long period of time, affecting management decisions. Hence, they should only be reached after the appropriate elaboration and at the highest level of the organisation.

As I have so often underlined, it should be borne in mind that the major responsibility of members of boards of directors is to make decisions in areas of broad policy

● affecting the progress and profitability of the operations, as well as
● selecting the executive and senior officers who will be expected to initiate, submit and execute programmes and means by which the corporation will attain its objectives.

To do so, the board of directors must have a clear understanding of what these objectives are, must have approved and be in agreement with them and must be capable of evaluating the performance of management in

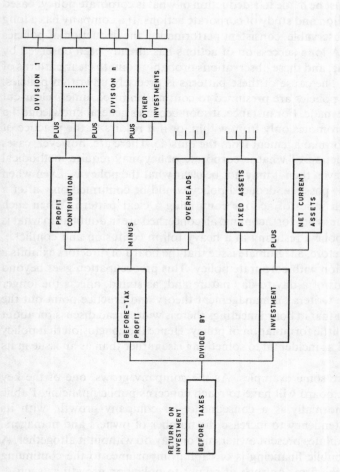

Figure 6.5   The procedure for calculating return on investment (ROI) should be well established corporation-wide and understood by every manager. This figure gives an example.

attaining the goals and objectives. Establishing policies and following through their implementation is a valuable exercise not only in terms of directing the firm but also in controlling it.

Knowledge of corporate policy is not always easy to come by. Unless policies are properly spelled out and presented in a written form, recourse must be made to a deduction of what is corporate policy, based on observation and study of corporate actions. If a company has a long record of observable, consistent performance, the deduction of policies is simpler. A long succession of actions has already been observed by many people, and these observations probably point to clear patterns of behaviour. The cause of these patterns is precisely unwritten policies. Often such policies are presumed to continue in force, unless clear-cut changes are made. For instance, it soon becomes general knowledge if a company promotes only from within, or if it resorts to the practice of taking senior management from the outside. There are, however, cases where deduction of what is corporate policy may require methodical study, and even then it may not be clear what the policy is. Even when deduction is possible, deduced policy would be confirmed only after a long-enough series of actions confirming a clear pattern. When such confirmation is not forthcoming, all concerned are in doubt as to what is corporate policy, resulting in a heavy toll in confusion and conflict.

It is, therefore, a legitimate issue that the board of directors exhibits a preoccupation with corporate policy. This preoccupation goes beyond the decisions of a day-to-day nature and, as stated, affects the longer term. Some writers on management theory and practice point out the curious fact that in board meetings there is widespread discussion about policy, but little formulation of policy. Hence the conclusion that policy is discussed as incidental to something else rather than as an issue in its own right.

Let's take some examples. As the company grows, one of the key policies the board will have to reach concerns public financing. Public financing normally is a consequence of company growth, with its associated tendency to increase the number of owners and managers. But it also dilutes present ownership or may do without it altogether. A policy on public financing is of capital importance to the continuing growth of the firm. As such, it relates to policy on growth as such.

Growth in company business is normally accompanied by growth in number of owners. Some of these owners cannot be active in company management or do not want to be. At the same time, the bigger the company, the more need is there to delegate decisions to professional managers. Growth, as well as survival, poses its own prerequisites. It calls for management – particularly board level management – to be innovative, to allocate resources for long-term planning. Plans for the future call for consideration of: possible new materials, new services, adaptability, low cost; performance in the hands of the user and satisfaction of the user; new methods of production involving possible changes in equipment; new skills and in what number; training and retraining of personnel.

A basic requirement for innovation is faith that there will be a future. Innovation is the foundation of the future and it can not thrive unless top management declares an unshakable policy of steady renewal, high quality and increasing productivity. Without such guidelines given by the board, line management and everyone else in the company will be sceptical about the effectiveness of their best efforts. Where top management does not understand the salient issues, or does not get personally involved, nothing will happen. That's how corporations reach a downturn.

There are examples of policy decisions at the board level which direct towards avoiding growth as an objective except as it is 'forced on us'. Other policies, not necessarily related to this, require minimising research and development costs except as needed to get current customer orders.

The opposite policy – to maximise research and development investments – is necessary if the board decides that the company should grow with the economy or faster – the objective being to improve upon the present share of market. The same is true of modernising the production line, moving into added markets and so on. Growth policies call as well for developing executives at a rate well beyond that needed for replacement. They may also suggest going after acquisitions which are attractive financially, whether in related fields or not.

As the foregoing examples suggest, problems of policy formulation arise as the board itself needs to unify its thinking on these matters. The board can also formulate policy to aid the line executives in their decision making.

Critical policy decisions have to do with capital expenditures which do not readily admit return on investment evaluation. This typically requires a critical review of the merits of each such proposal in relation to the estimate of the expenditure. It may also call for limiting the total expenditure to an amount which, in combination with the expenditures for other categories, will still meet the overall goals set for return on investment and other financial objectives. A standing board policy may, for example, specify that proponents of expenditures determine the return on investment in accordance with well-established principles. Such expenditures, for instance, must also be shown to have a strong prospect of assisting the corporation in meeting overall goals.

One of the toughest board decisions, particularly in family-type companies, regards the case of failure of the owners to supply strong managers. An unwritten rule in the business of family-owned companies` is that each generation produce one, and only one, strong man to lead the enterprise. Two or more strong men spur a contest for leadership. The absence of one strong man creates a leadership vacuum which the board should try to fill.

An interesting policy set by the Board concerns its own members, particularly, policy and practice in the selection of outside directors. Said the board chairman of a financial institution:

> In the 40 years of this corporation's existence the selection of outside directors has passed through many transitions. Initially, those stockholders who were willing to make a substantial investment in the company were recognized by being named to the Board. Usually, these would be individuals who had enjoyed some degree of success in their own vocations and who were known to exercise and believe in the basic principles of sound management and control.

But then, the same reference specified, as the company grew and as more of its equity capital was offered and acquired by the public at large, a more sophisticated policy for the selection of outside directors was developed, with personal investment in the stock of the company becoming a secondary consideration. Since consumer credit is a very specialised field of knowledge, direct experience in it has never been a consideration; but emphasis, rather, has been placed upon broad economic knowledge and experience, as well as understanding of the values of group interaction and exchange in decision making. The management of the company, with one exception of which it has now purged itself, has not followed the practice of placing on its board representatives of professional services which its activities require from time to time. At one time the corporation's counsel was a member of the board; this has been discontinued. The company never placed on its board a representative of its auditing firm, or its sources of credit such as other banking and insurance executives or security and brokerage firms.

POLICY-MAKING – JAPANESE STYLE

Policy formulation is not done in a vacuum. The reason why the first three chapters laid so much stress on strategic plans is because, when they are properly spelled out and constructive, corporate polices can nicely integrate with them. And sometimes this becomes mandatory.

Let's then follow the Japanese example. In high technology, the strategy followed by MITI (the Ministry of International Trade and Industry) is to include multiple competing firms in key government research projects. An example is the effort to develop a leadership in state-of-the-art Very Large Scale Integration (VLSI) electronic circuitry. Five major electronics firms were involved, and MITI distributed information to all of them, whose boards of directors appropriately shaped polices to that end. If the board of directors belongs to one of the ageing industries, its policy decisions should conform to the MITI strategy to lead domestic producers smoothly out of labour-intensive, low-value-added product lines, or out of that industry altogether and into new ventures. In Japan, this is achieved by allowing a growing amount of imports from Korea and South-East Asia. The United States and Europe are following the wrong strategy: the path of protection and subsidies leads to the scrap-heap. Yet in all the industrial countries the second- and third-generation labour force deserts these industries. In Europe they have been served, or partly served, by migrant workers from the rural parts of Turkey, Yugoslavia, Portugal and other countries. Similarly, in the United States the industries in Detroit and other northern cities are being served by migration from the Appalachian plateau and the South.

The plight of the Big Brown Industries is a great dilemma to all governments, as well as to the boards of directors of industries operating in this line of business. Allowing them to collapse would mean millions of new unemployed, including thousands of jobs in supplier companies. Beyond that, in the real world, you cannot destroy your steel industry and remain an industrial power of any standing. The boards of the Big Brown Industries know that and play accordingly.

On the other hand, neither is investing resources in the bottomless pit of inefficiency the right solution. Management reorganisation, full automation through robotics, new marketing techniques, along with computers and communications technologies, may partially remedy the ailing industries. But for this effort to succeed the board must be keen in new departures. New management, automation of the production processes through robotics, computer-based decision support systems, and worldwide marketing programmes might be successful if bundled together. However, the challenge remains to harness technology innovatively and to market experience – tasks which call for clear directions, ample financing, and the best in management skill. All issues are written in the range of the board's authority. A successful policy should also undoubtfully focus on economies in raw materials supply and on energy costs. Here, too, the private companies and the government can be partners – for the benefit of both.

In the energy sector, the MITI strategy is to simultaneously discourage non-essential consumption and encourage expanded supply by allowing gasoline prices to rise with world market prices. The United States abandoned price controls, while Europe's energy policy remains rather nonexistent amid the controversy between greens and nuclear energy proponents. In that sense, corporate policy cannot have a sense of direction against which to adjust and value its line.

These examples give evidence that the Japanese Government is very careful in shaping the parameters of markets and who may participate in them. Among the tools are incentives, research and development financing, productivity measures and controls over industrial standards – and these constitute gauges for corporate policy. Once a given market has been established in accordance with strategic specifications, MITI (unlike some European government bureaucracies) tends not to intervene in as much detail in the firms' daily decisions.[3] The state only rarely tells industry what equipment to buy, or what technology to introduce. These are corporate board decisions. But MITI routinely shapes the cost-benefit parameters of industry decisions by varying rates of accelerated depreciation, depending on the equipment involved. For instance, MITI influences industrial siting by providing infrastructure in favoured areas, rather than by directly ordering business into specific regions.

Policy-making through the price mechanism vastly reduces the need for regulatory bureaucrats, without causing the state to lose its grip on the evolution of industrial structure – and parametric approaches make the measures dynamic. An example may be helpful. In the early 1970s Japanese firms were allowed to depreciate investments for pollution controls by 60 per cent in the first year to assure progress against one of Japan's severe problems. Subsequently the rate was reduced to 27 per cent as the problem came under control. Boards of directors took good notice of the allowances for capital investment decisions.

At the same time, the industrial strategy followed by the Japanese Government did not prevent uncompetitive firms from failing. Even one of the top ten trading companies has been on the list of failures. But government policy did aim to ease the failure impact by advising failsafe and failsoft (Graceful degradation) solutions.

For instance, in consultation with industry, it was decided to scrap over 40 per cent of existing shipbuilding capacity, and MITI designated the facilities to be scrapped. A second example is the scrapping of much open-hearth steel and fertiliser capacity after 1973, seeing that the market dynamics have changed.

The Japanese do a good job in defining manufacturing strategy. They separate each product/market segment, defining one objective which becomes a guideline for board policy, depending on the relative strengths and weaknesses of the firm:

● high cost dependability,
● high quality, or
● flexibility.

Within these guidelines, in terms of new investment, board decisions should see to it that plant design, process structure and organisation meet objectives.

At a recent conference, an American executive put it as follows:

No significant sector of U.S. industry has a five-year plan for automating factories, much less a 10-year plan. Compare that with Japan which has a series of five-year plans. One company had a plan for a plant in 1970 that was to be remodernized five years hence. It was remodernized in 1975 and again in 1981. In 1986 the plant is scheduled to be torn out again, and it very likely will.

The point this executive made is that under current economic conditions, and the lack of appropriate incentives in the United States, it is difficult to get the commitment of the board to invest in new equipment, even though the old is obsolete. Besides that, with only few exceptions, both European and US companies look at the shorter term rather than the longer range. We made repeated reference to this fact in connection with the preoccupations of the board.

In Japan supply-side economics in the area of accelerated depreciation and demand-side policies (relating to government procurement and support for export) also help to reduce the financial risk involved in plunging ahead with new capital investment. Company boards buy this dual strategy and the results are very positive. While in the United States a heavy portion of the basic industrial plant is nearly forty years old, industry-government strategy in Japan sees to it that the average age of Japanese capital stock is half as old. Capital spending includes substantial replacement expenditures for new equipment capable of producing higher-value-added products with impressive productivity.

The bottom line of these strategic references is that raising the national competitiveness is a pressing concern. Incentives should be given to private and public companies to follow this line. This makes government-industry partnership a most important issue. Just as important, particularly in terms of export markets, is the ability to maintain in the longer run economic stability: from monetary policies to the cost of production. This is one of the current crisis problems in Europe and America. Deficit handling, the oil prices crises of the 1970s and the interest rates are held responsible. Less appreciated, but just as important, is the fact that boards of directors are not presenting management with the proverbial carrot-and-stick to get going. Yet the human donkey, as London's *Economist* aptly remarked, will not move until it sees a carrot in the front and feels a stick in its back.

NOTES

1. 9 November 1987. This reference regards an Arthur D. Little study.
2. D.N. Chorafas, 'Is Competition ahead? Then leapfrog them', *Computerworld Magazine*, 20 July 1987.
3. We will examine this subject in greater detail in Chapter 18, also emphasising strong and weak points.

7 Corporate Policy: Its Strategic Role

Policy is a fundamental guide, a general statement or understanding guiding the thinking of subordinates. General statements of policy are never specific, they are based on a philosophy or belief that serves to orient the actions of the company executives. More precisely, policies

- deal with broad matters, not detail;
- require study and thought;
- are approved only at the highest level of the organisation;
- extend over a long range of time;
- having been established, should be expressed in written text; and
- should be observed fully.

Within the enterprise, policy decisions offer 'the line' for the development of plans, and can be compared to the frame on which planning will be built. The existence of a certain policy eliminates on the part of subordinates the need for repeated decision making on routine subjects. The board of directors is deeply and continually concerned with policy. Not only do its members guide the action of others by policy, but also they themselves are guided by it.

Policy is generally regarded as a major instrument for the direction of an industrial enterprise or financial institution. Clear and well-communicated policies are cited among the most important tools of management. A company establishes policies so that the management and employees know generally what the position of the company is in a given situation. Three main types of policy can be distinguished:

(1) Policies that are established precedents;
(2) Officially formulated policies;
(3) Unofficially formulated policies.

Policies are not commands for action, but merely guides. They can be formulated at every echelon of management; obviously those bearing the most weight are the policies formulated by top management. The board of directors of a company passes down to the executive branch certain policies. The executive branch channels its actions along these policies and formulates other policies for the middle management.

Executives have shown a marked curiosity concerning policy and its place. Business and management research associations receive many requests each year for information on policy practices of other companies. It is a difficult subject for factual research as, to a great degree, it is one dealing with intangibles. Furthermore, policy is dynamic rather than static, taking different forms and often changing emphasis as the evolving need of the enterprise for guidance displays itself.

MAKING THE COMPANY'S POLICIES

Policy making is not restricted to large-scale organisations. While there is some tendency to recognise policy coverage as necessary in more areas than do smaller firms, the difference is not enough to be very significant. Nevertheless, if the need for policy coverage is generally felt by companies, both large and small, the requirements of present action are found to be much greater in the larger entities. The bigger the company, the greater the chances that policy will be formalised by written permission.

Two reasons are cited for this. First is the communications problem in the management of larger companies, which must publish fixed statements to ensure uniformity of understanding and interpretation rather than rely upon word of mouth, as the smaller management teams can do. Second is the increasing complexity of the managerial environment which presses hardest on the large companies, and which requires clear and consistent policy direction for uniform operating practice.

A good example of management policy successfully zipping down the line is one established by one of the financial organisations for whom I have been working as consultant to the chairman of the board. Figure 7.1 exemplifies this policy. The problem was personal computers and networks. The decision has been:

(1) Personal workstations (WS) should not be shared and their microfiles should be encrypted.
(2) Given security protection, networks and computer resources can be shared – always subject to authorisation and authentication prior to access.
(3) The personal computer at client site should also be dedicated to the client firm, but could be shared among its departments at its discretion.

SHARED RESOURCES

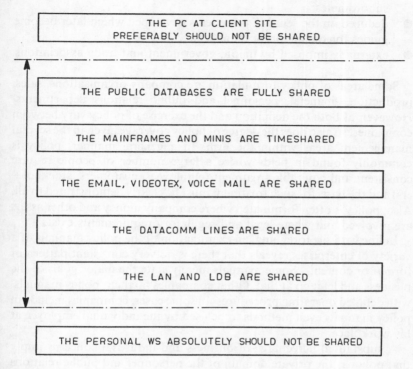

Figure 7.1   A clear policy must be established regarding shared and private
resources in computers and communications. The policy of a
leading corporation is reflected in this figure.

There are five good guides in policy making: the questions *why, what,
where, when* and *how*. All must be considered when any type of policy is
determined. In most cases, policy formulation is influenced by public
opinion and other conditions, internal and external. If public opinion is
unfavourable, then policy changes are usually brought about. Among
internal influences are advancements due to industrial research and
personnel relationships. External influences include governmental laws
and taxes. Harold Koontz, my professor of Business Policy at the
University of California, Los Angeles (UCLA), classified industrial
policy into that:

- originating within the enterprise to guide managers and their subordinates;
- deduced, in the sense of precedents developed which later become guides for the action of managers;
- externally imposed by union, government and trade associations

Some areas of policy formulation are company organisations, sales, production, financial, personnel and public relations departments. However, as both the definition and the exercise of policy vary between companies, so also does the degree of policy coverage given to the several management areas within the firm. In a general manner, policy is commonly found in fields where a large number of people require consistent and equitable treatment (employees, customers, stockholders) and the basis for such treatment must be clearly demonstrated to all. Also, policy is often formulated where company money and other assets are involved and where legal and regulatory requirements exist.

In line with the foregoing, an examination of the policy manuals of a variety of enterprises reveals that there is no very consistent pattern of format or contents. Some manuals merely state the major goals of the business and let it go at that. Other companies fill their 'policy manuals' with detailed operating procedures. In some cases, companies include in policy manuals even methods to be used by the individual employee at his workplace.

A substantial percentage of business and industrial concerns imply that policy is the private domain of the personnel and public relations functions. Some policy manuals include only personnel policy. Policies relating to public and stockholder relations are found to be fairly well developed; considerable attention is being given to primary company objectives and breadth of operations.

In financial control and accounting fields, policy coverage approaches that of the personnel field but, as a trend among companies, it is somewhat less broad and places more emphasis on factual, routine matters. The degree to which policy coverage focuses upon the areas of financial and accounting activity does not vary significantly among companies, although the general extent to which policy is formalised in written presentation is not substantially high.

The general sales and distribution field receives a certain coverage with outstanding examples the pricing and discounting policies, and customer service policies. Channels of distribution, advertising sales promotion and product quality are also pretty well covered by company policy.

Policy coverage in the field of manufacturing and production is weaker, and the variation between specific areas is greater, than in sales policies. Policies on quality control, production planning and production performance standards are the most frequently established. They are also the most frequently established. They are also the most frequently confirmed in writing.

Policies governing the conduct of research and development activities seem to be the least developed of any other area of business and industry. To a large degree, this may be due to the intangible nature of much of the research endeavour, and to the newness of the function. Many companies lack the experience to identify policy needs and guide its creation. Companies most commonly have research and development policies on the types of projects and on their selection and approval. Inversely, there is a marked lack of policy on the pay-out of projects.

WHO IS WHO IN POLICY MAKING

Policy making is influenced by the basic philosophy prevailing within the enterprise. Policy does not happen 'at random'. It is made by somebody, at some time, and on some basis. Information from a number of companies shows that within an industrial firm or financial institution, there is a substantial participation of executives in policy considerations. However, while policy perspectives are widely shared, the executive officer maintains a central and decisive position in the actual making of policy.

The board of directors enters the policy picture in the formulation of general company policies and in financial policy. All other fields receive relatively minor attention on behalf of the board. The company president gets into almost every area of policy development. There exists a general opinion in business that such development should be a major responsibility of the chief executive officer.

It is in the ranks of the functional executives that the intriguing variations in executive policy-making stature show up sharply. The sales executive and the financial executive emerge as two strong-men of policy-making in the ranks of the functional executives. The financial executive takes a leading role in policy creation in his own function and, through this, his influence is felt strongly in all other fields. In general company policy his voice is second only to the president's. In manufacturing and sales policies, his influence usually follows that of the functional executive himself.

In a variety of industrial cases, the manufacturing executive ranks a fairly close third in what concerns company-wide policy formulation. But his participation is somewhat more spotty in the various sub-areas of each function. In the field of his own function, namely manufacturing policies, he does not share the privacy of the financial and sales executives but receives moderate participation from all other functional executives.

The research and development executive also tends to show a relatively low participation in policy development in other departments and has somewhat incomplete participation within his own policy field. Formulation of research and development policy is usually shared to a substantial degree by all executives. This is interpreted by many to indicate that research and development has growing acceptance as a vehicle for general company progress, rather than being regarded as an isolated technical endeavour.

Subordinates interpret policy in order to make decisions which are in accordance with and not contrary to general company policy. The higher up the interpretation is made, the better the chance to clear the plan in an unambiguous way. To identify the difference between 'deduced policy' and 'deduced form', Table 7.1 presents in a nutshell the outcome of a planning study cited here by way of illustration.

Table 7.1   Deduced policy and deduced form

Policy	Deduced form
To expand mainly by development from within, after two decades of expansion chiefly through acquisition.	The public record of acquisition and spin-offs.
To lease or lease back, rather than to own many of the facilities.	Published accounts of longterm liability for leases, and published information on new facilities.
To centralise manufacturing facilities.	Over a span of years involving a 70% increase in sales, there was an actual reduction in the number of manufacturing plants
To decentralise distribution facilities.	During the same span of years, the number of distribution facilities rose by 45%.

'Deduced policy' is only clear after a long-enough series of actions has established a clear pattern. The real problem which prevails is that often actions are not old enough to draw conclusions from their effects. During this time many of these concerned are in doubt as to what is corporate policy. Such uncertainties result in confusion, conflicts and delays.

One form of testing policy is to ensure that the long-range plan conforms in its scope and procedures with the demands, requirements and objectives of the intermediate and short-range plans. Many intermediate-range (five-year) plans are in reality statistical plans, made to satisfy a corporate requirement but not used in the daily operations of the business. Such plans serve some corporate purposes but not as a 'forcing' function. They tend, rather, to hold together several short-range plans and bridge the time gap to the long-range plan.

The integration of plans projected in different time-scales often permits tests through feedback to gauge policy effectiveness. For example, product-line plans should be supported by projected sales plans, thus helping to create integrated business plans. An integrated business plan for a specific product line will:

● indicate the projected sales plan and the reasons for preference for specific goals;
● set projected costs and inform management when it can expect to achieve the plan;
● establish the profit management in regard to what should be achieved: (*a*) through technology; (*b*) through marketing.

Policy usually indicates that such a plan should have a well-established and standard format, provide the basis for co-ordination and control, and should not result in a crowded reporting system. In many companies, policy says that based on such a plan, a proper feedback can be envisaged within the context of the broader long-range plan. In turn the feedback or 'appraisal planning reviews' answer the question of when and to what extent the master plans should be modified.

Policies may also specifiy that appraisals are reached in accordance with the operating department to include: the size and characteristics of investments, an analysis of trends on product planning, pricing and distribution policies, and long-range examination of the current or potential markets which should be studied to determine profitability. The following paragraphs identify, as an example, significant accounting policies followed by corporations:

Principles of consolidation. The consolidated financial statements include the assets, liabilities, revenues and expenses of all significant subsidiaries. All inter-company transactions are (usually) eliminated in consolidation. Investments in companies 20 to 50 per cent owned are carried at equity in net assets, and the parent company's share of their earnings is included in income. Other investments are carried generally at cost or less.

Marketable securities are usually carried at cost or market, whichever is the lower.

Inventories. Inventory values, which do not include depreciation, are stated at cost or market, whichever is lower. Cost is determined generally on the 'last-in, first-out' (LIFO) method for US companies and for certain subsidiaries operating outside the United States. Generally, the 'average cost' method is used by all other subsidiaries.

Fixed assets and depreciation. Fixed assets are carried at cost. Expenditures for replacements are capitalised and replaced items are retired. Maintenance and repairs are charged to operations. Gains and losses from the sale of property are included in income.

Patents, trademarks and goodwill. Amounts paid for purchased patents and for securities of newly acquired subsidiaries in excess of the fair value of the net assets of such subsidiaries have been charged to patents, trademarks and goodwill.

Research and development. Research and development costs are charged to expense as incurred. Depreciation expense applicable to research and development facilities and equipment is included in depreciation in the income statement.

Income taxes. Provision is made for deferred income taxes where differences exist between the period in which transactions, principally relating to depreciation, affect taxable income and the period in which they enter into the determination of income in the financial statements.

Retirement programme. The corporation's contribution to the retirement programme in each year is based on the recommendation of an independent actuarial firm using the entry age normal method.

Net income per share is based on the weighted average number of shares of common stock outstanding in each year.

Key policy issues are likely to focus on organisational solutions, more particularly on the authority and responsibility lines between the Chief Executive Officer and the Financial Executive. But structural problems evolve.

FACING ORGANISATIONAL CHALLENGES

Like the overall objectives, policies are set by top management, by the chief executive officer and his staff with the assistance and concurrence of the board of directors, or vice versa. They represent the thinking and inclinations of the highest echelons who, however, cannot act without having a great deal of information and intelligence passed up the line from the levels below.

Setting policies and revising them calls for possession of such necessary materials as economic studies on current and projected trends in the firm's particular industry and the country as a whole, market research reports and forecasts, operating reports and costs, evaluations made by the management team, data on the performance of the company, variances in the current budget picture and, above all, a clear view of the future: *Where our company is heading.*

Armed with such information, top management sets about determining what goals it wants to achieve – and which policies should be followed to such end. It must concern itself with both long-term objectives and short-range goals the company must pursue in order to implement its plans. In many instances, as each twelve-month period is completed, the five-year plan is simply extended accordingly; thus it always remains a five-year plan.

But policies must be managed. It is not enough to set them once then forget about them. The environment changes, the market shifts, products get innovated, the company finds itself in evolution. It may be *our* first company, started as a relatively young consumer products company which has been marketing its products on a regional basis. As it continues to grow, it lays out an expansion programme which, at the conclusion of, say, ten years should find the company marketing its products on a national scale. It is only evident that past policies are in for thorough revamping.

Not only company growth and market shifts but also the change in our structural concepts can greatly influence the way we draw the organisation chart. A similar statement can be made of executive personalities and the way they look at executive activities handled through different types of posts and positions.

Figure 7.2 shows the evolution in organisational thinking from the 1960s to the 1990s. The relatively simple chart of line and staff of pre-Second World War years remained valid till the early 1960s, at which time new, more complex, relationships showed up. They were propelled

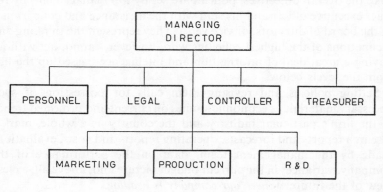

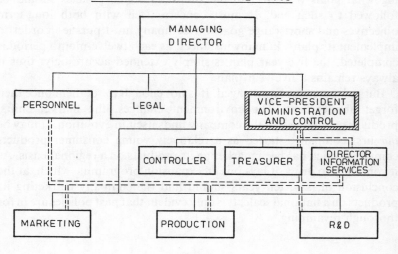

ORGANISATION CHART IN THE 1980s

PRESENTED AN EVOLUTION OVER THAT OF THE
1960s BY INTRODUCING THE TASK GROUPS (SPECIAL
STAFF) WHICH LED TO A 3‾D ORGANIZATIONAL
STRUCTURE.

ORGANISATION CHART IN THE 1990s

A FOURTH DIMENSION WILL SHAPE UP IN DECISION‾
SUPPORT CAPABILITIES, MAINLY FUTURE‾ORIENTED
AND DEDICATED TO:
- THE MANAGEMENT OF CHANGE
- THE NEW STRATEGIC DIRECTIONS (PRODUCTS,
  MARKETS, ASSETS, STRUCTURE)
- THE TRANSITION POLICIES (MEN, MEANS,
  MONEY)

THE GREATEST CHALLENGE IS NOT THE PROCEDURAL
CONVERSION - BUT
  1. THE CONVERSION OF PEOPLE TO THE
     NEW IMAGES
  2. THE MANAGEMENT OF
     - KNOWLEDGE
     - TIME
     - MONEY
     - KEY PHYSICAL ASSETS

Figure 7.2 During the last three decades (1960s, 1970s, 1980s) the organisational chart has undergone significant changes. Much more is
going to happen by way of restructuring during the coming decade.

in a significant way by divisionalisation, decentralisation and internationalisation, but also by the desire to avoid centrifugal forces and
ascertain management control throughout the whole range of operations. In the 1970s this became an accepted organisational form.

Precisely because this structure has become complex, often hiding
issues and operating units which deserve a great amount of attention, the
late 1970s and early 1980s saw the evolution of a *task group* (or, task

force) concept. Task groups are typically put together like the commando units of the Second World War. They are:

● Composed of very competent individuals.
● Receive a clear-cut mission on which they are accountable.
● Operate over a well-defined timespan, reach results and are resolved.

The late 1980s have seen a different organisational practice. It has been influenced by decision support, direct access to databases, multimedia communications, and the developing expert systems' capabilities put at management's disposition. Rapid change – and th need to manage it – had its impact. This new organisational form is still in flux but it will be structured in the 1990s.

This evolutionary tendency underlines the fact that organisation and structure is a domain where striking the right balance between stability and dynamic change has become most crucial. Theoretically, the organisational task is easy. It aims to provide the infrastructure in order to carry out administrative activities from different types of positions. Each of these types within the enterprise has a different range of duties.

At the top is a general office. There, senior executives and staff specialists co-ordinate, appraise, plan goals and policies. They allocate resources for a number of self-contained divisions. Each division handles a major product line or carries on the firm's activities in one large geographical area. Each division's central office, in turn, administers a number of departments.

Each of these departments is responsible for the management of a major function such as manufacturing, engineering, research, selling, purchasing or producing raw materials, finance, and the like. The departmental headquarters co-ordinates, appraises, and plans for a number of field units. At the lowest level, each field unit runs a plant or works, a branch or district sales office, a purchasing office, an engineering or research laboratory, an accounting or other financial office, and so on.

The basic types of administrative positions in the larger, multidivisional enterprise are thus: the field unit, the departmental headquarters, the division's central office, and the general office. These terms are typically used to designate a specific set of administrative activities. But while the terms may remain, their meaning and functionality changes. Most particularly the way these units are planned, directed and controlled evolves. Hence the stress put on existing structures.

Reorganisation often involves managerial changes. In the late 1950s, when I was working with IBM, there was a going adage that IBM's structure is like a hill of sand. Every three or four years, the adage said, God put his finger at the bottom of the hill and moved it. As a result, the grains which were at the top dropped to the bottom. Then God restructured the hill with his palms, and some of the grains at the bottom found themselves at the top.

Figures 7.3 and 7.4a describe two different organisational structures at IBM, separated from one another by less than five years. Subsequently, Figures 7.4b, 7.4c, 7.4d and 7.4e elaborate the organisation presented in Figure 7.4a in a summary form.

Emphasis is on the management of change. But change is often difficult for people and organisations. Therefore they resist it. Among the reasons for resistance applying to people:

- They do not see a need for the change.
- They fear what they do not know.
- They fear a loss of something: status, power, authority, freedom, responsibility, money, prestige, self-image.
- They fear their loss will be greater than their gain.
- They have a history of negative experiences with change.
- They fear lack of competency, an inability to perform the new task or function.

Sometimes, men and organisations react negatively to change because in the past change was forced on them or happened without explanation. They suspect or know the change will result in a new social structure. They realise change affects their personal value system: their own attitudes and beliefs, and they are afraid change will mean more responsibility or complexity. They want neither.

One of the issues to be preserved, if not enhanced, through successive reorganisations is the subject of *management control*. Also the focal point of control: Toward the past or toward the future?

Deriving its essence from five centuries' old accounting procedures, financial controllership was classically tooled toward the past. But already by the mid- to late 1960s, this concept was changing. From projects I was doing in 1966 and 1967 for the American Management Association[1] I recall corporate treasurers and controllers underlining that their focus started being towards the future rather than towards the past. In the elapsed two decades such trend towards future financial conditions and profits has been greatly reinforced.

At the structural side or organisational despendency, General Motor's policy assigns the financial executive under the direct authority

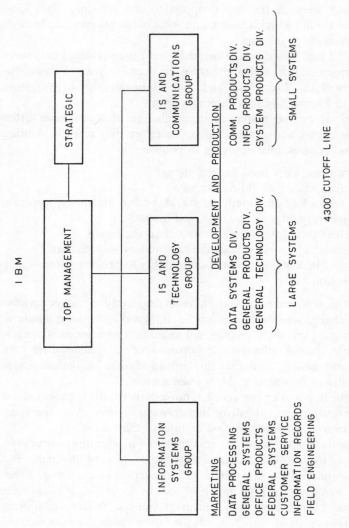

MARKETING

DATA PROCESSING
GENERAL SYSTEMS
OFFICE PRODUCTS
FEDERAL SYSTEMS
CUSTOMER SERVICE
INFORMATION RECORDS
FIELD ENGINEERING

INFORMATION SYSTEMS GROUP

IBM

TOP MANAGEMENT

STRATEGIC

IS AND TECHNOLOGY GROUP

IS AND COMMUNICATIONS GROUP

DEVELOPMENT AND PRODUCTION

DATA SYSTEMS DIV.
GENERAL PRODUCTS DIV.
GENERAL TECHNOLOGY DIV.

COMM. PRODUCTS DIV.
INFO. PRODUCTS DIV.
SYSTEM PRODUCTS DIV.

LARGE SYSTEMS

SMALL SYSTEMS

4300 CUTOFF LINE

Figure 7.3 The IBM organisational chart following a restructuring operation in the early 1980s, with a clear definition of cut-off line between large systems and small systems.

149

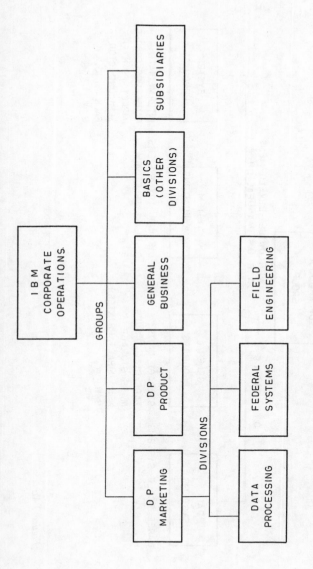

Figure 7.4a   **IBM** organisational charts prior to restructuring. The following four charts elaborate the responsibilities of each major division including the management of the foreign subsidiaries.

150

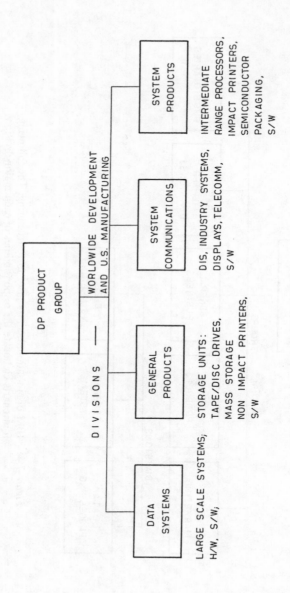

Figure 7.4b

151

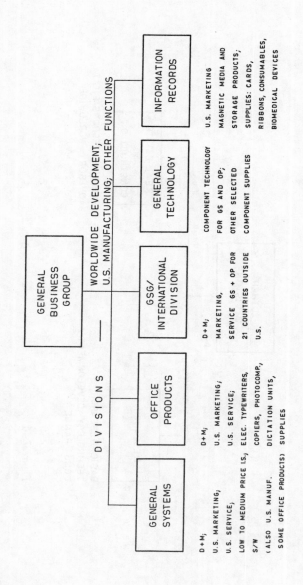

Figure 7.4c

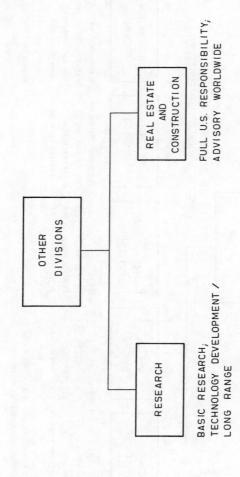

Figure 7.4d

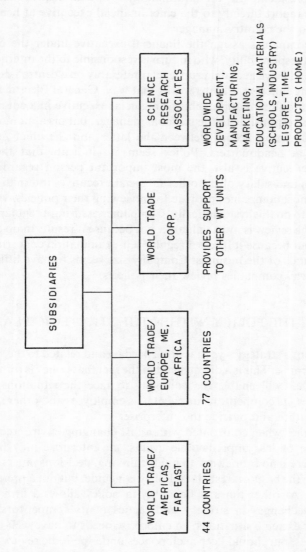

Figure 7.4e

of a finance committee, which depends on the chairman of the board – not the president. In the multinational operations, the financial executives report directly to the chief financial executive at headquarters, not to the country manager.

Other companies assign the financial executive under the country manager's responsibility, who in turn is responsible to the international division, and leave at a higherup level (preferably on a centralised basis) the auditing function. Philips works that way. General Electric follows yet another different approach: the financial executive in a country (or division) is responsible to the national manager, but his appointment is made in common accord between the latter and the chief financial executive at headquarters. Policy seems to indicate that the chief financial executive is also the most important person regarding the promotion and salary of the other financial executives internationally.

While most companies provide for reviewing their policies, very few are found to do this systematically. Companies assuring a regular review feel that the review is most valuable, not because it results in up-to-date policies, but because it forces a regular self-examination concerning the fundamentals of the business. Company size seems to have little to do with the way companies review their policies.

FITTING THE POLICY WITHIN THE STRATEGIC PLAN

Policy is not a strategy – yet it is influenced by and related to the strategy of an enterprise. This is a direct result of the fact that policy is formed in a manner that will enable the company to face the situations of the adversaries, its competitors, its clients, its employees and other relevant factors, within and outside the enterprise.

Sometimes when confronted with a fast-changing environment, and with more or less unpredictable events, an enterprise may have no policy: there is no framework to guide thinking, decisions must be made at once on the basis of fresh data. Policy is a guide, but not a prerequisite to action. At other times, a flexibility in policy allows a firm to face effectively changes in strategy and tactics of its competitors. Thus, except for extreme situations, an enterprise needs to have well-thought-out policies, but should keep such polices under periodic review and re-evaluation so that they do not become obsolete. We live in a dynamic environment. In business, in war, or in a game, policy decisions and plans may become useless, or even harmful, because of adversary action. As a consequence, the able manager changes his policies according to:

- the changes affected in the 'milieu' in which he is living;
- his forecasts for other changes and developments;
- his renewed objectives.

No manager should ever think of policies as being something settled and permanent. It is one of the highest managerial skills to be always alert and able to face every eventuality. Guides for action aply in 'normal' times, not in times of great upset and of switches created through the cutting edge of technology.

The impact of policy comes from the very nature of the business, industrial and financial enterprise. Broadly speaking, a business concern consists of a system of relationships which come into existence when the direction of resources is dependent on professional management. In times of crisis, the reserves in human skill the executive has at his disposal, or those he would be able to obtain at the moment, will be of great importance. Such reserves influence the degree of flexibility he will have in his operations. Company policies are often being made to reflect this very fact.

In the sense of industrial strategy formulation, the most important field for policy decisions is the one concerning the nature, type, design and make of the goods or services the company will offer to the market. This decision area is intimately tied up with the foundations of industrial strategy. The problems which necessitate policy decisions as to the product line of an industry can be classified in five categories:

(1) Type of products on which will be concentrated the productive potential of the company.
(2) Systems and methods for the production of goods or the rendering of services.
(3) Breadth and depth of research: product-wise, cost-wise, and also in regard to human potential.
(4) Price policy and credit policy.
(5) Problems of distribution and those of sales promotion.

Decisions on the subject of price policy require competent information as to the demand and the saturation of the market, and also as to the economic potential of the market, the position of the competitors, the potential of the industry, and the reaction of the market with regard to the products in question. Policy decisions with respect to product price need to consider not only the advertised prices but also questions of discounts, time payments, and of price differentiation – if this product is offered at different quality levels.

Product price is a dynamic subject and should be often reconsidered and re-evaluated. Changes in technology, new competition, price wars, sales promotion, shifts in demand and changes in taste, are some of the reasons calling for this revision. Forward-looking companies have always taken a global approach in the formulation of their policies, making sure that there is no contradiction between policies and strategies.

In a speech on General Motors' policies, Mr Curtice (former GM President) described some of the business policies of his company:

- increase dollar sales;
- increase market percentage;
- keep pace with, and support, the growth of the national economy;
- make the employees partners in business through incentive compensation plan;
- keep General Motors an operating not a holding company.

Some other company policies were also identified. For instance, in pricing civilian products: determine probable direct and indirect costs, allocate these costs to each unit sold, allow for sufficient profit making, set prices which are competitive and attractive to customers, do not rest on laurels. In producing for defence: co-operate actively with government, assume corporation's share of defence production load, endeavour to obtain contracts for more complicated defence products, concentrate production facilities on most difficult parts of products, spread work among plant locations.

The chief executive of another major company phrased as follows the basic policies of his firm: maintain a high degree of efficiency in operations; provide consumers with a variety of competitively priced products from among which they can choose those best suited to their needs; constantly scrutinise research to bring forth new and improved products; enable a vast number of people to share company prosperity; and provide the country with a manufacturing organisation that stands as a source of strength in peace and in war.

MAKING PROFITABLE USE OF SOMEBODY'S POLICIES

The following case exemplifies the opportunities presented to a company by studying the policies of its competitors. The executive team of a

US merchandising concern, looking into the subject of established business policies, found that while a lot of the traditional five-and-dime stores have been upgrading their merchandise and their prices, there were good chances for a chain of stores to expand by keeping prices and quality down. Having studied the strategic moves of its competitors, purchasing and merchandising policies were instituted. A pricing strategy was formulated so that no item in any store would be priced over $3.00. Also 'dollar sale days' were instituted, when 'Jumbo' bath towels sell at three for a dollar. At the same time this policy was instituted (1960) sales were close to $20 million and net profit before taxes was $482.000.

On the basis of this pricing strategy, policies were instituted regarding inventories. Unlike 'five and dime' stores, this marketing chain carries no basic inventory. Its buyers look for out-of-season, closed-out and discontinued items, or any others that they can get at a bargain. Only about 40 per cent of their merchandise carries a brand name. The chain goes after store locations in much the same way that they buy merchandise. Its stores are in low-rent areas mostly; management's policy is to look for bargains in 'discontinued' locations such as, for instance, those vacated by chains whose managers feel neighbourhoods are becoming run-down. How successful this approach is can be tested by the fact that the chain keeps expanding.

Similarly, industrial management can benefit by carefully examining another important area for the policy decisions of its competitors, one intimately related to their company strategies: the obtaining of capital. Even if management makes in advance an estimate of the necessary cash, there are always problems created over determining the best source of this cash. Will the source be internal or external to the firm? Cash problems are important to every enterprise, but in particular to those concerns to which much borrowing may lead to loss of ownership or control over the stock. A company thus may become vulnerable because of its very growth. The largest internal source of cash comes from depreciation and from retained earnings.

Because of the variety of facets involved in company policy making, it has often been maintained that business executives, along with politicians and military officers, are the principal policy decision-makers of the world. In helping a company to formulate its own industrial strategy, or in breaking the 'secret strategic code' of competitive industrial concerns, studies of established policies are most influential when connected to the governing or regulating of:

- public stockholder relations;
- companywide organisation;
- company size or changes in size;
- relations with government;
- relations with competitors;
- general breadth of operations;
- source of company funds;
- use of company funds;
- change to fixed assets;
- depreciation and valuation of assets;
- valuation of inventories and receivables;
- level of inventories
- product line(s);
- product quality;
- brand names;
- marketing areas;
- channels in distribution channels;
- advertising and sales promotion;
- pricing and discounts.

In any of these spheres of policy formulation, its careful study and analysis can give competition the advantage of 'established grounds' for judgement in deciding its own action. This may help the trial-and-error process of taking each step anew in an attempt to identify the strategy of the opponent. It also helps in capitalising on the opponent company's heritage of knowledge, and in breaking up the centrifugal force which could pull individuals together in a team.

Policy enables the individual employee or departments to act consistently over a period of time. This gives individuals, and the company, the quality of perseverance towards a goal. In turn, since people are directed consistently toward the same goal, policy makes it possible for executives to delegate authority. This comes about since executives are reasonably assured that individual employees will act the same as the executive himself would act over a given problem. In this sense, policy speeds company operations because executives are free to handle the unusual situations which might otherwise become bottlenecks. Delegation of authority passes routine operations down the line and gives the executive time to accelerate the handling of new and unusual operating problems. Well-established rational policies can improve communications within a company. Repetitive decisions are cleared from administrative channels, thus providing an avenue through which unusual situations can be passed to obtain new decisions.

For business and industrial executives, profit criteria in formulating policies are of fundamental importance. Non-profit motives include:

- to become the largest concern in the field;
- always to sell more than the last time period;
- to establish business statesmanship;
- to contribute to the advancement of industrial leadership;
- to ameliorate public relations;
- mere fun.

Any of these motives, or a combination thereof, can dictate certain policies. Yet in this modern age nothing lasts forever. Reasons of 'milieu', of resources, of technology, of market shifts, or sociological changes, of competition, and of scientific progress, impose the necessity of a continuous study and re-evaluation of the present policies within the framework of industrial strategy.

THE SUPPLIER'S PROBLEM: AN EXAMPLE

One of the major policy decisions that management often has to face is in the area of 'do' or 'buy'. That is, whether the enterprise will make with its own facilities all the parts needed for its product, or will buy them outside. Very often not only the small but also the large enterprise prefers to buy some parts, rather than enlarge its facilities in order to build every necessary component of its product line. For example, automobile manufacturers buy elsewhere the tyres for their cars. General Motors makes the AC spark plugs, but Ford and General Motors have special departments for 'styling', but Studebaker, over a period of years, was buying the services of Raymond Loewy. Citroën buys from subcontractors a large number of parts for its cars, including the motors. General Motors was selling hydramatic drive to competitors, such as Nash.

Reasons of cost of production, reasons of timing, and reasons of the manufacturing potential of the enterprise are among those that influence policy-making decisions in this area. Established 'do' or 'buy' policies help develop a major interdependence between manufacturers and suppliers. The interdependence of large and small business is reflected in a study made some years ago of 27,500 US firms that supply the goods and services General Motors uses to produce automobiles and other products.

Over 70 per cent of the businesses selling to General Motors divisions in the United States employ fewer than 100 persons and 45 per cent have fewer than 25 employees. Nearly 6,500 companies with fewer than 100 employees have sold goods or services to the corporation for more than ten years; over 600 of them have supplied General Motors for more than thirty years. Products purchased by GM from its suppliers include many unusual items. Lint is used for checking filtering devices in automatic washing machines, pork and beef rib bones for testing food waste disposers, hair for transmission gears, eyebrow tweezers for picking out lead wires in coil assemblies, and hog nose rings for fastening temporary identification tags to machinery. Other unusual purchases include marbles, tooth powder, pigeon traps and ground apricot stones.

This interdependence between the manufacturer and the supplier is even more pronounced in other areas, such as weapon systems. According to generally established policies, a weapon systems contractor must first decide how much will be developed internally within the corporation, and how much will be let out on a subcontract basis. The more 'in-house' development is done, the more diverse become the interests of the employees – for instance, airframes, structures, power plants, ballistics, electronics – and the more unwieldy is the project organisation. The more subcontracting is done, the more the prime contractor becomes responsible for items which he cannot actually control.

Varying approaches on the subcontractor problem are popular today. Some corporations have long been examples of the 'programme manager' approach. Douglas Aircraft was a weapon systems contractor who developed a large portion himself, but subcontracted major elements. Further up the scale of 'in-house' developers are corporations such as North American Rockwell, which with its various divisions (Airframe, Missile, Autonetics, Rocketdyne) stands ready to make most of the large components. The tendency is, however, away from the specialised industrial organisation which had been building up within US industry.

The supplier's problem has another aspect in terms of policy. Its salient question is inventory accumulation. Periodic policy switches by contractors (which have been given the cumulative name of 'inventory adjustments') may severely affect his production and employment. For instance, the most recent inventory adjustment in the United States has shown two impelling forces. One is related to the typical movements in inventory buying associated with the business cycle. The other reflects the efforts of business to economise on inventories by operating with lower inventory/sales ratios throughout the cycle.

Historically, the long-term trend towards lower inventory/sales ratios was interrupted in the early post-war period. With prices rising and many goods in short supply, there was every incentive to build up inventories. Since then, policies have changed many times: in the late 1950s and early 1960s industrial prices have been stable and supplies of most products have been readily available; hence there was less incentive to build up stocks. Ten years later inflation altered management policies: inventories accumulated, but first recession and then high interest rates altered the picture once again, trimming inventories to the lowest levels feasible.

As policies have been developed by industrial concerns enabling them to cut their stocks in order to reduce costs, management has been working to perfect new methods of inventory control. In some cases the use of computers has permitted savings by reducing the number of each size, colour and model that must be kept on the shelf to meet incoming orders. Certain countervailing forces have also been at work. In motor vehicles and other consumer durables, the proliferation of models, types and colours increases inventory requirements – and so does the slackening in demand.

Among the strategic moves taken by industrial concerns is the formulation of policies aimed to push inventories at the user's point. The so-called *zero stock* policy benefits retails but may end by accumulating higher stocks at the manufacturing level. To a surprisingly large measure, policy decisions in the inventory domain also show lack of uniformity among companies. Independently of what the books may be writing, management is not a science – it is still an art.

NOTE

1. *Developing the International Executive* and *Overcoming Communications Barriers in International Operations* (New York: AMA, 1967, 1968).

8 Qualities a Good Director Needs

Background qualities are instrumental in making a valid member of the board. Courage is one of them. 'Courage is not the only virtue,' an old Roman proverb says, 'but it is the one without which all others are meaningless.'

Business involves risks, and they have to be faced with courage. Businessman, are also subject to a fair amount of pressure and intimidation. When courage is not a basic personality characteristic of each and every director, *the company definitely has a problem: its future.* Lee Iacocca gives the example of a board membership which let itself be intimidated. Here is how he tells the story:[1]

But what about the Board? These guys were the illustrious guardians of the Ford Motor Company. They were supposed to constitute the system of checks and balances to prevent the flagrant abuse of power by top management. But it seemed to me their attitude was: 'As long as we're taken care of, we'll follow the leader'.

The second background quality is perspective. We are in a new economic age. We can no longer live with commonly accepted levels of stagflation, slow product-development, marketing mistakes, product defects, manufacturing processes not suited to the job, people on the job that do not know what the job is and are afraid to ask. These are damaging conditions to a firm. Among themselves they identify failure of management to understand the problems of the product in use. They reflect antiquated methods of training and ineffective guidance by the board. Also, in addition to being decision-makers, board members have to be motivators. Despite its inertia, an organisation has to move.

The third quality is the ability to apply one's own know-how to get results. Not every member of the board can understand and follow in detail all aspects of the business the company is in. But the board as a whole should do so and there must be at least two or three members able to dig on the same subject, so that a meaningful discussion can be had. Relating to his experience at Ford, Iacocca suggests in his autobiography:

Then I met with top management and our Board of Directors to discuss the fate of the Cardinal. In these talks, I got the impression that the entire company was confused about the car and that the senior people were only too pleased to have a young upstart like me make the decision for them.

Quite often in board meetings, the time devoted to a subject is inversely proportional to this subject's importance. Yet in any organisation the loss of market, falling apart of products, creeping mediocrity, and in the end financial collapse, is like an earthquake. Financial collapse is predictable. But if no measures are taken in time, when it comes it leaves a more destructive trail of corporate turmoil than an earthquake.

A VIRTUOUS MEMBER OF THE BOARD

'Virtue', Socrates said to Protagoras, 'is knowledge which cannot be taught.' But is it in human nature than men and women are virtuous? Are boards of directors seeking out and electing as members the most virtuous people they can find?

Ken Aubetta seems to give a negative answer:[2]

Instead, Board members asked: Is it good for *me*? Is Glucksman the likely victor? Only Peter Solomon, who was accused of being selfish, dared ask whether the coup made sense for the *firm*. The Board did not ask whether the coup violated the consensual tradition of a partnership, did not ask whether it was time for Peterson to move on, did not ask whether Glucksman possessed the qualities to lead Lehman.

There are other examples, for instance, the first-class passes airlines customarily hand out to their directors. As *Fortune Magazine* reported,[3] at TWA directors have received 'class A' passes, meaning that they and their families get free first-class space from which they cannot be bumped by paying passengers. TWA has even paid taxes on this income for its directors. While such corporate perks are not necessarily virtuous, they threatened to become a power game at TWA when the directors had to decide (in the summer of 1985) whether Carl Icahn or Frank Lorenzo of Texas Air would take over the firm. Lorenzo promised the directors they would retain such passes for life. Icahn made no such provision. The *Fortune* article suggests that James Freund, TWA's outside lawyer, phoned Icahn, ending the call with a request that the latter consider extending the same pass privileges that Lorenzo had offered. There is some evidence that Icahn said 'Screw the bastards'; other evidence suggests that he politely declined Freund's request.

A virtuous member of the board would have as first second and third goal the protection of the stockholders' equity and the survival of the organisation as a going concern. In the longer run, the two are inseparable though in the short term they may seem to deviate.

One of the virtues of a board member is to size up the organisation's strengths and weaknesses, then to induce the other members into taking measures to feed the strengths and strangle the weaknesses. Invariably this means placing emphasis on research and education – to better management, develop products, aid productivity in the office and in the plant, and successfully market from a low-cost production stand.

The board should lead and inspire. Decisions should come fast and be focused. Attention to detail is paramount. I once worked for the President of a major financial group who was more concerned with getting people to focus on an issue than on the outcome of that issue. Not having the subject focused on, risked destroying the firm in the long run.

Not all board meetings are focused. Far from it. 'The committee met weekly and talked about nothing,' says one former member of Lehman Brothers' Executive Committee.

> Pete would come in and say, 'I'm going to meet with the chairman of this or that company today. What do you guys think of that?' It was anything that was on Pete's mind. The committee was useless. If there was an operational issue, it was settled by the operating committee. If it was an important issue, Lew and Pete settled it.[3]

Next to this quotation, Ken Aubetta added in his book the following commentary:

> Peterson alone was CEO, the final authority, but he was not the boss. A partnership, he learned when he came to Wall Street, is not a corporation like Bell & Howell, with a pyramidal structure. Decisions often had to be made consensually. Moreover, the very nature of the marriage of convenience between Peterson and Glucksman necessitated compromise.

Compromise never serves long-term goals. Yet the ability to take the long-run view is another important quality of a board member. And so is the ability to make up his mind – and inducing others to do so. Today, no business can afford slow decisions and even more so, indecision. Furthermore, contrary to what textbooks say, most important decisions in corporate life are made by individuals, not by committees.

As President of the Federal Reserve Board, Paul Volcker has taken many successful initiatives. But such initiatives would have been unthinkable if he was not able to carry the Board with him. In August 1982 Mexico told the world that it was broke, unable to make interest payments on its roughly (at the time) $80 billion foreign debt. Volcker took command. He negotiated and cajoled to get the banks, governments and the International Monetary Fund to agree to a rescue package. 'He kept the whole thing from going over the edge,' says investment banker Felix Rohatyn. Said Charles Partee, a former Federal Reserve Board member: 'I think he likes a crisis. He never panics, he just digs and digs, trying to figure out what realistically can be done and when.'

That's good management. *Management is the ability to take a strategy and make it happen. Board members should demonstrate this ability in everything they do.* Precise goals, priorities, missions, budgets, timetables, are instrumental means in seeing through a strategy (Figure 8.1). The same is true of the technology, the environment, the focusing on opportunity. Policies as well as strategies projected for the decades of 1950 to 1970 are inappropriate today, where financial rather than real assets play the key role to survival.

Continuous vigilance is necessary. Even four years later, in mid-1986, the most immediate threat to the United States is still financial. Bankers fear a default by hard-pressed oil producers, notably Mexico, which by now owes $97 billion, or Nigeria, a $17-billion debtor. Mexico alone owes about $70 billion to US institutions, including Chase Manhattan and Bank of America. The banks, and probably the whole US financial system, would be staggered if Mexico were to walk away from its debts. And in 1986, bad loans in the American oil patch have joined the long-standing Mexican problem at the top of bankers' worry lists. Energy loans gone sour have already forced the federal bail-out of one major US bank, Continental Illinois, in 1984, and the latest surge of bankruptcies in the energy belt could at least cause some smaller institutions to collapse. The top US banks have an estimated $60 billion in oil and natural gas loans on their books, and more than half of the money has been lent to vulnerable small companies.

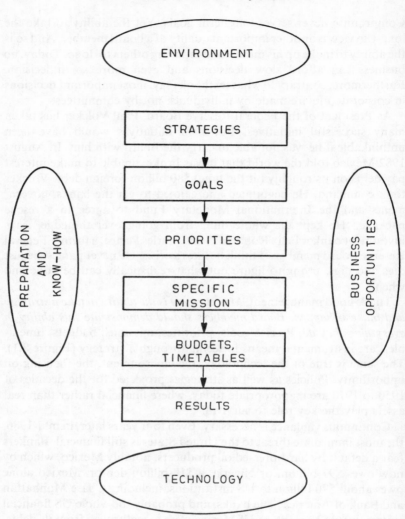

Figure 8.1 Environmental awareness, the analysis of business opportunities, an appreciation of technology, as well as preparation and know-how are the qualities of a good board member. They are needed all the way from the elaboration of strategies to obtaining results.

Corporate Boards and Government Regulatory Agencies have much in common in facing crisis situations. This demands from their membership bold views and departures from classical approaches. In the wake of the US oil crisis, for instance, the three Government Agencies that regulate banks – the Comptroller of the Currency, the Federal Reserve Board and the Federal Deposit Insurance Corporation – are asking Congress to relax laws that prohibit interstate banking. Reason: the regulators have begun preparing contingency rescue plans in which several big-city banks would stand ready to take over faltering institutions in the oil patch.

Part of the strategic planning process, in fact a major part, is to rethink what the company is all about. W. Edward Deming is suggesting to US companies that they rethink why they are in business. This is first-class advice – and a board member's responsibility. By way of example, Deming goes into further detail. He points out to management that most of the trouble with faulty product, recalls, high cost of production and service is chargeable to the system and hence to management itself. Effort to improve performance will be a disappointment until the handicap of the system is reduced. The board can lead in system change.

A corporation is part of the checks and balances making up the market system. The market rises and falls on the issue: Is there a payoff? Can management show that by providing the company services it fills a market need? Can the client perceive them as a worthwhile return on the investment? These are relatively simple questions which not always reach the level of the board. Yet, that's where the evaluation system should start, setting the pace for more detailed decisions to be done at management levels. Focused, often soul-searching questions are necessary as, in the real world, we do not face problems in an organised fashion. We must make decisions, even take calculated risks, when the data are not quite complete or accurate. To make up, we have to inquire. This, too, is an important quality for members of the board.

Yet another virtue is having the guts for new departures. 'To start anew with your tools . . . then you will be a man, my son,' Kipling wrote. Japan Incorporated put this advice into practice. As the record indicates, in their initial efforts to penetrate the US market, Japanese firms waged a frontal attack on US companies. The Japanese first developed a foothold in product markets where US firms were weakest, as well as in niches. They then rolled out their strategic thrust, building a strong product base and market position. This created the possibility for a frontal direct competition.

It takes courage to project and realise industrial beachheads, as Douglas MacArthur has demonstrated on the military front during the Second World War. The adroit sense of market orientation and the sequencing of able moves is an indisputable quality of board members, and the same is true of the shrewd appreciation of market flexibility. A board of directors worth its salt should seek the best way to enter and penetrate markets, or once having found an approach that succeeds, blindly stick with it. Board members must be adept at using a multiplicity of competitive weapons with varying degrees of emphasis: price, product quality, product features, aggressive promotion, service, distribution, product-line stretching, proliferation. The board should be instrumental in guiding its company on how to penetrate and win markets. This is not just the better way for survival. It is the only one.

Judging from this section's title, the reader might have expected me to suggest that virtue means immunity from conflicts of interests or, more precisely, from confusing the company's good with one's own well-being. While this expectation is right, it is also so evident that it hardly needs documentary detail. On the contrary, there are other issues often taken as secondary or even unimportant which need to be examined in detail – because they can make or break a good director, and eventually the company itself.

THE TECHNICAL KNOW-HOW OF THE BUSINESS

In many companies the members of the board of directors do not have technical knowledge of their products, their development, their manufacture, or the factors that determine product quality. Similarly, many firms don't really suffer from a lack of technology, but rather a lack of application of the technology that already exists. When such a situation prevails at the highest levels of corporate management, the benefits of products and projects cannot be easily quantified. Analysis done by others is one thing. Homework done by a board member is another – of immensely higher value. Not all members of the board of directors can be or become technology experts, yet technology has so much invaded every business quarter that expertise provides competitive advantages. Some members of the board will be lawyers, others bankers, still others marketing wizards. But if there are no chief technical officers, how will crucial decisions be reached?

Commenting on what it called 'GM's rocky road to cost-competitiveness', a March 1986 study by Paine Webber had this to say on the matter: 'GM is in a costly phase of implementing its long-term strategy. The company is seeking to become internationally cost-competitive over the next five to ten years by using a broad range of technological advances to reduce its manufacturing costs.' Of necessity, the Paine Webber study continued, technological change – be it introducing a new method of cleaning or a new fully automated stamping press – depresses productivity and hence squeezes margins while employees are low on the learning curve of a new process. Changing the basic manufacturing methods of a highly integrated, $100-billion company with manufacturing facilities in 39 countries throughout the world is a vast project.

Vast projects have to have the board's authorisation, but unless its members understand the impact they will not be able to reach learned decisions. If such decisions are randomly made, the board members will become their prisoners. Commitments will be haunting them for many years to come.

Even a bank has today a very significant high technology component, which can be strengthened or weakened by decisions made by the board. Cash management, home banking, automatic teller machines, and point-of-sale equipment substitute the classical brick-and-mortar branch offices that old bankers knew so well. Who will be making the investment decisions?

A role of the technology component is to create the appropriate infrastructure, so that the organisation is prepared to face opportunity. OPEC was successful for a dozen years because they caught the Western world unprepared. Oil was cheap, plentiful, efficient, and convenient to use, and we used it for everything. When it suddenly became expensive, we were not ready with alternatives.

It is not just a matter of authorising more money. Intimate knowledge of the business by the members of the board will demonstrate weaknesses the naked eye cannot detect. Just because technology moves so fast, even an engineering company encounters trouble if budgetary authorisations are not framed through guidelines. In 1980 Hewlett-Packard introduced its own personal computer, the HP85, and followed it up with nine other models. But the products were produced by five separate HP divisions. They ran different software, used three different keyboards, and were marketed in an uncoordinated manner. Result: they sold poorly.

Just because research today absorbs colossal amounts of capital, normalisation is very important in order to reach the broadest market, capitalise on mass effect in manufacturing, keep costs low, and also successfully promote sales. This is a different way of saying that the technical know-how of board members (at least some of them) must range from research and development to marketing. The company who takes control and reaches a critical mass in volume production first, owns a comfortable share of the market.

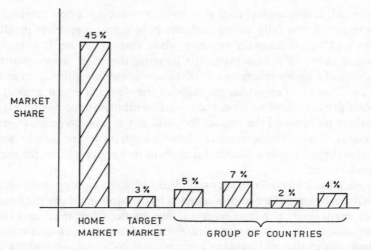

Figure 8.2   Market share is a valid criterion in evaluating how balanced is a company's sales effort and market appeal. This figure shows the unbalanced market share of a high technology company.

Company X had a first-class product and mastered 45 per cent of its home market (Figure 8.2) But in the United States which, the board decided, should have been its no. 2 in revenue, the company was able to attract only 3 per cent of market share. Four more countries accounted for 18 per cent among themselves. The other 35 per cent was spread in 100 countries around the globe. Most of these countries were no-growth markets. Also, local authorities imposed requirements which obliged a reworking of the software – usually a very costly activity. The product had escaped the decision-making powers of the board.

In the electronics industry, where competition is cut-throat, a survival strategy requires that the company achieves global cost parity with its competitors through volume production. An example is a technology-stretching 1-micron, 1-Megabit dynamic random access memory (DRAM). For some vendors, the 1-Megabit DRAM is spilling over to rest of their semiconductor business. Among US manufacturers, IBM first achieved volume production on the megachip. AT&T and Texas Instruments, the largest US commercial vendor of semiconductors, have been close behind. AT&T eventually is expected to make its chip available commercially to help it build volume, the key to low-cost production in an industry where price-slashing alone often determines the winners.

How much should the members of the board be involved in

elaborating such strategy? Most directors should understand the dynamics: if their company has been a leader in the field, then it must embark on an agressive strategy to recapture its lost global competitiveness. Without it, the company is destined to give chase as the semiconductor market slips away.

But should there be a frontal attack on the Japanese memory chip dominance, or the exploiting of specific markets? The board has to decide in full knowledge that there is a major growth potential for DRAM sales into computer, communications and consumer markets, with the potential for consumer electronics products to match demand by computer manufacturers. New generations of electronic products are growing away from past technology to higher levels of integration. The classic example is the VAX computer family by Digital Equipment Corporation (DEC). Thus, while semiconductor demand comes from increased shipments of new products, it also comes in a very different way with emphasis on custom integrated circuits and dwindling sales of standard parts.

Another major issue in being competitive – which requires members of the board with engineering backgrouind to appreciate it – is product quality. Chrysler Corporation increased to 40 per cent (from 25 per cent) the importance of product quality in its mix of bonus objectives. At the same time, it de-emphasised profitability, productivity and market share. Quite apart from the fact that high quality standards were instrumental in helping Chrysler to regain its market in the early 1980s, the bonus issue is in itself carrot and stick. Bonuses generally outweigh salary for top Detroit executives.

Not only do the authorisation, budgeting, and starting of new projects tax the board's decision-making abilities, but so also do project cancellations. Until the early 1980s Saudi Arabia was considered to be a rich man's land. Now, although it remains wealthy by any standard, it is by no means immune to the impact of cheap oil. Government spending, the engine that drives the country's economy, dropped from a high of $92.7 billion in the 1982 fiscal year to $54.8 billion in 1986. The drop in spending has slowed construction projects across the country, created an exodus of foreign workers, and overwhelmed the court system with bankruptcy proceedings. Only interest-free government deposits have kept many banks from failing. Said a top Saudi official: 'During the boom, the country generated tremendous wealth. Now the cycle is reversed. Every time we cancel a project, the ripple effect washes over the entire economy.' The same is valid with corporations. Project cancellations can have very negative effects.

While the board must have the courage to kill poor projects which sap the company's resources (human and financial) for no results, such decisions must be well balanced and fully account for the aftermaths. In a certain way, stopping a project midstream requires much more technical skill than authorising a new one. Starving a going project for funds is one way of killing it, but it is slow and inefficient. A more appropriate approach is board-level design reviews of major ongoing projects. To be successful, such design reviews require technical knowledge on behalf of those who make the go/no-go decisions.

Similar questions can be posed regarding investments. The payback period is haunting not only big firms – and such questions require technical expertise to be answered in an able manner. A small franchised dealer of the Spar chain found that for simple scanning equipment on its own, it takes four to five years to recover the capital. However, with PC and scanning, given the applications which were done, capital was recovered in one and a half years – including model cost. Many benefits came from online to suppliers and store management.

The technical skills the members of the board require are not a feature exclusive to high technology – as the case of a franchised food chain helps document. Commenting on the prospect of McDonald's, a financial analysis underlined that new products will enable the franchise to take market share from competitors and add to the frequency with which customers visit the restaurant. Other reasons were also given for the positive forecast. For instance, McDonald's willingness to develop more costly prime sites, resulting in higher-volume restaurants and faster growth in revenues from franchise fees. International profit margins were stated next, because they began to show the positive impact of economies of scale. Another factor was lower fuel prices. Still another, the consumer's overall income picture which brightened with the decline in oil prices, benefiting most the households of 25–35-year-olds, typical clients of the franchiser.

While some of the outlined criteria are financial, the impact of the technical factors, from new product to international marketing, should not be lost. Their relevance will increase in the future and invade all sectors of business. Overnight mail and freight delivery is an example. A relentless price war and foreign-expansion costs gradually cut into the operation profit margins. As *Business Week* relates it, with revenues up 24 per cent in 1986 to $3.2 billion, Federal Express continues to gain market share in its bread-and-butter overnight letter and package segments. But some people think up to 30 per cent of the letter business could be lost to facsimile machines and electronic mail as clients switch to online services profiting from advancements in technology.

The company itself employs some of the best solutions technology can offer, but competitors claim they are closing in on Federal's edge. Suggests United Postal Service (UPS) Executive Vice-President Kent C. Nelson: 'We are trying to leapfrog our competitors.' His company plans to install computers in its trucks that electronically plot delivery and pick-up schedules and track their location. 'The winner will be the company offering quality service at lowest cost' advises *Business Week*.[5]

What's the role the board of directors should be playing in guiding the hand of management toward a better investment plan design? The answer is: assuring the company maintains its competitive edge. And that takes lots of courage and know-how.

SALIENT PROBLEMS FACING MEMBERS OF THE BOARD

Of all the problems which the board of directors and its members should be addressing, one will be salient. This means the problem which must be solved first, either because of its importance or its urgency. Once this is done another of the problems behind it will show up in the front line. Salient problems are challenging. Some of them are recurrent. For instance, what is the real significance of 'product strategy'? What will our organisation do in twenty years? From where will the profits come? Who are the product strategists? What are their functions?

In a fast developing market with technology invading every walk of life, the board of directors must seek responsibility in product decisions. Should our company be a product leader in its every field of endeavour? Should our company develop all products through its own research and development? Or should it buy patents, or proceed through mergers and acquisitions? From motor manufacturing to banking, markets today are international. What are the effects of international industrial competition? What are the opportunities? Is there enough management skill to handle the new products and the new markets?

As I mentioned in Chapter 4, back in 1953 Louis Sorel taught me that product line problems are at the origin of many failures. During 35 years of professional practice I found this advise very sound. In Sorel's judgement, boards of directors were not paying enough attention to

- evaluating,
- innovating,
- streamlining,
- consolidating, and
- making cost-effective

their company's products and services. Yet from these products and services would come the money to cover the present and future cost of staying in business.

The work I did in the late 1960s and through the 1970s with Professor Albert Prinzing, then President of a multinational company, particularly focused on this subject: evaluating, innovating, and streamlining the company's product line. The focal point was a process of consolidation of products into product lines. It was permitted to:

- weed out marginal products,
- innovate to keep the line dynamic and competitive,
- restructure when the market indicated it was necessary,
- integrate all products into well-defined comprehensive groups, and
- push for low-cost designs able to be competitive from manufacturing, sales and distribution viewpoints.

Some product lines are more sensitive to good forecasting and able production planning than others. Lamps for instance are made of glass. Glass breaks. But lamps are also seasonal products. Figures 8.3a and 8.3b give an example. Frequently resetting the product lines ends in significant scrap and this should be avoided. The better way is to forecast market demand. Computer-based simulation helped in making sales projections. It also assisted in the co-ordination of sales projections with production planning and inventory management.

In June 1966, I was invited to a High Technology Symposium held in Frankfurt by Chase Manhattan. Dr David Rockefeller, then chairman of the board, presided. In one session the question was about Concorde, at that time still to get its market test. Asked Dr Rockefeller, 'Do you think Concorde will be a commercial success or a failure?' I said: 'A commercial failure, because it is loaded with unnecessary costs – so they told me at the British Aircraft Corporation.[6] Dr Rockefeller said: 'Yes, this too. But more than that is the fact that Concorde comes only in one size. It is not designed to become smaller or bigger as the needs develop and as the market demands' (Figure 8.4). Then he added: 'Any product of high technology which is stuck at one size is a failure. It does not have market breadth on which to distribute the huge R & D expenses.' I never forgot this lesson.

While, by any measure, motor vehicles are mature products, they are not immune to this rule. In the mid-1980s Detroit had two objectives. It expected to cut costs by buying and reselling cars instead of making them. And, as they reduced manufacturing, the Big Three also tried to shore up sales by becoming better marketers – reacting to customer

175

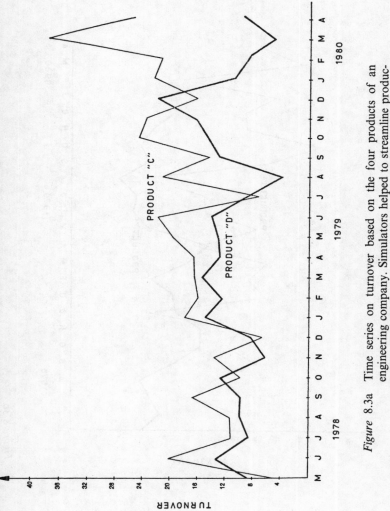

Figure 8.3a Time series on turnover based on the four products of an engineering company. Simulators helped to streamline production planning and avoid waste in terms of scrap.

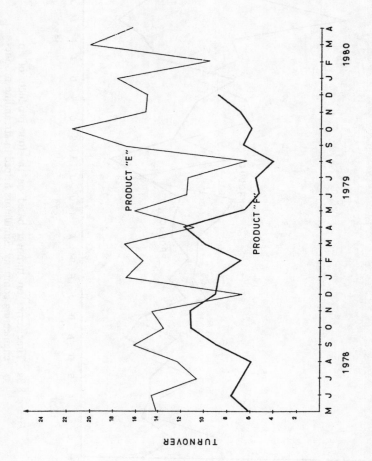

Figure 8.3b

AN ADVANCED TECHNOLOGICAL PRODUCT MUST
BE DESIGNED TO:

    – FIT DIFFERENT MARKETS

    – DEVELOP INTO A COHERENT PRODUCT LINE

    – USE STANDARD COMPONENT PARTS

    – MINIMIZE MAINTENANCE REQUIREMENTS

A GOOD EXAMPLE IS THE BOEING

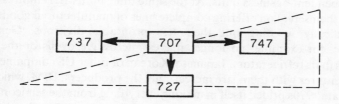

A BAD EXAMPLE IS CONCORDE

MONOLITHIC PRODUCTS DON'T SUCCEED,

NEITHER DO THEY RECOVER THEIR DEVELOPMENT COST.

PRODUCT CONTINUITY:

    – SPREADS THE R+D/M INVESTMENTS

    – PERMITS A BETTER MARKET FOCUS

    – PROVIDES A MASS EFFECT, AND

    – PROTECTS THE FLANKS AGAINST COMPETITION

Figure 8.4   The Rockefeller principle is that a high technology product must be offered at different sizes to appeal to different segments of the market, thus helping to recover development costs and make a profit.

drives instead of forcing them to react to their own designs. 'Times are changing,' said Donald E. Petersen, Chairman of Ford Motor Company 'We need less emphasis on having all the answers and more on being sure we ask the right questions.' Financial analysts expect that Detroit's radical turnaround will cause 30 per cent of domestic motor manufacturing capacity (representing at least 2.5 million cars) to disappear within five years. As a result, the United Auto Workers estimates that 118,000 of its automobile plant and supplier jobs will be lost by 1990. That's 7 per cent of the 1986 total, when this estimate was made.

As the industry dynamics change, so should evolve the director's thinking. To be attacked successfully, salient problems require brains which can adjust to the new environment as new conditions unfold. Solving tomorrow's problems with yesterday's views leads to disaster. Smaller size is part of the new perspective. The huge, rather monolithic, industrial corporation which dominated the US economy is giving way to independent business units. At the same time, industrial empires that prided themselves on offering complete lines of manufactured goods are methodically weeding out their less profitable divisions. General Electric, for example, no longer makes microwave ovens or the ice-makers in its refrigerators. Japanese, Korean or other US companies, or joint ventures with them, are increasingly the producers. IBM, which as of the late 1970s prided itself in making everything from the semiconductors to the software used in its computers, embraced a different strategy, encouraging each manager of a business unit to look outside as well as inside the company to find the lowest cost commensurate with quality.

Such changes call for a different mentality by board members. Andrew Carnegie, Henry Ford and John D. Rockefeller owned not only huge factories but the raw materials that fed those factories. With the distribution network an integral part of the aggregate, *vertical integration* (the control of all the key aspects of a given business), was the foundation for the rise of the Continental European and American industrial power. But now it is realised that big size does not necessarily mean big profits. And it is also found that several of the corporate managers lack the skills to run the expanded operations. The same can be stated about the members of the board.

Survival sees to it that a new generation of managers – having contemplated the advent of global markets, rapid technological change and short product life-cycles – is questioning the faith in the omnipotent corporation. As this questioning gains momentum it is leading towards a restructuring of the Western economy. With the waves of change sweeping away old concepts, solving the salient problem becomes much more difficult. This is not just a 1986 reference. Every time financial and industrial trends change in direction it has been that way. As a result many industries find it difficult to understand the business they are in. As the study of industrial history helps document, too many companies do not understand what their true business is. The railways, for instance, thought they were in the railway business, not the transportation business, allowing the motor vehicle, freight and airline industries to take over their customers.

Creeping bureaucracy also played its role in this process. Staff jobs became a haven for raging mediocrity, as many boards have failed to appreciate that one of their key duties is to see that 'homo bureaucraticus' does not take hold of the organisation. 'Work increases to use up available resources, regardless of real jobs to be done.' This law has special relevance to the power manoeuvres found in a bureaucracy that is subjected to fluctuating political forces.

The more likely reasons for failure are to be found in the chronic immobility of the system. Those in power have no interest in relinquishing it, and nowhere else to go. Those in waiting fear they will damage their chances by pushing. The entire apparatus has an interest in preserving itself by preventing change. But change is coming, want it or not. In US industry today a new spirit of the search for efficiency helps explain the huge increase in divestitures. It underlines also the corresponding surge in joint ventures and other alliances between domestic and foreign companies.

Restructuring the big corporations is also significantly altering the way they are managed. One of the most noticeable changes is the effort to develop closer, long-term relationships with suppliers. Many companies are sharply reducing the numer of suppliers they do business with, even as they buy more parts from outside vendors. They want to make themselves important to their suppliers, thereby increasing their leverage. At the same time, the suppliers are being given an unprecedented amount of responsibility. They are now frequently involved in designing the parts that they have been asked to manufacture. A. O. Smith Corporation, for example, designed the engine subframe for the Sabre, Ford's newest mid-sized car.

But new horizons and new directions carry a commensurate amount of risk – and the board should be aware of it. Saturn Project, Detroit's well-publicised attempt to save small-car production, is in trouble. Announced late in 1983, Saturn was supposed to be built in the United States at Japanese-like costs. However, the first car in the $5-billion project won't appear until 1990, and GM says it will be priced higher than the bargain-basement model that was originally promised. General Motors executives also are questioning the basic premise behind Saturn: that advanced production technology is the key to make the car more competitive, prompted by the Toyota joint venture which stunned GM by achieving Japanese-like efficiency with careful management rather than exotic automation.

If these are the symptoms, what can be stated as being the background reason for them at the board level of decision making? First comes lack of information on the latest developments and on alternative means and possibilities for doing business. Staying with the motor vehicle industry example, between now and 1990 Japan alone may introduce four times as many models as US companies.

The second reason is habitual thinking and resistance to change. These are always major factors in falling behind when 'time-honoured' methods and approaches are followed, lower efficiency and diminished survival capabilities are almost always the result.

Third is the sort of spirit which makes a member of the board think: 'My problem is unique.' Failure to learn from other companies' experience and faults is a generally negative attitude. It becomes more so, faced with the challenge of research and the character of change. This kind of thinking, defensive in its essence, is most often a source of trouble.

The fourth deadly sin for a board member is reluctance to seek advice, and its opposite: getting the wrong advice. Both are common pitfalls of industry and both contribute to wrong decisions, lost opportunities, spoiled time, higher costs and lower efficiency.

THE GRAIN OF SAND IN THE OYSTER

You cannot argue with success, and H. Ross Perot is a success story. He sold his company Electronic Data Systems (EDS) to General Motors in October 1984. Since then, the Texas billionaire emerged as GM's most unorthodox director, till he quit the automaker's board in December 1986.

'He has livened the board meetings up quite a bit,' says Charles Townes, a physics professor and fellow GM director. When in February 1965 the Winston Churchill Foundation bestowed its leadership award on him (Prince Charles went to Dallas to present it), Perot searched for an apt summation of what he was. He told the dinner audience that he once dreamed of being a pretty pearl, but with his jug ears and crooked nose that seemed unlikely. Then he realised that his lot was to be the grain of sand that irritates the oyster enough to make the pretty pearl. 'That's what I am,' Perot said. 'An irritant around here. I stir things up.' At GM, fellow directors say that Perot can be a talking idea-box at board meetings. And he himself admits, 'I will always be a proponent for push, push, push, harder, harder, harder. That's my nature.'

Correctly, Perot does not mind offending tradition. As a motto at his office suggests: 'Every good and excellent thing stands moment by moment on the razor's edge of danger and must be fought for.'

When the GM computer experts to be absorbed into EDS told Perot that they felt more secure at General Motors, he answered them: 'Get up in the morning and look in the mirror. You are your own job security. This is a business, not a social service.' And the advice stuck, for most of them.

At General Motors, Ross Perot can be testy. He sneers at its cumbersome bureaucracy. He teases executives who whimper about the competition. He talks a lot about how Toyota 'outperforms us in every way'. GM employees, he said, 'come from an industry that complains about the playing field not being level. In my view, the playing field is never level.' GM Chairman Roger Smith also made clear his intention to shake up the sleepy GM bureaucracy, and so for some time he welcomed Perot's views: 'He always has comments on car quality and styling and everything else,' adding that Ross Perot has been learning plenty about cars.

When GM people wander into EDS checking up on finances or on marketing, Ross Perot handles them the way bureaucrats should be treated:

> Some well-meaning guy from General Motors will show up and want us to do something. If it is a good idea we will do it. If the man comes down and just wants us to fill out forms, then we don't do it. They are all good people, but their little view of the world is of cluttering away in some little corner and their first impulse is to make us look like them.

One of the now established business traditions Perot would not abide by is scheduling. 'I refuse to program myself,' he says. 'For most business people at my level their schedules are like a dentist's. Mine is not.'

The way he started his company in June 1962 was itself untraditional. His theory was that companies knew they needed computers but did not know what to do with them. EDS would design, install and operate them. With this he made one billion dollars out of an original $1,000 investment. Now what EDS is trying to do for GM is save it money by overhauling its fragmented computers and communications systems. Before this major revamping there were 95 data communications networks and more than 106 data centres. EDS is working to reduce that to 18 data centres and one digital network.

The experience is quite like that of other major corporations eager to renew themselves and reorganise their infrastructure. In 1985 Bank of America started a major programme to integrate 64 different networks throughout the world (the majority of which were in California) into one logical structure. It takes both foresight and courage to make such major changes.

From policy making to the shedding of bureaucratic approaches and the integration of the computers and communications infrastructure, the adaptive corporation must face new realities. The board of directors must lead in this major change. It must also appreciate that its most valuable members are those who know how to be the grain of sand in the oyster.

Alvin Toffler aptly suggests,[7] 'instead of being routine and predictable the corporate environment has grown increasingly unstable, accelerative, and revolutionary'. This makes the financial, commercial and industrial organisations most vulnerable to outside forces. Small inputs can trigger vast results. Nearsightness at the board level, and the non-availability of a querying, stirring-up spirit – by at least some of the board members – put even large corporations beyond repair. Many will disappear or be absorbed by others between now and the end of this century.

One man alone cannot bring in the change. It takes a team at the top of the pyramid to do it. Two good examples are:

- The turnaround which has not materialised at the Burroughs Corporation (now Unisip after the merger with Sperry/Univac) and in contrast
- The rescue, restructuring and new departure at Chrysler.

Since 1980, when W. Michael Blumenthal took command of Burroughs, he tried hard to rejuvenate the company's computer offerings. He slashed its overheads, focused its attention on lucrative new markets – but still failed to garner either significant profits or a larger share of the computer market. What is missing, Blumenthal once contended, is critical mass. There is also a worldwide management problem. Unlike Chrysler, Burroughs did not succeed in presenting a new management image. What is more, quota based on quality rather than quantity after six years has not yet been established.

Burroughs cannot fight its immediate competitors, IBM and DEC, head-on – just as Chrysler could not fight GM and Ford on a similar ground with a hope of winning. But Burroughs' Board has not shown an understanding of what makes a competitive advantage in the computer business and, for the company's misfortune, the grain of sand was not in the oyster. Customers complain about an absence of sophisticated

software. They also say that the company is in desperate need of
telecommunications skills and the kind of high-volume, low-cost
manufacturing that was at the root of IBM's remarkable revival in the
first half of the 1980s.

At these trying times, like all major waves of change have brought in
industrial history, it is important to strangle our weaknesses and feed
our strengths. We must challenge our own most fundamental assumptions, and we must renew. Confidence in the company's survival is
critical – and, therefore, strategic. 'We are trying to eliminate the fear
factor,' Blumenthal said, referring to the fear among Burroughs'
customers that the company will wither leaving them with multi-million-
dollar computer orphans. But the fear factor will not be eliminated by
wishing it away. The faltering Sperry (now merged into Burroughs),
ailing Control Data, and Honeywell's troubled computer division, can
tell a story in this regard.

A company may broaden or shrink its product line, but if it does not
reconceptualise its mission it will not succeed. The board must pay much
more attention to acid tests. They will tell about *the fit of the organisation
to the problems facing it.* The rising curve of high technology, accelerated
innovation and stiffening competition affects the corporation's:

● clients
● key personnel
● products
● markets
● production and distribution processes.

A key role of the board of directors should be *thinking the unthinkable.*
This means challenging the obvious and reconceptualising the corporate
functions. No board can afford to be blind to, or unaware of, what is
happening to our entire way of life.

NOTES

1. Lee Iacocca, *An Autobiography*, Bantam Books, New York, 1984.
2. Ken Auletta *Greed and Glory on Wall Street: The Fall of the House of
   Lehman*, Random House, New York, 1986.
3. *Fortune*, 17 February 1986, p. 23.
4. Ken Auletta (1986).
5. 6 November 1987.
6. Who, with Aerospatiale, designed the Concorde – and they should have
   known the facts.
7. Alvin Toffler, *The Adaptive Corporation*, McGraw-Hill, New York, 1985.

9 Training the Corporate Directors

If success is what happens when preparation meets opportunity, then it is a self-evident truth that the board members should be trained. Even the best-run companies can experience trouble in periods of rapid expansion and in times of profound technical change. The number one priority today is more education of the users of high technology tools and, as well, of the decision-makers. As end-users become more educated, they call for integrated, generic systems that allow them to magnify the value of their time. This is most important for members of the board. Many companies have set their sights on establishing an edge in high technology. This requires preconditions: one is the ability to appreciate the role of technology in a changing business context; another is managing within a constantly changing external environment – successfully confronting changing markets and new competitors. Still another prerequisite is computer literacy.

Lifelong learning at the top level of management is *innovating*. If a company is not the number one, it has to innovate. This is valid of marketing, where it must find market niches that have not been exploited. But it is just as valid of know-how. Whether in finance, insurance, merchandising, or manufacturing, the smaller firm cannot go neck-and-neck with the number one. The number one competitor is too big. The smaller firm has to outflank him.

Five years ago, Mellon Bank of Pittsburgh, the USA's twelfth largest bank in terms of assets, began a programme designed to make all of its employees, from the newest clerk to the Chairman of the Board of Directors, computer literate. The training programme, which includes instruction in the fundamentals of computer operation, the use of personal computers and the use of inquiry/response languages, was one of the first of its kind to involve employees at all levels of a major US corporation. Computer literacy was part of a larger programme that also included evaluation and selection of professional workstations to be installed in the offices of all members of the Bank's middle and upper management. The objective has been to increase the number of people in the Bank utilising computers in their day-to-day activities from 30 per cent (most of whom are branch tellers) to 70 per cent within two years.

Quite significantly, both of these innovative programmes were mandated by the then Bank's Chairman of the Board, J. David Barnes. Dr Barnes and many other executives do realise that technology compounds the need for training in order to upkeep a corporation's intellectual resources. If lifelong training is necessary for the professionals and the managers, it is even more so for the members of the board of directors.

TOP-LEVEL TRAINING IN ORGANISATIONS

The lower levels of supervision and the clerks in an organisation are seen as mainly passive individuals, able to execute a job and to accept directions, but not able to influence policy matters. On the contrary, top management is the body of policy-makers. They should be trained in:

(1) Finding problems. It is management's job to work continually on the system which they command.
(2) Instituting modern work methods and providing the necessary technological infrastructure.
(3) Deciding on improved means of policy making and of strategic planning.

The responsibility of top management must be changed from sheer numbers to quality. Improvement of quality will automatically improve the productivity of policy-makers.

(4) Create a structure in top management that will push every day towards a more competitive performance.
(5) Drive out past habits so that everyone can work effectively and break down barriers between departments.
(6) Institute a vigorous programme of education and retraining at all levels in the organisation.

Organisations receive attitudes, values and objectives from their policy-makers. Their motivation, a necessary component of an active participation in an organisation behaviour system, is different from that of middle or lower management – and difficult to separate from their know-how.

While hardly any employees experience complete congruity between personal and organisational objectives, the potential contrast of motivational factors and attitudes is very significant at top management level. The board members' know-how directly influences decisions, filtering through opinion and perception issues which are at the centre of every explanation of human behaviour in organisations.

The ability to master the computerised enterprise of the future will be an essential ingredient of success for tomorrow's managers. This is much more true of people responsible for strategic planning, for setting policy, and for deciding the main directions. Board members who fall behind in technology are cutting themselves out of the mainstream. They are not participating in what will be the predominant business orientation of the near future. Hence the importance of an educational programme in high technology, which will explain its evolutionary nature and be based on a flexible, productive curriculum.

Several assumptions can be made about the nature of the learner. Learners play, by definition, a dependent role. They engage in an educational activity to acquire new matter and they are subject-centred in their orientation to learning. But while low-level learners are motivated primarily by grades, threats of punishment, or possibilities of rewards, board members are (or should) be motivated by the upkeep of their own know-how. One primary task of the trainer should therefore be to devise ways of making the learners pay attention to the significant developments affecting their careers and the course of the organisations which they run.

The upkeep of know-how imposed by a fast-moving technology must be made within the perspective of adult learning. This is the field of *andragogy*. Only in the 1950s did research begin to focus on adult learners for a comprehensive theory of a lifelong upkeep of skills. During the last thirty years there has been a substantial number of unversity-level programmes offered on a cross-industry basis. Most of them were instituted to give industrial executives the opportunity to participate in broadening their educational horizons. Such courses are customarily designed to help executives deepen their understanding of top management responsibilities. They also range into broader topics such as economic theory, international affairs and political theory. These subjects go a long way beyond the traditional management training and are concerned with the business environment.

An important additional opportunity presented by executive development courses is exchanging ideas with senior executives. Regular programmes by universities present the advantage of a higher calibre teaching faculty and of association with the management background of other companies. The drawback, however, is that being designed for a general appeal they do not necessarily meet the needs of every company and management team in the most efficient manner.

For the stated reasons, university courses should be seen as a complementary measure and not as a substitute to the company's own executive development programme. Furthermore, in this particular chapter we will not discuss this type of programme, but one definitely oriented to top management.

Training top executives is a rigorous and serious undertaking. It should be based on fundamental understandings. In my training classes some ideas came from clinical psychologists interested in discovering the conditions under which people are able to change their behaviour. Carl Rogers demonstrated that people are most likely to change when they accept that the locus of responsibility for change resides in themselves. Abraham Maslow found that people are most likely to change when they feel safe enough in an environment or relationship to risk experimenting with new behaviour. Other findings discovered that universal developmental stages occur throughout life and that transition (or crisis) involved in moving from one stage to another is one of the major sources of motivation to learn.

Sociologists and social psychologists have supplied additional knowledge concerning the many social forces that affect learning. Cyril O. Houle found that adults who continued to learn independently fall into different categories. First, there are goal-oriented learners, that is, people who must have specific goals to guide them in their learning. This is the largest group. Second, there are activities-oriented learners. They enjoy learning and engaging in discussion with other people regardless of the goals. Houle's findings contradicted the traditional academic idea that all learning should be pursued and enjoyed for its own sake, and alerted adult educators to the need to build their programmes around the learners' goals.

With precise goals to be satisfied in terms of a lifelong activity of knowledge acquisition, learning is becoming a normal, almost universal part of living during adulthood. When adults undertake learning on their own, they become aware of the need to know or be able to do something, diagnose the specific knowledge skills, attitudes and values needed to achieve their goals, and translate their diagnosed needs into learning objectives. The more knowledgeable people, as members of the board should be, plan strategies for using their own resources: they implement a plan, evaluate learning outcomes, and their sense of self-direction often conflicts with the traditional practice of the teacher telling the students what they should learn.

Proactive learning differs markedly from the following of fixed curricula. It also requires marketing the curriculum to a multifunctional audience. Such a programme should:

- focus on the educational needs of the end-users of the new high technologies;
- demonstrate that success or failure is not simply a function of the technology, but is highly dependent upon the skills and understanding of those using the technology.

The key concept is that effective use of the technology depends on the kinds of educational strategies devised by planners prior to actual implementation. By knowing in advance the typical evolutionary learning process associated with high technology, the organisation can develop proactive measures designed to meet increasingly complex end-user educational needs.

Targeting key executive, managerial and professional individuals within the organisation, and presenting effective educational packages, increases the probability of successful implementation. Constructing effective long-range education ensures the ongoing results and a further evolution in the organisation.

THE STRENGTH OF A COMMITMENT

A theory of human nature states that the strength of a person's commitment to a decision or an activity is in direct proportion to the extent that he or she has participated in making the decision or planning the activity. Hence, with andragogy, we should encourage learners to share in planning their own learning matter. This leads to different learning experiences from those classically known. In traditional pedagogical practice, the teacher is expected to take full responsibility for the teaching–learning transaction. With andragogy, the teacher is more a catalyst than an instructor. He is a guide. He cannot really make a person learn; he can only help that person to learn.

Focusing on issues is an integral part of adult learning. Management able to focus on issues stays ahead of competition. In fact, it is more important *to focus on an issue* than the outcome of that issue. Not having the subject(s) focused on, risks destroying the firm – in the long run.

Adults are what they have done. They derive their identities from their experience, describing themselves in terms of their occupation(s), skills, travels and achievements. As such, adults have more to contribute to learning situations.

- They have a richer foundation of experience with which to relate new knowledge and skills, but also
- they have acquired fixed habits and patterns of thought.

The first issue sees to it that learning often acquires meaning when related to experience. The second can, however, be negative, as adults are often less open-minded than young people in their learning practice. Hence, greater emphasis must be placed on techniques that tap the experience of the adult learners. Group discussion, case studies, simulation exercises, laboratory methods and role playing are all examples. Skilful teachers have always explained new concepts and broad generalisations with illustration from the learner's experience.

Educators of adults must have an orientation towards learning that differs from the traditional path. Traditional educators are primarily concerned with logical development of subject-matters from grade to grade according to levels of complexity. Andragogy requires that adult educators are primarily aware of the current concerns of the individuals (and institutions) they serve. They should be able to develop learning experiences that will address these concerns.

Skilful learners apply what they acquire in their daily business. Adults often have a perspective of immediacy of application towards most of their learning. In this sense, they should see andragogy as a process of improving their ability to cope with life's problems.

Strategic planning is a good example of a learning environment. Learners (and, in this case, members of the board) may be requested to:

(1) Evaluate competition: *our weaknesses, our strengths.*
(2) Make forecasts: identify threats and opportunities.
(3) Critically analyse company policies and their limits.
(4) Identify possible target actions, and estimate effects.
(5) Determine investments for each strategy, likely profit levels, possible risks.
(6) Develop alternatives then choose among them.
(7) Define management control and set control points.

An important ingredient to successful andragogy is to convince the participants on the wisdom of taking notes. Rarely during board meetings have I seen people taking notes on what is being discussed. Yet this is fundamental for understanding. It is one of the McNamara principles, as stated in Chapter 4: 'The discipline of *writing* something down, is the first step toward making it happen.'

Other objectives in training programmes for senior executives may be to identify increasing productivity opportunities through office automation; develop a better managerial approach; evaluate investment; effectively examine technical and organisational items.

The new twist of industrial history brings up matters of culture apart from high technology. Some competitive situations indeed emphasise the shrinking corporation rather than growth. The ability, for instance, to close down factories in a way which is neither disruptive of normal operation nor brutal in terms of labour relations should not be taken for granted. There is a new managerial career developing called 'director of plant closings'. Not only the changing industrial landscape but also the merger rush has resulted in additional closings that might not have taken place otherwise. In the past, corporations have been promoting people who opened up plants successfully. Now they seek to find more people expert in knowing how to close plants. This led to a joke about a company going through three management stages:

- risk-takers start it,
- caretakers manage it, and
- undertakers preside over its death.

This is a new conscience in the art of management. We must always be ready to re-evaluate our plans and commitments, to chop off dead wood even if major investments have been made in a given line. Wise investment advisers preach this line: 'Don't only take profits. Take also your losses.' For industrial corporations, the wisdom of abandoning existing property – and the method of doing it – must be taught. The board members must learn from other cases and an educational programme should see to it that this is done.

I am underlining these references to impress that technology transfer is not the only subject for andragogy – though, as we will see in the subsequent sections, technology transfer is a major part of it. Andragogy should definitely include what I call *the 4-P prescription*.

The first P is *Planning*: the skill to set a purpose; devise a scheme for reaching it; provide the needed resources; assure the know-how, time, money, key physical items. Planning includes the able scheduling of resource usage, and the programming of actions so that the goal can be reached. These are skills which must be taught. If the board of directors wishes to be in command of the situation, and of the company, it has to have the skill to do it. Election to the board is often made because of the representation of equity, as a way to link to other industries (banks, insurance), for legal advice, or sometimes for public relations, not for decision-making skills. Nothing says *a priori* that the member of the board is a born manager, or that he has acquired planning background – though this may be the case. He probably has experience, but lifelong learning serves both himself as a person and the company to which he addresses his services.

The second P is *Power*: precisely, the ability to control people and things; exercise influence; act; force; affect strongly; perform; produce results.

The third P is *Predictability*. This is the quality of having a clear policy and sticking to it. The board of directors is a policy-making body and it may sound awfully redundant to train its members on policy making. Yet, my personal experience suggests that making policy and *seeing through* all implications of such policy is not necessarily the same thing.

The fourth P stands for *Persuasion*: the art of setting a firm belief or conviction; also, promoting a particular belief; inducing adherence to it; providing reasons to persuade. Any policy becomes that much more easy to observe when we can:

(1)   Create an image;
(2)   Project the effects;
(3)   Explain, demonstrate;
(4)   'Sell' the wisdom of following it;
(5)   Train in its mechanics;
(6)   Implement without upheaval;
(7)   Maintain to keep it actual.

Organisations may be ossified (the majority) or open to change (the minority) depending on the way the 4-P prescription is applied. Any policy has so many more chances to succeed when the organisation behind it commits its resources to the attainment of the goals it has established. Such commitment starts and ends with the board of directors.

COMPUTERS AND COMMUNICATIONS: END-USER TRAINING

Training in the new technologies is one of the subjects which should feature at the top of the list of a training programme oriented to the board of directors. Such training should not be theoretical. It should involve a good deal of hands-on experience and focus on the information requirements of board members. These will to a large extent be answered by an Information Centre (Infocenter) implementation.

In 1985 a large well-known organisation questioned its personnel, from the clerks to the members of the board on the degree of satisfaction they had with the information systems organisation. Figure 9.1 provides the answers. At the time this project took place, the 'now available'

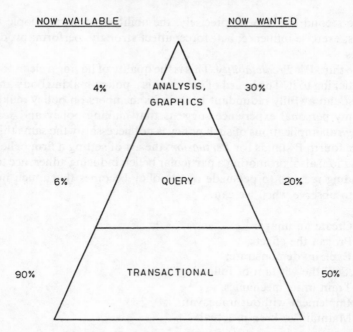

NOW AVAILABLE   NOW WANTED

ANALYSIS,
GRAPHICS

4%   30%

6%   QUERY   20%

90%   TRANSACTIONAL   50%

Figure 9.1   A leading organisation asked its computer-literate employees
(managers, professionals, clerks) to vote on what they wanted *now*
in terms of information systems capabilities. The difference
between what was available and what was wanted is most
significant.

online capabilities in the system divided into three classes: transactional
(90 per cent); query only (6 per cent); and analytical tools with graphics
(4 per cent). To the question what else the users would like as support for
their business: 50 per cent responded they were satisfied, 20 per cent
wanted query features, and 30 per cent wanted advanced analytical
tools.

Advanced analytical tools were particularly requested by the decision-
makers, including members of the board. The upper management levels
in an organisation have more to gain from able decision-support tools
(Figure 9.2), but their availability is not synonymous with their usage.

User training is a subject indivisible from the good implementation of
computers and communications. A valid example in this direction is
given by the Mutual of Omaha (Nebraska), the leading insurance
company which has today in operation more than 1,000 PCs at
managerial and professional positions. The Mutual of Omaha spent

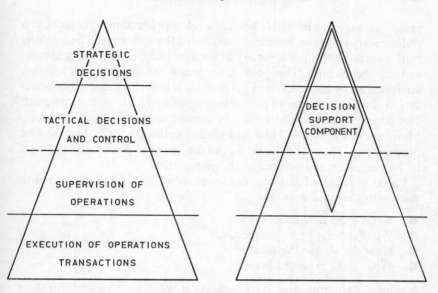

Figure 9.2   Decision support systems cannot and should not be designed the same way for the different levels of the organisation. Stratification is important as each level has its own requirements.

several years developing its management-directed information centre activity. The planning, development and application phases were done on a dual basis handling in parallel:

● conception of the Infocenter and its services;
● education for the services offered by the Infocenter.

Both issues evolved over time. The same is valid for the question of what an organisation can do with office automation, and how far it can go. The office automation (OA) studies at large, and the Infocenter implementation in particular, started with a basic premise: insurance is a labour- and paper-intensive activity. Hence, able solutions must provide an answer on how to apply the available technology appropriately in order to gain both on the labour and on the paper front.

Mutual of Omaha starter in 1981 with its Infocenter operation. First, there were timesharing (TS) users. Then the personal computer (PC) announcement by IBM changed the conception. Many people without access to TS asked for and got a PC as an intelligent workstation.

Since the beginning, management conceived that one of the top issues in a successful Infocenter operation is management education. As a result, the policy was established to develop programmes (initially at a rudimentary stage) on *computer literacy* for the end-users. The teaching staff is versatile and has a variety of backgrounds: educators, communicators, technicians. The goal is to break the barrier which today separates many managers and professionals from the computer resources, to accelerate the use of such resources and to make it more efficient. Not surprisingly, computer literacy created interest in learning more. Many managers asked: 'How do I really use the product?' They see the productivity. They need the skill. And they want to do something about it. The initiative thus passes to the end-user.

Faced with the educational challenge, Mutual of Omaha decided to start with the fundamentals:

● What's the new concept?
● What's the systems perspective?
● How do we use the tool?
● What's the expected benefit?

A pilot programme was developed. As it went on, its administrators found different levels of literacy even among managers. The motto became: 'You must learn to verbalise before you can understand.' Hence, the programme first defines OA, PC, mainframes, databases, communications, PC links to mainframes, integrated software, expected advantages. A key point is to teach the management of change. This is done in a manner non-menacing to the careers of the attendants. The theme is: 'How computers and communications may help *you*'; and also: 'What you can get out of them'.

Once the first literacy steps are successfully done, there is a new theme: 'How you can take ownership of the future'. The next phase is managing technology for *your* benefit. This way, managers and professionals are softly led into the system perspective: what the automated place could look like. Scenarios are developed.

As the experience at Mutual of Omaha documents, for any organisation undertaking a computer literacy programme, the challenge is: 'How to bring all this together. How to balance needs. How to teach senior management to understand a computers and communications language.'

As the programme unfolded, the management of the insurance company has seen with satisfaction a new approach to work. Authorities on management have taught this approach for years. In order to determine which tools to apply, Peter Drucker advises asking the question: 'What business are you in?' This pushes managers to examine their business critically: 'We had not thought of that before.' Another critical question Drucker asks is: 'What do you need in order to do your job better?' This pushes managers and professionals into thinking what they currently have and what they are missing. Able answers to these questions open opportunity for automation. The next cycle of training gives an overview of systems architecture: 'This is where you are going to be in a short period of time.'

At the Mutual of Omaha, throughout training, information systems are presented as a utility function. The participants are asked: 'How can you translate the information for yourself?' This approach uncovers human factors. It also helps demonstrate to the users why new technology requires new skills in:

● communications;
● database organisation;
● analytical approaches to management problems.

The third part of the computer literacy programme is a workshop. The high theme is: 'How to draw a blueprint for the future'. Case studies are done on how to implement workstations (WSs) and their software. In parallel, the trainers want to get out the feelings of participants. Quite often, this approach reveals that prior to the computer literacy programme frustration dominated, because most managers tried to use the tool before they understood the fundamentals:

● what it is all about;
● what it can do;
● what it cannot do.

The programme attempts to reconstruct available notions – and to enrich them – by focusing on user needs: 'Let the needs define the tools.' One of the methods is to teach how to prioritise your opportunity list. This is a hit list for OA.

To recapitulate, this management-orientated computer literacy programme sets the specification stage: tool definition, then selection. It demonstrates how the selected tool should be used. It helps the participant develop a blueprint with a state-of-the-art system. It explains maintenance update, and it proceeds with hands-on training.

In a data processing (DP) organisation with more than 1,000 people, the Infocenter employs 36 specialists of which only 5 are in the computer literacy effort. This small group, which accounts for 5% of DP employment, has been able to see to it that high technology is given, for the first time, to people who don't have preparation for it.

Computer literacy programmes help break down the barriers which separate current management from the technology at its disposition. Informing on what is and what can be or cannot be done is the best approach to gaining acceptance. Practical examples help, and the same is true of hands-on experience. No company can continue to prosper with computer illiterates at the management level. The time to manager-change and prepare for the future is now.

OBTAINING HANDS-ON EXPERIENCE

We all know that leadership is a decisive factor in business success, but we do not always appreciate what it takes to obtain leadership. Just like the effort of penetrating global markets, using technology in an effective manner calls for foresight and for insight. It also necessitates guidance on work priorities.

The examples of the Mellon Bank and Mutual of Omaha come from the financial sector. A first class reference on top management computer literacy is United Technologies. In 1982 Dr Gray, then Chairman of the Board of Directors and CEO, instituted a hands-on training programme on PC-based personal workstations. Such a programme was implemented top-down in the organisation. The first to take it were the members of the board. Then came an impressively large population of senior executives earning more than $100,000 per year: in all, 1,100 people. Here are the main points of a synthesis of several programmes offered by corporations to their top management.

All teaching is done strictly through interactive videoforms. The first day, in the morning, the theme is:

● *What's your hardware*: video (colour, black/white, high/low resolution); cursor on video (also mouse); keyboard (pocket calculator, PC); microprocessor; central memory; floppy (don't flex it); hard disk; printer
● *What's your basic software*: operating system; database management systems (functions only); data storage and retrieval (introduction only); fourth-generation languages; applications packages; horizontal software; communications routines

All this is taught in an easy-to-follow, comprehensive manner. Still on the first day, in the afternoon, the theme passes on to applications:

● Explanation of and practical implementation with spreadsheets

● Applications examples, such as portfolio management (personal, company's own), loans (analysis of company balance sheet and economic account); collection/employment of funds ('What if'); treasury management; amortisation plans; foreign-exchange decisions; interest-rate variations

All cases studies are prepared in advance by the teaching staff. All operations are supported by help screens.

The second day, in the morning, the time is devoted to two tasks:

● Redoing the same exercises accomplished through spreadsheet, but in graphics
● A brief introduction to word processing for electronic mail, and message preparations for electronic mail

In both cases, the practical examples dominate. On this second day, the afternoon focuses on:

● Introduction to data communications (protocols, PC-to-main-frame links – help screens only),
● Electronic mail in effect.

The third day sees further applications. This is a day-long implementation with one or (maximum) two complete exercises based on the company's own environment – and how personal computers, integrated software, PC-to-mainframe links can be of assistance. Exercises are being prepared in advance, with all data and help screens prestored.

An integral part of this third day is communication with public databases on behalf of the participants of the computer literacy course. Public databases extend the capability of managers and professionals to search for and locate the information needed for making decisions or for completing analytical tasks which they have undertaken.

The board must formulate coherent policies about learning how to use the tools technology makes available – and should provide the first evidence of a successful implementation. It makes management sense to do so. To give a leadership position to the company, it is necessary to establish a *comprehensive strategy*. The change of some people and PC purchases will not be enough to establish a new direction. There should be a cut-off date, for instance two years from now, beyond which no manager can get promoted without being computer literate. The best test of how he is using technology revealed by the results which he obtains.

For applications of computers and communications at the board level, there should be no software written in a classical sense, only commodity programs (vertical and horizontal) and fourth-generation languages. Some chief executive officers have become experts on how to use these tools. At Bangor Punta, the Chairman and CEO, Mr Wilson, uses his PC and local area network not only for company communications, but also for property management of his own.

When it comes to management training, graphics should be used as the backbone. Graphics is management's shorthand and it nicely fits an exception reporting structure. Management by exception has been preached for 30 years. Now we have the technology to put it into effect. These are steps to be taken if a company really wishes to become the leading edge in its industry.

It is evidently advisable to start with the right funding of the programme, and the board should see to it that this is done. It is not enough to have computer literacy goals accepted and subscribed to. It is also necessary to ensure the funding. With funding we can get the technology – and whoever has the technology controls the future.

An illiterate in computers and communications in the Western world is not very different from an illiterate in the written word living in an underdeveloped country. Whether computer illiteracy is encountered in the bush or in boardrooms, in Black Africa or in the rich Northern Hemisphere, it characterises those who do not intend to survive. Achievements in terms of technological literacy are the best documentation of this last statement. Experience helps demonstrate that those companies which train their people well in the new technology move ahead of their competition. Nowhere can the appreciation of technology be more valuable than at board level.

While training in the new technologies, the senior people at the top of the organisational pyramid should also redefine their role. After all, they are the best qualified to understand that, without lifelong learning, *experience becomes obsolete faster than it builds up.*

10 Satisfying the Information Needs of the Board

'Getting the right information is a substantial part of the job,' says Irving Shapiro, former Chief Executive of Du Pont. 'The basic ground rule is that you cannot be taken by surprise. You get lots of information and most of it is totally unnecessary. The organization tends to want to give you the good news and not cough up the bad news . . . To manage well,' Shapiro suggests, 'you have to get the message across that whatever the story is let's get it on the table fast so there are no surprises. But it doesn't always happen that way.' 'No one wants to be the messenger and get his head cut off,' adds Robert J. Bies, Professor of Organization at Northwestern University's Kellogg School of Business.

Getting the right information at board of directors level is hardly a simple task. Although managers say they do not want to be surprised by problems, few employees want to be the bringer of bad tidings. And most boards are hardly doing the system-tuning to let the right information through. Figure 10.1 presents one solution which I have applied with success.

Leaving aside the want of board initiative, it takes a lot of hard work for a corporation to change the non-information habit. Many companies still punish those who deliver bad news. As a result, it is an exception for managers to tolerate and even want bad news. This compounds the issues involved in setting up an effective computers and communications system - in spite of large expenditures made to improve the company's information infrastructure.

As far as fundamental reasons are concerned, experts in organisation behaviour are basically of two schools of thought over what companies can do to ensure that managers get the bad news along with the good. One school says the solution is cultural, in other words, an atmosphere of open communication and trust has to be created to overcome the tendency to report only good news to senior management. A corollary to this approach is that tangled information problems will solve themselves. The other school holds that a structural solution is the key to effective communications. With this approach, the experts argue that safe channels have to be established to make sure that both bad news and good news flows to the right managers. They believe that a structure

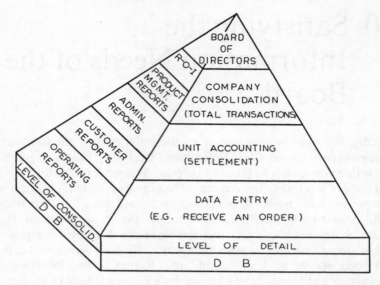

Figure 10.1 The organisational pyramid must be served through the appropriate computers and communications support. This goes all the way from data entry to consolidation necessary for the board of directors.

conducive to early detection of problems is a flat hierarchy. Too many management levels obscure the facts.

We have properly underlined the fact that one of the issues to be approached in an effective manner through computers and communications is the flattening out of the organisation. Too many hierarchical levels in an organisation are management fat. Ably used computers and communications contribute in increasing the span of control. Citibank has done just that in measuring the benefit it has obtained from its large investments in office automation. While prior to such investments the average number reporting to a manager (span of control) in the Citibank hierarchy was five, subsequently it has become seven. The next goal is eight. In other words, not only should we properly define the type of information the board needs, but also the information channels to effectively restructure the organisation.

INFORMATION FOR USE AT BOARD LEVEL

'The free flow of information,' said John deButts, former Chairman of AT&T, 'boils down to the relationship between the CEO and his reporting people. No one was criticised for bringing bad news to me, because you cannot run the company any other way. And I had a lot of bad news brought to may attention.'

Quite independently of the installed computer power, the first ingredient of successfully informing the members of the board is their own attitude towards open communications channels. This attitude rests on organisational, cultural, social, political and other frequently ignored factors.

As a research project which I conducted with my graduate students at Washington State University helps document, conservative organisations maintain that information should be furnished to board members through 'normal' channels of the company. According to this school of thought, board members should direct their requests for information through the proper channels, in order not to disturb normal operating functions or to waste time with individual members of the staff furnishing them with special information. Progressive organisations take a different view. To them, the information to be provided to the board should come both through normal and through special channels. The latter include audits made at the board's (or at the president's) request by independent organisations or expert consultants.

Progressive organisations would both look at the overall picture and dig on details, as warranted, case by case. Conservative firms consider that, in most cases, summarised data should be adequate to bring to the board's attention. Normally, this sort of communication is done on a monthly basis. However, many companies see to it that any substantial changes or important information is given at the time of happening. Ongoing procedures in many organisations foresee that board members should request information through executive channels responsible for providing the information. This is particularly valid for financial reports, operating results, cash flow, capital requirements, future prospects and other related data.

Here is how one of the organisations participating to the aforementioned research project responded to specific queries. The open-eyed reader will appreciate that such answers are near-sighted, ultraconservative, self-destructive, and border on misinformation:

(1)   *Q.*   Do you feel that board members should have more, less, or the same information as the president?

    A.   *Less, so that the president can have the upper hand on the board.*

(2) *Q*. Should board members have free access to all company information, or should all information to the board come through the president?

A.   Board members should not have free access to all company information, and information to the directors should come from the president (this will help doing filtering, editing and make-up).

(3) *Q*. Do board members need only summarised data or should they be able to get raw data and do their own summerisation?

A.   Information that is pertinent for board members' use should be summarised.

(4) *Q*. How timely is this data, as of now? last week? yesterday?

A.   Timeliness depends on the type of information. If it is for information only, it could be as late as a month old. But normally data furnished the board should be current.

(5) *Q*. If board members have limited access to company data, at what level of management should this access reach? Vice-presidents? Middle managers?

A.   Board members' access should be through the president. But the information should be no lower than the corporate vice-president level (in other words, the board members should just be framed with the information senior management wants them to know).

(6) *Q*. What specific classes of information do board members need?

A.   Financial operating results, quarterly financial progress against plan, periodic market trends, significant labour happenings, and government and court rulings.

(7) *Q*. How much detailed information should be in each class?

A.   Information should be general in nature. If additional detailed information is necessary, the board members can request this through the president.

   No wonder many companies go to the rocks because of limited access to both qualitative and quantitative data. Yet such access is necessary to assist the board in performing a truly professional job. Lee Iacocca,

Chairman of Chrysler's Board, is right when he says in his *Autobiography*: 'I often wondered: where was the Board when all of this was going on?' The way he relates the Chrysler story is that when he went to his first board meeting he began to understand the problem:

> Chrysler's Board of Directors had even less information than their counterparts at Ford – and that is saying a mouthful. There were no slides and no financial reviews. Riccardo [the former chairman of the board, Chrysler Corporation] was giving a little pitch from the back of an envelope. This was hardly the way to be running the tenth largest corporation in the country.

It cannot be repeated too often: the members of the board should have a well-organised body of information starting with graphical and order-of-magnitude data, but extending through menu selection to all necessary qualitative and quantitative detail. One leading corporation established as a policy a one-page snapshot with twenty pigeonholes: two are tabular and eighteen graphical. Behind each one of them stands full and detailed documentation, to be interactively available in case it is necessary.

However, business highlights should not be 'just a summary.' They should be highly accurate, factual and well documented. This takes a great deal of preparation. Any company which is in to 'quick fix' solutions is not going to give its board, and its top management levels, the information they need to reach decisions.

Traditional data processing people who lack a basic understanding of the concepts underlining top management information are going to make a lot of mistakes:

● They do so anyway, when asked to go beyond what they feel comfortable with.

● They are also going to resist change and try to force all top-level decisions to fit the facts they can manipulate.

● They are classically unable to see beyond the scope of 'electronic data processing' (whatever this means) which inhibits other forms of analysis and evaluation.

● They bring with them the elitist attitude that programming is a high-priest function – while in reality it is a function which turns talented people away from the computers and communications careers.

In their depth of obsolescence, classical 'electronic data processing'-minded people have little patience for creative documentation. They

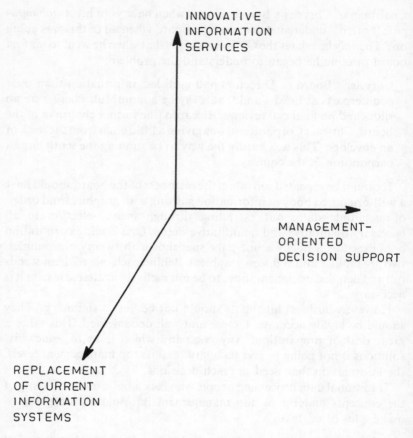

Figure 10.2   The major investments should be done to promote innovative information services. Next in line of interest comes management decision support. The replacement of bread-and-butter programmes and equipment is of low importance.

feed management whatever *they feel* it needs and to hell with anyone who says they do not want to have it in that manner.

A change of attitude is absolutely necessary and *innovation* should play a leading role in it. Modern computers and communications systems develop along three axes of reference as Figure 10.2 suggests:

1.   *Innovative information services* addressed both to *our* firm and to *our* clients. They make feasible *new products* which are highly competitive, low cost, and can be first-class income earners.

2. *Management-oriented decision support* tools. They range from simulation models and spreadsheets to analytical query capabilities. *Expert systems* play a leading role in this class.
3. *Replacement of current information systems.* While improvements should be an integral part in renewal, the emphasis here is on cost effectiveness, with return on investment the criterion for decision.

Figure 10.3 shows the chart into which can be condensed a study I did with a leading organisation to supply a policy tool for investment decisions. The emphasis of this study has been focused along this third line of reference. Different criteria would be applied to the other two domains.

For instance, timeliness and accuracy of information as well as the ability to reach for further detail when necessary, are among criteria relative to management decision support. The same is true of breadth of information. The source of data provided to outside and inside directors should be both internal and developed by independent outside sources, both professional regarding our own company and within the industry at large.

All information should be available on request to the board members including copies of audits, reports of examinations by governmental supervisory authorities, special studies and evaluations by brokerage houses and credit analysts. There must be no problems and no bottlenecks in providing information to the top of the corporate pyramid.

THE MISSING INFORMATION

Because the members of the board are very busy in other undertakings, they often do not realise that they lack information. Yet in a well-run company there must be no significant differences in information given to inside and outside directors. They should receive the same reports and analysis, plus special studies as necessary.

This is not the typical case in industry. Inside directors have ready access to reports, data, and other information relating to their management responsibilities that is not automatically furnished to outside directors. As a result, inside directors are better informed and have more details on matters presented at board meetings because they are involved in company affairs. When this happens the contribution by outside directors is very limited.

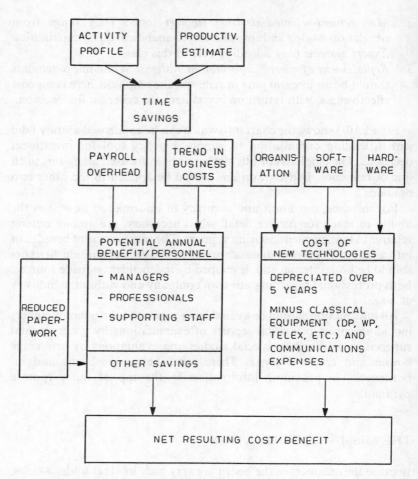

Figure 10.3   Cost/benefit analysis should be made on the basis of company-wide policies which are properly spelled out. This figure gives an example.

Since the members of the board are very busy, every care should be taken in improving the ways information is transmitted, received, read and understood. The board should also make it a policy to periodically conduct an autocriticism with the aim of performing creative evaluation of its own actions. This has often proved more difficult than it sounds because it touches the ego of different personalities. Here is how Iacocca relates his effort at Chrysler:

When I became chairman, I moved in on the Board members very gradually. I was not crazy enough to point my finger at a group that had just hired me and tell them: 'It's your fault.' But once or twice I did ask the Board, as politely as I could: 'How did management ever get their plans past such a distinguished group of businessmen? Didn't you guys get any information?'

This is an elegant way of conducting an autocritique: 'Did you members of the board get the right information? Has it been read and understood? How did it influence your decision process?'

Misinformation and no information applied at board level have in common a deep distrust of the company's managers' own decision process. Defensive attitudes usually reflect:

● Personal emptiness;
● Wrong-doing.

Such wrong-doing can range from inactivity to insecurity or also conflict of interest. In either case, the company pays the bill.

The way defensiveness expresses itself in real life can be attested by the answer received from a financial organisation to the aforementioned research:

It is obviously impossible to furnish the president with all of the detailed information that divisional and departmental vice presidents use in their day to day administrative operations. For the same reason, it is impossible to furnish directors with even the detail in summary form that is available to the presidents.

Failing on purpose to appreciate the need for all books to be kept open – even if they will be needed only exceptionally – this respondent was to add: 'For Board members on a continuing basis to have raw data and do their own summarizing, would tax their time, energy, and ingenuity to a point of no return' or, alternatively, help them understand what is going on.

Said another respondent:

The basic function of the Board of Directors, in my view, is to carry out its responsibilities to the shareholders of the corporation. This means reviewing regularly company policies, analyzing the results of operations, observing the extent and value of long range corporate planning, and, most importantly, judging management on a continuing basis, both as to incumbents and individuals in line of succession.

Now we start talking business. As another corporation was to comment: 'data submitted to board members (whether at regular intervals or at request) should be current. They should be presented by comparison with projections and objectives, including:

- financial condition and position;
- operating results;
- share of the market;
- profit margins;
- trends in relation to competition, and so on.

Every company has a different aproach, but there should also be somewhere in the corporate organisation a means by which directors have the opportunity of direct contact with several levels of management. In some cases this is accomplished by having individual department or division heads make specific project reports direct to the board and submit to questioning by individual directors. In other cases, there is a periodic (often annual) review by a special committee of the board which, in conjunction with the auditor, receives a report covering the prior year's operations from all department and division heads. There are also interviews with management people. Following this, the committee makes a report to the board which is also independent of top management reporting.

For many industries, particularly those in high technology, annual investigations are inadequate in finding causes of poor performance and correcting them. Furthermore, cost cutting should definitely be a goal in these investigations and the same is true of project control – from research and development to marketing.

Unless this process of handling control information is automated, it will consume an inordinate amount of time of the corporate directors and of the operating departments of the organisation. Used in an able manner, computers and communications provide the needed solution to this issue. Figure 10.4 is the block diagram of an interactive management control system designed to focus on costs and profitability. Starting from the premise (properly underlined in the preceding chapter), that all board members should be computer literate, online access will permit them to analyse cost benefit performance and evaluate results in an acceptable fraction of their time.

The theme I underlined here is mental productivity. When I emphasise

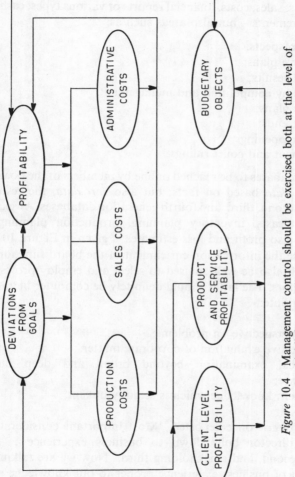

Figure 10.4 Management control should be exercised both at the level of highlights regarding the execution of policies, and at the level of detail in connection with operating results. This figure gives an example on the latter.

that board members should be fully informed and make their independ
ent study prior to reaching decisions, I don't mean that this should or
could be done by paper and pencil. These are palaeolithic approaches,
though still widely practised in many corporations.

Computer-based decision support to the board should not only
include profits, sales, costs, financial reports of various types, cash flow,
capital requirements – but also areas such as:

● future prospects;
● alternative plans;
● expected results;
● progress by competition and management;
● strategic plans;
● market trends;
● labour happenings;
● government and court rulings.

The future databases to be reached online by members of the board will
involve *hard data* based on facts, but also *soft data*, the results of
projections: second, third, and fourth generation databases. An example
involving forecasts, inventory planning, production planning and
control, and also profit and loss estimates is given in Figure 10.5.

To enhance the information enrichment of the board functions, the
chairman will also be well advised to select and employ professional
outside directors. The latter should definitely be computer literate and
able to contribute:

(1) A new perspective on problems;
(2) An objective evaluation of corporate matters;
(3) Analytical examination beyond broad and deep business
     experience;
(4) Polyvalent knowledge which is steadily upkept.

As *Business Week* once reported, 'Most important consideration in
selecting a director boils down to business experience . . . with
reputation second, and stockholding third.' Now we are talking of a
different sort of business experience proper to our knowledge society
which brings analytical capabilities beyond the proverbial objectivity to
board meetings.

Board policies and procedures designed for success in an industrial
environment are largely inappropriate today. The board of a modern
corporation can carry out its specific duties of approving objectives,

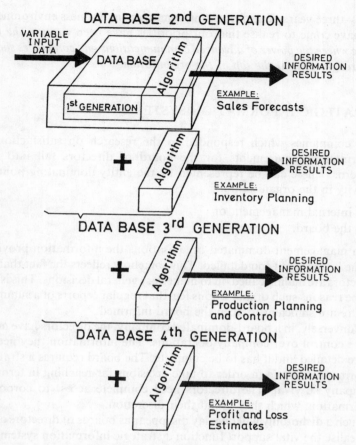

Figure 10.5   Properly exploited interactive databases can provide valid support to management decision. This example ranges from sales forecasts to profit and loss estimates.

monitoring progress, evaluating performance, shaping strategic plans, if it has both specific knowledge about what the company is doing – and the tools and metrics to replace approximation, feeling and guesswork with facts, measurements, projections and an analytical methodology.

Quite often, the main problem of information discrimination for the board arises from the consideration that its members' need for specific information can be met only by the channel of management. Another serious problem is that corporate directors often lack technology tools which secretaries, salesmen and tellers now have at their disposal. After thirty-three years of implementing computers in business environments we have come to realise that our priorities have been wrong. *The first place where the power of advanced communications and computers should be brought in is at the top of the organisation.*

STRATEGIC INFORMATION SYSTEMS

The companies which responded to the research on satisfaction of information requirements for the board of directors fall into two patterns. These can be represented by the entity dominating political activity in the organisation:

- internal management or
- the board.

In management-dominated organisations the information provided to the board is not too detailed. This somehow reflects the fact that the directors are mainly called on to make very general decisions. This is one of the reasons such organisations feel that regular reports of a summary nature are sufficient to keep the board informed.

Conversely, in a board-dominated company, the directors have much more control over company operations. The information they need is more detailed and it has to be complete. The board requires a strategic information system in order to take decisions far-reaching in terms of company survival. The directors need complete access to corporate information, which they use at their discretion.

Such a dichotomy will one day disappear as boards of directors come to realise the vital support function a strategic information system can provide. 'Strategic' is synonymous with business opportunity. The structure of strategy-development proceeds from the environment to the corporate mission. Both the business environment and the mission shape the strategy and, ultimately, the plans and tactics of the organisation.

This requirement for consistency dictates the role of the information management function. This function is strategic in the sense that its own, proper *mission is derived from corporate strategy, not corporate plans.*

- If information management has the capability to create strategic advantage, it must influence corporate strategy.

This requires a formal, corporate strategic-planning function that includes the management of information technology.

● Corporate strategy cannot be developed without reference to the use of information technology.

Computers and communications today constitute the corporate infrastructure. Within such a perspective, some information system applications may be simply operational. Others should clearly be part of the corporate strategic mission.

The strategic information system put at the disposal of the board should help identify critical functional areas. It should:

(1) Make feasible acid tests on financial operating results as well as longer-term financial projections.
(2) Help in interactively evaluating financial progress against plans, but also in testing market trends.
(3) Inform on breakthroughs by competition, significant labour happenings, government and court rulings.
(4) Assist the director ,in examining and experimenting on future prospects.

The information provided by a strategic system will be used by the board in making decisions which typically range from the selection of competent management to profits and their distribution; stockholder relations; competitive forces; quantity and quality of product, distribution and service; public relations and advertising; study of economic factors significant to future performance; handling of government relations and of employee plans.

Strategic information systems are no trial-and-error approaches. The board members must receive information on all financial and operational conditions of the corporation. Computers and communications must ensure that a wealth of information can be made available timely, efficiently, and at a reasonable cost. Technology today permits rapid collection, analysis and distillation of the results of the business.

It is therefore surprising to see how many companies are not using computer-based management information systems, and how education as to their importance on high technology lags behind – particularly at the top of the organisational structure. Said one board member: 'We do not know enough about a computerized management system to determine whether or not it would be valuable to our meetings.'

Companies which pioneered in computer literacy at the level of the board found that a strategic information system is instrumental in:

(1) Examining future business prospects;
(2) Determining short- and long-term policies;
(3) Experimenting on financial matters, such as assets, investments, business cycle, and so on;
(4) Evaluating company progress: quantity and quality of output, attainment of goals, productivity, low cost performance;
(5) Seeing through the actions of key personnel;
(6) Managing by exception.

These are key issues concerning policy-making bodies. In order to establish policies, the members of the board need to be analytical about long-range goals, busines trends, and future business prospects. They must also be able to ascertain that policies are being carried out and to what extent they are successful.

Whether the board feels responsible for supervising the management rather closely, or acts more as a maker of policy, information is a core subject. The members of the board of directors must quickly grasp the major issues of discussion, expertly dissect them, and make wise judgements. Each subject must be described, understood, and analysed, before the board can reach a consensus of the meeting. Ably used computers and communications are a significant aid to mental productivity.

The decision on how to design a strategic information system, appealing at the board level, cannot be reached lightly. Critical questions should be asked before the design starts: What is the function of the board of directors in corporate management? How is it organised? What does it do? What are the information needs for the decisions which it takes?

Many of these decisions relate to corporate image. There are significant discrepancies between a company's image of itself and that held by its customers. Such differences can be critical in terms of future impact. For example, a firm that feels it is technically superior in an era when cost is becoming the significant competitive factor may find that its *quality* image is very important to its future.

In general, company image may be assessed in two basic fields: *product* and *organisation* to manage the resources. The strategic information system should reflect on both of them. Key product references involve:

● price;
● novelty;
● quality;

● reliability

Information the board requires along these lines goes all the way to project management skills and capabilities, as well as the ability to meet the customer requirements.

Organisational requirements on which the directors must have information typically involve:

(1) The ability to manage change: from planning to control;
(2) The personnel quality, including the upkeep of skills;
(3) Responsiveness to client demands;
(4) Integrity in terms of operations;
(5) The ability to foretell and adjust to market forces;
(6) Negotiating skills.

To define the important dimensions of product organisational image, directors must do the proper testing. Results might, for instance, suggest that the firm has potential problems with the degree to which management is interacting with customers – or with the products' appeal to the market.

Online exception reporting, backed-up by an equally interactive access to detail, is a sound approach to the design of strategic information systems. Management information should not be confused with operational data. It has totally different requirements, as demonstrated in Table 10.1.

There is always a problem in making sure that adequate information is available to directors, while at the same time not overburdening them to the point where they might find it difficult to handle the material. As cannot be repeated too often, technology today helps ensure that directors are well-enough informed to exercise good judgement. The able use of technology is particularly instrumental in:

● reducing the amount of board meeting time, by providing directors with the opportunity to inform themselves ahead of time;
● minimising the element of surprise, helping board members to think things out and back up their case with facts and figures;
● significantly improving the quality of board meetings.

The computer should be seen as a communicator, agenda-maker, time management engine, able presenter, and decision support tool. Raw data can be overwhelming, exhausting, and in many cases less meaningful than graphical information.

The strategic information system should be designed to filter through

Table 10.1   Managerial *v.* operational requirements

	Managerial	Operational
1. Information	*Synthetic *Stable *No RT, RET *Graphical *Historical Trend *By exception *Multidimensional Models *Integration of key forces	*Detailed *Volatile *RT update *Numeric *Mainly positional *Massive — —
2. Volume	*Low	*High
3. Applications	*One shot *Ad hoc *Heuristic *What if *Unstructured *Modular *Visualisation *Colour *Fast response (1 to 2 secs)	*Repetitive *Predefined *Algorithmic *Computational *Structured *Stream oriented *Originally paper *Black and white *Normal response

4. Communicating	*More communicate
	  than compute
		*More compute
		  than communicate

5. Databasing	*High security *Individual database *Closed user group *Public databases	*Normal security *Shared database — —

6. Life Cycle	*3 years, using
	  what exists
	*6–7 years, with
	  what is in labs
		*6–7 years, using
		  what exists

Notes
RT = real time.
RET = real-enough time (e.g. 24-hour cover).

both qualitative and quantitative data regarding the current state of the company including assets, projects, earnings. Different presentation thresholds must be established. At one level, visual and narrative summaries of the discussion matter should be given in highlight. At a lower threshold, sufficient depth must be provided so that the directors understand the matter, its alternative solutions, their weights, and recommendations supported by the management.

These references have a common background. The information for management is an integrated, computers and communications based configuration of: people, procedures, software and equipment, designed to satisfy the information needs of management. Such satisfaction should occur at all levels.

LAYERS OF DECISION SUPPORT

Certain companies have strategic information systems that failed because they do not meet the criteria under discussion. Often these systems are developed on the basis of a mentality which says: 'Let's collect all data that we can concerning competitors, technology, markets, products, equipments.' But then they don't know what to do with the information. Quite often, the results are voluminous and unmanageable. Thus they have little real value. As companies invariably find, unless information systems rate highly by well-established criteria, they are not worth the effort required for their development.

Properly managed, computers can help all the way: from data collection, storage and retrieval, to proper information handling. Many firms use computer models to develop forecasts and present them in a way easy for directors to comprehend. Such models are used for strategic decision making.

Strategic information systems should support answers to 'What if?' questions. Since the advent of Visicalc, almost ten years ago, 'what if?' questions can be effectively answered with spreadsheets. We now have sophisticated integrated software available. This is a model-oriented system designed to help in strategic information criteria. Spreadsheets, databases and graphics assistance have developed into business models able to handle interrelated projections on profits, return on investment, sales, revenues – but also to structure and evaluate typical operating statements. Polyvalence is one of the characteristics of software available for decision support. Valuable issues, tyically present to top management, can be experimented upon, prior to decisions being made. What would happen if we went out of a given segment of our business over the next two years? If we begin producing redesigned products for a given niche? How important may be the combined effect of our proposed improved warranty and the anticipated improvement in our parts and service sales-generating capacity?

However, the board does not only need quantitative results but also answers to sensitivity questions. The latter show what factors are important and unimportant. This is, in fact, one of the prime values of business models: classical, mathematically oriented analyses seldom isolate a single factor, or sets of factors, in terms of their relative importance.

One study I have done at board level unearthed an image that was really surprising to the executives: an honest and technically competent organisation that lacks marketing aggressiveness. Another image study revealed that a given firm's products were rated high in terms of operating characteristics:

(1) Performance;
(2) Reliability;
(3) Ease of maintenance;

but low in product development effort within stated costs and schedules. A subsequent *strengths and weaknesses* evaluation documented among the major strengths:

- technical expertise;
- machine capability;
- maintenace and support;
- an international sales force.

But it also identified that major weaknesses have been:

- low market share;
- lack of product standardisation;
- high-cost manufacturing;
- high price image.

A strategic information system must lead towards not only the analysis of strengths and weaknesses, but also their assessment. This plays a crucial role in supporting competitive capabilities, revealing opportunities, and providing for risk control. Assessment is the *alter ego* of forecasting, which is typically provided through decision support. Forecasting offers insights which result in the development of a strategy for, say, the company's marketing effort. For instance, differential activity can be forecast for various market segments in different parts of the country. This, coupled with marketing and distribution costs analyses, may show that a uniform nationwide strategy would be clearly inferior to one which took advantage of low distribution costs for some products in some areas.

Valuable at the corporate operational layers, such information is still important at the board level – but it is not enough. The board needs assessment leading to concise statements of the most significant strategic items related to, say, various client groups or environments which affect the organisation's choices. That is why we should provide both qualitative and quantitative decision support systems for top management. The directors require mechanisms through which the current situation and future opportunities can be assessed, reflecting the influence of such forces as:

- competitors;
- the market drive;
- its potential;
- a company's own management;
- its products;
- the organisation itself.

Strategic information involves the recognition that much of it will emanate from new sources, often external to the firm. This implies that environmental information must be collected and processed in ways to render it into a form suitable for the support of strategic choice. Stacks of competitive annual reports and volumes of papers describing emerging products or technologies are not suitable for direct use by the board of directors. As guidance for strategy formulation, data in raw form is almost useless. Information is analysed, evaluated data. At the board level, evaluation should be made for some specific strategic purpose or use. Yet, too often, the information developed for the support of strategic planning is so unfocused as to be of little use. In the human mind, an original idea has a living meaning. It connects with experience and produces conviction. Decision support systems for top management must account for this fact. Computer-based decision support must assist, not cripple, the art of thinking. The thinking process will be impaired if we confuse data with ideas, or mistake information for 'knowledge'.

Long-range planning is modelling exercise, extending well beyond mere numbers to mirror the organisation of a business. Knowhow is more important an organisation asset that other labour, material, and capital requirements. A decision-support model should tie concepts together and suggest relationships between:

- people (our clients);
- people (our own);
- products;
- money.

It is important to realise that, without an understanding of the real world, the best model is useless. Hence the key to constructing workable decision systems is a strong sense of how the world works and what is important. With these factors in mind, the computer can help to develop insight and foresight. Sensual contact, intuition, the chemistry of personal contact, articulated judgement and aesthetic taste are part of the decision-making process. But properly used, the computer helps us plan and control and – in some cases – understand. It handles logical structures, manipulates assumptions, selects data – all of our own making and choosing.

THE NEW COMMUNICATIONS MEDIA

The new communications media brings us closer together than we ever have been before. Broadband communications see to it that culture once only available at the centre of big cities now spreads to the four corners of the country. In doing our business we are more prone to communicate rather than commute. Computer message systems can substantially reduce the number of interrupting telephone calls a senior manager receives, without lessening the amount or timeliness of the information received. And the messages can be scanned very quickly.

There is another advantage of message systems. The sender can file the message electronically, by whatever criteria he desires and have it saved for whatever period of time wanted. Such message systems provide an easy audit trail and historical record.

Changing our message media changes our way of life, since the way in which we communicate casts the language we use. And the language shapes our minds. The city life itself is vastly transformed as old industries phaseout and new perspectives take command. In the 1940–45 period, the Pittsburgh area of the United States alone produced more steel than the then wartime Germany and Japan taken together. This enormous production power has been dismantled. New centres characteristic of the knowledge society have taken the place of the old. If the Silicon Valley with its 3 million inhabitants was an independent state, it would be the thirteenth most important economic power in the world.

Such vast transformations require far-reaching decisions by the board of directors, which simply cannot be made the way we used to think and work thirty, twenty, ten or even five years ago. *The nascent industry of the post-industrial society needs the most brilliant brains – and they must themselves be assisted by high technology to produce knowledge-based assets.*

The core subject is no longer automation, though automation has given remarkable results. In 1985 Japan produced ten times more automobiles than in 1975 – but with the same personnel. This is the effect of automation and robotisation. But technology is moving on. For the last dozen years of this century, artificial intelligence rather than automation will make the difference. The emphasis will be on *expert systems* to magnify the mind's capabilities; on human windows for better man-machine communications; on artificial vision to enhance the robot's sight.

Expert systems are people's amplifiers. An expert system is a *practical solution* able to handle complex problems; tackle issues requiring a high level of human judgement and expertise; communicate with their users through an effective dialogue. Expert systems ask questions, give advice, and justify it.

Machine intelligence started with the appearance in quick succession of writing, calculation, and mechanisation in the ancient Greek world. The trail leads through medieval Italy, Renaissance Germany, and Victorian England to fundamentally new approaches developed in America and in Japan. It revives and transforms an ancient craft which in the intervening centuries has never been completely stamped out.

By the beginning of the twenty-first century, we will return to an economy which will be much more similar to the agricultural than to the industrial era. Man will be better integrated with nature thanks to personal electronics. The process of de-industrialisation has begun; that of the knowledge society is well launched. Within ten years, a person without fundamental understanding of computers will be as limited as the person today who cannot read or write. That much has been said at the conclusion of Chapter 9. It is a good sign that computer literacy at the senior management level is on the increase. On 4 November 1987 *The Financial Times* published the results of a study and report sponsored by the British Government under the headline: 'Suppliers fail to meet needs of top managers', and the opening paragraph was that the computer industry, including suppliers and data-processing specialists, is failing to deliver what the UK's top managers want from information technology.

'What is lacking,' Michael Wiltshire suggested in his article on the government study, 'is an appreciation of the way managers really work. The chief obstacles to the more effective use of information technology (IT) are human and organisational, rather than technical.'

Many of the managers interviewed in this study were strongly aware of the amount of work and the cost associated with creating and maintaining a database or other information source. Yet there was the considerable disillusionment about the ability of DP departments to understand and deliver reasonably quickly what was wanted, while the report also showed 'a continuing significant level of interest in information technology in British boardrooms.'

Another reference made by the same issue of *The Financial Times* is worth retaining. It concerns the Midland Bank decision to abandon the development of massive banking software being implemented for it by Hogan Systems, the American software firm. This decision seems to have been controversial for a number of reasons, the most important being that Midland is going through a systematic transformation in commercial and systems terms.

The new suite of programs would have been called 'Megabank', but the new chief executive in charge of information technology, Gene Lockhart, pointed out that the contact with Hogan had been signed before he took over. He explained that Megabank was not the way he wanted Midland's IT to develop. The change comes at an opportune time as emphasis is no longer placed on massive data processing but, rather, on networks and databases – and so is competitiveness.

The new communications are *multimedia*. They integrate voice, image, graphics, text and data. They include effective approaches to networking. When flow of knowledge is vital, networking is equally so. A major barrier to entrepreneurial innovations within the modern corporate framework is lack of information.

The new communications media aim to reduce this imbalance, but they cannot substitute for everything, for instance, for organisation.

Another barrier to innovation is the organisational hierarchy itself. A hierarchical hang-up is manifested by the inertia of the managers in power, whose tendency is often to neglect, sequester, or smother the entrepreneurial spirit. The challenge to the board of directors is to *open up the system*, to welcome unconventional thinking while still maintaining control.

11 The Savage Competition for Strategic Products

Survival in a dynamic industry has often been linked to management guts. Though this is a necessary ingredient, it is not enough: cost-effective products with market appeal, steady innovation, significantly low-cost manufacturing, and a worldwide network able to tap the growing markets are the other four pillars of success.

Industrial history teaches us that products die: a steady development effort is necessary to upkeep not only the product line but also the process which makes these products, so that

- product-line renewal can be steady;
- production costs are the lowest.

From computer-aided design (CAD), to computer-aided manufacturing (CAM) and robotics, technology makes feasible this goal. But technology is not enough. The board of directors and the top management of the firm must aim in this direction: it is the only way to face a savage competitive environment.

Figure 11.1 brings into perspective an example of product-line development which characterised a computer and terminals manufacturer over the last ten years. This product line was not streamlined. There were significant overlaps. In terms of cost and capacity, the company's new product line (N) was designed to substitute for the whole range of current equipment. Care was taken to do so in a cost-effective manner. This substitution came none too soon, as the market share of the company in reference was shrinking while the market itself was on an expansion course.

Not only must the board of directors see to it that the product line is properly and continuously:

- renovated;
- pruned;
- tuned;

but also marketing perspectives should dominate such product-oriented activites. The personal computer market gives an example. Facing slower growth in most personal computer markets, vendors are heating up the fight for the schoolroom. In the United States there is about one

223

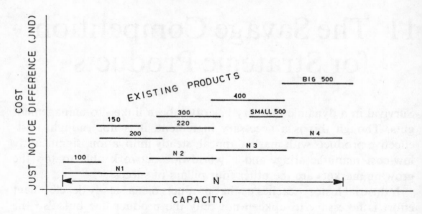

Figure 11.1   A company's product line should be streamlined. In this connection a computer manufacturer replaced several overlapping
products with a line featuring upwards compatible new announ-
cements (Note that 100, 200, etc. stand for product identifiers of
the old line. N is the new product line).

classroom computer for every 40 students (mid-1987). That ratio may be
one for every 20 by 1990. PC manufacturers are stepping up their school
marketing programme. As in all education-industry sales of technological equipment, manufacturers are betting that when children or
their families go to buy machines of their own, they will choose what
they used in school. Thus donating or deeply discounting computers for
education helps seed the market. But only low-cost producers are able to
afford deep discounts.

SIZING UP THE MARKET

Co-ordinating the development of the company's products with market
drives is a never-ending task in which the members of the board of
directors should be involved. The more sophisticated the clientele
becomes, the more demanding it is and the faster the market change. The
general manager of a French bank was to suggest, in June 1986, that 35
per cent of the transactions his institution did in the first five months of
that year were for products which did not exist eighteen months later. In
such an environment, profits are not made by outguessing the capital
markets, but by being close to their pulse. Understanding, let alone
forecasting, foreign exchange markets is not one of the skills a serious
banker lists on his resumé.

There are two strategies between which the board of directors must choose in order to put the company's course on the right track. For small firms they are alternatives. For major firms, they are complementary as a whole, but alternatives by product line:

(1) Niche markets, where innovation is the criterion for success.
(2) Mass markets, where low cost *and* high quality make a company succeed.

In mass markets, production volume is vital. Without it a company would lose the leading edge of design capability. In the semiconductor business, for instance, until you get to a volume of 1 million or 2 million per month you are still in the pilot stage.

Niche markets call for a different strategy, focusing around pre-market-entry activities. Successful companies spend much time analysing market opportunities and acquiring a deep understanding of where their forthcoming product fits.

It has already been underlined that big companies can benefit from both strategies. Before entering the US market, Sony sent teams of designers, engineers, and other specialists to study how to design its product to suit American consumers' preferences. This is a stage that goes well beyond market research and into product design.

Niche markets exist where there is business opportunity but not enough volume to attract the giants. Their able identification may result in a radical change of careers and/or product lines. Eliot C. Clarke was a senior Vice-President at Morgan Guaranty Trust. He is now a deer farmer in Millbrook, New York. Clarke chose deer for economic reasons: 'This is the only profitable form of farming I know.' This is the story of *boutique farmers* who have carved out a highly profitable niche supplying speciality fruits, meats and vegetables. They are cashing in on Americans' increased concern with nutrition, boredom with a diet of processed foods, and new-found taste for the exotic: the young urban professionals who want fresh, high-quality products. While the number of mainstream farmers in the United States is declining (400,000 of them, or 8 per cent of the agricultural work force, changed jobs in 1985), boutique farming is very much on the rise. It is a niche market, accounting for less than 1 per cent of the country's agricultural output, and it is strongest in the North-East, California and Florida, all of which have available farmland that is close to sophisticated urban markets.

Mass markets ask for a different type of treatment. They call for a strategic marketing plan that integrates all key elements: product, price, sales, distribution and promotion. The Japanese give an example on how mass markets can be exploited. When they began to export again (after the Second World War), they faced strong US and European competitors who dominated many world markets. Their products could not match those of the competitors in terms of:

- technology;
- global marketing networks.

The Japanese strategy has been to compete on price because of the labour cost advantage which then prevailed. While US firms concentrated on sophisticated products carrying high prices and high profit margins the Japanese offered simple, small and more-standardised products at lower prices and profit margins.

This typically mass-oriented strategy was to build volume and drive cost down early in the product life cycle. In the copy-machine industry, for instance, Ricoh, Canon and Sharp introduced much smaller machines than Xerox. Sony and Panasonic did the same in the consumer electronics market. Honda and Yamaha designed smaller motorcycles. Such mass-market-oriented strategy paid dividends. Today it is clearly evident in market entries into other industries, such as computer and medical electronic equipment. In the latter case, the Japanese entered the United States and world markets with a low-cost, stripped-down version of competitors' equipment. Toshiba introduced an X-ray computerised Cerebral Tomography (CT) scanner at 40 per cent less than General Electric's model and without some costly features that customers would not necessarily miss.

On the other hand, in order to exploit a specialised niche within a mass market, some Japanese companies attached foreign markets by offering products with more features and functions than their competitors did. This strategy was applied in the case of technical products with short life-cycles where new-product development was the key to success.

Many products start as niche market ventures, then reach wide acceptance. The telephone, for instance, needed twenty years to reach 1 per cent market penetration. Videotex was commercially introduced in the United States six years ago, but because of fuzzy market-focusing its potential may never be realised.

Market should, indeed, be one of the key preoccupations of the board of directors. This statement is just as valid with high technology firms as it is with settled industries such as publishing – a case in point being the failure of *TV-Cable Week* of Time, Incorporated. Market research and initial projections showed that the magazine would need 60 per cent market penetration among cable subscribers, and that was an implausible figure. The plan to sell the magazine with the co-operation of cable operators was unworkable. The operators (a fractious bunch) feared that Time Inc. was already too powerful a force in the industry. They worried that subscribers would be spending money that might be spent on other services. In fact, the promoters of *TV-Cable Week* knew that they were working with untested assumptions. They called for a small-scale market test but were turned down. The operating executives of the TV magazine grew increasingly convinced that the project faced insoluble technical, editorial and marketing problems, but their warnings were ignored by senior management – which is a good prescription for how not to succeed. This is not just a publishing failure reference. It is a case which dramatised what top management involvement means.

PRODUCT PRICING

One of the most serious decisions facing the board of directors is product pricing. College books teach that pricing decisions are reached by calculating direct material, direct labour, manufacturing overheads, marketing and sales expenses, the research and development budget, financial costs, administrative overheads, and a fair profit margin. Nothing could be more untrue.

Pricing decisions are made by the board, but are set by the market. As Dr Ralph Barnes, one of my professors at UCLA and former Ford executive, taught us in his seminars: 'The Board of Ford reads the GM prices, and sets a policy of doing a similar product at lower cost. Otherwise Ford cannot survive.' Product pricing is set by the market – which magnifies top management's responsibility in

● swamping costs;
● improving quality.

In 1979 Chrysler had to sell 2.3 million cars and trucks to break even. And they were selling 1 million: the company was going to the dogs. In 1982 the Lee Iaccoca management reduced the break-even point to 1.1 million. And they were selling 1.4 million. The *tough cost-cutting* and rationalisation measures did part of the needed miracle. The other part was contributed by *betting on quality* to beat competition. As it has been stated, under Iaccoca's leadership the Board introduced quality as part of the quota. Starting at a 10 per cent weight for quality, in early 1986 quality reached a full 25 per cent in terms of quota impact.

Product quality means:

- greater uniformity, dependability and customer acceptance, but also
- higher output per hour, per unit of raw material, and of the production capacity as a whole.

Errors and variations result in high cost – with loss of competitive position as a result. Faults stay in the system until reduced by management, yet their combined effect is usually easy to measure.

Some individual causes of low quality must be isolated by judgement. Others may be identified by experiment: some by records on operations and materials suspected of being offenders, down to a worker or a machine. Statistics help detect the existence of causes. But the emphasis to be put on quality is the responsibility of the board.

Taken at the level of the board of directors, pricing decisions are not limited to costs, quality and profit margins. Other basic criteria enter the picture. For instance, a basic problem with the internationalisation of industries is that when disinflation gets to the point where producers realise that:

- other people really can produce large volumes and
- they are willing to take market share away without regard for profitability,

the day has arrived when price wars are possible in virtually every product area. Such price wars have to be forecast, and their aftermath precalculated, well before they arise. Otherwise it will be too late to react. This, too, is a board of directors responsibility.

A company should be betting on even modest improvements in key areas to produce gains in performance. American, German, Italian and other equipment makers install Japanese just-in-time inventory control systems to boost service and profits. Others are issuing their salesmen with portable personal computers so they can call in orders daily. The tactic aims to improve customer service, but also to assure faster turnover.

Reconstructing what classical textbooks suggest about costs and profit margins, Figure 11.2 suggests a three-way classification:

(1) Manufacturer's cost of goods sold;
(2) Selling costs;
(3) Operating margins.

Industry leaders swamp item No. 1, expand item No. 2, and keep item No. 3 healthy. It is not easy. But this is precisely what a market-and-profits-oriented business would do.

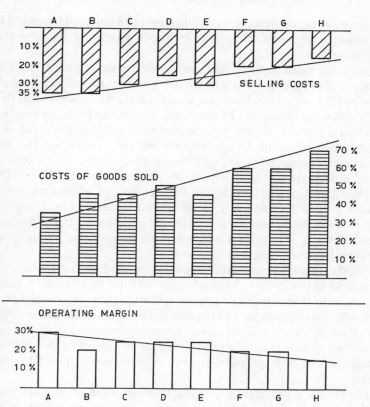

Figure 11.2   The expense structure of eight computer manufacturers is contrasted to one another. The better off is vendor A, the worst off vendor H.

Potential price wars make it wise to be steadily on the look-out for the origins of high costs. In a service economy, for instance, labour costs are far more important than in manufacturing, where robotics is replacing the former direct labour costs. Carl Icahn, the new TWA owner, found this out the hard way. 'I never said they (the stewardesses) were not breadwinners,' he suggested after taking control of the air carrier. 'That is completely untrue. What I do say is that we cannot compete with airlines that are paying half what we are for flight attendants.' Indeed, at the time this reference was made, the TWA average personnel costs stood at \$35,000 to \$40,000 per year per flight attendant. People Express and Continental were paying around \$18,000. 'I tell you categorically that TWA would have gone into Chapter 11 if I had not come along and gotten wage concessions,' Icahn concluded (The object of Chapter 11 is to protect companies from their creditors permitting their eventual restructuring).

In a deregulated industry, like airlines, the market sets the price. What is expected of management is to cut costs to meet the market price and have profits – or perish. Even the 'state supermarket' understands that.

In 1984, in Socialist France, the government let nationalised aluminum group Péchiney move out of steel and chemicals and chop losing diversifications to concentrate on core business. The then Chairman, George N. Besse, held Péchiney's costs to a 24 per cent rise over three years, as sales jumper 39 per cent to $4.3 billion. That produced profits of $70 million in 1984, compared with losses of $575 million in 1983. Subsequently, Besse became Renault's Chief Executive and reduced the nationalised French motor manufacturer's operating losses of up to $125 million a month. This showed what really tough, good management can do.

Another upstart French entrepreneur is retailer Edouard Leclerc, who runs a $6-billion-a-year chain of supermarkets. In a series of battles against industrial cartels and government restrictions, he slashed prices and defied his opponents to take him to court. In recent cases Leclerc won the right to sell designer clothing manufactured by Daniel Hechter, as well as upmarket beauty products made by Christian Dior. Official distributors of these products tried in vain to keep them off Leclerc's shelves.

The Leclerc action greatly benefited the French consumer. He sells gas and diesel oil at rock bottom prices, and is ready to enter any lucrative market. One of his successful market attacks has been the government tobacco monopoly, which allows only designated outlets to sell imported American cigarettes. Leclerc is now importing them, unwrapping them, repackaging and selling them under his own pricing scheme.

These are not decisions which can be delegated to subordinates. Pricing issues decide the life or death of an organisation. As such, they are by excellence the responsibility of the board.

THE MINICOMPUTER AND MICROCOMPUTER MARKET: A CASE STUDY

There are sectors in the computer business which are currently generating the most explosive business opportunity. Since the early 1970s the lower end products have created new markets and served as the business base to bring new users into the industry. They also made some new rich companies out of yesterdays' unknown entities. The impact of such product introductions has not always been clearly appreciated. After the successful 1981 entry into the PC arena by IBM the market started getting full with micros: there were a few far-out runners and many followers. The 1981 to 1986 period saw a steady decline in central processor-based terminals, reflecting new business challenges confronting computer manufacturers as a group. At the same time, there has been a user trend towards applications solutions.

In the first half of the decade of the 1980s four primary markets accounted for the growth of the installed base:

(1)   The market for word processing, electronic mail, and office automation at large.

The forerunners expanded their share. The followers significantly dropped in market penetration. Such results help pin-point possible winners in the consolidation phase which invariably follows.

(2)   Industrial automation, with micro-mini systems extending beyond their initial instrument monitoring function to be used for the actual processing of the collected data.

Here, the market leaders of the 1960s (IBM with the 1800 series, and General Electric with the 4000 series) which dominated process control applications did not follow up on their initial success, leaving the market wide open to the small minicomputer companies (of the 1970) which became computer giants. An example is DEC.

(3)   Scientific data processing/laboratory control. This has been the first and most important application for micro-mini systems.

Small computers have always been widely used by engineers in the laboratory to monitor equipment. As the capability of the smaller processors rose, they came to be used to process the results as well, instead of feeding the monitored data to a larger and independent mainframe for analysis.

(4)   The evolution of computer-based training had a notable impact on the educational market. It revealed that the lower-end microcomputer vendor can take over in force.

In early 1986 Apple controlled an estimated 54 per cent of the US segment of this market, followed by Tandy with 18 per cent, Commodore with 16 per cent and IBM with 3 per cent. The remaining 9 per cent of the pie was shared by many others.

Education is a fast-growth market at a time where the computer is seen as a teaching aid for everything from reading and language arts in primary schools to mathematics and physics in secondary schools. The savage competition in the school business finds its justification as vendors appreciate that computers become more and more an instructional tool. This favours the more powerful personal computers commonly used in business – particularly the IBM-PC-compatible machines sold by AT&T/Olivetti, Tandy, Commodore and IBM itself. In many secondary schools, typing classes are giving way to word processing laboratories where students use personal computers as they will in the workplace. More complex products and networking capabilities are part of its plans. Competitive thrust on a larger scale of decision making is at a premium as schools are not making piecemeal decisions anymore. The trend is away from the discretion of a school principal and towards a district-wide decision.

Decisions relating to product characteristics are often instrumental in determining the results which follow. Compaq's success defied the predictions of computer industry analysts. Making clones of IBM computers proved to be a short cut to disaster for most companies that have tried it, but Compaq's approach has been unique. Compaq is not a clone-maker, insists Rod Canion, the company's president. Instead, as Compaq puts it, its products conform to the business personal-computer market standard established by IBM. With each of its products, however, Compaq has added something lacking in IBM's PC. Compaq made its name by introducing, early in 1983, the first portable IBM-compatible personal computer. Although IBM later announced its own portable, Compaq still dominates this market sector. Canion suggests that, according to private research, 58 per cent of *Fortune* 1000 companies say that computer dealers are their primary source of supply for personal computers. (The *Fortune* 1000 is a list of the 1000 larger US companies. The *Fortune* 500 are the top 500 of the 1000 list).

Business customers apparently want to create systems with peripherals and add-ons from different manufacturers without having to shop around. Individual manufacturers cannot match the low-overhead, high-quality sales and support of the dealer, Compaq maintains.

What the markets which have been identified have in common can be phrased in the following five key points:

(1)   Worldwide market appeal;
(2)   High volume manufacturing for large numbers of users;
(3)   Ample applications software support;
(4)   Capillarity in marketing channels;
(5)   A swift establishment of a customer base.

Once a customer base is established, the producer should care for profitable add-on and upgrade business. But the most fundamental requirement is the worldwide basis of operations. 'It is an illusion to think that you have to cooperate only with European companies – you have to have the concept of being a world company,' says Olivetti's Carlo de Benedetti, who sold 25 per cent of his firm to AT&T and brought out Exxon Office System's distribution network for Olivetti's own electronic office equipment.

For European companies, worldwide operations mean an entry into the United States – half of the world computer market. For US firms the 'must' markets are both in Europe and Japan. We will return to this issue.

In a fiercely competitive environment, such as the one we are considering, operating plans must be clearly integrated into long-term growth estimates and strategies. Without such integration, there is a major danger that organisations perceive their goals as deferrable and also distort the identification of their problems.

The process of translating goals into current operating requirements must focus on the real issue: Can *our* company match the market's price/performance curve while maintaining margins and growth? The answer is not easy, but with good planning it can be done. Figure 11.3 presents two frames of reference. Both focus within the critical period for supremacy in the mid-range computer market (1981–5):

● estimated value in billions of dollars
● estimated population of installed equipment (in thousands)

in the IBM 4300 v. DEC VAX market competition. Starting from one fifth the 4300 base, within $4\frac{1}{2}$ years VAX has closed the value gap in terms of installed base – and nearly doubled the head count v. the 4300. This is a telling story and should become a classic frame of reference in a highly competitive market. Above all it is the story of a successful product against a giant marketing organisation: the David v. Goliath of the late twentieth century.

All manufacturing and marketing organisations should confront the challenge of price/performance. Whole industries such as:

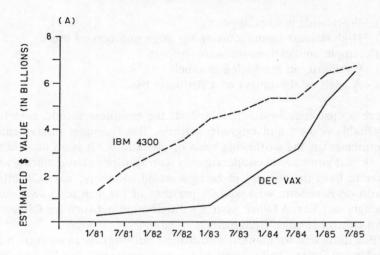

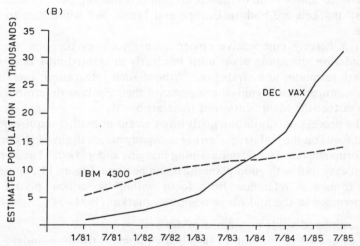

Figure 11.3   In the 1981 to 1985 timeframe DEC made a determined effort to overtake IBM in the medium-range computer market. Figure 11.3A exhibits the estimated total system value; Figure 11.3B the estimated system population growth of VAX v. 4300.

- calculators
- cash registers
- accounting machines
- typewriters
- printing engines

have been radically altered, even absorbed, by the rush of digital technology. Formerly distinct markets now overlap. Products once separate, from semiconductor components to computer systems and communications, now merge. As a result, the long-term vision of the future is not nearly as important as the ability to implement on a short-term basis programmes which incorporate that vision. Goals and strategies are only relevant to the extent that they *influence* and *change* current decisions.

Each major break in the underlying technology has been accompanied by the entrance of new competitors, developing new applications for computers. In the 1970s it was the 'minis'; in the 1980s the 'micros'. The rapid pace of change in technology contributes to the trend. As the mini-micro sector continues to experience rapid growth throughout the economy, niche-competitive strategies become increasingly important as determinants of success.

The competitive standing of micro-mini manufacturers in terms of units constitutes an important indicator of market position:

- Intense competition has usually limited the profitability of initial processor sales, with gross margins running as low as 25 per cent.
- The vendors generally make most of their money later, on upgrading and on peripherals.

The development and exploitation of a new opportunity requires the creation of an entirely new marketing effort which is protected from the biases of already existing operating departments and product lines. With galloping technology, markets can be easily lost when companies maintain their basic sales-and-marketing orientation until it is too late to capture the new opportunity.

PLANNING FOR BRINGING TOGETHER PRODUCTS AND MARKETS

What was said about the minicomputer and microcomputer business is characteristic of many other products and markets where new technology dominates. Examples are software, communications, biotechnology, space, new materials, and new energy sources.

Let's take software as an example. The product is American in origin. There are very few European software products and none has gained widespread acceptance. A similar statement can be made of Japanese software. Taking Europe and America as poles of comparison, what's the reason for the discrepancy? What are the limiting factors to the growth of a European software industry? In terms of population, Europe is a bigger market than the United States, but there are language barriers limiting each national language to less than 60 million people. There are also other reasons:

(1)　The general structure of the computer market in Europe is not conducive to integration.
(2)　The market fragmentation seems to persist.
(3)　A medieval capital market inhibits imaginative investments.
(4)　Obsolete university systems fail to bring up new technologists.
(5)　Obsolete legislation fails to support proprietorship of the products.
(6)　There are few large-scale computer companies to compete internationally.
(7)　With the possible exception of Olivetti, there is no computer company in the European continent with a worldwide appeal.

Here is the case of bringing together products and markets in a happy marriage. Gianfranco Prini, of Delphi, asked twenty-five computer companies in 1986 to send their previous year's annual report and to supply some additional figures. He got a sample of fourteen out of this request. What Prini found is that all US firms (9 out of 14) have a uniformly distributed international organisation. When they decide to go global, they do it very seriously. They cover the entire geographical area to which they appeal – for instance not only Singapore but the whole Asia/Pacific area.

In Europe there is, Prini found, a much less than necessary development of new products able to compete in the world market, but there is also a great diversity of market place policies reflecting an unfavourable climate for European firms. Table 11.1 brings these facts into perspective.

As far as computer products are concerned, Europe is the only fairly open market – which puts European-origin companies at a disadvantage. The reason for the last statement is that the North American market (United States and Canada) is fairly closed and the Asia/Pacific market is very closed (with the exception of Australia). With North America being first in market size, the outcome is obvious. It is no accident that IBM derives 57 per cent of its income from North America, 15 per cent from Asia, and 28 per cent from Europe, which is in the middle of the range of the income earned from each market by all US computer companies.

Some conclusions from the results of the study are inescapable:

Table 11.1 Computer market by geographical region

Geography:	US and Canada	Europe, Middle East	Asia/Pacific
Status:	Fairly closed	Fairly open	Very closed*
Market size:	1st	2nd	3rd
Source of income:			
IBM:	57%	28%	15%
All US companies	55–60%	25–30%	10–15%

* Except Australia, but Japan accounts for nearly 90% of that market.

(1) The European market size is roughly half the US market size for mature information technologies.

(2) For new technologies, it is less than half.

In other words there is a time delay in bringing technological breakthroughs to application to Europe.

(3) European computer companies contribute *less* than 5 per cent to the total worldwide computer business – if *mature* technologies are considered.

(4) None of the European computer firms was found to have a clear strategic marketing plan for its products.

There are also barriers set at the beginning of this century which are still around to impede economies of scale through market penetration. In the communications industry, for instance, such barriers consist of a diversity of incompatible local standards imposed by each country's own post, telephone and telegraph (PTT) authority. (A French joke suggests that PTT really stands for 'petit travail tranquil'.)

An example helps to show what this means to company profits. Not long ago, AT & T installed Dimension 85 (its digital PBX) at Hoffmann-La Roche, the large Swiss chemicals and pharmaceuticals company. To change the software to conform with Swiss regulations, AT & T paid twice the price of the system.

Nothing short of a wide marketing network with

- open distribution channels for the high end of the product line, and
- dealers for the low end,

permits a company to obtain a large market coverage. Here again, a Japanese reference is intriguing. In some US markets, Japanese firms did not copy the distribution channel of US rivals, but instead developed a system more suited to their long-term marketing mix.

For instance, when some new Japanese entrants launched a major onslaught on the US copier market in the mid-1970s, they sold their products through independent office-equipment dealers rather than through a direct sales force, as had been the practice of Xerox, the industry's long-term leader. Many Japanese firms gained access to US markets by having US companies distribute their products under US brand names. Sony began exporting its transistor radios through US companies in the 1950s, before it established its own distribution network. Fujitsu and Hitachi entered the US market by selling their small computers through US producers such as Amdahl and National Semiconductors. As they got a market beachhead and developed confidence in themselves and their products, the Japanese began to establish their own overseas sales subsidiaries. This way, they were able to gain managerial experience and strengthen their marketing position. Established sales subsidiaries became the centres for further development of overseas marketing networks. But all this requires a thoroughly elaborated marketing plan.

What we are discussing here is by no means limited to high technology. Any industry is characterised by a concentration of sales (and often, but not always, of profits) in a relatively small client group.

- In banking, about 80 per cent *of profits* come from 20 per cent of the client population (originally from Bank of America, this ratio has been verified throughout the European banking industry).
- In the cement industry, 14 per cent of the client bases accounts for 78 per cent *of sales*. (Figure 11.4)

The fact that product characterisation and market targets are very intimately related is not very often appreciated. Yet, without a clear product/market definition it is not possible to focus the board's attention on business opportunity.

BETTING ON COMPETITIVE ADVANTAGES: THE QUALITY CHALLENGE

We underlined the importance of a valid, well-thought-out marketing strategy. Just like IBM, once Japanese firms gain an initial foothold in

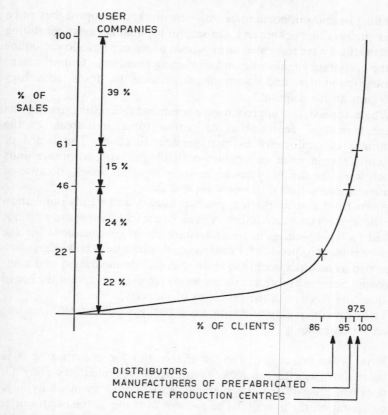

Figure 11.4   Based on statistics of the Italian cement industry, this figure shows Pareto's Law in a twentieth century setting. The 39 per cent of sales is done to the 2.5 per cent of clients.

the foreign market, they diligently set about filling out their product line, to reach an increasingly broader segment of the market itself and to exploit its potential. This is tantamount to saying that they recognised that a broad product line is necessary for long-term success against local competitors already occupying the more profitable market segments. At the same time, they bet on quality. Not everybody would want small automobiles, motorcycles, or televisions – but everybody would want a quality product.

This polyvalent strategy has not yet been analyzed by multinational companies as it should. For many, the implementation of global operations comes from ideas dating back to the extracting and distilling industries. Management has not yet fully grasped the problems it faces, blending business opportunities with new marketing approaches and a solid engineering background. On several top-management consulting assignments I have suggested an approach which can be followed online to the corporate engineering and marketing resources. 'Online' means through computers and communications using the tools technology now puts at our disposal.

Where applied, this approach gave commendable results. Its benefits range from the identification of critical functional areas, to the assurance of conformity to management directives. The board of directors should open an interactive diaiologue with corporate units which were like far-away castles in years past but which, because of communications today, can now be next door.

Apart from able marketing, product quality and steady innovation are the winners on which to bet. A modern competitive industry cannot afford to be superficial in its understanding of specifications for the performance of its products. Principles of the theory of knowledge, often regarded as inconsequential in textbooks on administration and management, become lively and gravely serious to the members of the board of directors faced with the problems of industry.

To start with, quality problems are not always well defined. Denning takes an example:

> What is the meaning of the law that butter for sale must be 80% butter-fat? Does it mean 80% or more in every pound that we buy? Or does it mean 80% on the average? What would we mean by 80% butter-fat on the average? The average over our purchase of butter during a year? Or would we mean the average production of all butter for a year, ours and other people's purchases of butter from a particular source? How many pounds would we test, for calculation of the average? How would we select butter for test? Would you be concerned with the variation in butter-fat from pound to pound?

These questions are no pastime in mathematical science. They concern the proper definition of a product. Unless they are unambiguous, properly understood, and metrics established in a scientific manner, the discussion about quality is more fiction than fact.

Yet product quality is today a subject about which practically everybody in the Western world starts to care. Quality has multidimensional product attributes. Reliability is heavily emphasised by many new high technology entrants. The members of the board of directors cannot meaningfully discuss product quality till they master the subject. But neither can they afford to abdicate their responsibility. To paraphrase Clemenceau's famous dictum: 'Quality is too important a subject to be left to the engineers.'

In the knowledge economy characterising the Western countries – from electronics to banking – quality is tantamount to service. Survivor companies must be highly service-minded and go out of their way to accommodate customers who have a problem. Even mature industries show that need. Nissan Motors, for example, after deciding to enter the US market, carefully studied the experience of European imports, especially Volkswagen. This study clearly showed that adequate provision for parts and services was vital to the success of imported cars. Nissan digested this lesson to assure customers of prompt and efficient service.

Nowhere is product quality more important than in the new industries. Cetus took a novel approach in product and market strategy that could lead to an entirely new generation of diagnostic tests. Its scientists developed a series of chemical steps that literally clone the target DNA if even the minutest amount is present in a sample. The quality prerequisites are evident if we recall that this process produces up to a million copies of the DNA the probe is looking for.

The board of directors should appreciate that a company destined to survive must show its capacity to furnish a sequence of product improvements in performance, function, styles, features and quality. Such devotion to product improvement should be reflected in a firm commitment to listening to and learning from one's own customers. Qualified company personnel must spend long hours in discussion with customers about:

(1) What limitations and weaknesses exist in the present product offerings;
(2) What's the wanted quality level or which the customer will pay;
(3) How much functionality should be included in upgrade;
(4) How products might be improved;
(5) How the customers might react to possible product modifications.

Once collected, these perceptions, wishes, attributes, complaints, and suggestions must be extensively analysed for insight into user needs. They should form the basis for potential product development.

Product development never occurs in complete isolation. Products are developed and modified with particular markets and customers in mind. It is not necessary that the conception of the market and its evolution be

explicit and detailed at the research level. But detail should characterise
product design and market feedback.

ZAITECH: THE RISK OUTSIDE MAINSTREAM BUSINESS

Precisely because competition along a company's main line(s) of
business is often savage, top management sometimes looks for extra-
curricular activities. This policy is risky for two reasons. First, the
product markets management enters are outside established company
competence and therefore a slippery and risky terrain. Secondly, though
apparently profitable, they potentially involve more unknowns than the
company imagines and more risk than it can afford.

The best example is *Zaitech*. In Japanese it stands for *Financial
Technology*, but in reality it is financial speculation proper for the
'Casino Society' in which we live. As *Business Week* was to state under
this heading on 16 September, 1985, 'Only when fear overcomes greed
will the casino society rein itself in. The question nagging all concerned is
how big a jolt is needed to alter the seductive calculus of speculation.'

The basic point of that issue (back in 1985) had been that the US
evolved into a nation obsessively devoted to high-stakes financial
manoeuvring as a shortcut to wealth. Simply put, the volume of
securities market transactions had not only soared beyond economic
purpose but had imperilled the economy by overburdening an
inadequately capitalised financial system.

The October 1987 stock market crash world-wide proved right the
1985 prophecy. In London Sir Kenneth Berrill, chairman of the British
Securities and Investments Board, warned that 'the whole securities
business now needs international collaboration.' And this is just as true
of Tokyo, New York, Frankfurt, Paris, Milan or any other major
exchange.

In Tokyo, Zaitech had its first victim, Tateho Chemical Industries,
about a month and half prior to the 1987 stockmarket crash (precisely,
on 2 September), but in October the world-wide near panic gave the
chance to find out how many other companies, besides Tateho, have
been playing Zaitech.

According to the *Japanese Economic Journal*, 'Almost all manufacturers have become involved in an effort to survive the harsh downturn
that followed the increase in the international value of the yen'. In other
words, Japanese corporate managers have sought to offset operating
losses with gains from speculative trading in financial markets. Up to a
point they have been successful. *The Financial Times* presented a
fascinating picture which is given in Table 11.2.

Table 11.2   Risk and opportunity with Zaitech

Company	Zaitech profits ($ million)	% of pre-tax profits
Toyota	1,098	48
Nissan	877	107*
Matsushita	797	61
Mitsubishi	320	58
Sony	270	107*
Sharp	213	81
Toa Nenryo	159	25
Sumitomo	149	46
Nippon Oil	145	106*
Sanyo Electric	124	10

* Zaitech profits in excess of 100% of yearly profits – hence, covering losses in the main product lines.

In other words, well-known established companies like Nissan (motor-vehicles), Sony (electronics) and Nippon Oil actually lost money from their mainline operations in 1986. They made profits out of Zaitech to cover losses and pay dividends. The game can be profitable as long as the stock market goes up – but times have now changed.

Tateho became Zaitech's first victim when it announced that its liabilities exceeded net assets by about $25 million as a result of $141 million in losses in the fall of the Japanese bond market. The concept is not totally new. In the US there is a former billionaire Mr Hunt, who is now rumoured to have *negative assets* of $2.5 billion (liabilities exceeding net assets) as a result of losses in trying to corner the silver market. The game, though, becomes frightening when it is applicable not to a person but to a large corporation.

The risk starts from the fact that much of the increase in asset values is linked to the overvaluation of the stock market itself. Companies which speculate in the market can be double losers: Both their portfolio and their own stock can be subjected to a sharp drop. This would in turn be disastrous as a typical publicly quoted nonfinancial company in Japan made 30 to 40 per cent of its profits in 1986 by investing its reserves in the rising stock market.

The most eminent danger is that if stock prices continue to slide, they may push major Wall Street, London, or Tokyo brokerage houses into insolvency. That could transform a stock market crisis into a broader financial panic. Furthermore, the speculative use of debt and other forms of leverage is pandemic in the financial world.

Speculators have become overleveraged and must borrow more to avoid default. Intense competitive pressures are forcing companies to restructure, acquire and merge. All these activities tend to reduce equity and expand debt.

During 1920 Charles Ponzi of Boston promised to pay 50 per cent interest for the use of deposits for 45 days. This was based on a plan to arbitrage foreign exchange between actual depreciated exchange rates at which foreign currencies could be bought abroad in 1920, and the higher fixed rates at which International Postal Union coupons would be redeemed for US stamps in the United States. The calculations were purely window dressing. Ponzi took in $7.9 million (in money of the 1920s) and had only $61 worth of stamps and postal coupons on the premises when he was arrested.

Zaitech and the Casino Society have a great resemblance to 'Ponzi finance'. They are types of financial activities engaged in when interest charges of a business unit exceed cash flows from operations. The Ponzi game, that is, the repayment of debt with the issuance of new debt, is usually played by a borrower who has some control over the price in the market in which he issues his own personal debt. Mr Hunt should write a book on the limits this experience entails to save other investors from misfortunes. It's a contribution that should be highly appreciated at the boards of directors of corporations inclined toward Zaitech.

Tateho failed because its securities speculation in Japanese bonds futures led to large losses. But it should not be forgotton that the typical industrial company in Japan can have loans up to 80 per cent of its assets. The law allows it, but it is an unstable system.

Corrections in Japan's domestic market will have a major effect overseas. Japan accounts for roughly a fifth of world savings and about a third of world stock market capitalisation. The Japanese have more than $300 billion invested overseas, much of it in liquid investments. Potentially, this is a much more serious threat than Third World debt which currently stands at $1 trillion.

There are reasons for management's search of an escape mechanism to stimulate profits. Japanese steelmakers, for example, are biting the bullet. The soaring yen stimulated imports of Korean and Taiwanese steel. Most of Japan's big five steelmakers have already squeezed their variable costs as much as they can, so now they are announcing plans to cut fixed costs: By the end of 1990 they will shut down eight of Japan's 34 blast furnaces.

Petrochemical companies in USA, Europe, and Japan have cut capacity by 15 to 20 per cent since 1982. The Japanese petrochemical industry completed a 36 per cent reduction in combined ethylene production capacity in 1985. Meanwhile, global demand for petro-chemicals is strong. Chemical sales to the packaging industry is one reason. For instance, Campbell Soup is planning to use plastic cans for some of its products.

But, overall, the late 1980s contrast with the expansion period of the early 1980s when financial assets led physical assets as a means for embodying wealth. That is precisely why Zaitech could claim many more victims. And Japanese corporate managers are not the only ones playing Zaitech.

Some US bankers and savings and loans executives, particularly in Texas, have been playing poker with the chips in their balance sheets for years. US regulators are spending billions of dollars to keep the gambling losses from hurting depositors. Leveraged buyout and junk bond players are still winning. But if economic growth suffers, they could be big losers as well. And we could all suffer.

As the events of October and November 1987 demonstrated, any major movement of the US and of the Japanese stock markets affects the demand for the dollar. World-wide it makes the dollar less attractive. In Japan in particular it alters the wealth of Japanese investors. Thus repercussions make tidal waves in all continents. They are not confined to the United States or to Japan.

Robert Gilpin, of Princeton University, thinks of the dangers embedded in the fundamental weakness of a world monetary system based on a Japanese-backed dollar: He warns that 'an inevitable conflict exists between continuing Japanese provision of American liquidity and the confidence of the market in the dollar.' If the world loses faith in the relationship, he adds, 'the Japanese-financed American hegemony may also one day collapse along with the possibilities of a stable international political order.'[1]

Back in the 1960s President Reagan's limousine was surrounded by student demonstrators carrying signs saying 'We are the future.' Reagan, who was then governor of California, held a piece of paper up to the window that said, 'I'll sell my bonds.' Today many com-panies have taken the road of speculation and everyone is selling his stock.

It is bad management to look for quick gains and destabilise the company in the process. Trouble starts at the national level. Public attitude helps keeps innovative thinkers out of the race and promotes pop-economic thought. That is, ideas promising good times with no sacrifice or discomfort. These include big savings through 'better tax collection,' protectionism, and philosophies of soak the rich and the corporations. As Mark L. Melcher aptly stated:

> The public is not looking for a great leader who wants to put the country's economic house in order. Instead, it seems to want someone who sounds and looks like a politician, but either does not have the clout to rock the economic boat or does not want to. And, of course, it is getting just that.[2]

NOTES

1. *Business Week*, 5 October 1987.
2. Prudential Bache Securities bulletin, September 1987.

12 The International Corporation

For international operations a company has to determine which of its products, either actual or potential, it can successfully market abroad, and what areas hold the greatest promise. It must examine the different arragements for breaking out of the confines of the domestic fields and choose between them. Above all, it has to select and train the management personnel to do the job.

International operations are both a reason and a result of the changing aspects of industrial strategy. Even for companies who in the past had international facilities, the activities overseas have changed considerably in the last fifteen years.

The extractive was once the principal type of foreign operation. Companies of the most-industrialised countries looked abroad for the raw materials which they needed, like oil and minerals, and set up enterprises to secure them. With the changes brought about by the shrinking world (given impetus by the Second World War), accelerated international travel, better communications, the evolving tastes and economic conditions in many countries, and the two oil shocks of the 1970s, formerly predominant factors have been deeply altered. More firms with goods to sell are discovering profitable markets abroad and are moving in on them. But the movement is selective and successful ventures are well-timed.

Business and industrial enterprises with appealing products increasingly find themselves with previously unavailable or unrecognised opportunities outside the borders of their homeland. The way the international industrial and marketing complex stands today, American, Japanese, German, Swiss, Swedish, but also English, Dutch, French, and Italian companies has gone beyond export-mindedness toward international industrial empires.

Figure 12.1 contrasts the new multinational perspective to the old and makes evident how much more enlarged the new one is. What all these companies have in common is an acute need for a multinational, integrated management team at the top that thinks in terms of worldwide commitments.[1] This is deadly necessary not only for an efficiently co-ordinated day-to-day effort but also in order to provide a sound basis for forward planning and for corporate growth and survival as operations cover an increasing number of countries abroad.

NEW PERSPECTIVE

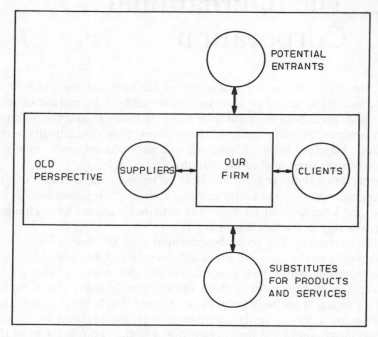

Figure 12.1 The old management perspective was limited in scope. Today the board's decisions should consider not only the company they run but also potential entrants to the market as well as substitutes for current products and services.

The crucial aspect of the multinational effort can be appreciated if we consider that the industrial world is currently undergoing radical changes in the distribution of population, its age groups, developing drives, purchasing power and productive capacity. But as markets turn toward an international perspective, they also become more selective. This increases the level of commitment which is necessary – and calls for new types of organisation and structure.

INDUSTRIAL ORGANISATIONS AND MULTINATIONAL COMMITMENTS

Management's role in international industry and trade often starts at the evaluation of the wisdom of an investment: whether capital and skill should or should not be invested in a particular country. If management chooses to invest, then the extent of the investment must be determined. The typical way is to have the decision to invest conditioned by the consideration of some six main factors:

(1) The size of the market;
(2) The nature and extent of existing competition;
(3) The customer's acceptance potential of the company's products;
(4) The political and economic atmosphere within the country or area;
(5) Questions of tariff, import quotas, exchange restrictions, and restrictions on remittance of profit;
(6) The existing and projected general regulations.

The answers a thorough study would give, would help to determine certain basic strategic moves – starting with whether there must be any local ownership interest at all and the structure of the subsidiary the company may wish to organise in the foreign country.

Before a commitment is made, a considerable number of more detailed crucial questions need to be answered. Ironically, companies engaging in international operations have to face a good deal of the problems relating to their own structural matters, and to the personality clashes which do exist. This is a direct reflection of the fact that the large corporation today is highly politicised. Its managers are continually looking inward to catch any shift in the power constellation, so that they can adjust to it before they find themselves on the losing side.

It is not too often appreciated that the corporate power game is a major handicap in successful worldwide business. So is job-hopping. Many executives know their place until they come up with a good idea. At that point they quit and pursue it on their own. At the same time, executives handcuffed by the corporation attend endless meetings to defend turf and learn to avoid risks at all cost. In such a culture, even successful risks often are not worth the trouble to the man who takes them – yet international operations call for much more on-the-spot risk-taking than the domestic. The best control plan is one along three axes of reference served through a steady, timely and accurate flow of information based on computers and communications (Figure 12.2).

The performance of an international subsidiary gets tested sooner and more frequently because of the diverse market, higher local competition and relatively smaller size of the unit – as compared to the big parent company at home. The success of IBM is often attributed to the fact that the computer giant is remarkably close to its markets.

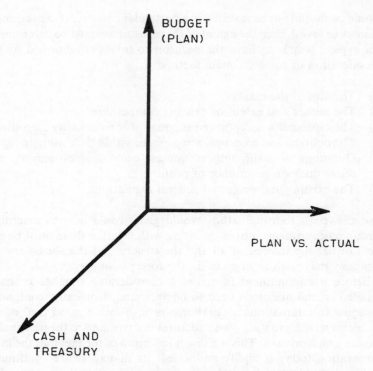

Figure 12.2   While a financial plan as well as cash and treasury evaluations are important, just as vital is a steady comparison of plan v. actual. Results should preferably be presented in a graphical form.

To run a multinational business successfully, management has to:

(1) Pay great attention to people by assigning the human resources responsibility to top-ranked executives.
(2) End the tradition of measuring individual performance against an 'ideal type', which doesn't really exist.
(3) Recruit and integrate local talent.
(4) Link performance to compensation and greater opportunity for young people with good brains, speaking many languages and having a policy of hard work.

A vital element in international operations is a policy of renovation. Organisations tend to get old, just like people. But an internationally minded firm has to have a plan to keep its structure at home and abroad young, flexible, and creative. One of the keys here is that every division head and chief of national operations has something to contribute to the success of the organisation. So the board of directors has to listen to people who work for the firm. This flexibility factor is a basic equation which can be seen in a company's multinational business. 'Half our business is outside the U.S.,' explains Richard Love, director of international marketing for Hewlett-Packard, which has major facilities in Mexico, Singapore and a number of other countries. With this being the case, how can a domestic board of directors effectively run the 'other 50 per cent' of the business?

Even the proper definition of goals, authority and responsibility for the domestic operations is not enough in a multinational sense. A serious consideration of business problems involves the examination of organisation and structure within each and every country of operations.

Structure means internal organic arrangements upon which are established the relationships between persons, functions, the physical and logical resources of a going concern. Business has always been delimited in its significance by:

● its organisation;
● its environment;
● its objectives.

Organisation denotes a process, and relationships associated with this process. International business operations do not come into existence spontaneously. They are the result of the creative efforts of management – efforts which must reflect country culture, market, products and overall competition. While in the United States a company can gain market share by cutting costs, different criteria may prevail, country by country, abroad. The same is valid of establishing manufacturing operations abroad:

(1) A company can simply pick up stakes and shift an existing operation overseas as Atari did, or
(2) Grow volume production abroad through a carefully worked-out plan.

This is to a large degree what the more successful international companies have done. They start out in their country of origin with a manufacturing capacity and, as their volume grows, they maintain that plant but also move abroad, building facilities for the volume overseas.

Alternative approaches are:

(3)   Buy a local company in the target country and integrate it into the current corporation's system.
(4)   Establish a joint venture either with a local company or with another international firm operating there.

While cost cutting may be the basic reason for moving manufacturing abroad, well established firms choose to keep a domestic facility for their new, technologically advanced, products. They have to have their manufacturing operation closely coupled with their engineering during start-up since there are always problems. There may be other reasons for moving some of the manufacturing abroad, apart from reducing labour costs. Usually the new arrival is granted full exemption from all corporate taxes for up to ten years, receives large cash grants for worker training, and is fully exempt from import duties on parts and materials.

Another 'advantage' some organisations conceive is the perk of management being able to fly down to another country in midwinter or to get some golf and beach time after checking out the plant. Serious companies, however, don't go in for such folly. Today, two trends in manufacturing investments are outstanding:

(1)   *GM and IBM type*: Heavy automation investments to increase product quality and swamp costs in the United States – in order to retake control of the market.
(2)   *South Korea, Pacific Basin type*: Apply automation to capitalise on low-cost labour.

Emphasis increasingly shifts to brainpower. Can there be low cost brains? The answer is definitely NO!. As Robert McNamara once said: 'Brains go where they are appreciated.'

THE MULTINATIONAL COMPANY'S RIGHT STUFF

Whether in domestic operations or internationally, market growth is a matter of getting organised. No market can grow at a steady rate (as opposed to temporary jumps) faster than it is possible to absorb and use the product. The challenge in international operations comes from the polyvalent approach it requires to be at the right time with the right product in the right market.

International operations have a very significant impact on corporate culture. There is an evolving business code for globalised companies.

This code is forged out of roughly sixty years of international experience – counting the decades between the two world wars and the post-war years. As with any process, the business code for globalised companies is steadily refined. What started as a British, Dutch and German practice, was followed up by American and more recently by Japanese globalisation efforts.

The rule of thumb for Japanese international firms is: if it costs less than $100 to produce, make it in South-East Asia. Otherwise build a plant as close to your export market as possible. But apart from the well-known business opportunity analysis which needs to be done, there are cultural problems to face all the way up to the boardroom. 'We already have simultaneous translation at our sales meetings,' observes Fujitsu's President Takuma Yamamoto. 'As we become more multinationally oriented, we are bound to become more cross-cultural. True, this will cause some problems, but the end result should be favorable.'

Business perspectives make it clear that any sizeable move abroad will boost the economics where these companies operate. The following are some examples of what leading Japanese corporations are doing.

Internationalisation is one of the three main pillars of Toshiba's new corporate strategy. 'We chose to internationalize because we concluded an export-oriented approach is no longer viable,' explains President Sugiichiro Watari. 'We decided to accelerate internationalization because of trade friction and the yen's high value.' Indeed, the mainly export trading companies of Japan are paying dearly for the yen's high value. The mid-1986 estimate has been that profits drop by 20 per cent or more at big exporters: Casio Computer, Hitachi, Mitsubishi Electric, Nippon Electric Corp (NEC), Seiko, Yamaha Motor and many others. Until this change in strategy, most of Toshiba's overseas production has involved colour TVs, electric ovens and control panels. In the future, the company will also manufacture abroad such advanced items as semiconductors and video tape-recorders (VTR).

Nippon Gakki is a different kind of company. Although it is diversifying into high-technology electronics and sporting equipment, it remains pre-eminently the world's largest producer of musical instruments, under the Yamaha brand name. The company has seven overseas plants, including one in Georgia and another in Michigan. 'In twenty years, two-thirds of our production should be overseas,' predicts President Hiroshi Kawakami.

Komatsu already has factories in Indonesia, Brazil and Mexico. It is now establishing plants in Tennessee and Britain. Its president Shoji Nogawa acknowledges that the yen's dramatic revaluation has forced

Japan's heavy-equipment giant to come up with a new corporate strategy. The company is now:

- reviewing its product line.
- developing new, more competitive products,
- investing in robots and other advanced industrial machines;
- shifting more production overseas.

'At present roughly 5 per cent of our production is overseas,' Nogawa estimates. 'In three to five years that figure should be 30–35 per cent.'

Ricoh has also a global outlook. 'We have the lowest export rate and the highest overseas production percentage of any company in our strategy,' says President Hiroshi Hamada. 'Today over 15 per cent of our total production is outside Japan. Half our cameras are made in Taiwan. In five to six years we expect 70–80 per cent of our office automation equipment will be manufactured in the countries where it is marketed.' Ricoh moved overseas in the mid-1960s, first to Korea and Taiwan, later to the United States. Now the company has five overseas production facilities, including two in California and one in Britain (of Ricoh's 3,600 overseas employees, half are in production). 'Over the next two or three years,' Hamada remarks, 'apart from R&D and keeping up existing production lines, we will make no new investment in Japan. It will all be overseas.'

Brother Industries has about 15 per cent foreign production and that number could double within five years. Says its President: 'I see a need for manufacturing facilities in the United States and in Europe soon. When we were operating overseas we try to forget we are a Japanese company. We like to use local equipment and employees to benefit the local community.'

Canon started clearing a 180-acre factory site at Newport News, Virginia, with production scheduled to start in 1987. With a total investment of $120 million, Canon expects the plant will employ 1,000 and make 20,000 copiers a month by the end of the decade. It selected Newport News because of the land, location and proximity to New York. Canon USA's President Fujio Mitarai, who has spent twenty years in the United States, notes that at present exchange rates, labour costs are about the same as in Japan, while land and material prices are cheaper.

This globalisation policy is part of a dynamic change taking place in Japan's industrial structure towards the twenty-first century – which is just thirteen years away. In late 1985 the Japanese Government commissioned a blue-ribbon study group chaired by the former Bank of

Japan Governor Haruo Maekawa. The goal of the Maekawa Committee was to examine the mid-term aspects of liberalisation and the structural adjustments needed in the Japanese economy to achieve greater international harmony. Although the Committee's report released in early 1986 did not carry the weight of policy, it laid down a set of principles intended to guide future policy discussions in and out of the government.

The Maekawa Committee argued that Japan must make a historical transformation in its traditional policies on economic management and the nation's life-style. Ther can be no further development for Japan without this transformation. It set as national goals:

(1) Reduction of Japan's current account imbalance;
(2) Reorientation of Japan's economic structure towards international co-ordination;
(3) Enhancement of the quality of life;
(4) Arrival at a level of international responsibility commensurate with Japan's economic position.

It also emphasised Japan should strive for economic growth led by domestic demand, and recommended several practical reforms to stimulate private consumption.

Another study group was appointed by MITI to draw up the basic concepts of Japan's industrial society in the twenty-first century. This committee took a tough look at the structural causes of Japan's trade imbalances, the need to develop the high technology and information industries required for the third industrial revolution as well as the Japanese life-style.

The high point of the second research effort was the identification of specific steps the government could take, such as increasing disposable income and worker free time, improving housing, providing incentives for direct overseas investment, technology transfer and basic research and development. It also suggested that the government should give assistance to foreign investment in Japan and encourage more foreign companies to become suppliers to Japanese manufacturers. 'The report is unique in the history of MITI,' observes MITI's Fukukawa. It anticipates what Japan must do to maintain full employment: namely, move into industries on the technological frontiers and expand service industries. It suggests a dynamic change will take place in Japan's economic structure towards the twenty-first century.

The move into the twenty-first century is the multinational company's 'right stuff'. And the same is true of national policies which should be globally oriented. Europe, the United States and Japan are just as wealthy. They have the economic and political resources to develop their knowledge industries and, with them, a philosophical survival posture. The difference is whether or not they are using these resources in the right manner.

Where is there evidence that a nation's multinational companies are on the road to achieving world technological leadership in more than a handful of their segments? Or evidence that they are allocating resources in order to recapture and maintain a technological level superior to that for foreign competitors? If competitors outstrip a global enterprise in terms of their commitment to development of both product and process technology, then this company is doomed. On the question of global position, what evidence is there that hiring the usual nationals as managers abroad is a policy relegated to the past?

Human relationships will be increasingly important in the multinational competitive environment. 'I did not fully appreciate how significant personal relationships are until I realized the New Year's calls by corporate leaders on their customers were highly personal,' observes Mr Moody of AT & T. 'It shows a depth of relationship and investment of personal interest. There's a lot of message there for foreign firms about "Japanizing" their company and the long-term investment of resources and capital.'

FINANCIAL CONSIDERATIONS IN AN INTERNATIONAL STRATEGY

Though its goal may be sales and manufacturing, the multinational company has many characteristics to be found in financial institutions. It operates in different currencies and appeals to markets which are not only at various levels of maturity but also at inflation, deflation or stagflation within the same maturity level.

The first preoccupation of the international firm should be with the world economy. Which way is it moving? What's the most likely forecast? What kind of management decisions are necessary given that perspective? As of mid-1986, for instance, the world economy was in the fourth year of an economic recovery. The oil slump and soft commodity prices put an end to the struggle against inflation (at least for the time being), creating good conditions for an extension of the current business cycle. During 1986 the dollar was weakening against other major currencies (sterling, deutsche mark, yen, swiss franc) raising – on the US side – hopes of balancing the current account; and in the other countries fears about losses of exports.

After a pause in the upswing during the initial months of 1986, the pace of expansion looked set to accelerate in most countries in the second half-year, continuing at least until the end of 1987. Growth rates in the major economies were pretty well aligned, but Japan was likely to substantially underperform its long-term trend growth. That was the forecast. What about reality?

A year and a half after these forecasts were made is a good time to look back and judge their accuracy. Japan did underperform its long-term growth. So did other major countries. But the American balance of payments did not improve in any significant level while the huge budget deficit of the US gave to the financial markets world-wide a reason for a slide which approached the limits of panic.

By November 1987, in the United States, the Federal Reserve Board was forced to choose between stabilising the dollar with higher interest rates and averting a recession by pushing rates down. It came to that. And it became increasingly evident that the path back to stability was going to be long and arduous.

In spite of reassuring steps policy makers were taking, no study, commission, congressional hearing, press conference, or slippage of the tongue could alter certain undeniable facts. If anything, it made them worse by increasing the nervousness of the financial markets. The US is a net debtor nation. It owes $400 billion to foreigners at the end of 1987 and, because interest payments keep rising faster and faster, it could owe $700 billion by 1989. Current estimates talk of a $1 trillion US debt by 1990. That is 25 per cent of the gross national product of the United States.

Those figures are so huge they hardly seem real. But what they mean is that the US, which has been accustomed to setting its own agenda, has become dependent. That is likely to mean a lower standard of living – and not only in the US. Unavoidably, the whole world will be affected. Policy making at the board level has to be very sensitive to these facts.

The board of multinational corporations and those nationals who lean on export must also monitor very closely the co-ordinating polices of major nations – even if they are often deceiving. There are marked differences in fiscal and monetary policy approaches, though since the celebrated Group of Five and Group of Seven (Finance Ministers) meetings, governments have frequently expressed the desire for increased co-ordination of policies. When it comes to synchronising monetary policies there is clearly no full accord.

High-minded calls for international co-operation are destined to achieve little, because governments often fail to make good on international economic promises when domestic considerations get in the way. The Louvre agreement, for instance, entered into troubled waters because commitments to co-ordinate policies have not been implemented by the different countries with sufficient vigour. As Marc E. Leland, who was the assistant Treasury secretary for international affairs during President Ronald Reagan's first team, was to comment: 'The danger with coordination is it promises too much and delivers too little.'

Figure 12.3 presents the heavyweighters in the world economy. The most remarkable change concerns Japan, as it moved from fifth to second position. In fact, the distance between first and second is much smaller today (160 per cent) than it was at the beginning of The Second World War (234 per cent). Notice that the economic data are converted to different currencies as of mid-1986 when the study was made. Such statistics evidently change with the sharp change in parities – particularly as of late 1987 – but this reference to changing parities is valid in $ *vs* other currencies – not so much among the other currencies themselves.

Since the United States not only has been, but also remains, the front-runner – albeit a weakened one – looking at the US economy the careful international company would find that, since the middle of 1984, the US economy has grown at an annual rate of only 2 per cent, which is well below the long-term trend rate of around 3.5 per cent. The mainstay of this growth has been personal consumption, while capital spending and foreign trade clearly exerted a restraining, if not outright negative influence on growth.

Personal consumption in the US is propelled by the young urban professionals (yuppies) with a marked preference for quality products and love for imports – which explains the steadily negative balance of payments. For some time there has been no sign of any acceleration in economic activity, except figures reflecting the involuntary accumulation of inventories in the business sector. The impact of military spending, which acts as the flywheel of the economy, has been discounted since 1981 with the high military build-up set by the Reagan Administration, financed through astronomical budget deficits.

As of 1987, the only major new trend in the United States is *speed buying* with the goal to accelerate consumer spending. Designers of shopping malls are moving toward smaller facilities that *allow faster and faster spending*. These are projected for the mom who has 'plenty of money but no time.' We should place this in the context of a nation that:

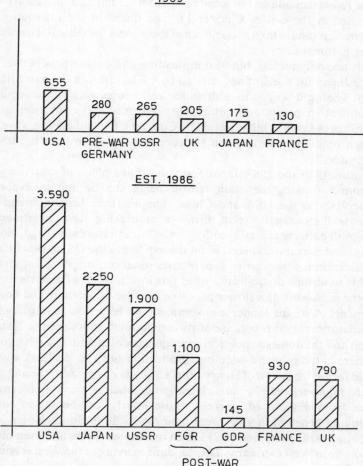

Figure 12.3 A July 1983 study identified the heavyweighters in the world economy. Two frames of reference at nearly 50 years difference have been examined. Notice the reversal in relative economic importance of the different countries.

- Has seen consumer debt rise 40 per cent in the 1984–87 timeframe while disposable income has increased only 22 per cent.
- Has experienced during the elapsed seven years of the Reagan presidency (1981–87) the doubling of the national debt.

These references add to the scene of world-wide financial instability we examined at the end of Chapter 11. The board of the international corporation should take good notice of them. And the same is true of the larger national firm.

It is not only useless, but also misleading and counterproductive, to blame Japan for the declines suffered by US industry in the past fifteen years. The right way is to address the real causes such as inadequate investment in plants and equipment, research, and education. If a harshly protectionist bill is passed by Congress, it could bring a wave of foreign retaliation hurting the US economy far more than the trade deficit does.

During 1986 and 1987, Japan found itself in a phase of much slower economic growth, the main reason being the decline in exports, particularly to the USA and China. The less than brilliant trend of business discourages export firms from making new investments, thereby depressing capital spending – while South Korea, Taiwan, Hong Kong, and Singapore rushed to fill the gap left in the US market by the decline of Japanese exports. Japanese personal consumption finds itself unable to absorb domestically what was lost in terms of exports, since income is growing at a slower pace due to reduced overtime and bonus payments. Also, the Japanese government has been slow in introducing stimulatory measures because of its commitment to reduce the budget deficit and the domestic political consequences of abandoning this goal.

There is today world-wide overproduction but soft demand, as the world forgot the lesson of Henry Ford's $5-a-day wage: *Mass production can be supported only by mass consumption.* Mass consumption cannot result from millions of workers whose hourly 'compensation costs' (including benefits) in 1984 were typically $1.38 in South Korea and $1.27 in Brazil, compared to $13.69 in the United States and even more expensive in West Germany. The standard of living of the West is bound to suffer.

This makes it necesary for the international company to take a detailed look market by market. Which countries have recently been experiencing the most rapid increase in labour costs per unit of output in manufacturing and which the slowest?

The United States have seen diminished economic growth and declining wages:

● from a weekly average of $201 in 1973,
● to $167 in May 1987, in constant 1977 dollars.

This represents loss of purchasing power, less job security, and reduced public services. In sum, a declining standard of living.

By contrast, West Germany experienced an increase in wages by 4 per cent in 1986 and 4.5 per cent in 1987. Manufacturing labour costs are only one element in the total price level. But manufacturing costs are of particular importance in international trade. *The Financial Times* was to comment (19 November 1987) that it is striking that for both 1986 as a whole, and 1987 to date, British manufacturing costs have risen less than German ones. Morgan Guaranty Trust estimates that German industrial workers now average $18.07 an hour in wages and fringe benefits, v. $13.69 in the US and $12.19 in Japan.

Some people believe that West Germans have the right formula for their kind of economy. Our policy is not to increase 'capacity, but to rationalise and modernise production,' says Axel Kemna, chairman of machinery manufacturer Gildemeister. Critics suggest that Germany is underconsuming and underinvesting. It has become a saturated economy with an ageing population. But others agree with the German position. Because the German population isn't growing, the German economy does not need to grow, advises Akira Nambara, a director of the Bank of Japan. In Paris, Alain Minc, president of Cerus, is of the opinion that: 'The Americans are putting the question to the Germans in pure Keynesian macroeconomic terms. The real issues are deeper. The Germans can get richer and richer with a stagnant economy.'[2]

Business Week presented an interesting comparative study focusing on three countries, with four criteria in mind:

(1) *Inflation* in Germany is low: 1.6 per cent for 1987 *vs* 1.4 per cent in Japan and 3.2 per cent in the US.

(2) But *unemployment* stays up: about 8 per cent *vs* 2.9 per cent in Japan and 7.3 per cent in the US.

(3) *Exports* are hard-hit. The 1988 projection talks of *minus* 0.2 per cent for Germany, *minus* 0.8 per cent for Japan, but plus 0.8 per cent for the US.

(4) *Growth* is sluggish (a 2.3 per cent average annual rate in the 1983– 87 timeframe, *vs* 3.6 per cent in both Japan and the US).

As a result the estimated growth rate for 1988 in Germany is somewhat less than 2 per cent. The US does not fare much better. Projections indicate a 1.2 per cent growth rate. Of the three countries only Japan may reach a 2.8 per cent growth rate in 1988.

These are issues of vital interest to the members of the board in their decision-making process. 'Nestlé's 1988 budget would have to take into account current monetary and economic uncertainties,' said Helmut Maucher, the managing director. But, enumerating the group's trump

```
┌─────────────────────────┐   ┌─────────────────────────────┐
│                         │   │                             │
│         U S A           │   │        GERMANY              │
│                         │   │                             │
│  1. MARKETING           │   │  1. QUALITY WORK            │
│                         │   │                             │
│  2. INNOVATION          │   │  2. STANDARDISATION         │
│                         │   │     AND NORMALISATION       │
│  3. SOFTWARE            │   │                             │
│     DEVELOPMENT         │   │  3. SYSTEM ENGINEERING      │
│                         │   │     (POWER NETWORK)         │
│                         │   │                             │
└─────────────────────────┘   └─────────────────────────────┘

            ┌─────────────────────────────┐
            │                             │
            │          J APAN             │
            │                             │
            │  1. FAST PRODUCT            │
            │     IMPROVEMENT             │
            │                             │
            │  2. COST/EFFECTIVE          │
            │     MANUFACTURING           │
            │                             │
            │  3. WORLD MARKET VIEW       │
            │                             │
            └─────────────────────────────┘
```

Figure 12.4   Three topmost characteristic strengths of the economies of the
United States, Germany and Japan.

cards – continuing rationalisation of production, increased spending on
marketing, promotion and research, and a very solid 'war chest' in cash –
he hoped it would be able to keep earnings at about the same level.[3]

Besides the prevailing financial characteristics, knowing the personality, financial background, and culture of each country of operations is
very important. There are typical strengths in the different economies
which must be studied, analysed, and capitalised upon. Figure 12.4 gives
an example.

If the board's basic mission is to enhance corporate profitability, and
it is, then bargain-hunting information should also be brought to its
attention. A case in point is the so-called 'Giscard Bonds' in France,
which proved a gold mine for investors, paying 66 per cent in 1985. The
controversial but alive bond issue was floated in 1973, when Giscard

d'Estaing was still finance minister. Both principal and interest payments were linked to gold. As the gold price soared, so did the Government's costs. The bonds brought FFr. 6.5 million into the treasury but have cost FFr. 22.6 billion in interest payments alone. French officials figured that by maturity in 1988, the issue will have drained the state of up to FFr. 110 billion. That's about 1,700 per cent of the money Giscard Bonds brought to the Government – the difference being the investors' profits.

Financial markets cannot be examined in a valid manner without a careful consideration of protectionist barriers. After all, the strength of markets and of currencies interests the board of the multinational firm to the extent that it can channel its products abroad – and quotas have nine lives. Both the starting point and the trend in quotas should be examined, globally and in each country of operations. Import quotas have an insidious tendency to become self-perpetuating, merely because the protected industry in the importing country fails to adjust, but also, if not primarily, because it keeps up its political lobbying against free trade.

Quotas become a fact of life to which whole market-places eventually adapt. The importer's commitment to a distorted mix of price, volume, profit margin, product design and local sourcing becomes established to the point where he prefers the quota system to continue. Japanese car makers, for instance, typically export between 25 per cent and 33 per cent of their car output in the US market. Till the yen became overpriced (mid-1986 and throughout 1987) the Japanese motor industry made high profits in the United States, which helped finance an intense price war for the Japanese consumer in the home market.

But with the forecast of a new environment with changing parities and protectionist measures, several Japanese car companies invested in manufacturing capacity in the United States. If, taking their position into account, the Japanese industry and government decide that their best long-term marketing strategy in the US is to continue with self-restraint, it will be hard for anybody to make a forceful case against the investment.

At the same time, Federal Trade Commission economists David G. Tarr and Morris E. Morkre documented, among other findings, that the Japanese curbs cost American consumers $1.1 billion annually in the form of higher prices, or an average of $394 per car (1981 to 1985). They also found that the cost to the economy of protecting 4,600 US jobs was $240,000 per job, per year. This is the other side of protectionism.

Another significant report was made by economist Michael C.

Munger. He concluded that the domestic recession from 1980 to 1982 and the relatively high level of wages in the automobile industry were far more significant factors than foreign competition in the industry's decline before the import curbs were negotiated with Japan.

FACING INTRACORPORATE PROBLEMS

While the day-to-day decisions in managing an enterprise are the responsibility of the professional managers, the board cannot escape the responsibility of assuring that the multinational network of the company runs like a well-oiled machine. This is not always the case, and it is surprising how many inter-divisional frictions exist, many of them arising from what should have been plainly impersonal factors.

A good many of these factors look as if they have nothing to do with international operations whatsoever. Pricing and profit allocations is a good example. Particularly in decentralised operations, where all divisions are profit oriented, none of them is willing to make or accept a transfer price which might penalise its ability to meet the division profit objectives. Resistance is magnified when such objectives are the basis for an executive evaluation and compensation plan. Intracorporate pricing problems may even arise when a company tries to allocate income from licensing and technical assistance fees received from abroad. The domestic research and development division, for instance, would look for a financial motivation in providing the international division with the necessary know-how.

Poor solutions to this profit-allocation problem have often been tried with dubious results. One approach calls for both the domestic divisions concerned and the international division to receive full credit for all income earned abroad. In this case, it is the company's financial people who are at a loss.

The reason for paying so much attention to the internal or structural problems of the corporation is that before engaging in international ventures a firm should first set its home and aims in order. An analysis along these lines could even reveal errors and gaps in the operations at home, in general organisational matters and in the higher-up personnel.

Disappointments abroad tend to be interpreted under a magnified perspective. Like any expansionist move involving potential wealth and power, international operations tend to create severe political strains within the corporation. If this is true at the start of business abroad, it becomes even more so when the international sales and profits grow to substantial sums – say at or above 30 per cent of the company's business.

Because of failure in the initial organisational setting, a company may never give to the international division its proper balance. The man in charge of the international operations, and his immediate associates, may find themselves in a position of 'a separate, but not quite equal group' within the corporate structure. When, as often happens,

- the top international executive is not a member of the executive committee; and
- there are no international, known and respected businessmen sitting on the board of directors,

international operations do not have a voice in the policy-making body of the corporation, in spite of their income-making activity and the profits which they bring. It is precisely for this reason that in the following chapter, on organisational perspectives, the job description of a board of management for international operations will be outlined. This makes it feasible to give to each country of operations the attention which it deserves, in accordance with the market's size and drive.

The importance of this call to greater prudence and a more rational structure will be better appreciated if we recall that international companies now employ 45 million people – of which 40 million are in the main industrialised countries. Here they account for one-third of both manufacturing and service employment. In Great Britain, for instance, one in every two people in manufacturing works for a multinational company.

At the same time, the fact that business and industry are still far behind in management and organisational research as to the rational way of handling business problems with a worldwide span hardly escapes the attention of the board. Surprisingly little has been done so far to close the gap. And because research on how to organise and manage a worldwide industrial entity has been sadly lacking, nobody can really profess to have the answers to all of the problems. Admittedly, problems and opportunities in managing international operations vary from company to company as to their very nature. This further helps exemplify the tensions in the inter-divisional and country-of-operations relationships we are referring to.

For the international corporation, competition between its product divisions has varying implications. If these divisions are engineering, manufacturing and marketing different lines, there is less to be said than in the case where their success depends on close collaboration. Still a basic question of rationalisation to be answered is the relation between the domestic product division and the international division as such.

- Should research and development be done only at the domestic level?
- What about niche markets abroad?
- Should each of the domestic divisions be given an international arm?
- What about the necessary co-ordinating activity by country of operations?
- How will the marketing funds and associated drive be channelled to the foreign markets: individually or by division?
- Who will be responsible for manufacturing investments and scheduling responsibility? for cost control?
- Who will be facing the labour problems abroad: the domestic product division, the international division or each country of operations?

In 1973, for instance, executives at Eastman Kodak, the photographic products company, heard an internal talk on labour relations. 'Today our biggest fear' the speaker told them, 'is the international trade union movement. Its long-term objective is to have full colllective bargaining with multinational corporations.'

Fourteen years on, that seems nearly laughable. International bargaining remains a distant union dream, while the growth of the multinationals' sophistication has outstripped the desperate efforts of unions to match their strength. At the same time, little impact has been made by governments, let alone unions, on companies' freedom to:

- open and close plants;
- switch investment between countries;
- wield economic and political influence.

But there are exceptions. Unions representing Ford workers in Britain, West Germany, Spain, Belgium and Portugal are threatening to support industrial action 'up to and including occupation' if Ford closes a European plant. A rare 'success' has been achieved in saving a Coca-Cola bottling plant in Guatemala City from closure after a 12-month occupation and campaign by the International Union of Foodworkers. This involved strikes at Coca-Cola plants in Sweden, Norway and Mexico, along with short stoppages in Italy and a consumer boycott in the United States. At Kodak itself, a 'European Kodak Workers' Conference' has been pressing – unsuccessfully – for talks on investment plans and lobbying the EEC to investigate the company, in response to fears that Kodak is systematically running down plants across Europe.

Shopfloor representatives have also been trying to develop inter-national links, with mixed results, in companies like Unilever, Philips, ICI (Imperial Chemical Industries), Talbot and Merck. As a result, companies are keeping a wary eye open, knowing that the growth of multinationals leaves unions no option but to carry on trying to operate internationally.

Management attention is further necessary as international compan-ies not only integrate production between countries, but also become more sophisticated in their ability to shop around for cheap labour. American Airlines and Bank of America, for instance, ship cartons of data forms to Barbados and Brazil to be keyed into computer terminals, and then relayed to central records offices by satellite. Texas Ins-truments, Control Data, and IBM develop software in India and teletransmit it to the United States and other markets via satellite. Wages in India are 10 per cent of those in Europe and America for roughly equal skills. Smith Corona, the US office-equipment maker, has taken shopping around a step further: instead of moving factories, it is shifting the workers. It is bringing 149 young, unmarried South Korean women to work at its Singapore plant, living in company lodgings.

While such moves can be decided by some executive down the line with the know-how to take the initiative, it is unthinkable that the board of directors does not know about them and approves them. This is a different way of saying that decisions with corporate-wide implications must be taken with full knowledge of the situation. They should be reached at the top level of the corporation: the board itself.

NOTES

1. See also the discussion in Chapter 13 on the *International Board* I helped institute in a foremost multinational industrial enterprise.
2. *Business Week*, 23 November 1987.
3. Financial Times, 19 November 1987.

13 Organisational Perspectives in Multinational Business

In every corporation, whether national or multinational, the number one goal of organisation and structure is to permit more efficient communications. Communications flow in two ways: top–down as orders and directives; botton–up as information which will permit successive management layers to make documented and factual decisions. Both sides of the information flow must be fast, accurate, and unobstructed. Computers and communications can play a key role in this regard, but they will not substitute for rusty or poor management. Throwing money at the problem is no way to a solution.

While these statements are always valid, they do also help to size up corporations. Coping with information demands posed by national business is a pillow on which few companies can rest comfortably. It is full of uncertainty and difficulty – but also full of challenge. Analytical, and occasionally unconventional, thinking is required by executives who must be adaptable and competent. They should understand business and social conditions abroad. More than that, they must learn entirely new patterns of thought and behaviour if they are to cope successfully.

In some countries, companies have to compete with state-controlled industrial combines; in others, with privately owned monopolies. Not only do industries vary, but also the laws and regulations of business are far from being the same from country to country. The variety and complexity of multinational business are infinite. This is a basic reason why even companies which have made great strides abroad have not always found the climate favourable to their evolution.

Companies usually complain of trade barriers imposed at the frontiers, and correctly. Many of these trade barriers have been erected in the most ramshackle way imaginable. Still, while trade barriers are an impediment, the salient problem lies in communications. It is not just a matter of establishing and serving some communications channels. The requirements go much deeper, all the way to the human relations. A thorough examination of what it takes to establish a valid and functioning human organisation should be the starting point in examining organisational perspectives. All other issues are subsequent to this requirement.

OVERCOMING COMMUNICATIONS BARRIERS

Communications barriers exist between people – not just between organisational units. They may be due to different cultures, language problems, jargon and semantics, different taste and personal distaste, aggressive or defensive attitudes. In all these cases the chemistry does not work well.

When communications barriers have a low profile, we usually say that people, and therefore organisations, can communicate. But the way to start a communications study within a multinational enterprise is to consider that these barriers exist – then study ways and means for overcoming them.

Twenty-one years ago, in 1966, I made a world-wide research project on the communications subject for the American Management Association. Information for this study was obtained through lengthy interviews and correspondence with 143 people in 17 countries. Of these participants, 114 were company executives: 42 presidents, vice-presidents and other officers, 39 directors and senior managers, and 33 other members of management. The other 29 were consultants, government officials and academicians. The participants were situated in four continents.[1] The following references highlight in the results.

The first obligation of a multinational corporation is to create sound policies to guide communication. Since such policies must be applicable throughout the company's operations, they must have enough flexibility to cover immediate situations that are characteristic of each country.

To tackle multinational problems in an able manner, management must face head-on communications challenges, instead of shying away from them. Most executives working abroad – whether they are American, Japanese, English, Swiss, German, Italian or French – said that they had great difficulty communicating with headquarters. Subsequently most headquarters executives responded that they had no feeling of communication barriers between themselves and the subsidiaries. This lack of sensitivity should be a danger signal to corporations. The way to start examining communications barriers is by accepting the fact of life that there *is* a communications problem in the operations abroad. If headquarters don't see it, that's too bad.

The reason for underlining these facts is the need to bring to the attention of the board of directors the weak linkages in running the corporations. Satellite channels will be used to bring together the corporate executives in New York, London, Zurich and Tokyo. But is the human component ready to receive the message?

Men seasoned in international business know from experience that people sometimes fight one another not because they misunderstand a situation but because they understand it only too well. This was confirmed by a horde of examples provided by the aforementioned research in 17 countries.

Some of the senior executives whom I met abroad indicated that they had done everything possible to inform others about their situations, but they were met with silence, irrelevant responses and compromises. And, although some of the compromises were consistent and based on sound business principles, they did not necessarily result in greater efficiency.

In each corporate subsidiary that was visited, executives remarked that their subsidiary had its own special needs, demands and problems. To say that these are only policy or procedural differences would be to deliberately oversimplify the situation. Psychological factors are very important, since they tend to widen the gap between headquarters and the subsidiaries and cloud communications. In many companies that have suffered from ineffectual communication, executives have refused for psychological reasons to be pushed into spending money for new systems or changing procedures – when they could have found very sound policy or procedural reasons for refusing.

Companies that try to control the communications jungle with budgetary tools may find them more of a disadvantage than an advantage, as emphasised by one international executive: 'Budgetary strings are proving to be more useful to the meak and the ignorant who want to abide by the rules than to people who are willing to sail close to the wind.'

Once the most basic communications layer is well served, it is time to streamline the physical aspect of information exchange. In this regard, the best advice is to eliminate communications on mirror subjects, which represent half the paper going through the pipeline. Chopping the dead wood out of communications will sharply alter the cost of information handling, while making an efficient framework possible. To improve the quality of communications the multinational corporation should:

- critically examine their characteristics;
- determine their frequency;
- study their impact in terms of end results.

Although this may seem obvious, it is rarely practised, since most communications networks grow like wild cacti.

The able use of computers and communications comes precisely at this point. Supposing the corporate executives work through intelligent, multifunctional computer-based workstations, we should see to it that they definitely have any-to-any connectivity – and that they are attached on *one logical network*, no matter how many physical networks are beneath it.

Let me, however, repeat what I have so often underlined: it is men, not machines, that make the organisation tick. We must make the image of communication reflect the nature and structure of the organisation. Many corporations have confirmed that this is more difficult than it sounds.

Communication does not necessarily follow classical organisational patterns; in fact, the clash between them is sometimes very apparent. At times, forgetting the human component results in great inefficiencies, especially when companies do not plan and prepare for worldwide expansion.

One of these inefficiencies is the cost of misinformation. A basic axiom about communication in international companies needs to be stressed at the outset: able information exchange can be achieved by:

- lowering fences;
- opening channels;
- minimising paperwork;
- keeping messages brief and to the point.

It can also be achieved by:

- decentralising the foreign subsidiaries;
- evaluating their performance on the basis of profit and loss and ability to meet objectives.

Purposeless reporting often gives companies a distorted picture of the progress abroad and leads them to serious miscalculations.

The board of directors may be misguided into believing that international companies can solve their communication problems simply by introducing faster methods. Although computers are bound to play a role in the future, they will be subordinate to human imperatives – and this is what the present section aims to underline.

Every company should be interested in efficiently solving the communications problem which I have presented. Evidently, this is all the more important for larger firms where control is more difficult to exercise because of size. Catastrophies occur when firms shrug off shocks and danger signs. Where this happens, the fault lies with the board of directors and the chief executive officer. They have been isolated, buffeted, disconnected from their markets, seldom knowing anything is wrong until it is too late.

SOURCES OF PRODUCTIVITY AND INCOME

Raymond Barre, the former French Prime Minister, once suggested that: 'Companies must admit once and for all that it is not the strong franc, but their own management that explains their export problems.' 'This statement could not be closer to the truth, and the board of directors should take notice.

Often companies choose to go international, not in order to expand their geographical dimensions and cover new markets, but only to capitalise on cheaper labour. That's not good management. Cheaper labour for its own sake is an ephemeral advantage, and cheaper labour may have other strings attached to it, for instance, lower skill and lack of tradition. The board of directors should appreciate it is not only the absolute level of wages that counts, but also the productivity which goes with them.

Another mistake often done at the board level of multinational corporations is to believe that product and marketing patterns which prevail at the country of origin are valid, or nearly valid, in all other countries of operations. Nothing is more untrue. Product design requirements, product use patterns and market appeal vary widely from one continent to the other. Also, from one country to the other, as a US manufacturer was to discover when it studied patterns on microcomputer usage (Figure 13.1).

More investment, especially in advanced technology, is often seen as the key to raising the competitiveness of industry. Yet the explanation for low productivity lies not only in the amount of investment in new plant and machinery, but also in the way the plant is used. It is in the down-to-earth field of production management:

● proper scheduling,
● optimisation of resources,
● avoidance of frequent machine breakdowns,
● valid maintenance procedures,
● adequate attention to quality,
● proper quality control procedures,

where performance is demonstrably better than that of competitors. Deficiencies appear to stem from low technical competence on the part of managers, foremen and workers concerned with the production process. While the members of the board of directors are not supposed to go down the production line to correct such deficiencies, they should be aware of the company's weaknesses wherever they exist. In an

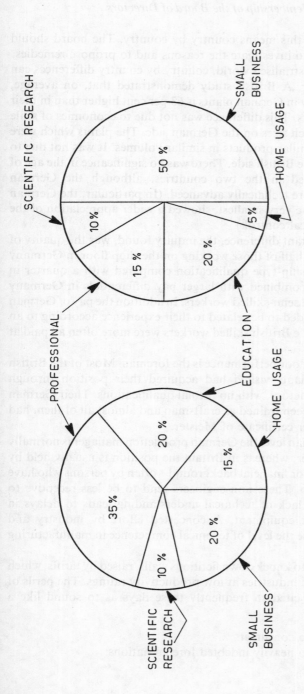

Figure 13.1 Pie-charts on the use of microcomputers in the United States and in Europe. The most striking differences are in the professional employment of personal computers and in the small business domain.

international firm, this means country by country. The board should command studies to investigate the reasons and to propose remedies.

Even in the industrialised world, country by country differences can be far from minor. A British study demonstrated that, on average, labour productivity in German plants is 63 per cent higher than in their British counterparts. This difference was not due to economies of scale such as greater batch sizes on the German side. The plants which were compared made similar products in similar volumes. It was not due to overmanning on the British side. There was no significance in the age of the machinery used in the two countries, although the German equipment was more technically advanced. (In particular, the German companies, even the very smallest, showed a wider appreciation of the benefits of numerical control.)

The most important difference, the inquiry found, was the quality of manpower. About half of those working on the shop floor in Germany had an apprenticeship-type qualification compared with a quarter in Britain. This was combined with larger pay differentials in Germany between skilled and semi-skilled workers. In addition the pay of German skilled workers tended to be related to their experience according to an accepted scale, while British skilled workers were more often all paid at the same rate.

Crucial to shop floor performance is the foreman. Most of the British foreman in the plants visited had acquired their position through experience in the factory, with no formal qualifications. Their German counterparts had been trained as craftsman and almost all of them had acquired the higher certificate of Meister.

Above the foreman level the German production manager is normally a graduate engineer, whereas in Britain the position is usually held by people with a sales or financial background – often by persons who have learned on the job. These non-engineers tend to be less receptive to innovation. Their lack of technical understanding leads to delays in installing complex equipment. A concerted effort by industry and government to raise the level of technical competence in manufacturing is urgent.

Just as urgent is to knock down fictitious walls, raised by tariffs, which keep countries and industries at low productivity ratings. The perils of protectionism are cited so frequently these days as to sound like a familiar litany:

● the damage to consumers;
● the damage to heavily indebted foreign nations;

● the damage to the country's own exporters who might face retaliation

What is not stated with enough vigour are the risks for the companies whom trade restrictions are supposed to protect.

Since the board of directors often finances the lobbying for protectionist measures, its members should understand that relief from tough foreign competition may temporarily benefit protected industries. But they clearly run the danger of becoming fat and lazy:

● too comfortable with artificial prosperity;
● too loath to improve productivity;
● too willing to ignore shrinkage in their markets.

Eventually, they would become more vulnerable than ever. Furthermore, some of them risk widening the cyclical swings in the demand for their products.

The cyclicality of some basic US industries, for instance, may be increased if through formal voluntary quotas US companies fail to match imports in price or quality. In such a case, US firms cede major slices of markets to foreign competitors for good. Once foreigners expand sales, they are likely to keep their prices low, upgrade their products, and retain the increased level of sales. Then, with imports remaining fairly steady, US producers could degenerate into residual suppliers, forced to absorb a disproportionate percentage of the swings in overall demand. As a result, industrial instability would be increased.

These are notions which should not escape the attention of board members, but they often do. Otherwise the pressures exercised on the government to impose quotas for foreign producers could not be easily explained.

Take the small but pivotal machine-tool industry as an example. It seems to be slipping into a morass. In 1985 imported machines seized 36 per cent of the US market, up from 13 per cent a decade ago. Moreover, their market share rose every single year despite wide fluctuations in total US sales. American machinery makers now want quotas limiting foreign producers to 17.5 per cent of the US market. But quotas would give a firmer, though smaller, slice of the market to imports, and US industry's wild cyclical swings would be aggravated.

In a short-sighted manner, it is understandable that import-battered sectors, such as textiles and shoes, are attacking the problem of foreign competition through lobbying for quotas. What they fail to understand is that, in effect, they are creating another problem. In handing foreign rivals a relatively stable slice of the market, they are increasing their own insecurity. They keep capital and labour tied up in sectors condemned to low returns and to lay-offs. And they lose their chance of becoming really competitive.

It takes a board of directors' decision to become truly competitive – from funds to brains and guts. A multinational company cannot permit itself to be competitive in one market and uncompetitive in others. Stripped to their fundamentals, its policies must be universal. For instance, US multinational corporations in the automotive market should have the goal to become so competitive as to export cars to Japan – not just to recover the market share the Japanese motor manufacturers have taken in the US market. As a goal it is *do-able*, as the Japanese export drive helps document.

The growing need for such an international perspective can be better appreciated if we consider that before the end of this century probably 500 of the most dynamic international companies will control two-thirds of the industrial wealth of the world. Only the fittest would enter this class. The concentration of power brings stiffer competition. Such concentration is even greater if we bring into account the projection that about 50 organisations will control more than a quarter of the total wealth. This group will typically include up to ten entities from each of the key sectors: banking, insurance, computers, communications, systems integrators, construction firms, motor manufacturing and machine tool/robotics. Figure 13.2 shows the number of the more important multinational companies, their country of origin and its share in the multi-national business. Though this number is today in excess of 800, mergers, acquisitions and consolidations are powerful forces behind its reduction.

In each and every one of the previously mentioned industries survival will call for the highest grade management talent and for open lines of communication. Only well informed wizards will be capable of holding in one piece:

- multi-billion-dollar corporations,
- organised along multi-product and multinational lines,
- coping in an efficient manner with the mega-problems which are expected to result.

The management of change, flexibility and adjustments to the ever-developing conditions are major assets. Many corporations are too large to get along in a world of dynamic change with the best communications system. Top management becomes out of touch. Senior executives lose

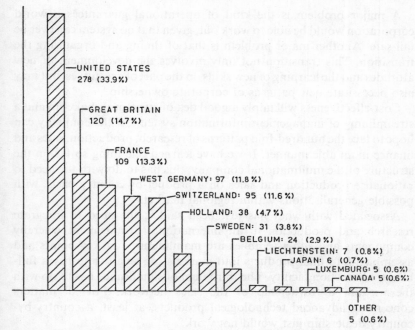

UNITED STATES
278 (33.9%)

GREAT BRITAIN
120 (14.7%)

FRANCE
109 (13.3%)

WEST GERMANY: 97 (11.8%)

SWITZERLAND: 95 (11.6%)

HOLLAND: 38 (4.7%)

SWEDEN: 31 (3.8%)

BELGIUM: 24 (2.9%)

LIECHTENSTEIN: 7 (0.8%)

JAPAN: 6 (0.7%)

LUXEMBURG: 5 (0.6%)

CANADA: 5 (0.6%)

OTHER
5 (0.6%)

Figure 13.2   Statistics on the national origin of international companies. The US dominates, followed by Britain. West Germany and Switzerland are surprisingly at par. Japan is still behind.

the loyalty and respect of their key middle managers – the more so in a sprawling worldwide empire.

DESIGNING A WORLD CORPORATION

Companies said to be oriented toward a world-corporation approach look, by definition, at the entire international market as one unified area of operations. They reach out everywhere for business opportunites, from people to money and products. The idea may sound simply wonderful, but there really is more to it than might seem at first to be the case. For one thing, the questions which are raised in terms of multinational operations now take a new weight: 'Will a centrally located staff, which until recently was interested in one market, a staff interwoven in an age-old philosophy of doing business, be able to stand up to, say, a hundred-country challenge?'

A major problem is the kind of operational guarantees a world corporation would be able to work out, given that no system can ever be fail-safe. Another major problem is that of timing and organising the transition. This transition not only involves the development of new attitudes and the learning of new skills on the part of executives, but may also necessitate new patterns of corporate ownership.

Cost-effectiveness will imply a good dea of structural shake-up and a streamlining of management information systems, if the company can hope to face the hundred-fold patterns of research, production, sales and finance in an able manner. If we have learned one thing so far on the structure of the multinational company, this has to do with the need to rationalise production and sales on a product-by-country basis, with possible generalisations within regional markets.

Associated with what has just been said is the need to integrate research and production in an international arrangement whereby components and sub-assemblies are manufactured at key points and assembled into final products into markets too small to justify a full-blown production facility. The third item of significance has to do with the wisdom of ownership of the sales network. For all matters concerning advanced technological products, at least, a country-by-country dealership just would not work.

Due emphasis should also be given to the need to centralise financial matters in the corporate headquarters. Here we would tend to favour the DuPont and General Motors approach, dividing the financial from the operating network – and thus availing top management with an efficient means for information feedback and unbiased control. At least until a worldwide industrial *esprit de corps* is developed, centralisation of decision would be particularly beneficial in the areas of investment planning, capital budget co-ordination, and the use of capital sources. This does not contradict what was said on the need for board members to get international perspectives and/or to create a separate international board of management. Indeed it reinforces the background reasons for this distinction. If in the last analysis key problems are to be centrally decided, to counterbalance the centrifugal forces at work in any organisation, then both international perspective and knowhow must be at a high point. At the same time, running the financial and operational networks separately facilitates to some degree both adaptation and control.

Operation-wise, an independence of the financial network would tend to give greater regional autonomy in research, manufacturing and marketing, though here again some functions such as product planning, reliability and sales quotas would need to be centrally co-ordinated. Within this framework, it is also reasonable to say that when the line and staff groups of the foreign subsidiaries are built up to an acceptable point of efficiency, they should enjoy a greater degree of autonomy in making operating decisions.

Among worldwide corporations, some have consistently pursued, and with good reason, another item of great significance: the exclusive hiring, training and usage of local personnel, from the top executive level downwards. IBM, for one, has almost centred its operations on the training and the development of able indigenous personnel. These include not only the employees of engineering, manufacturing, sales and service divisions, but also the chief executive of each operating country and his immediate assistants. Only some 0.2 per cent of the IBM World Trade employees outside of the United States are US citizens. Most of them are working on assignments in area headquarters and provide the bridges with the parent corporation.

Not only it is very important to nurture local personnel, but it is also the right time to do it. There is today in most Western countries a new guard. It is energetic, bold, financially sophisticated, and committed to getting ahead through hard work rather than family connections. While many of the old executive stock have strong ties with heavy industry, the younger generation is cashing in on the explosion of the service economy and the opportunities presented by emerging technologies. Such go-getters simply do not belong in any old-boy network.

A major role in this change of minds is being played by the technological innovation which is making its way through to daily working lives. The proportion of information workers in the US economy rose from 49 per cent in 1962–72 to roughly 60 per cent in 1986. (European statistics stand at about 50 per cent.) There is now more capital investment for each information worker than for each manu-facturing worker. Communications networks link together the multi-national corporation, and information workers are by excellence communicators. At the same time, there is a feeling of insecurity which paradoxically clusters people into multinational lots. How different this is from the beginning of this century!

Stefan Zweig describes the turn-of-the-century confidence in his book *The World of Yesterday*:

> When I attempt to find a simple formula for the period in which I grew up, prior to World War I, I hope that I convey its fullness by calling it the Golden Age of Security. Everything in our almost thousand-year-

old Austrian monarchy seemed based on permanency, and the State itself was the chief guarantor of this stability. In this vast empire everything stood firmly and immovably in its appointed place. At its head was the aged emperor. Were he to die, one knew (or believed) another would come to take his place, and nothing would change in the well-regulated order. No one thought of wars, or revolutions, or revolts. All that was radical, all violence, seemed impossible in an age of reason.

Our time, at the end of the century whose beginning Zweig described as the 'Age of Reason' has little to do with stability. It is the 'Age of Knowledge' and knowledge implies steady change.

It takes a major upheaval to bring a new epoch into being, and this is just as true of nations as of corporations. Vienna was delivered from the Second Turkish Siege in 1683 by a victorious battle. But the Turks also gained as defeat led to political renewal. While the general who led the Siege of Vienna was invited by the Sultan to commit suicide, the new Turkish empire was characterised by *meritocracy*. The slave people owned by the empire took over the reigns. The change brought about by the Sultan's initiative extended the life of the empire for about 250 years.

Meritocracy is once again the key to survival, and the core of the world corporation. That is why clear-eyed international organisations push through ambitious management education programmes. Their goal is to improve competitiveness but also to tie the system together. The teaching forces the participants to reach the painful recognition that management skills make the difference in:

● ability to practice market segmentation;
● product positioning;
● marketing techniques.

Such programmes initiated by multinational companies focus on individual and company-wide learning. They are involving strategic and organisational skills as well as marketing. Without steady comprehensive training, the country-by-country operations risk having a poor grasp of marketing, lack clear strategies, and consist of inflexible and loosely connected departmental and geographic empires organised along traditionally functional lines.

No company without the commitment to build this sort of educational capability can call itself multinational. A company's products and technology are purely transient but the human capital stays. It is the human capital that really differentiates companies from one another.

Just as important to the world corporation is the creation of a common language and the setting of strategic and organisational concepts. The same is true of the ability to respond quickly to change, and also to initiate it. The world corporation must be prepared to change the strategy quickly, and the organisation with it. Here again, the board of directors must take the initiative and show the way. Until this is done, change would stall.

Experience in this sense is positive. Said the executive of a company which has been able to revamp itself and experience a turnaround: 'Two years ago organizational changes stunned the company, and people went into the state of paralysis. Now we are doing them all the time.'

A BOARD FOR MULTINATIONAL OPERATIONS

One of the principal problems to be studied by the board of directors is the criteria and parameters that determine the policies and actions needed for international operations. Also important is to establish the level of detail in terms of involvement, and the media and channels used in the international scene.

In my consultancy I have examined different solutions. One of the most successful is that chosen and implemented by a West German firm with operations in sixty countries and factories in a third of them. The solution was the establishment of a separate board, subordinate to the principal one. There were good reasons for this choice which was made by Professor Albert Prinzing, then president of the company.

The international board operates from a certain geographical distance. Therefore its decisions and policies require an effective methodology. In the case of the multinational firm referred to, experience dictated that a board dedicated to multinational operations achieved better reliability of results. Figure 13.3 reflects this reference plotting for one of the main countries of operations, revenues and employment against time. Through the instrument of the International Board, investments were followed on an individual basis rather than being lumped together in an amorphous chapter 'overseas' as the practice usually is with multinational companies.

Focussing country-by-country, and having been given the mission to make these country-by-country operations work as a network, permitted the members of the International Board to acquire a broader knowledge of the situation in which each subsidiary operates. This is a valid step toward the possibility of better management. It was enhanced through the constitution of the international board.

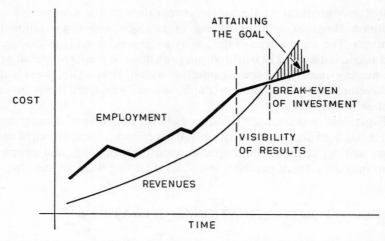

Figure 13.3 To bend the curve of employment a leading organisation embarked on an ambitious automation programme. Attaining the goal has been preceded by a phase where results were highly visible.

Since the beginning it was decided that the international company, instead of trying to control every detail of worldwide operations, should set objectives. Both factors are important:

● They influence communications;
● they affect the acquisition and retention of able executives.

To increase the sensitivity of headquarters – hence of the international board – to foreign conditions, managerial positions at the international division were filled with executives who had experience abroad. Several managerial jobs were allocated to foreign executives in the service of the firm. In other words, it was found to be a good practice to invite subsidiary managers to attend courses or other planned meetings at headquarters lasting several days at a time. This way the international board members could meet their counterparts around the world and develop a common base of thought, principles and aims. This approach was instrumental in giving the members of the international board a much better background in business approach than their frequent but short visits to other countries could provide. It also offered them the evidence that the basic operations of the foreign subsidiaries were no different from those that each one of them knew from his country of origin.

Effective problem solution was another advantage. Many problems can never be really solved until the board of directors includes men with multinational experience – not just the flying tourist type. The international board had only people with these qualifications. Said the president of another firm who saw the experience:

To us, this has not happened yet. If you examine the type of men of the Board of our multinational company, you will find only one who has had international experience. Members are picked for their banking connections, their business or governmental associations, and their proved experience in domestic operations. But not for skill in international practice.

Table 13.1 outlines the established *responsibilities* and *indicators* of the international board. The responsibilities present the most important functions. The indicators explain in a few paragraphs how these functions should be interpreted.

NOTE

1. D. N. Chorafas, *Developing the International Executive* and *Overcoming Communications Barriers in International Operations* New York; (sponsored and published by the American Management Association, 1966 and 1967 respectively.

Table 13.1 The international board

Responsibilities	Indicators
1 Acts as a clearing house for capital, skill, and experience, in (*a*) marketing, (*b*) manufacturing, (*c*) finance and personnel.	● Reflects the local operations, synchronising their aims with those of the central corporate authority. ● Assists in corporate strategic planning through study and evaluation of general economic trends and future developments at the international level and by country of operations. ● Helps in balancing the corporate business strategy by shifting the centre of gravity of activities and profits from one territory to another. ● Acts as the review board for new products and techniques of manufacturing developed by domestic operations and those of the subsidiaries abroad with R & D facilities. ● Consults on warehousing problems, procedures and investments in regional/country stocks. ● Assists the chairman of the board and the president in fact-finding missions. Also in seeing through initiatives originating in board meetings and affecting the operating subsidiaries.
2 Acts in an advisory capacity to the chairman, the president and the members of the board of directors, in directing foreign operations on a profit centre basis.	● Helps in appraising foreign operations and in running the international division on a profit-centre basis. ● Suggests needed organisational surveys to be carried out by the three main divisions of the international staff: marketing, development/manufacturing, and finance/administration/personnel. ● Advises the board of directors on top organisational planning for all international activities. Decides on this issue and implements its decision, after consultation with the board. ● Assists in developing objectives and policies; and in adapting domestic management practices to foreign operations.

- Advises on human relations studies (including public and industrial relations) to be carried out by finance/administration/personnel.
- Consults on executive development programme, management inventory studies, and executive compensation plans.
- Reviews and evaluates appraisals of alternative methods for supplying foreign markets.
- Assists in handling (*a*) international trade agreements; (*b*) foreign exchange controls; (*c*) procedural and policy studies affecting corporate international operations.

---

3 Assists in the definition of efficiency measures in implementing marketing approaches and in establishing objectives for sales achievements.

- Supervises the development, installation and administration of methods, procedures and facilities required to accomplish sales objectives and marketing programmes.
- Screens the international price list proposed by the corporate vice-president of marketing prior to approval by the corporate board of directors.
- Proceeds with sales volume and cost analysis estimates, including discount policies.
- Evaluates the wisdom of analytical studies made to determine whether corporate products made for domestic operations can meet foreign demands.
- Investigates trade conditions prevailing in foreign countries and studies their effects on the corporate business.
- Looks for opportunities for greater market penetration and the exploitation of new foreign fields.
- Examines and recommends improvements in existing products, where desirable, to meet competitive conditions.

Table 13.1 The international board—*continued*

4 Evaluates established international sales quotas and submits periodic reports in conjunction with same.	● Helps the board of directors' international marketing by area and by country's (*a*) share of the market; (*b*) annual growth in sales; (*c*) profit margin. ● Examines forecasts concerning annual sales by country of operations; develops accordingly policies and marketing plans; authorises sales, advertising, sales promotion and products service. ● Keeps abreast of sales surveys to determine market potentials as a function of available and coming products, local taste and living conditions. ● Examines the co-ordination of: (*a*) manufacturing and (*b*) sales perspectives of international operations. ● Provides the corporate board, both informally and in report form, with statements of results achieved in comparison with programmes and budgets – in international operations. ● Screens opportunities for licensing arrangements for overseas manufacturers.
5 Recommends to the corporate board policies governing promotion and advertising.	● Consults on international advertising, the appropriate internal departments and outside agencies (abroad) and makes policy and/or action proposals suitable for international markets. ● Advises on new trade marks. ● Consults on the development of special unit packaging required for specific markets. ● Evaluates the findings of market research on international sales perspectives and optimal advertising approaches, making documented proposals to the corporate board. ● Co-ordinates the flow of visits of international distributors and customers to domestic and foreign plants. ● Co-operates with industry groups directly interested in international trade.

6 Advises the corporate board on market orientation regarding the product lines which are offered abroad.

- Evaluates the composition of the product line in foreign operations.
- Consults on the marketability of new products developed both by domestic R & D and in the foreign laboratories.
- Periodically reviews and screens the existing corporate worldwide product lines.
- Consults on the most profitable 'product mix' to secure sales performance abroad.

7 Guarantees that the international manufacturing network will be at all times at top operating condition.

- Helps the corporate board of directors in allocating the necessary funds among subsidiaries to lower the unit cost of production.
- Evaluates all activities concerning manufacturing; production planning and control; plant engineering; and purchasing abroad.
- Promotes the transmission of needed technical information which must assure a two-way communication from domestic to international and from abroad to domestic.
- Suggests needed procedural steps so that all foreign subsidiaries receive regularly the information pertinent to the manufacturing, tooling and processing requirements.

8 Advises the corporate board on how the international subsidiaries can perform a responsible job in the economical manufacture and shipment of products according to the approved production budgets, while meeting quality standards.

- Supervises the engineering work done abroad so that it is in total co-ordination with the R & D operations domestically and in selected countries.
- Reviews the technical organisational structure to guarantee the best interests of the corporation.
- Helps the headquarters staff in locating and correcting deficiencies in quality, wherever they may arise.
- Evaluates factory inventory control by country of manufacture, deciding on reorganisation whenever necessary.

Table 13.1   The international board—*continued*

9 Assures that all international investments are according to corporate policies.	• Examines the financing of export shipments, the return on investment and the profits to the corporation from such shipments. • Investigates issues confronting 'free export', especially the small capital base from which most dealers abroad operate – and takes corrective steps. • Helps identify capital requirement needs, forecasting profit margin possibilities, and deciding accordingly. • Assists corporate management in conducting consolidated cash flow studies and cash requirement evaluations. • Helps in supervising the cost/savings estimates, and takes steps to improve them. • Evaluates financial performance by country, region and consolidated, against the plans approved by the corporate board of directors.
10 Helps the corporate board in guaranteeing that the financial, administrative and personnel operations contribute to the realisation of the strategic plans.	• Assists through its advice in establishing and maintaining corporate financial goals and policies. • Provides a basis for developing relationships with each financial community of company operations abroad. • Examines and reacts to negotiations on financial agreements with leading institutions abroad. • Helps in setting performance standards for effective manpower planning. • Advises on whether or not the subsidiaries abroad are staffed with qualified people, and on the corrective action which is necessary. • Consults, evaluates, and decides on the needed management skills and specialities throughout the international operations. • Advises on personnel hiring and training in all subsidiaries abroad, meeting challenges in human resources. • Consults the corporate board of directors on matters concerning salary administration including: job description, salary evaluation, salary structures and performance appraisal.

11 Helps the corporate board of directors assure that each region and country of operations attains all financial company goals and objectives.

- Advises the corporate board on the development of short, medium, and long-range plans concerning international operations.
- Supervises and consults on whether financial systems are applied in a consistent and homogeneous manner throughout the corporation by means of (a) management audits; (b) financial analysis; (c) cost control; (e) expense reduction programmes; (f) the implementation of management information systems.
- Compares existing with anticipated requirements defining new management positions in terms of responsibilities, functions and duties.

14 The Big Corporations' Fear: Litigation

Big corporations, particularly the international companies, have a constant fear of litigation – and for good reason. With their operations in five continents, working in countries of totally different legal systems and customer mentality, litigation can become a nightmare. But international operations are not the only source of legal problems. For some firms, even in their own country of origin there has been the chilling impact of court action, with sky-rocketing legal costs and a heavy burden on the time schedules of their senior executives.

Taking IBM as an example, the rumour has it that the company spends an impressive 2 per cent of its yearly business in legal actions the world over. Pressed by governments, its competitors, and some of its own clientele. IBM has often faced expensive settlements.

Litigation is a totally different world from that in which the welfare state and friendly politicians have influence. As the presiding judge in a recent US decision put it: 'There is no authority for, and no logic in, assuming that either party to a litigation is entitled to a certain percentage of favorable decisions.' Litigation is tough, costly, and its outcome far from certain. It has always existed, but the wave of litigation really started in the mid-to-late 1960s. As an example, Table 14.1 presents in a nutshell the history of ten years of IBM court cases in the United States (1968–77).

The decade of the 1970s discovered the easy access to courts, which has been a fact of life for centuries, and encouraged the legal action – the few against practically every big firm. In the early 1970s, for instance, General Motors found itself as a defendant against a class action brought on behalf of 'all persons everywhere now alive and all future unborn generations' charging GM with pollution and seeking $6 trillion in damages.

There is fact and fiction associated with liability suits. One of the myths is that the easier it is to collect damages, the more protection consumers have. In some fields, like health care, ease in collecting awards has done more harm than good to the bulk of consumers by slowing the development of important new technologies. As Frank E. Samuel, Jr, President of Health Industry Manufacturers Association, Washing DC, pointed out in a letter to *Business Week*,[1] under the

Table 14.1   Ten years of litigation

1968	*CDC* v. *IBM* filed; IBM seeks settlement.
1969	DOJ* suit filed. Pre-trial discovery begins.
1971	*Greyhound* v. *IBM* filed.
1972	*Telex* v. *IBM* filed; *Greyhound* v. *IBM* dismissed; *Greyhound* v. *IBM* appeal filed; Judge Edelstein assigned to the DOJ case.
1973	*CDC* v. *IBM* settled; *Telex* v. *IBM* decision; *Calcomp* v. *IBM* filed; *Hudson* v. *IBM* filed; *Marshall* v. *IBM* filed; *Memorex* v. *IBM* filed; *Transamerica* v. *IBM* filed; CDC database destroyed.
1974	*Telex* v. *IBM* appeal filed; *Telex* v. *IBM* appeal decision; *Telex* v. *IBM* Supreme Court appeal filed; *Marshall* v. *IBM* settled; *Telex* v. *IBM* settled; *DOJ* v. *IBM* discovery ends and trial begins.
1976	*Memory Technology* v. *IBM* settled; *DOJ* v. *IBM* trial enters 2nd year – 29 witnesses, 133 trial days to this date.
1977	*Sanders* v. *IBM* settled; *Calcomp* v. *IBM* dismissed; *DOJ* v. *IBM* enters 3rd year – 42 witnesses, 330 trial days to this date.

*US Department of Justice

patchwork of confusing – often conflicting – state laws, many juries award damages against manufacturers even when it is not clear that their products caused injury. Hence, rather than pushing the frontiers of medical science, manufacturers are playing it safe, channelling research away from avant-garde technologies.

LITIGATION UNLIMITED: ITS SOCIAL IMPACT

Starting with the decade of the 1970s civil suits filed in the US federal courts grew by an impressive 84 per cent over the 1960s. At the same time, litigants are becoming constantly bolder. A legal study estimated that if the growth rate of federal appeals remains constant, by the year 2010 there will be 1 million appeals decided each year, requiring 5,000 judges – up by a factor of 50 from the average number of federal appeals judges available in the decade referred to (1970s). Such litigation statistics are staggering. If appeals run at about 10 per cent of the total cases initiated, that would mean the courts could be hit with 10 million cases annually. And the costs of litigation have sky-rocketed as companies are hit with more lawsuits that take longer to complete.

Even when a company wins a case, it loses financially because of growing defence costs. A court case also distracts management attention. Often, it brings uncertainty to management decisions, thus bringing important projects in jeopardy. The social impact from these facts is not necessarily appreciated. Yet they are the hidden costs of litigation, which often outpace the more visible costs of fees and associated expenses. What is more, the hidden costs are being paid both by the firms and by society – which is just as true of the real costs of the legal system itself.

Another of the hidden costs is the impact of delays. For industry litigation can breed interminable delays, during which plans for important projects must be shelved or even killed. With the number of cases brought to the attention of the courts on the increase, the always notorious delays in the legal process have grown worse. And there is a social impact from the fact that the legal system is being co-involved by the process which tends to make litigation the primary method of treating all significant problems in our society.

Delays due to litigation can have a far-reaching effect as businessmen factor into their decisions the potential of conflict in court at every level:

● the government;
● the stockholders;
● the public – that is, consumers at large;
● the environmentalists.

Unlimited litigation presents unpredictable, tough, potentially gigantic financial hazards. In the area of product liability, the risks have been especially marked. But antitrust and securities cases can have similar dangers.

Like a typical taxi ride, costs are incurred throughout the course of a court action, not only at the end. Starting at the beginning of the litigation process itself, there is the cost of lawyers' time during the lengthy pre-trial manoeuvreing known as 'discovery'. In the mid-1970s a $2 million settlement of shareholder suits against several of Gulf Oil Corporation's former officers for operating an unlawful political slush fund, yielded only $300,000 for the company. The balance of $1.7 million went to lawyers on both sides of the controversy. For the better known law firms, the entry price is over $1 million. 'No major law firm can afford to handle a case worth less than $1 million,' said a top lawyer. While the largest companies might in the last analysis afford these costs, few smaller companies can do so.

Then there is the ongoing cost, which itself can be sizeable. Solutions will necessarily be piecemeal because they usually respond to multifaceted legal problems with no single or simple root cause.

Quite understandably, any general strategy to combat the rising tide of litigation must take account of:

- technological advances;
- demographic changes;
- a vast wave of new legislation;
- a judical revolution that has produced thousands of new claims and new plaintiffs.

In response to the growth of population and the spread of an ever more complex technology, a massive amount of legislation has been pouring out of Congress and the state legislatures. Some estimates put *the annual total of new laws* from US legislatures at 150,000. Scores of environmental, consumer, health, safety, and civil rights statutes have opened the doors to new legislation – and from there to state and federal courts. Therefore, it may come as no surprise that in one single year the federal district courts in Kentucky and West Virginia reported that cases filed with them increased more than 50 per cent. 'More people are convinced that companies are selling more defective products than years ago,' a legal expert was to remark. As Judge Hufstedler stated: 'Discovery rules permit a rich opponent to paper a poor one to death.' Bundling together a host of small claims against a company consolidates the damages sought – and makes it worth while for lawyers to take on the litigation.

All this creates a vicious circle. As we will see in the *US* v. *IBM* section, under the Federal Rules of Civil Procedure, private litigants are free to call on their adversaries for the documents hidden in their cabinets and databases. Of course, they are just as free to take depositions from all witnesses. In the various antimonopoly cases against IBM, from the late 1960s to the late 1970s, discovery led to 64 million documents being pulled from the company's files. No lawyer can or will pass up the opportunity to study such documents – and this both for professional and for financial reasons.

Liberally interpreted discovery rules can produce extensive delays and staggering costs. It is also becoming a favourite tactic of persons suing corporations to ask for specific directors make depositions. Thus, they are taking them away from their work over relatively lengthy stretches of time – while lawyers and judges struggle to determine the facts in fields which are extremely complex and technical.

Such is indeed the background of the *US* v. *IBM* case. 'Judges,' said the Court of Appeals in refusing IBM's claim of prejudice against Chief Justice Edelstein, 'while expected to possess more than an average amount of self-restraint, are still only human. They do not possess limitless ability, once passion is aroused, to resist provocation.' The Court of Appeals was further to add that given the 'seemingly interminable length' of the IBM case, 'even the most stoic might well lose patience. . .' As a bad case comes never alone, in January 1981 the EEC Commission challenged IBM for violating antitrust rules, abusing its dominant position in Western Europe's multi-billion-dollar computer market. 'IBM is confident that we have fully complied with the rules of the EEC and, in the course of 1981, we will respond formally. Later, depending on how the EEC reacts, there could be an appeal to the European Court of Justice in Luxembourg,' an IBM spokesman said at the time in Paris. Prior to this case concerning IBM's promise for closer collaboration with European suppliers, the legal battle extended through years in an otherwise sterile environment of claims and counterclaims.

In this, as in so many other trials, in no way can society be said to be the winner. The earlier 'disclosure of interconnect features in IBM equipment may be important commercially to some of IBM's competitors, which are also commercial firms being in business for a profit. But it does not benefit society as much. Yet society has to pay the cost of litigation, as the court system through which this case went is in the budget of the European Community.

INTERPRETING THE SHERMAN ACT

The Sherman and Clayton Acts in the United States were to protect consumers from paying the price of being at the mercy of suppliers who are dominant in their industry. That essentially is what the various antitrust charges against IBM have been about. Size and the risk of a monopoly have been at the base of litigation against IBM and, at other times, against AT&T, General Motors, or other large firms. Since the IBM affair is now closed, we can look back and reflect over what has been accomplished by the court action. 'Practically nothing' would be a pragmatic answer. But some would even say it was counterproductive.

In 1968, IBM had between 60 and 65 per cent of the world market for mainframes and was practically no player in the minicomputer arena. The so-called BUNCH (Burroughs, Univac, NCR, Control Data, Honeywell) controlled the balance of the market in the United States – a little less abroad, accounting for local vendors. DEC was a tiny player focusing on a niche. Almost twenty years later IBM and the IBM compatibles control between 80 and 85 per cent of the market. IBM itself strengthened beyond the 65 per cent point towards 70 per cent. Another 15 per cent or so of market share is in the hands of IBM-compatibles. They basically have their origin in the Fujitsu-Hitachi

Project M, financed in the early 1970s by the Japanese Government.

Governments are now at the beginning of a period that will see them awarding huge contracts. They will be very large and run over long periods of time. But they will also be crucial to the survival of computers, communications, and systems firms who need them to develop the` knowhow for solution-selling during the next decade.

So we need to rethink our priorities and the criteria which we use in spite of – or even because of – the Sherman Act:

- Is megacontract research and development part of an attempt to monopolise the market?
- Who benefits from the fruits of huge research and development expenditures?
- Are these fruits made available to customers?
- Should research and development be oriented to competitive market solutions?
- Is this process followed by a sweep of the corporate adversaries?

Legal historians have vigorously debated what Congress actually had in mind when it passed the Sherman Antitrust Act. Senator John Sherman, who was said to have been somewhat reluctant about the whole antitrust matter himself, may well have put it best when he said of the law that was named after him: 'All that we, as lawmakers, can do is to declare general principles.'

This is, in a few words, the background of the litigation which has seen the Department of Justice bring IBM to court for the third time. The practices the US Department of Justice (DOJ) sought to establish were that IBM:

(1) Used 'fighting machines', in the form of such prematurely announced systems as the 360/44, 360/90, 360/67, and the 2319 A and B disk drives;
(2) Bundled software, services and hardware prices to lock in its customers and lock out competition;
(3) Offered educational discounts to orient educational institutions to IBM systems and standards;
(4) Tried to establish an overall control of the data processing (DP) industry standards.

The IBM defence, led by Attorney Thomas Barr of Cravath, Swaine & Moore, answered that the general purpose market defined by DOJ was not relevant because it excluded products and services that were competitive to those of IBM: 'The practices IBM used were natural and lawful responses to both competition and the needs of the marketplace. The Telex decision had proved how relevant the peripherals submarket was.'

Over the many years this case rolled on, the market itself changed very significantly. From the late 1960s to the early 1980s there has been an earthquake in the computer market and it still continues. The whole world is evolving toward IBM's *de facto* standards in:

- communications protocols;
- hardware compatibility;
- basic software.

The huge investments in research and development did not create a monopoly. They broadened the market. More business opportunities became available to competitors. But were the competitors ready to grasp them? McClellan aptly comments: 'The BUNCH lulled themselves to sleep. While they napped, things began to happen. The microprocessor hit with full force. Specialty markets proliferated. The industry shifted. IBM transfigured. Customers wondered. Yet, the BUNCH slept on.'[2]

Of course, there are exceptions, and in a number of cases litigation is used by the companies themselves to further their aims. In late 1987, for example, the Digital Equipment Corporation (DEC) spent an estimated $1 million arguing bitterly over the terms of a proposed Air Force computer purchase. DEC lobbied Strom Thurmond of the Senate Armed Services Committee and Bill Chappell, Jr, chairman of the House Applications defence subcommittee, and filed official protests. But in the end, the General Services Administration (GSA) rejected the company's attempt to fundamentally alter the Air Force's proposal in a way that would have enhanced its odds. Still, as *Business Week* commented,[3] the delay may buy DEC some time to ready the new software it needs to improve its chance of capturing the Air Force bid. 'It was money well spent,' said a company spokesman.

Apple Computers, too, lobbied greatly to head off a proposal that would have limited Army purchases to IBM-compatible computers. 'It buttonholed key congressional leaders, pleaded with the GSA, and brought Army officials to its Reston (Va.) headquarters to see its Macintosh computers. Finally, Deputy Defense Secretary William H. Taft IV ordered the policy amended,' suggests the same issue of *Business Week*.

REVEALING THE TECHNICAL SPECIFICATIONS

IBM has a contention system, its defence lawyers said in the US v. IBM case, in which one group proposes a plan and another challenges. As stated during the hearings:

> It is not unusual when you take a large number of people like that, that from time to time someone within the IBM corporation will have a thought or write it down on a piece of paper which is not the most brilliant thing in the world . . . but it is not that which, it seems to us, your Honor should take as the intent of the IBM corporation.

From the early days of the trial, Judge David N. Edelstein (who also was the judge in the 1952 case against IBM which ended with Consent Decree in 1956) pushed both sides to get the show on the road. For the next three years, after its beginning (1968–71), the Government and private plaintiffs shoved tons of documents around and asked IBM for more. IBM asked the industry and the Government for everything they had. A battle that spanned five years began when IBM protested that it couldn't release documents that it considered privileged client–attorney files. IBM made an appeal, lost the appeal and handed over the papers.

One thousand witnesses and potential witnesses gave depositions on aspects of the case. Some complained that they were being asked to produce records of what they had done from the day they first thought about computers.

In 1974 the Department of Justice expanded its list of triable issues to include monopoly of the compatible peripherals, sub-markets and abusive practices against leasing companies. IBM protested, to no avail.

In 1978 the DOJ brought up a proposal which IBM seems to have found unacceptable. Among the possibilities for injunctive relief from the alleged monopoly was a suggestion to force IBM into announcing a standard bus interface, that could be changed only after pre-announced disclosure. Both technologically and financially, this amounted to a plug-compatible manufacturers' (PCM) heaven, the more so if the next generation of IBM equipment developed as then predicted: bus-oriented with complementary but separate internal processor modules.

Understandably, IBM refused the 'offer'. The Department of Justice pressed on, extending rather than altering its proposal, which put IBM on the defensive, fielding the antitrust division's ideas for settlement to avoid upsetting its long-term business. Precisely, it proposed:

- That IBM undertake the maintenance of other manufacturers' equipment – on the grounds that, typologically, in 50 per cent of the United States only IBM maintenance service existed;
- That IBM provide advance notice of technical characteristics – well prior to announcement day – to the peripherals manufacturers and other manufacturers;
- That plug-compatible capability be offered at a point prior to the channel.

Competitors wanted interface information sooner than first shipment – and they were asking to know how to interconnect in other ways besides a channel interface.

IBM's line of answer has been that technical specifications are changed up to the last moment prior to announcement. It also said that other means of interconnect than those currently applied require knowledge of the entire machine architecture.

Ironically, ten years later, IBM itself challenged the notion behind its own answer. In 1986 it offered the European Computer Manufacturers' Association (ECMA) the specifications of Logical unit 6.2 (LU 6.2)* and they rejected it. (LU 6.2 is a key SNA protocol roughly corresponding to the presentation level of the ISO/OSI reference model).

Leaving aside the fact that the rejection was technically irrational (and contradicted court moves ECMA took in the past against IBM), it also made bad business sense. As ECMA members would privately admit, the true reason for the rejection was that if LU 6.2 was accepted, they would have found themselves three years behind IBM. At the same time, the same ECMA membership had no alternative to offer or to adopt. So instead of three years they risk finding themselves six years behind IBM.

This example has been referred to in order to show that some of the people (and firms) who abuse the judicial system have no alternative options to put forward. They are simply negative. They are also technologically illiterate because, as the LU 6.2 case documents, they fail to understand that in the computers and communications industry of the future, a logical soldering iron (software standard) is far more important than hardware interconnect.

Survival depends on forging ahead, not in hanging on old assets which have in the meantime lost most if not all of their income-making power. A significant survival factor is, as well, the ability to shift and take leadership in new fields, like software sales; or in fields which already exist yet still have mileage. Maintenance is an example. But maintenance is a market with its own characteristics. Responding to the obligatory maintenance of competitive equipment, IBM management said that the real question is not whether or not this will open up the 'other' 50 per cent of the country to competition but, rather, that it is totally impractical. Indiscriminate obligatory maintenance is impractical, IBM said, since it is hard enough getting adequate support personnel for its own equipment. Besides, it cannot do a good service for the machines of another 100 manufacturers.

As the decade of the 1970s rolled on, twenty-five lawyers from the Antitrust Division of the Department of Justice examined witness at the trial, but

- only one examined more than five;
- nine examined only one or two.

Of the six government lawyers who signed the original complaint, none remain with DOJ. Of the ten lawyers who signed the trial brief, only one junior lawyer hung on, with the 1980 lead attorney for the government being the fourth assigned to the case.

In the spring of 1980 former Solicitor General Bork called the IBM case 'the Antitrust Division's Vietnam.' IBM's top lawyer blamed the Division's lack of management and control for assigning inexperienced lawyers to the case, and for letting a case which could have been tried and over within a year turn into a perpetual 'discovery machine'.

Yet, in spite of some verbal fireworks the fact remains, as many observers see it, that IBM too tried to gain from the rules governing the judicial system. For over ten years its strategy was to seek a settlement which, like the 1956 Decree, focuses on a frozen moment in the emerging technology, a moment in the past. Ingeniously, such a consent decree could try to spell out rules for polite and open competition. In 1956, the Court decreed competitive status for the card-tabulating market – but IBM's business was already in computers. By 1980 IBM's business was shifting beyond computers into software as a major income source, with know how and communications the more distant perspectives. In that sense, it was a consent decree which set forth the rules for open competition in the general purpose mainframe market of the late 1960s and 1970s – which were already past. And justice was done.

What was then to be the result after many years in court action – particularly in view of its dismissal? One of the principal problems in *US vs IBM* has been that there never was a meaningful definition of the issues in the legal contest. Yet this case cost the US government (and the taxpayers) millions of dollars. Has it all been in vain? It is just as legitimate to ask the opposite question: Had the antitrust action ended in breaking up IBM, would the result have been positive, or at least worth while?

To answer this query we can look at the break-up of AT&T. Then the answer would be an unqualified, flat: NO! With local tariffs going up for the consumer and the best telephone network in the world in pieces, it could be no other.

What's then the whole essence of antitrust? Is the avoidance of monopoly the real goal? Fundamentally, the issues are deeper and touch the structure of a system of laws which must now face a radically changed environment.

As Western society moves toward de-industrialisation with knowledge becoming the new criterion of power, what's the role of an antitrust law. 'The new empires are the empires of the mind,' Churchill was to remark. This is a more basic issue for Congress (not for the courts) to decide than the fate of the *US* v. *IBM* or *US* v. *AT&T* processes themselves. 'If the judge did not form judgments of the actors in those courthouse dramas called trials, he could never render decisions,' an Appeals Court was to remark. But can a judge form judgments outside the context of the course society is now taking?

LEGAL PROBLEMS WITH INFORMATION TECHNOLOGY

Artificial intelligence (AI) is a new field in the computers and communications industry. It is also a fast-expanding field, at least in some of the areas which it includes. Expert systems, natural languages, and artificial vision are examples. Other AI branches are robotics and voice recognition/synthesis. If differences in what hardware can or cannot do and well-known software supports lead to legal problems, it will be interesting to see in the next five years the legal problems which will result from new technologies. Many of these problems will have in the background the still ill-defined notion of raising standards of fast-developing, new software products.

To start with, it is not uncommon that programming products are being built but do not work according to what is written in the system analysis. Either the analyst did not understand the user's wishes, or he did not explain himself well, or the programmer did not follow the analysis. As a result, the programming product lacks a clear applications viewpoint. Few people in this industry seem to realise that if we build poor products, this will lead to:

- disappointment of expectation;
- the establishment of low standards;
- reduced sales and, therefore, low funding for further work.

The subject is intricate. Should the law set different standards for AI producers and vendors than for other business people? The answer is: NO! However, a lower level in terms of sophistication, but also better established – classical data processing software – has:

- no legal standards;
- no test method(s).

Subjects regarding fitness (in reaching goals), quality, robustness, bugs, efficiency, vendor liability, etc., are left unanswered, thus creating the preconditions for future litigation.

There is a similarity between sophisticated software constructs and the drugs industry. In both cases, we deal with the fringes of human experience; hence the needed code should help set the standards the vendor would have to meet.

While all this is valid for a variety of software constructs, it is just as true that in new fields there are more subjects which can be open to litigation. There is no law today governing expert systems, but there could be two solutions:

- a passive mechanism;
- an active approach.

A *passive mechanism* would look after a code of practice for expert systems products, to be administered by a professional association. Typically, this will involve a panel investigation of complaints followed by sanctions. However, the very fact which makes this approach necessary also weakens its impact. There is today no legal remedy because, being a new field, expert systems has a large volume of misinformation. Many cases may fall in a grey area: no clear breaking of law, but . . .

An *active mechanism* would require preregistration of products with well-defined specifications, including applications perspectives. But it

- will be expensive to administer;
- will be difficult to predetermine standards for;
- will present problems of confidentiality of AI software.

That is why many people maintain that a code of practice is a better approach to follow – at least in the first instance.

Legal regulation of software products is anyway an involved business. Intelligent software (AI) products do many things which are both

- unseen to the naked eye;
- unknown to the average user.

The protection mechanism should give the average user the capacity to recognise the fault, as well as to evaluate the effects of the fault.

From this point on starts the implementation question. Self-regulation may be fine, except that the machinery is in the hands of the producers. As a result, the users may not have confidence in it. For this reason, other experts suggest that legal regulation is a necessary complement. Furthermore, legal regulation is more formal and sets a day when a final, pace-setting judgment will be made. On the other hand, self-regulation and legal regulation may come in conflict.

Talking of legal measure in a broad sense, the law offers two solutions:

(1) *Contractual provisions.* Their object is regulations of instance between two parties.
(2) *Court provisions.* They should include the mechanism for evaluating conformity to standards (specified by law), and provide for penalties, leaving the decision to the judge.

There are parallels with other professions: accounting records must be shown in a 'true and fair' manner. This is the letter of the law, but some years ago the question came up in England on what is 'true and fair'. True and fair varies with the sophistication of the society and the understanding of the people living in it. Examples in accounting practice are:

● inflation accounting;
● the valuation of stocks.

What's more, new guidelines may or may not find favour with accountants. And there are further problems with a certification procedure: who should do the certification?

The answer to these questions is not a matter the board of directors can be excused for ignoring. Whether it sets policy for a computers and communications manufacturer or for an organisation using high technology, litigation resulting from imprecision (and indecision) is too serious a matter – and it should be treated at the highest decision-making level.

IS SOFTWARE A DANGEROUS ACTIVITY?

This is a problem which has not yet been addressed in a legal sense. But other issues have been treated and might serve as a reference. In New

Zealand, for instance, road accidents are institutionalised as part of a possibly lethal activity: *driving*. The law specifies that all drivers contribute to a fund. Persons involved in an accident do not need to prove whose fault the accident was. They will anyway be compensated by the fund if they establish they were part of such accident.

Such a course could be followed if a legal connection is established between hardware/software procurement and insurance coverage. The computer machinery vendor should be obliged to disclose to his clients:

- what the wares he sells can do;
- what they cannot do;
- where the limitations are;
- what might be harmful.

But, because computers and communications technology develops very fast, codes of practice have the same problems as the information systems industry as a whole: 'When it works, it is obsolete.'

Not surprisingly, the expert systems can be used as help in legal advice, keeping all matters in an actual status. Not long ago, a research project found the law was not logical enough on the subject of artificial intelligence projects. But another expert system, an intelligent retrival mechanism, has been of help in legal cases.

Alternatives examined in the preceding section can now be re-evaluated under this section's heading. Self-discipline by the software industry will basically mean action by a trade association. Such a solution is similar to procedures which exist with advertising and publishing, but with software it does not seem to carry great weight.

The industry itself can take action to protect itself and its clients from catastrophic issue. The nuclear industry has done so (at least in the West). But then came Three Mile Island and Chernobyl. A nuclear plant can only operate if covered by insurance. If the right possibilities are allowed for, in the light of recent events, the cost of insurance can be so high that the plant can no longer be profitable. So, commercially, insurance costs can stop dangerous products being put on the market.

With self-regulation through industry associations, there is also a risk that its institutionalisation turns into a cartel, with big firms trying to close out small ones starting up with brilliant ideas and first-class products-to-be. From the risk of cartel action to the fact that a vendors' association will need long time to develop its own reputation and market confidence, this solution is not so appealing. Anyway, it is not an issue to be solved overnight through the producer's own action.

The alternative is to let market forces decide. In this case, a unified standard does not seem a good proposition. A better solution is compulsory insurance. A software company must then convince an underwriter to issue insurance. This being a private business the standards will be dynamic. Underwriters may in turn request a certification laboratory, like the United States' National Bureau of Standards (NBS) to do the definition job:

- it has (or should have) the know-how;
- it commands a persuasive authority;
- it can constitute a focal point of reference if cases come to the courtroom.

The court itself has problems of adjustment. Judges and members of the jury know what a car is and could judge cases of car accidents. But they usually have no such experience with computers.

These alternatives rely on the fact that the role of law is to protect the weak against the strong. It is therefore also proper to consider precisely the opposite case. Take a small software company and a big client firm: Who is the weak? Who is the strong? Neither should we forget that a voracious user of software is the ultimate consumer. But even if he uses high technology in his work or for pleasure, the state of knowledge of consumer as compared to state of knowledge of vendor are very diverse. Hence legal protection should be provided.

It is also important to redress the difference of knowledge – and here lies a major ethical action which can and should be undertaken. With artificial intelligence software entering the market, such action should include (if not actually focus on) the differences which exist between classical software and expert systems. With expert systems, programs change dynamically. As a result, the degree of complexity in finding out what happens increases by order of magnitude. If the legal system is not tooled to deal with high technology at large, it surely is not ready to handle this case. Significant preparatory work is necessary on the technical side.

Companies which work on major software projects for the military have also other legal issues to look after. Contracts farmed out by the Strategic Defense Initiative (SDI) are an example. The German–American contract specifies that firms which take SDI contracts will be subject to the laws of both countries. What many companies do not know (or appreciate) is that US laws are much more restrictive on dissemination of information. Following Watergate there have been new US laws which have severely tightened cases regarding dissemination of official data. At the same time, there is a likelihood of strategic restrictions being used as tariff barriers. This will tremendously complicate litigation.

Nor is the consumer software market to be taken lightly in a legal sense. In countries where consumer associations are strong, litigation can be murderous to the vendor. The lack of knowledge by consumers about what, say, expert systems can do and how, is protective to him when consumers act individually, not as a group. In a sense, over the last few years, some consumer groups have taken the initiative. They are currently doing a rather good job in evaluating spreadsheets, database management systems (DBMS), and word processing (WP) packages. Still, users are dissatisfied because they do not always know what they are buying nor how to employ it in order to get the best results.

There is, of course, a major step between the officialisation of certification procedures and the active pursuit of rules which are legally valid, cover all quality issues relating to software, and can be used as such in case of litigation. In the last case, the direct assumption of responsibility is a vital reference – and in this sense current trends are far from uniform.

There is first of all the *California paradigm*. It is quite likely that the law in California will see to it that a computer program, particularly artificial intelligence, may be regarded as a legal person. Machine-developed software would fall under that category. This is still some time away, but it has recently become a possibility. It is also likely that the owner of AI software will be the person to hold responsible for profit and loss. In other words, in California the law may start recognising ownership by 'inhuman' persons as contrasted to human persons or other living beings. There may then come a day when expert systems become such entities and that society recognises them as such.

There is on the other hand the *British paradigm*. IBM and ICL now want to have ownership of machine-developed software. In that case, the company as owner will be liable for damage.

The California paradigm is a far cry if we care to recall that, at present, we don't even have laws for software copyright protection. But it can happen.

What's the effect of the California or the British paradigm on profits and losses, company responsibility, customer impact and possible litigation in each case? The answer is far from evident. After proper study, the decision on the course to follow should be made by the board of directors. It should be uniform, legally valid, technically documented, and as far-sighted as technology permits.

NOTES

1. 19 May 1986.
2. Stephen T. McClellan, *The Coming Computer Industry Shakeout* (New York: John Wiley & Sons, 1984).
3. 23 November 1987.

15 Mergers, Acquisitions and Disinvestment

In the search for product diversification, many industrial concerns have chosen mergers as a logical method. Fundamentally, product diversification can be seen as a means of providing a degree of corporate security or, as is usually the case, of continuing company growth. But often mergers and acquisitions bring under the Corporate fold unrelated product lines or exotic services that management finds difficult to control.

During the last twenty years, management has looked to *diversification* as a living, dynamic force, capable of providing new dimensions in company growth, *if* properly administered. In a number of cases, experience has shown that this *if* should be given careful consideration, a finding which led to the concept of *disinvestment*.

Diversification can never succeed if approached on a hit-and-miss basis. A rational, organised approach might be:

(1) *Vertical*: The goal is the integration of the sales dollar with design and manufacturing made in-house, from the systems level down to assemblies, sub-assemblies and components.

(2) *Horizontal*: This is oriented to product lines (and usually markets) with a certain common ground (or similarity) between the products offered, such as substitutes for and complements to one another.

(3) *Conglomerate*: This includes all other types of product – and market-oriented variety; it stresses diverse ventures and aims to protect company profits if rough weather develops in the main line(s), basically a hedging philosophy.

In terms of strategic planning (and also management-wise) vertical integration makes more sense than horizontal. It is also the earliest form of the two, having its origins at the beginning of this century: the time of galloping industrialisation. The German form of industrial 'Konzern' is based on this concept; but in its international application, taxation has been the moving gear (a basic factor which faded away with the application of the value-added tax).

Among the known advantages of vertical integration is normalisation

307

in product design, better control on inventories, avoidance of delays by suppliers, and the ability to call back in-house for manufacturing (during the lean years) of contracts which have been given to suppliers. But vertical integration also has its limits.

The concept of wide diversification has led to the notion of the conglomerate. Heralded as the way to do business on a national or multinational scale, the attractiveness of conglomerate ventures began to fade. By taxing management resources in a range of diverse product lines, it ended by reducing effectiveness. At the same time, companies found that rough weather may develop not only in the main line but also in the acquired products – with a compound and often detrimental effect.

At the peak time of the conglomerate approach, wondering about the many and diverse product line, people asked Thornton, the patriarch of the philosophy and maker of Litton Industries: 'What's the product Litton makes?' He answered in one word: 'Money'. And to those puzzled by the company's buying thrust, Thornton suggested: 'We don't buy companies – we buy time.'

But it also takes sixteen hours work per day, seven days a week, to hold an industrial empire (any empire) together, and when the original genius gets tired or disappears the empire risks falling to pieces. Conglomerates were news in the 1960s and, quoting from Voltaire's works, 'In the case of news,' observed the patriarch of Ferney, 'We should always wait for the sacrament of confirmation.'

DIVERSIFYING THE PRODUCT LINE

Although mergers and acquisitions are a major form of company growth, surprisingly little is known about the underlying factors and rational criteria. Despite an expanding flow of information about individual acquisitions, there is a notable lack of concrete data on the efficient basis for evaluating possibilities and alternatives. Also, little is known on how mergers and acquisitions affect the financial position of a company – in a way useful in making a longer-range strategic plan.

In a similar manner, in spite of the fact that there exist many theories about the relation between mergers and monopoly (or mergers and concentration), the gaps in information are so great that they have supported widely varying estimates of the shape, trend and effects of merger operations. Experience, however, can teach us a lesson. Failures in conglomerates have in common the inability to make tough decisions.

Many mergers have been based primarily on hopes and dreams. Management failed in outlining beforehand the financial impact of the deal and the resulting responsibilities. This led to a hydra complex in research and development, incompatibilities in manufacturing, non-integrated (if not disintegrated) marketing networks, and the hiring of too many people as though the different divisions were trying to solve unemployment single-handledly. They did not market aggressively. And the business that came to them was not very profitable.

Good, solid management rests on the guts to make all the tough decisions that have been put off. Clean up the bad business, slim down the staff, define the prime market(s) and begin aggressive selling.

That's no news to managers who have learned through the years that they just have too many tough decisions. This is true with products, people and loans. Further, we are not doing a division, an executive, an employee, or a loan applicant a favour by going against good sound principles and giving them a third and a fourth and a fifth chance. We have just got to have some values and principles and stick to them. Tough choices are the number one characteristics of good managers; they mean steady tough times – and tough times should develop tough-minded people.

A management team made up of tough-minded people is likely to be direct and vigorous because its members know what their values are. Easy times do not force people to probe internally and make tough choices. Unchallenging times tend to teach people that it is easier to slide around tough decisions instead of making them. Eventually diversified companies develop a 'traffic problem', pointing in conflicting directions. Little by little, this process erodes vitality and the ability to perform. Besides, the less we understand about our values, the more confused our lives are; the person who has clarified his or her values will perform consistent and decisive *acts of courage*: the courage to say what has to be said and to do what needs to be done.

Values indicators are not enough to run a widely (and, often, thinly) spread-out company in terms of product lines and multinational marketing activities. Such indicators are goals, purposes, aspirations, attitudes, interests, feelings, beliefs and convictions; but many are likely to be contradictory to one another and to cause internal conflict. Goals and plans must be sorted out, and quantitative standards developed, tested, cross-evaluated and implemented. They must cover:

● products and their vitality (Figure 15.1 gives an example based on the time-span 1940 to 1962);

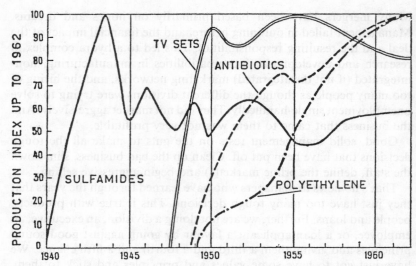

Figure 15.1   All products show a curve of vitality. A 1963 study compared four
products and provided interesting insights on their vitality curves.

- geography (national, multinational);
- infrastructure (research and development, manufacturing, marketing);
- financial staying-power;
- specific targets;
- management skill to see these goals through.

The reasons for a diversification policy (product-wise, or multinational) must be spelt out. It is not enough to look into company growth through mergers and acquisitions within a vague concept of geographic expansion – diversification. We must consider predominant product (and/or topological) diversification aspects. In the majority of cases, both geographic and product aspects are present in mergers and acquisitions, although in varying degrees and offering various possibilities.

And there are a number of governmental rules and regulations to cope with. Geographical mergers seem, for the time being, to involve the least resistance on behalf of governments. Many such mergers have international aspects, although there also exist intra-national geographical mergers. Examples of the former are offered by the 'big rush' shown in the 1960s by US companies which, by merger or acquisition, got a good hold in the European Common Market – and the inverse rush by Japanese and European companies (German, Swiss, English, French) experienced today in th US market. There are also legal aspects to cope with.

The law governing mergers and acquisitions changes slowly, but its interpretation changes faster – according to the whims of the time. In the late 1960s to late 1970s, in the United States, after having enjoyed some years of welcome, mergers came up for a careful antitrust scrutiny on behalf of government. This mood was part and parcel of a wider antitrust action which saw some fifteen years of antitrust activity by the Department of Justice against IBM, and the break-up of AT & T. But with the Reagan Administration the winds changed. There has been an end to IBM's odyssey and the early to mid-1980s saw again an explosive growth in mergers and acquisitions. Financial analysts have commented that this explosive merger activity is a documentation that corporate assets are a cheap buy. Though some acquisition activity is speculative there is also a rationality in integrated product line – as the General Electric – RCA merger documents.

Product mergers, it has already been stated, are classified as horizontal, vertical, or conglomerate. A horizontal merger involves the acquisition by one company of a competitor. As far as antitrust violations are concerned, this is the easiest kind of case to prove in court. It can readily be shown that the number of competitors has been reduced and that the market share of the acquiring firm has been enlarged. For nearly fifteen years, the courts have been fairly liberal to the government in their answers and, as a result, big companies have been shying away from horizontal mergers – though the practice started again with the consolidation which took place in the early 1980s in the oil industry.

In a vertical merger, a manufacturer typically may pick up either a supplier or a chain of retail outlets. Again, regarding antitrust enforcement, the government may try to show that elimination of the retail outlets forecloses this market to other manufacturers, or that the acquisition of an important source of supply gives the acquiring company cheaper materials while shutting off competing manufacturers from the same source.

The conglomerate merger is one in which a company diversifies by buying a firm in a field new to the purchaser. Here, proving anticompetitive effects is a difficult problem. It is, nevertheless, true that this system of classification is not clear-cut. For example, it is rather uncertain whether acquisition by a manufacturer in the western United States of East Coast facilities for making similar products is a horizontal or a conglomerate merger, although it is clear that it involves geographical expansion aspects. Nor is it certain whether the acquisition of a manufacturer of women's dresses by a manufacturer of men's suits is horizontal or conglomerate.

Acquisitions by integrated companies may well be both horizontal and vertical, as, for instance, in the case of a steel products manufacturer that acquires a company owning steel mines and mills. Despite its ambiguity, the three-way classification can be used as a guide to merger patterns that have been put to test by the enforcement agencies. Statistically, horizontal acquisitions have been questions far more often than all others taken together.

EVALUATING THE POTENTIAL OF A MERGER

The criteria for the evaluation of a potential merger as to its profitability often vary widely, depending on management drives, company finances, and the nature of the merger itself. The difficulty of an accurate evaluation increases with the increase of company complecity, and there is no formula to prove the case. Management makes the difference.

Usually the early steps to diversification are simple: as many as half a dozen company executives may gather to consider the prospective company, its products and its financial condition. At this stage they may have no more than published annual reports or other data available from public sources to guide them. If it is a closely held company which does not publish its financial data annually, the principal source material is likely to be an investment broker's statement.

While this may be an oversimplified approach, it doesn't take long to stack the company up against pre-established criteria. At this stage, management is more likely to reject than approve. In fact, when the finding is affirmative, it is merely affirmation that management may commit the company to the expenditure of additional time, effort, and money to do a more thorough analysis. The aims of a strategic plan do not spring out automatically (Figure 15.2) and management may discover that what it got in an acquisition is a Pandora's box.

Studies show that one of the main reasons for acquisition failures is sloppy competitive analysis, not poor legal and accounting audits. Even among larger corporations acquirers often lack proper and unbiased information on the target's

● profit margins,
● growth rate,
● market position,

- management skill,
- internal controls,
- image as seen by the market and by competitors,
- customer base, and
- quality of suppliers.

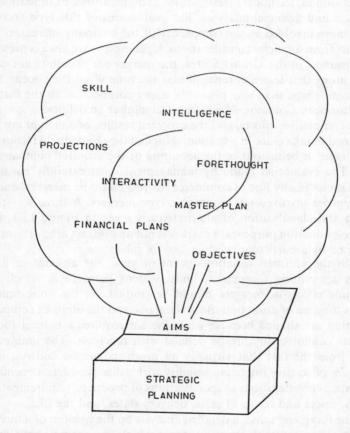

Figure 15.2   Strategic planning aims to control situations which, if left to their own, could become explosive. Mergers and acquisitions are a specific area of reference.

The more sophisticated acquirers tend to know what the required information is and where it should come from. But most companies fell victims to packaging and structuring deals. They do not do their homework in a factual and documented competitive analysis, thus ending with significant discrepancies in a target's financial and market position.

Full-scale appraisals vary according to the company's type and to the nature of information required to make a sound decision. As with other evaluations, overnight judgements cannot be relied on as a substitute for market studies, technical investigations and operations, examination of products and financial analyses. But evaluations of this type become much more involved as the complexity of the company increases.

Apart from financial considerations, legal aspects are always present. For instance, in the United States, the merger act prohibits not only acquisitions that lessen competition at the time when they occur, but also acquisitions that may probably lessen competition in the future. The European Common Market has set similar guidelines.

The competitive effects, and the expected results, of a merger are not presumed to take place in a vacuum. Nor can they be deducted from the size, shape, or behaviour of the acquiring or the acquired company as such. The evaluation made by management must carefully consider expectancies in any line of commerce for product-type mergers, and in all countries involved for geographic-type mergers. A three-way projection and classification of alternatives is given in Figure 15.3. For merger-evaluation purposes, a market is not an abstract area arbitrarily delimited by a particular product and its substitute.

From the antitrust-violations point of view, the absence of fixed merger-act criteria for market limits widens the area in which the economic effects of mergers should be studied. At the same time it widens the area of discretion. Both the scope and the limits of company discretion are shaped because while the act requires a market focus, markets cannot ordinarily be defined with precision. The ambiguity arises from the fact that virtually all products can be laid out in a spectrum of relative interchangeability with other products, depending upon such considerations as specifications of products, requirements of buyers, prices and terms of sales, delivery dates, and the like.

In the foregoing sense, a detailed analysis on the wisdom of a merger will be concerned with the advantages which may come about from every major factor involved in the merger or acquisition. The same can be said about the respective disadvantages. Under advantages, management usually wants to know the answers to such questions as:

● Will the merger, or acquisition, result in operating or staffing economies?

● Will it contribute to a more efficient system of sales and distribution?

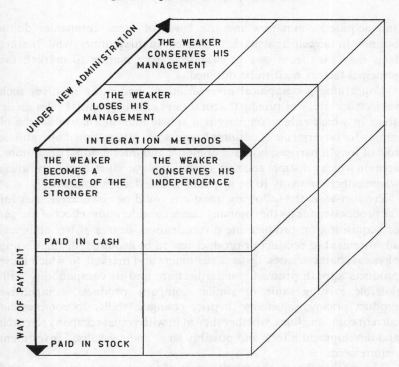

Figure 15.3 Multifunctional approach followed in acquisition studies by a leading corporation. Way of payment, integration methods, and goals under the new administration make the frame of reference.

● Does it contribute towards the company goal by diversifying the markets, or the customers within markets?
● Will the merger or acquisition bring to the company new management blood, which will enable it to build on what it already has?
● Will the merger or acquisition give additional financial strength and earning power?
● Does it have tax advantages as a justification?

Factors taken into account in such evaluations may, for example, include company size, market share, company rank, oligopoly, market dominance, changes in price competition, increases in concentration, possibility of vertical integration, opportunities to enter new markets, and the like.

Most, if not all, merger decisions to be reported to the stockholders, the government, or the public, may well begin with a summary of facts concerning the size, operations and marketing methods of the acquiring and acquired companies and the kinds of other companies doing business in the principal markets affected. In this manner, while market facts may vary from case to case, and from market to market, the principal factors need to be outlined.

Concerning geographical diversification, evaluation involves such subjects as: areas of principal actual sales effort; potential sales areas; areas in which either company is a substantial alternative source of supply for buyers; role of customs barriers, for international operations; role of freight barriers, both for domestic and international operations; areas in which a distinct and non-substitutable product is sold; and areas where either company to be acquired is an effective competitor.

Product-wise, the following questions could be considered: uses for the products made by the company under consideration; effect of merger or acquisition on product-line diversification; degree of technological advancement of product or product-line to be acquired; distinguishing physical characteristics; distinct customers and markets to which these products appeal; product standardisation, and its compatibility with possible existing same or similar company products; competitive product pricing; sensitivity to price changes; ability to complement current company lines; whether they fit in with actual company research and development effort; and possibly large and specialised investment requirements.

The market shares, the relative sizes of the merging companies, and the like, do not represent statistical certainties from which the competitive effects of a merger can be judged. They are only variables whose stability and significance vary from case to case, depending on the nature of the merging companies, their products, their geographical operations, and more importantly their competitive aspects, behaviour, and management skills.

Mergers and acquisitions should not be done strictly for growth's sake: this is the philosophy of the cancer cell. The basic criterion must be *industry leadership* – and this is an issue of quality and concentration on areas of strength. As Peter F. Drucker aptly suggests: 'Any business needs to know its strengths and base its strategy on them. What do *we* do well? What are the areas in which we perform? Strengths are always specific, always unqique. One gets paid only for strengths; one does not get paid for weaknesses.'

THE NEW ACQUISITIONS POLICY

Mergers are *à la mode* from time to time, with four waves outstanding: at the turn of the century, in the 1920s, in the 1960s, and in the 1980s.

- In the first, the trusts swallowed up every company they could to build monopolies and stifle competition.
- In the second, small companies got together to meet the competition of the giants.
- The motor of the third has been product diversification (in an increasingly competitive market) and the challenge of international operations.

The oil industry mergers which took place in the 1980s (fourth wave) were to a considerable degree also motivated by speculative fever, as we will see in the section on corporate raiders. But they were also a reflection of the fact that for some oil giants it became more expensive to search for new resources than to acquire another company's existing deposits and, with this, the other company itself.

Other reasons have also been present. In the case of the Burroughs–Sperry merger, Dr Blumenthal, the Burroughs President, stated that his goal was to create a critical mass which can master a large-enough share of the computer market in order to compete with IBM.

In yet other cases, profit-making companies look on the tax losses recorded on the books of a concern which is losing money, as a big inducement to merge. The loss can be used at the internal revenue service desk to offset the taxes on their own profits; and the inverse can also be true. Probably the best-known case of this dates back to the early 1950s when Kaiser:

- got a loan from Bank of America to buy Willys-Overland (a profit-making concern);
- merged it with Kaiser Auto (which had incurred severe losses);
- recovered Willys's tax money, paid the loan, and kept the company.

Most likely, in the coming years, the underlying reason for a great deal of industrial mergers will be fear of being caught with a single product in an age of rapid technological change. There is a realisation now, as never before, that new products are a vital source of new profits. Industrial concerns can get a new product through research and development, or they can go out and buy it. Research and development might take several years. A merger, management hopes, can do it overnight. Then when the opposite is the case, the direction become one of disinvestment.

Product diversification is both a reason and a result of new marketing times. In earlier days, a corporation was expected to stick to what it knew best. Stringent antitrust laws now discourage fast-growing companies from mergers with companies too close to their own fields.

Result: many firms are forced to move into an entirely different line in an effort to increase their profit margins. And, if successful, once they have made such a move they find it even easier to continue diversification.

Like any other managerial action, a diversification programme must be well managed. To be successful, it must be more than 'seizing opportunities' by making quick decisions whenever a company or product line is offered for sale. The cornerstone is the 'evaluation' of whether or not and, *if* yes, on *how much* the acquisition of a new product line could lead into new fields that mean opportunity.

To prevent faulty moves, management should seek out the disadvantages of a specific transaction as carefully as the advantages. Before commitments are made, both the cost of the new product line, and its future financing, should be carefully considered and compared against expected profits or other advantages. Some criteria for the subject evaluation have already been presented in the preceding section. Diversification-wise, the product market need not be so broad as to encompass all products produced by either company, or all substitutes for these products. It does not need, either, to be so narrow that related products of the two companies appear to have no economic connection with each other.

For instance, an American textile manufacturer caught in the ailing textile industry has set a record since 1955 of twenty-nine mergers into such fields as electronics, automotive parts, aluminium products and optical equipment. Textiles, once constituting the sole source of income, now account for only 16 per cent of company sales. At the same time, company profits have tripled. A different example is given by two companies: the one sells and installs broadcasting and closed-circuit television equipment; the other manufacturers television monitors under its own name, and private brand names, and produces other closed-circuit television and broadcasting equipment. The merger has been in the form of a stock exchange.

Some 60 per cent of all mergers are still within the same basic industry. The growing trend of the 1960s towards going outside, buying new products, new management, or new scientific brains, by taking over small to medium-sized companies is, for the time being, a spent force, as management came to realise that widely diversified mergers do not offer 'sure' solutions to the troubles or shortcomings of a company. Nor do they automatically guarantee growth and a big rise in earnings.

When the merger business is overdone, the cause of disinvestments eventually arises. Some disinvestments take place to streamline the product line, and are a sharp reversal of the acquisition policies directed towards the conglomerate concept. As such they seem to be financially beneficial to the parent company: or at least that's the way the stock market looks at them. When Boise Cascade 'disinvested' itself from its money-losing, ill-fated real estate venture, its stock went up considerably. Other disinvestments are made to raise cash and help support the main product line: Lone Star did so by selling its profitable wood products division to meet the capital budget of sky-rocketing investments for new cement factories, which hit the $100 million market.

Some disinvestments take place as part of a concept of 'dimensioning'. An example is given by Genesco Incorporated, which has been steadily reducing retailing operations, divesting itself of Henri Bendel stores, a Manhattan shop for elegant, expensive apparel; its nationwide 122-store H. Kress variety division, its 28 Roos-Atkins clothes shops (in California), and its Post drugstores in Houston. Such a move leaves the company with only footwear stores and four menswear outlets.

Mergers can be generally beneficial in an expanding economy (when business is good), as they can contribute to expansion by encouraging the release of money tied up in a matured industry into a younger one. But in this sense they look more like venture capital: the go-go business of the 1960s and of the 1980s. Putting up capital to start risky high-technology companies has, in fact, made a glorious comeback in the United States.

THE CASE OF STATE INTERVENTION

To get a hint of the attitude of the US Government, as an example, toward business mergers and acquisitions one must look at the action taken by the Justice Department. For instance: Coca Cola and Minute Maid; Campbell Soup and Pepperridge Farm; Burlington Industries and James Lee; Minnesota Mining and Manufacturing and Warner-Lambert Pharmaceutical. Three things are in common in these ventures. Each of the acquiring firms is a leader in its own field and each ventured from its main line into new products: Campbell from soups to bakery products; Coca Cola from carbonated drinks to frozen juices; Burlington from textiles to carpets; and Minnesota Mining from abrasives and adhesives to drugs. Thirdly, in every case, there might be some threat of concentration of economic power.

Yet in only the last one of these cases has the plan to merge actually run into a serious stumbling block. When officials of Minnesota Mining and Warner-Lambert started talking of a merger in late summer 1960, they decided to seek informal clearance from the Justice Department. No problem was anticipated; the department has never brought suit against the merger of firms making unrelated products. Although the Government at first said its opinion would be forthcoming quickly, it then informed the two parties that the investigation would take longer than expected.

The implications of this unexpected hitch reach across the breadth of the corporate community, which has long assumed that mergers solely for the sake of diversification, rather than picking up competitors or suppliers in the acquirer's own field, were free of antitrust peril. Add to this the Federal Trade Commission attack on Procter and Gamble's (1957) acquisition of Clorox Chemical and you get into the puzzle: the soap-maker went outside its own field in buying a bleach producer? or the two fit naturally together in a general 'cleaning and washing'? Because of its economic strength, merchandising experience and advertising ability, the Governmental opposition argued, Procter and Gamble would enlarge the already dominant market position of Clorox.

A question thus arises on the odds that any particular acquisition will be attacked by the Federal Government. Vulnerability to governmental scrutiny has shown to be greatest if the two companies operate in the same field. If they do not, vulnerability appears to depend on whether the acquisition enhances the market power of an already dominant company or makes it substantially more difficult for suppliers to find outlets that are not under the control of their competitors or for buyers to establish independent sources of supply.

The Government argues that although in itself diversification can be a very healthy thing, diversification by merger can have certain anti-competitive effects. This opinion is presented on the grounds that a diversifying acquisition removes an otherwise potential competitor, and that it might also materially affect the existing competitive pattern of the industry being entered, so as to erode the last vestiges of a previously viable enterprise. In the way it seems to be shaping up, the basic test can be phrased in five questions:

(1)   Does the acquiring company have great financial power?
(2)   Does it have ready access to capital for expansion?
(3)   Is it using a hefty advertising budget?
(4)   Does it possess an established retail credit network?
(5)   Does it tend to shadow the market so that competitors in the industry it is invading will not be able to hold their own?

It is only obvious that because of governmental opposition, a strong temptation develops on behalf of industrial management to look for sure and simple methods of predetermining what mergers will be questioned and when a challenge is likely to be sustained. Attempts have been made to find tests that could be applied to a limited set of facts concerning the acquiring and acquired companies, but these cannot be generally efficient since they would have to be based on an assumption that specific sets of company attributes, such as products and size, for example, determine the effects of a merger.

Shifts in units of measurement used in evaluations of type, causing at times substantial shifts in the apparent structure of an industry and in the apparent market share or rank of the acquiring or acquired company, tend to make such tests less dependable. The government's reasons for using one unit rather than another are rarely explicit. It is frequently unclear as to whether a unit of measurement has been selected for its relevance or for its relative availability. In most cases production, capacity or sales figures, or some combination of these, have been applied:

- In the Du Pont–General Motors case, the market was defined in terms of dollar value of sales of automobile finishes and fabrics by Du Pont to General Motors and in terms of General Motors' dollar requirements for these items.
- In the Bethlehem Steel case, the principal unit used was ingot capacity in tons, with dollar value of sales a close second.
- In the Crown Zelerbach case it was production tonnage.
- In American Crystal Sugar case it was the dollar value of sales.
- In the *Farm Journal* case it was circulation and dollar value of advertising.
- In the Brown Shoe case it was the dollar value of production and retail sales of shoes;
- In the Erie Sand and Gravel case it was the sales in cubic measures of sand.

The relative scarcity of major companies operating in the relevant markets is also noted as one of the reasons for governmental disapproval of a merger. Thus, the small number of integrated steel companies receives emphasis on the Bethlehem decision; and the small number of significant competitors played a major role in the findings in the Crown, *Farm Journal*, Erie Sand and Gravel, and Reynolds Metals decisions. Conversely, the number of competitors did not receive specific attention in the Du Pont, General Motors and American Crystal decisions.

Obviously related to the scarcity of major competition, is the possibility of dominance of a market by a company before or after the

Membership of the Board of Directors

respective merger or acquisition. Although not clearly defined, 'dominance' appears in these cases as a blend of statistics on the relative size of the acquiring company and other information, such as its tendency to be a price leader, its tendency to set the price pattern for competitors, or its ability to influence opportunities for other companies to come into the market.

The form of competition most frequently scrutinised by the US Government is that of price competition. Attention is focusing on areas of:

- the elimination of a price-cutter in the industry;
- possible excessive price-cutting by a vertically integrated company coming into a market composed of smaller non-integrated companies.
- the acquisition of advantageously located facilities that give a company an opportunity to reduce prices below those of less advantageously located competitors;
- the enhancement of the market position of a price leader and potential increases in the tendency of other companies to follow a price leader;
- a general lessening of competitive probing for increased sales through decreased prices.

For instance, in the Reynolds Metals case it was found that after acquisition of Arrow Brands (a manufacturer of aluminium foil for the florist trade) by Reynolds (one of the principal aluminium-foil producers), Arrow cut prices on florists' foil to a point that was evidently below Arrow's cost of production. The Government held that Arrow could not have maintained its price at so low a level for so long a period on its own and further held that such pricing was evidence of Arrow's market power achieved through acquisition by Reynolds.

In the American Crystal case, by contrast, the court concluded that the competition of American Crystal and Colonial had been prime forces in the price-conscious industrial sugar market and that co-ordination of the sales activities of the two companies would reduce incentives to price competition by American Crystal and Colonial as well as by their competitors.

To date, some cases of governmental intervention in industrial mergers and acquisitions deal with situations in which it may be more difficult for suppliers to find independent outlets; for buyers to obtain a merger; or an acquisition is likely to make a difference to companies formerly doing business with the acquiring or the acquired concerns.

Where the relation between the merging units is a vertical one (supplier–buyer), it may well be that companies with which one of the merging units did business may be cut off. This, in itself, does not invalidate a merger, but the law applies if a narrowing of sources or outlets may substantially lessen competition or to tend to monopoly.

When opportunities to enter a market by new companies are feeble or lacking, the loss of a present competitor because of merger or acquisition is bound to receive careful consideration. Regardless of whether an acquisition itself changes opportunities for entry, the US Government has in more than one instance examined facts on past entry and factors determining opportunities for future entry. For instance, in the Bethlehem Steel case, government investigators found that the prospect of a new entrant to replace an absorbed Youngstown Sheet and Tube were practically nil, either in terms of capital investments or of experience.

In the United States since 1935, only two new integrated steel companies have been established in the iron and steel industry, Kaiser Steel Corporation and Lone Star Steel Company. Both companies entered the iron and steel industry with substantial government assistance and together account for only 1.6 per cent of total industry ingot capacity. The new entrants have made no real dent as far as the larger integrated companies are concerned, in the sense that over the twenty-two year period, 1935–57, no new entrant has become one of the twelve largest integrated steel companies.

Generally acquisitions of whole companies or whole divisions have been challenged by the United States Government with greater frequency than partial acquisitions. Horizontal acquisitions, where the acquiring and acquired companies are competitors, have been questioned more frequently than vertical or conglomerate acquisitions. Also, governmental investigation of merger cases, although it affected a wide range of industries and geographical areas, involved far more manufacturing than other segments of the economy and it concerned national rather than regional or local markets. A very careful examination of these 'trends in thinking' by government officials can offer to industrial strategy-makers good grounds on which to bypass the rules of the game.

A CHANGED ENVIRONMENT

The reason why within an international industrial perspective the policies of the US Government are so important is three-fold: first, by attacking the multinationals at their home base, antitrust law imprints on top management's mind a certain line of conduct which has a good chance of being reflected internationally.

Second, other governments tend to look to the US Department of Justice for precedence on how to deal with large-scale industrial concerns and financial institutions. In the 1960s the Common Market Executive set up an Antitrust Division which (though the Common Market may deny it) is to a considerable degree modelled along the line of its American counterpart. Something familiar can also be said of the different governments trying to establish a viable national industry able to compete with the multinational giants, particularly in advanced technology such as computers. France, Brazil and India are examples.

Third, there is now emerging a new reality which may invalidate all previous thinking on the subject as outlined in the foregoing examples of American antitrust activity. Market and industry structures change, and many number two and number three outfits, by trying to keep going on an *also-ran* mentality, are increasingly becoming marginal.

Let's look at an example. In November 1980 Boeing carried a gigantic commercial coup that raises interesting questions of public policy. Delta Airlines ordered sixty of Boeing's new 757 jet airliners, for a ringing $3 billion, with delivery beginning in 1984. That establishes a solid base for the 757, one of the next generation of airliners designed for high fuel efficiency. But Boeing's momentum presents a daunting obstacle to the tentative plans of its two competitors: McDonnell Douglas and Lockheed. If they decide not to develop further generations of civilian jet aircraft, is that good or bad? The only competition for Boeing would then come from Airbus Industries, the French–West German partnership, and there we would have an international polarisation of an industry which used to be widely based.

A better known example is, of course, the automobile industry now dominated by General Motors. The main competition about which GM has to worry is coming from Japan. As markets are increasingly extended throughout the world, the normal processes of industrial growth begin to have a new meaning. As industries mature, they have also tended to consolidate into fewer and fewer big companies.

The greatest challenge comes when this process takes place on a world scale and each of those surviving companies is likely to operate under a different flag. In terms of preserving the cherished competition within, say, the US market, political and economic authorities do face a shrinking range of possibilities: doing another Chrysler bail-out and committing large public resources to keeping three major manufacturers in the automobile industry, the jet airliner business and so on. There is the alternative of assuming that there will eventually be only one survivor, with increasingly close ties to the government – in the European manner – as it sells abroad. That's a total reversal of past policy. And if there is only one national producer, its connections with the government will grow progressively more intimate. What's the preferred course?

16 Venture Capital and the Board

The road to telecommunications leadership is already littered with the bleached bones of computer vendors who didn't make it. The road to computer leadership is covered with the skeletons of start-ups, but also with limbs of large corporations who failed their entry into the market. Whichever way one looks, and in whichever industry, a similar story can be written. For the larger company it takes about three major failures to bring it down. But for the small firm, and more particularly the start-up, the first major failure may be the end.

Then why is money available in venture capital, when the risk of failure is so great? Two answers can be given to this query. First, there is also the probability of success, and venture capitalists carefully scrutinise where they put their money – though no scrutiny can ever *guarantee* success. Typically, a venture capital firm in high technology will examine hundreds of business plans. Between 1 and 5 per cent of the submitted plans are funded, and in some venture capital companies the percentage is much lower.

Second, venture capitalists are investors. Investors are people who manage investment funds, looking at whether to buy stocks or bonds and when to sell them. In doing so, they take risks. Venture capitalism is another form of risk-taking in the search for greater profits.

To be sure, there are differences. Classical investors look at a company from the outside. *Venture capitalists* are primarily oriented towards how a company:

- runs;
- solves the problems of its developments – from products to market perspective;
- faces the problems of competition;
- attacks the issue of technological change.

So a venture captialist looks at business from the inside. An investor examines a company's five-year or ten-year track record and what the ratios are. The venture capitalist looks only at the future.

While the bulk of Wall Street's capital remains invested with big corporations, its heart is with the new ones, especially those run by defectors from major companies. Other new Wall Street heroes are raiders who would fire top management and carve corporate assets for profits.

THE BOARD OF DIRECTORS LOOKS AT VENTURE CAPITALISM

There are two different reasons why a board of directors may be interested in venture capitalism. First, many large corporations today not only follow closely on developments relating to high technology start-up firms, they also take an interest in some of these companies. General Electric is an example in the United States. Siemens is an example in Europe. Many other well-established firms have set up and manage a venture capital fund. Whenever this is the case, the board of directors should take a keen interest in it.

Second, and the most obvious, the board of directors may actually be the policy-setting body of a venture capital fund. Though many venture capitalists are private individuals, a board action is a realistic case.

Venture capitalists have a gambler's nerve and a prospector's nose for gold. They have prospered by investing in small, unknown companies, then capitalising on the bull market that has sent the Dow Jones industrial average to one new high after another in the 1985 to 1986 period. Contrary to the rather widely held belief, venture capitalists are not traders. Their investment is risked for a period of several years in anticipation of long-term gains. Therefore venture capital companies require a business opportunity analysis and five-year plan from the start-up, at the time of funding.

Milestones to measure success are a critical feature of the plan and are proportional to the individual nature of each company. What happens to the fortunate 1 per cent to 5 per cent of the business plans that are funded? Roughly one out of ten makes it big, two may break even, five are a burden and always need money, and another two go bankrupt.

Is this score good or bad? To give an answer we must compare it with something else, book publishing being as near a parallel as one can get. In the long run:

- Some 5 per cent of a publisher's list makes it big, as against 10 per cent in venture capitalism;
- Another 20 to 25 per cent break even or make a tiny profit;
- 70 to 75 per cent of published books are a dry hole.

So book publishing fares a little worse in terms of probabilities, though the few books that hit the jackpot make enough profits to keep the publisher prosperous.

There are reasons for a start-up going bankrupt, of which these six are the most important:

(1)   It is undercapitalised from the beginning.
(2)   The basic business concept has no potential for success.
(3)   The business ground is not an original idea.
(4)   It has a marketing man at the top and no research and development.
(5)   It has research and development skill, but no marketing.
(6)   It is managed by plain average people – no thrust, no high skill.

Half the reasons relate to human capital; that's why having the right people is the primary factor a venture capitalist looks for in a business plan. This includes the chief executive officer, his prior profit and loss responsibility, and a seasoned team in the fields of finance, research and development, marketing and operations. Without the right people, you get nothing.

Next in importance comes the exciting proprietary technology with its extraordinary market potential. That market potential is generally defined as having a sales perspective of $20 million to $50 million at the end of the five years – starting from zero. Hence, when the venture captialist looks from the inside, he is asking questions about:

● human capital;
● exciting products;
● market demand;
● cost factors;
● volume relationships;
● competitive positioning;
● what financial resources are needed to acquire a staying power.

One variety of venture capitalism is *venture nuturing*. It involves managerial assistance from the investing corporation as well as cash, and sometimes also marketing, manufacturing and even additional research. Venture nuturing helps in some way answer the question 'How does a fledgling company reach a level of prosperity?' Jim Treybig, President of Tandem Computers, who, in addition to receiving venture capitalism money to found Tandem, had several years of experience working for a venture capital firm, puts it in these terms: 'I've always had people better than I am working for me.'

Whether we talk of a start-up or of a going enterprise, we have to have people who are good at creative, strategic thought. We need people with the ability to sell – but also with backgrounds in finance, research, development and marketing. At a premium are people with tenacity, faith and drive. Glamour people rarely make it. They are overconfident and they are afraid to get their hands dirty. People with no sense of timing fail; a lot depends on timing, for example, when to introduce the prototype. Even good timing can go sour if timetables are not respected. If development takes too long, the firm cannot raise the money. The same is true about slippages in marketing plans.

Another form of venture capitalism is *venture spin-offs*. Usually this is the by-product of a large corporation's own research and development effort, spinning off a new business if management feels it does not fit too well within its own mainstream activity.

Venture merging is the term used to describe the deliberate attempt to piece together all the various approaches to technological venturing. Some large corporations, for instance, are in the process of transforming themselves from a huge, single-product company into a new technological giant in communications, computers, electronic office equipment, advanced materials and energy devices.

Internal ventures occur when a corporation sets up an entirely separate greenhouse division within itself to develop radically new products or to enter different markets. Management hopes that this approach might provide 'small company conditions', with ideas incubating and growing before having to stand on their own feet.

Finally, *new-style joint ventures* are the case when large and small companies go into projects together. The small firm is providing the ideas, entrepreneurial enthusiasm and flexibility. The big corporation offers the capital and the worldwide marketing and service back-up.

THE VENTURE CAPITALIST'S DRIVING FORCE

One of the reasons people find it so exciting to do business in venture capitalism is that entrepreneurship flourishes there. Start-ups have innovative programmes and, given good management, they provide incentives. They also minimise the red-tape that can get in the way of business growth. Entrepreneurship gives a vital boost in a small business's development programmes. This is just as essential as capital in helping people with ideas.

Unlike the commercial banker who lends money for interest, the venture capitalist is a partner. Typically he takes an active role in management during the early phases of growth. Sometimes the venture capitalist has to step in to run the company in a troubled period. Ideally, investor and inventor combine forces in synergy. Each pushes his partner to greater creativity in developing the product and finding markets while, at the same time, successive rounds of financing can accelerate as a company starts taking off.

Negotiations often require from four months to over two years. 'When we investigate, we call everyone,' says National City's Mr Sherwin. 'We use consultants, trade associations, government data, economic studies – everything we can think of. We take a long time. Not because we are stupid, but because we are thorough.'

In the beginning, the histories of successes and failures are similar: gather a technical staff; announce the breakthrough; get the money and spend it; go public. Then:

- announce new breakthroughs in even more glowing terms;
- watch the stock sky-rocket to ten times the opening price;
- spend the money raised at the public offering;
- Take orders – then deliver some hand-built models as prototypes.

From that point on, the histories of successes and failures divide. After the prototype level, the success story would go into series production to fulfil the market demand. They will babysit the product, train the client, get his acceptance and use such acceptance as point of reference. Success stories will typically be fast moving, keeping ahead of competition, thinking of the successor to their product even when the latter is at the prototype stage. Above all, they will bet on quality.

Failure-prone start-ups will be quick in announcing reasons why their product is not being delivered. They will borrow more money, leaning on their now fearful investors to come up with guaranteed loans, debentures or preferred stock to 'protect' their investment. In this failure-prone class also fall companies ready to abdandon the originally touted breakthrough and frantically seek other products or workable business plans to salvage the firm, using the new money they have got. Then they will 'go into Chapter Eleven' as quietly as possible, emerge wiser than before and seek new adventures. They will leave behind on Wall Street a fear of new ventures in that particular field that might endure for a decade.

In spite of this fear, multiplied many times over by the diversity of fields venture capital addresses, in 1985 the US venture capital market bet some $3.2 billion on fledgling businesses. This has been the prime

financing source for hundreds of small companies involved in biotechnology and other high-technology products. In every instance on record,
the moneymen are searching for good ideas. In the 1983 to 1986 period
alone, venture capital clubs have been started in two dozen American
cities. Domestic and foreign banks, investment houses, non-profit
research institutes and private entrepreneurs are backing some 1,200
venture funds in 1986.

As pay-off for the inherent risk in this business, venture capitalists
want control of the firm they are financing – as much as 80 per cent of the
stock of an unproven start-up. Said Richard Bannon, partner of
Cardinal Capital Development Fund: 'For one thing, we don't want the
owner to be able to sell the business out from under us. The exit
mechanism is particularly important to us because we must return the
invested dollars to the partners – in cash or traded securities within ten
years or so.'

After taking control of a successful start-up, venture capitalists
capitalise on the public's seemingly insatiable appetite for shares in
companies selling their stock for the first time. New companies are
rushing to take advantage of the buoyant stock market. In 1985 alone,
nearly 900 companies made initial offerings of stock, raising $12.8
billion (US statistics). That is nine times more capital than was raised by
new firms in 1982 and even more than the amount for all the years since
1971 put together.

Mutual funds and pension funds, big institutional buyers and
individual shareholders have all anxiously sought to invest in the new
firms. But not all venture capitalists emerged winners. Some saw the
sunny prospects of their companies turn sour in a matter of weeks, their
paper profits vanishing just as quickly. Sometimes unjustified enthusiasm pushed up the price of some high-technology stocks to 80 times
their earnings, compared with about 16 times earnings. Then many of
the fast-rising new issues fell faster than they rose.

Changing fortunes is one reason why in the quest for financing, a
business plan is essential. Venture capitalists will not consider a
company without one. Owners profit from compiling them because they
are forced to think about where their business should be going and how
to get it there. There are people who will do a business opportunity
analysis and a business plan for a fee, but investors worry that
entrepreneurs who use finders to write the business plan are delegating a
task they should be handling themselves. In fact, prior to making his
business plan the entrepreneur should acquaint himself with the ways
and means venture capitalists use to judge companies, as well as those of

the market. What potential users want such a product? What do they want it to do? Market potential is particularly important. Michael Sherwin, President and General Manager of National City Capital observes that many entrepreneurs underestimate the importance of determining whether a market even exists for their product.

A business plan addressing the vital questions facing a start-up company need not be lengthy. Sometimes the back-ground of the entrepreneur himself can be the prime asset or liability. At least one venture fund dismisses entrepreneurs who come from big companies, on the premise that such people have become too used to assistants and safety nets. Most fund managers also try to get an idea of the founder's family. If there is some doubt that the wife/husband may balk at the prospect of her husband/wife working 15-hour days, seven days a week, plus heavy travel, they do not give backing. The risk for their capital increases by so much.

ROADBLOCKS TO VENTURE CAPITALISM

The roadblocks to venture capitalism can be both cultural and financial. Not long long ago, there was an investigation in Denmark into 'who starts a new business'. Its results indicated that people with an academic background are not prone to go into business on their own and start a new enterprise. Some not clearly identified reasons seem to indicate that university education

- reduces personal risk-taking;
- tempers the entrepreneurial activity.

Another study pointed to the fact that persons trying a start-up are driven by product opportunity rather than market opportunity. But venture capitalists invest primarily for market opportunity – and rightly so. Also on the motivational side of the picture, a study was to point out that investing in people who are negative to their current job is a bad venture. A good venture is manned by people positive to their current job, who have the thrust to capture a market further than their present job permits. As Bernard Tapie, one of the successful young European entrepreneurs suggests (in the French Press), 'Create companies and earn big money through entrepreneurship. Dare to think big!' 'I am no superman,' he says. 'I am just a professional who knows how to do his job.' And he adds: 'The rewards of business are not simply money. It is the pleasure, the game, liberty, mobility, the possibility of creating. I believe in dreams, risk and laughter.'

There are not many who do so, and here come also the financial problems facing European venture capitalism:

- There is no established way of disinvesting (going public).
- There are no easy sources of obtaining capital at the right time, with continuing investment sources.
- The appreciation of need to invest in prototypes, in order to start the marketing activity very soon, is not present.

These three points illustrate the fact that there are no people ready to jump on an opportunity involving high risk (cultural problems).

There are some governmental sources for financing European high-technology projects, like the British Alvey and the EEC Esprit. But Alvey is currently running out of money and so was Esprit I – though new projects came up like Esprit II and Eureka.

Other issues are of a marketing nature. For instance, the practical impossibility of signing large original-equipment manufacturer (OEM) agreements. The large European company is very conservative with start-ups. Furthermore, there is a

- market fragmentation, from language to custom problems;
- difficulty in hiring good experienced managers for start-ups in quantities necessary to grow solid new businesses;
- tough time in going international, because US and Japanese markets are fairly closed.

European start-up companies must try twice as hard as their American counterparts to succeed in competition. Because the culture has been very different for long decades, the new technologies are very hard to legislate for, to market and – most importantly – to do solution selling.

CAPITALISING ON VENTURE FUNDS

Investments in entrepreneurial companies are often made for reasons other than pure profit. This is particularly true of corporate funds which focus on a broad range of emerging companies at various stages of development. In this case, one of the most common objectives for corporate investors is to identify windows of opportunity in new technology. Large companies have learned that alliances with smaller, fast-moving units are a good way to get a window on the change and innovation affecting some of their own markets.

A similar goal is to learn about new markets for the existing business.

The exposure that a corporation can gain by partnership with a smaller company often brings a new perspective to traditional market expectations. It also leads to tapping an emerging supply of new or related products. New products developed by an emerging business can extend the corporation's product line and market share. They provide inside information on potential acquisitions and help enhance corporate image.

Investments made in emerging companies can make a corporation more exciting to its current and potential shareholders, and can also increase the value of its stock. Equally, it helps in cross-fertilising managers, developing a more motivated management team. In some cases such cross-fertilisation can prevent a brain drain of managers leaving for more exciting jobs. In fact many established corporations are instituting separate, · independent business units to simulate an entrepreneurial environment. They find that these *intra*-preneurships can infuse risk-taking and creativity into otherwise slow-moving cultures.

The benefits to the start-up firm may, in some cases, be substantial. A corporate partner can help in several ways. Bigger corporations can lend a hand in strategic planning, marketing, distribution, research and development, manufacturing, and lines of credit. Known, well-established corporate investors lend credibility in the market-place to a start-up firm. From being nobody, it becomes somebody. Original equipment manufacturers (OEM) agreements with an established company can provide extra assurance to potential customers who are concerned about whether a new company will stay in business. Another asset is the possibility of raising additional capital from the corporate investor. This is usually easier than going through financing with venture capitalists, while the risk of losing control of the company is less – though by no means non-existent.

There are also snags. Burroughs became both a significant customer of Convergent Technologies and a minority shareholder when the two companies struck a deal. But this helped neither company in an appreciable manner. Exxon literally strangled the small business-equipment firms it absorbed. After its acquisition of Zilog, the best people (including the founders) left. To all practical purposes, glamour start-up Zilog went down the drain – at least in terms of innovation.

Another risk is that usually big corporations approach smaller companies with an all-or-nothing attitude. Because the cultures are too different, acquisitions often create clashes between corporate and entrepreneurial elements.

A better deal for the start-up is minority equity investments. Yet often these are cautious steps to gauge value before making a total commitment. In fact, toehold investments grew in popularity as corporations began to appreciate their strategic potential. At a fraction of the risk and cost of an acquisition, larger firms ally themselves with smaller, developing proprietary technology or penetrating new markets. At the same time, corporations are getting a better idea of how to manage and benefit from their investments in start-up or fast-growing small companies.

While many large corporations know their way around on how to capitalise on venture capital, the economy too stands to profit. By 1986 venture capital available in the United States totalled more than $14 billion and an US Government study of 72 companies showed just what impact this money can have. With the help of $209 million in venture funds, the beneficiary companies reported:

- decade-cumulative sales of $6 billion;
- 130,000 new jobs;
- $900 million in exports;
- $450 million in tax payments.

The message should not have been lost on business and political leaders. Yet the recent tax reforms in the United States seem to remove much of the financial incentives for venture capital, killing the goose that laid the golden egg.

A post-industrial economy needs innovative companies to solve rising unemployment rates and to meet the technological challenge. If the entrepreneur is a cornerstone in any emerging programme of economic change, the venture capitalist can be regarded as his financial twin.

In Europe, venture capital largely functions not across borders but within individual countries. As a result, the products have a limited market, a narrow horizon in earnings, and are too expensive to sell. Because of the fragmentation and lack of co-operation, the average size of an investment in Europe is much smaller than in the United States. The ventures themselves tend to forgo the export opportunities that a foreign financial partner can bring them. Still, in the proliferation of private funds, Britain has a long lead, accounting for roughly two-thirds of the total dollar value. West Germany has the fastest-growing pool of funds, many of them aided by local governments trying to attract companies and jobs to their regions.

No European country can provide a market big enough to support a strong venture capital portfolio by itself. Funds in every country have to band together so they can help each other develop the companies they invest in. The flow of investment capital across European borders is a slow process. Yet there is a definite need for fast pace in doing deals, assessing technology, spotting managers and helping new companies find markets.

In spite of some exceptions, the United States remains the focal market for venture capital. Half of Europe's pool in this field is being drawn into US companies rather than invested at home. Frederick Adler, a venture capitalist based in New york, estimates that 40 per cent of the funds in his US investment portfolio come from a nationalised French bank. Foreign, mainly European, funds provided 27 per cent of US venture capital last year, second only to pension funds which contributed 28 per cent. Part of the reason is that Europe has a lack of real knowledge about venture capitalism and is cool towards risk-taking in the old continent itself.

PROFILES IN VENTURE CAPITALISM

Though the idea was as old as the royal financing of fifteenth-century explorers, modern venture capitalism is generally dated from 1938, when Laurence Rockefeller put up the money to transform a troubled division of General Motors into Eastern Airlines.

Venture capital in the United States became big business in the 1960s during the electronics boom associated with Silicon Valley in northern California. One of the best-known practitioners is Arthur Rock, whose successes include Apple Computers and Intel. His fortune is believed to exceed $1 billion. 'He's made more than just money, he's made companies, without ever touching a tool,' says George J. W. Goodman, the American economics writer whose books are published under the name 'Adam Smith'.

'Management, management and more management. That's the key to success in venture capital,' says Peter A. Brooke. He stresses that venture capitalism is hands-on work, radically different from commercial banking and even investment banking. 'In the high technology markets,' Brooke says, 'new products have to develop fast. An entrepreneur needs help of all kinds, especially with contacts to help him sell around the world from the outset.'

Venture capital cannot instantly create high-technology businesses that will replace smokestack industries. It needs seasoning to mature, and the right culture to grow.

Brooke became a venture capitalist in the early 1960s. He worked as a banker, then became manager of the venture capital department at Bessemer Securities Corporation. In 1968 he formed TA Associates, which is one of the largest venture capital partnerships in the United States with $1 billion in investments. TA's portfolios are dominated by high-technology companies, mainly in microelectronics and, to a growing degree, biotechnology. In 1977 TA financed the Tandon Corporation, now the leading US producer of floppy disks for small computers with sales approaching $500 million. In 1973 it funded Federal Express, which specialises in overnight delivery of parcels throughout the United States and which is now worth $2 billion on the stock market.

TA Associates has an international network of independent venture capital funds in Europe and Asia. Started in 1981, this network groups a dozen funds with nearly 300 million dollar's worth of investments. Members include several Advent Funds in Britain, Advent Belgium, Four Seasons Venture Capital in Scandinavia, Techno-Venture in West Germany, Alpha Associés in France and Horizonte Ventures in Austria, Advent Techno-Venture Investment in Japan and the Southeast Asian Venture Investment Corporation in Singapore.

These ventures have a common, underlying concept: that an innovative idea and entrepreneurial leadership are as valuable as financing. And the same is true of expert advice. Headquartered in Munich, Techno-Venture relies on technical advice from Siemens in selecting investments. 'Initially, we had trouble with Siemens' inclination to want to grab promising ideas for itself,' commented the Techno-Venture manager. 'But we finally persuaded key officials that new, small companies would develop projects faster and better. Now they give good advice and keep their hands off.'

Benjamin Rosen is a major investor in Lotus Development and Compaq Computer. He worked for Coleman and Company, a New York securities firm, for Morgan Stanley, and then published an electronics-industry newsletter. In 1981 he launched his third and most successful career as venture capitalist.

Rosen started two venture capital funds with L. J. Sevin, founder of Mostek, a semiconductor manufacturer. Sevin Rosen Management's $2.1 million investment in Lotus Development turned into a holding worth $70 million when the company went public in late 1983. The fund invested some $2.5 million in Compaq, the portable computer manufacturer whose portable wares run like the IBM PC. When Compaq went public, in late 1983, that investment was worth $40 million. Another star

338   *Membership of the Board of Directors*

performer was Osborne Computer till it went down the drain with the fund losing $400 thousand.

Like a knowledgeable venture capitalist, Rosen is not a passive investor. He became Chairman of Compaq and takes an active hand in other ventures. He also sees far more deals than other venture capitalists in companies he participates in. Picking the probable survivors is a tough job, whether you are an analyst, venture capitalist or market researcher. Yet some rules of thumb are considered valid. 'Any company that we put money into must have an aggressive new product policy,' notes Rosen in *Business Week*. 'A new company typically needs to expand its product line in three to four years,' explains another investor in *Business Week*. 'Of the 80% of the companies that won't make it, half will sell out due to the lack of an encore, a second big product.'

Much of the fortunes Sevin, Rosen, the other venture capitalists and the men whom they finance are making come from the public offering of shares. The founder of the terminal and desktop-maker, TeleVideo Systems, owned 29 million shares in his company, each valued at $18, when it went public. On paper his holdings were worth $520 million.

Lotus priced its shares at $13 each when the company's liquidation value was 48 cents per share. TeleVideo's tangible book value was 68 cents per share when the price was set at $18. When Kaypro sold 4 million shares of stock at $10, the value of the company at that time was little more than 20 cents per share. In fact, the Kay family originally offered to sell shares in their portable computer company, Kaypro, for up to $18 per share. Their holdings of 28 million shares would have been worth $504 million. But after intense negotiations, pension-fund managers and other investors refused to pay more than $10 per share. The value of the Kay family stock dropped to a mere $280 million on paper.

The offering price for the stock of new companies is determined in a series of private negotiations between the Wall Street brokerage houses and their customers. The resulting price is a balance between supply and demand. The relative valuations dropped after several high-technology stocks lost some of their glitter in the wake of the losses posted by Texas Instruments, Mattel, Atari, and others.

Some investments turn sour, the firm on which they bet does not ignite the market. One company that tried to go public but faltered was Androbot, manufacturer of several types of consumer robots. It offered to sell stock for up to $12 per share, seeking an infusion of $1.5 million in new working capital. But the offer was withdrawn as a company official explains, 'due to market considerations'. One money manager suggested that the company's poor financial health was more a factor. 'I was shocked to see this as a deal,' he said, 'and further shocked that Merrill Lynch would be associated with it.'

Hardware is just one of the hot products on which to make or to lose a fortune. Software is another. Mitchell Kapor, founder of Lotus Development, dabbled as a disc jockey, an instructor in transcendental meditation and a mental-hospital counsellor prior to getting into the millionaire's row. He got an Apple II computer, wrote two programs for charting, sold them to a software distributor, then with backing from venture capitalists he founded Lotus Development in 1982. Within a year the company's 1-2-3 integrated software became the industry's bestseller, making Lotus the second largest independent software company in the United States with estimated annual sales of $40 million. Kapor held some $70 million worth of stock when Lotus went public.

Neil Hirsch is the founder of Telerate Systems, an electronic financial information service. He spent two years studying business but then dropped out and started hanging around stock-brokerage offices. There he had the idea of speedily transmitting financial data to individual customers. In 1969 Hirsch formed Telerate to track the prices of volatile commercial paper and send them electronically to customers' video terminals. Some 11,000 subscribers in the United States and overseas pay an average of $700 per month for the service. When Telerate went public, Hirsch held shares worth $67.5 million.

Arnold Bernard, creator of the Value Line stock-rating service, is not a youngster like the other millionaires. His first job was writing theatre reviews for *Time* (in 1925). During the Depression he managed money for some clients and worked on a stock-rating system. This, in 1935, he turned into the Value Line Investment Survey. Today, 112,000 subscribers pay Value Line $365 a year for an assessment of 1,700 companies. Bernard's stock in Value Line was worth $145 million when the company went public.

Walter Gilbert is co-founder of Biogen, a genetic engineering firm. He spent most of his life working with genes. While a Professor of Molecular Biology at Harvard, he won the Nobel Prize in 1980 for his work in exploring the DNA molecule. Then Gilbert and eight other scientists decided to capitalise on their knowledge. With $750,000 in venture capital they incorporated Biogen in Curaçao. The firm produces interferon, a substance that is being tested against a variety of illnesses, ranging from cancer and herpes to the common cold. The main product line is gene-splicing – with a broad potential impact from genetics to agriculture. Gilbert and his wife hold shares that were worth $12 million at the public offering.

Not every venture can be successful, and there is a $1 billion story which went bust. That was Daniel Ludwig's Brazilian dream. In 1970, the German-born US shipping magnate paid a visit to the Amazon jungle. He liked what he saw and bought a piece half the size of Belgium.

During the 1970s Ludwig poured into his Brazilian venture $1 billion to realise his ambition of turning the virgin forest into a profitable wood-pulp enterprise. Then in the early 1980s, under a transaction being worked out in Rio de Janeiro, Brasilia and New York, a group of Brazilian companies, backed by the Government, took over Ludwig's Jari project.

Daniel Ludwig bought his tract of 4 million acres (1.6 million hectares) in 1967. It lies just south of the equator, part in the lower Amazon state of Para and part in the neighbouring territory of Amapa, by the Jari river. The main aim was to produce wood-pulp for paper, a commodity becoming increasingly scarce. The Jari project sought to exploit the forests without wrecking the ecology. The plan was to plant trees and to farm them efficiently. The new plantation, covering 250,000 acres (100,000 hectares) of land, included pines, eucalyptus and the gmelina, a quick-growing tree from India. Ludwig bought a pulp-processing plant in Japan and towed it round the world and up the Amazon to the heart of Jari. Other projects included large rice-growing fields, herds of water buffalo and cattle, as well as smaller agricultural plans. Jari turned out to contain an estimated 150-million-metric-ton deposit of kaolin, a white clay used in making porcelain and paper. To serve all these operations Ludwig built 60 kilometres of railway, 500 kilometres of main roads, 4,000 kilometres of secondary roads, six small towns, three airfields and a port.

Yet despite the determination and energy, Jari has yet to pay dividend on the billion dollars Ludwig put into it – $650 million of investment from his business empire and $350 in foreign credits. The tropical Amazon soil was found to be much less fertile than expected, resulting in lower yields, and the Asian trees adapted less well than hoped. Above all, the Brazilian Government was hindering Jari with breaucratic obstracles. A one-man ownership of such a huge tract of land also provoked attacks from some politicians, who demanded nationalisation of the project.

THE CORPORATE RAIDERS

The corporate raiders are a different breed of venture capitalist. When they bid millions to take over a company, they don't really want to buy it. They are merely putting a company in play, hoping to sell out at a high price.

Corporate raiders are bold and typically act as if they knew something the rest of the investment community does not know. T. Boone Pickens, the Chairman of Mesa Petroleum, is not a man to pick solely on companies his own size. One of Mesa's latest quarries, Phillips Petroleum, was fifteen times bigger than Mesa. Though smaller than other companies Pickens stalked, like Gulf Oil, Phillips was still much too big to be taken over easily.

Among corporate raiders, Pickens is sometimes hailed as a crusader for shareholders' rights. He appears often on television in the United States as an apostle of capitalism. His takeover battles with Cities Services, Gulf Oil and General American Oil were against, he says, 'professional managers who believe they own the company'. They have grossed him and his friends around $500 million. The money has come from *white knights* riding to the rescue of the beleaguered companies. But Pickens's battles have also made $9 billion for the companies' other shareholders.

In Wall Street jargon, a *white knight* is a supposedly friendly deal saving a takeover from an unfriendly bid. Either way, the company ends in somebody else's hands. The *poison pill* is a different business. Poison pills normally involve preferred stock with special rights attached. This is triggered on an unwelcome bid, thereby making it prohibitively expensive for a predator. Some Wall Street experts look at them as a way to even the balance of power between the raider and the target. Others disagree.

For T. Boone Pickens, however, the poison pill is one of the most potentially damaging approaches that could hit corporate America. In fact, he has warned that, if used on a large scale, it could place control of Corporate America in the hands of a few people interested only in keeping their jobs.

Greenmail is a technique used in a number of cases involving the acquisition of a block of a company's shares. It's a sort of kickback. Companies justify greenmail by stating the express or implied threats of disruption of the company's business. In such circumstances, these firms have repurchased their shares on other terms more favourable than those available to other shareholders. Yet the Phillips battle highlights the difficulty of defining just what consititutes 'greenmail.'

Phillips promised to pay T. Boone Pickens $53 per share in cash for his stake, whatever happens, while Phillips shareholders receive paper said to have a value of $53 per share. Pickens vigorously denied that this is a form of greenmail but some of the institutions were not sure and prepared to vote against the recapitalisation plan.

To see the financial impact of such a defensive offer, let's recall that in the Phillips case, T. Boone Pickens and two oilmen from Midland, Texas, bought 8.98 million Phillips shares for $37 a ⅜-share. They then offered to buy another 15 million for $60 a share. Phillips tried to fend off Mesa, first by fighting in the courts. It obtained temporary restraining orders by alleging that Pickens violated the Hart-Scott-Rodino Act when he acquired 5.8 per cent of Phillips shares without making a filing to the federal trade commission.

In a personal affidavit, Joseph Fogg, Managing Director of Morgan Stanley, alleged that Pickens' purchase of Phillips stock violated a standstill agreement signed by Pickens with General American Oil in 1983. In this agreement he promised that for five years he would not buy General American's shares or try to control the company. At the time, General American was owned by Phillips. While legal moves are part of the defensive action, a financial offer which is very lucrative to the raider is another defence.

Pickens was not the only Phillips Petroleum raider. Another was Carl Icahn, the 48-year-old Wall Street financier. He, too, has a low opinion of corporate management, which he describes as generally inadequate. Icahn is a fervent believer that what he is doing is good for the US economy. 'A lot of U.S. managements fly around in their jet planes and go to their hunting lodges where they live like nobility of old. But they do not own the company,' he says, arguing that one of the great problems of the economy is the lack of management answerability to shareholders.

Phillips Petroleum, TWA, Eastern Airlines, Cities Services, Gulf Oil are examples both of corporate raiding and of the takeover fever that swept through some of the United State's biggest and most traditionally managed industries. Airlines have been for long on the sick list as the US oil business tries to come to terms with falling oil prices and sharply reduced demand. In 1984 alone, Chevron, Texaco and Mobil spent $29 billion buying Gulf, Getty and Superior Oil respectively. One can write a script on the sorts of problems Wall Street and big business are wrestling with on both sides of the corporate raiding arena.

Irwin L. Jacobs is a Minneapolis takeover artist who for some years threatened to buy many big companies but has bought only a few small ones. But with his 1985 agreement to buy American Machine and Foundry (AMF), a $1.1-billion-a-year industrial and leisure products company, Jacobs became a significant conglomerator. In April 1985 Jacobs acquired a 7.5 per cent interest in AMF through Minstar, a public company he controls. He then phoned W. Thomas York, AMF

Chairman, to say he might want to purchase its Hatteras boat division, or possibly all of AMF. According to what was later learned, York was distinctly not interested and added: 'We don't pay *greenmail*.' Within weeks Minstar tendered for 12 million shares of AMF at $23, which would have given Jacobs's company 50.5 per cent ownership.

AMF's response was an elaborate dosage of *poison pills*. In addition, Morgan Stanley, AMF's investment banker, began to shop around for a *white knight*. Minstar sued to stop the poison pills, and AMF counter-sued. In federal court in New York in June 1985 District Judge Mary Johnson Lowe held for Minstar. AMF's lawyers promised an immediate appeal.

Like Pickens and Icahn, Jacobs presents himself as a champion of shareholder interests, pointing out that in case after case shareholders get a better price as a result of a takeover, hostile or otherwise. But he insists he opposes greenmail: 'I don't want it, I don't believe in it – but I wouldn't necessarily refuse it if it were forced on me.'

There are also differences among raider tactics. While Pickens and Icahn typically go after one target at a time, Jacobs trains his sights on several simultaneously without indicating his precise purpose. 'We are an unpredictable group. The problem people have with us is that they don't know which way we are going. If I lost that, I would lose a great asset.'

We have spoken of white knights and poison pills as defence measures. Another variety is the so-called employee stock ownership plan (ESOP). This allows employees to take a stake in a company on more beneficial terms than are available to outside investors, because of official tax privileges. A key element in Phillips's defences, for example, was the biggest ESOP in the United States, after recapitalisation permitting Phillips employees to own between 32 per cent and 42 per cent of the company's equity. The ESOP argument goes like this: 'The employees will have a significant economic interest in performance. This should help ensure its success and thereby benefits all stockholders.' However, many of the big institutional investors are worried that the concentration of ownership in the hands of the employees will work to their disadvantage over the long term.

In a way, the theme of many exertions in corporate raiding seems to be: how to succeed by failing, or how to make a fortune through thwarted takeovers. The debate over hostile takeovers frequently engages their artists. They rarely turn down a public forum to air their views, and sometimes appear before a Senate subcommittee on take-overs.

Raiders do not reveal their art in public lectures and in committee hearings, but the careful observer can find four rules that govern the approach to takeovers:

(1) Spot something of value: a company with substantial assets, cash flow, or both, whose shares are undervalued.
(2) Move with speed and stealth.
(3) Always be flexible; ready to buy more or to walk away abruptly, to sue or be sued.
(4) Be willing and able to buy the company you ostensibly want.

That cost Icahn his ownership and deep involvement in TWA. When asked how anyone can possible want to buy all these companies, Jacobs responds, 'It's like the case of the young fellow walking down the street. He wants all those attractive women he sees, but some he wants more than others.'

Some arbitrageurs show significant management skills. Carl Icahn works with a staff of just eight assistants – already a very positive reference, given the industrial empire which he runs. He is a quick learner who is imposing his work ethic on some of the largest and most troubled US corporations. Icahn (estimated net worth: $700 million) is simultaneously juggling four daunting turnaround projects: the born-again TWA, the bankrupt Texaco, the resurgent USX, and the revived ACF.

As *Business Week* (8 Feb 1988) was to comment, Carl Icahn's demonstrated management know-how made him the most credible of US raiders, one whose spartan style of running a company is both inspiring and chilling for corporate America. Observes Paul Tierney, 'When Carl goes after something, you can be pretty certain he will pursue it to the death.'

Take TWA as an example. In 1985 Icahn won a bitter seven-month tug-of-war with Texas Air Chief Frank Lorenzo. In 1985 TWA's losses were a cool $150 million. In the process, he passed up the chance to turn a quick $150 million profit on his $310 million investment. That forced him to prove another of his maxims: *executives with their own money invested in a company do a better job of running it*. In 1987, TWA made profits.

'You must have a high tolerance for stress to survive in this business,' suggests one of the artists in corporate raiding. He knows nicely why. When the market collapses many promising deals in corporate raiding become disastrous. A good example with Australian dealmakers was given by *Business Week* on 9 November, 1987.

The article first brought under perspective the historical reference. Taking advantage of easy credit, beer barons Alan Bond and John Elliott, and financier Robert Holmes à Court built empires by searching the international market for undervalued companies. In case cash flow and dividends from their targets did not cover new debt, they traded on rising stock markets to earn the needed cash. But as the article suggested: 'The game's over now.'

Holmes à Court seems to be in the most precarious position of all the Australian raiders. Analysts believe the Bell Group which he controls had paper losses exceeding $1.1 billion. Its investments included 10 per cent of Texaco and 15 per cent of Standard Chartered PLC. More trouble came at the end of October 1987 when Merrill Lynch & Co. suddenly withdrew as underwriters of a $750 million, low-cost debt financing. The pullout could leave Holmes à Court to cover loans, estimated to be 210 per cent of shareholders' equity.

Bernard Baruch is rumoured as having said: 'Wall Street is a crap game and all the world's a casino with players making entrances and exits until they lose their shirts and pants. That's why they say no matter who wins Leona Helmseley never loses.' That is true of all stock-markets. 'The nice thing about the stock market is that you never see the money when you invest it and you never see it when it is gone,' suggests Art Buchwald, and adds: 'I originally went into the market for greed. But it was only last month that I discovered I was also entitled to a lot of pain.'

17 How Successful is a Consolidation Policy?

As the opening chapters properly underlined, the goals of industry are in a steady evolution. Not only are the big brown factories a disappearing species in the developed world, but also the employment landscape itself is rapidly changing. Seen under this aspect of economic and financial restructuring, mergers and acquisitions have a totally different perspective. They become the means for the consolidation and the restructuring of our economic system.

It is under this aspect that the board of directors should evaluate and decide on an acquisition policy. The Western economy is entering a very favourable period with reasonable stability in the background. It is the time to revamp and modernise the industrial system which served us well for over 100 years:

- Most countries will experience a 2 to 3 per cent annual expansion for the next ten years.
- New research projects are set up to serve as technology transfer mechanisms into the twenty-first century: from the Strategic Defense Initiative (SDI) to the Microelectronics and Computer Development Corp. (MCC) in the United States to Esprit and Eureka in the European Community, Alvey in England, Gesellschaft für Informatik und Datenverarbeitung (GMD) in West Germany, and ICOT (the New Generation Computer Project) in Japan.
- Many countries have for the first time the opportunity to design and start to implement an industrial policy for new technologies.

This policy investigates and exploits fields which will be important by the end of the century. If focuses on opportunity.

New leading economic indicators are on the rise and they point in the right direction. Inflation is now under control – between below 1 per cent (Germany, Switzerland) and the 4 per cent level (United States, France), with only few exceptions (UK, Italy). Revenue per head is on the increase, yearly at the 3 to 6 per cent level. The cost of labour, as a percentage of the cost of goods sold, stands at 14 to 15 per cent and is shrinking.

This has some evident effects on employment, with unemployment standing at the 7 to 10 per cent level (with one exception: the UK). But it is mostly structural unemployment, the result of the rate of change. In the Western world we went:

- from 40 per cent of the population employed in manufacturing
- to 20 per cent of the population at the present time;
- the next step is 10 per cent.

Our society cannot adapt fast enough to absorb the difference. But no country (let alone company) can afford to solve the unemployment situation single-handed. For the country which tries to do so alone, it will be political suicide; for the company, economic hara-kiri. The solution lies in an international co-operation among developed nations.

THE PARADOX OF LIVING IN OUR TIMES

Whether the company is big or small – local, regional, national, or international – whether it works in the financial, manufacturing or marketing industries, it cannot avoid the fall-out of the internationalis-ation of business activity. The impact of the international industrial and marketing perspectives may be large or very small, but the way to bet is that they will always be there.

A similar statement about impact can be made of units as big as continents, through states and countries to units as small as townships. Those who know how to restructure themselves and live with their times, also know how to survive. The others who, through inertia and probably unwillingness to close a needed course, let themselves drift, end up in lots of trouble. *Restructuring, moving ahead,* and *knowing how to survive* are the key words for the years to come. They are concepts just as valid for company boards of directors as they are of municipal councils, state and country governments. Restructuring should definitely include strategic use of technology. Figure 17.1 presents a matrix approach I am employing in evaluating, stating in terms of technological impact at the companies I am working with as consultant to top management.

Fifteen chapters in this book have given plenty of evidence not only that the key players in the world economy have changed in the course of the last forty years, but also that some of the basic commodities have lost their former glamour. If decolonisation had not taken place in the liberal winds which prevailed after the Second World War, it would have been a 'must' today to get rid of economies which are just a drag.

Metals and oil are the cases in point. In the Western world the gross

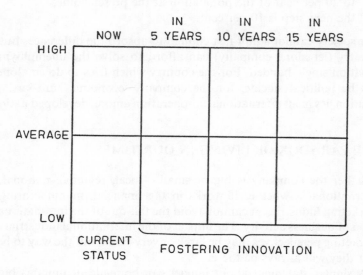

Figure 17.1   The strategic use of technology must be properly planned. This matrix has been very helpful in classifying current and coming projects, as well as in evaluating strengths and weaknesses.

national product (GNP) is rising, year by year, but metal demand is not. The reason is that in the developed world the roads, railways, and major infrastructure are already built, whereas in the underdeveloped world there is no prospect of building them. This is primarily because of low commodity prices which are often such countries' major source of income. Low hard-currency earnings are making the importation of much needed technology and capital goods impossible to afford. Meanwhile, in the developed world our standard of living is rising, but in a way that does not require massive quantities of metals. In the developed world we have our energy-generating systems in place. We now care about our information systems in our communications – which require knowhow, not massive raw materials.

In the developed world, growth is service-oriented with higher disposable incomes being expended on such items as holidays abroad, long vacations, home computers, and improving the general quality of life. However, such activities do not consume large tonnage of metals and, even when money is spent buying items such as cars, computers and washing machines, miniaturisation, recycling and substitution by plastics has cut back unit metal consumption.

As a result, there is the vicious paradox which leads to increasing GNP and increasing standard of living in the Western world, coupled with static metal consumption affecting the underdeveloped countries. Those countries which need to use metal cannot afford to do so, while those who can afford to do so do not greatly need to do so.

The Western world has now reached a level of stability, and stability is more important than an unpredictable high-growth period followed by stagflation. It is the stop/go which kills. This is not to say that there are no problems to be sorted out, but we should be looking at them as opportunities. We should also be learning by the experience other nations have had. Europe, for instance, starts facing some of the same problems and opportunities that the United States had some fives years ago. In the decade after the 1973 oil shock, the United States created 16 million new jobs and Japan added 6 million. Yet Western Europe has had practically no growth in its work force. Unemployment, which as recently as 1971 averaged 3 per cent in European Community countries, more than tripled. European economies expanded just 5.6 per cent between 1979 and 1984, as against 10.5 per cent for the United States and 21.7 per cent for Japan.

At the same time, the world is facing an on-and-off debt crisis, with the strain of debt-service payments proving too much for the fragile political systems of the lesser developed world. As Guido Carli, the former Governor of Italy's Central Bank, pointed out: 'Rather than expanding growth opportunities, the industrial powers have crowded the Third World almost entirely out of capital markets, forcing those nations to revert increasingly to barter arrangements to obtain needed imports.' The corporate board cannot afford to decide without full account of the debt crisis. It's a time bomb regularly defused through recycling and other measures so that it does not explode. But it may.

Arnaldo Musich, President of the Buenos Aires-based Foundation for Latin American Research, has been more optimistic, asserting that although the debt problem is far from resolved, considerable progress has been made. Musich noted that Latin American countries have successfully rescheduled payments on $100 billion of their $370 billion foreign obligations. In 1985 the Latin debt total grew only 2 per cent, meaning that for the first time in many years the debt actually declined about 2 per cent in inflation adjusted terms.

There are also other problems. Whether in the industrialised countries or in the lesser developed world, unemployment hits the untrained people. Of the trained people there are not enough to hire. But the profile of trained people itself has changed. Literacy no longer means knowing how to read and write – it means knowing how to live with high technology. This leads to the notion of *functional illiteracy*.

Estimates of functional illiteracy in the United States run as high as 20 per cent. In spite of its notoriously difficult language, functional illiteracy in Japan is closer to 1 per cent. The Japanese outpace other nations because of:

(1)   The ability to understand and apply the information they possess.
(2)   Their successful and profitable adaptation to the leading technologies of the day.
(3)   The skill to cultivate and refine creative discoveries made by others.

These are, in the twenty-first century, signs of a nation on the move. Typically the British and the Germans are great in creativity, but not necessarily in the marketing of the products which they develop. That is the American speciality – the area where the United States gets high marks.

The coming years will be brutal when they encounter such dichotomies. International competition will be savage in exploiting weaknesses, but will reward the ability of a nation, company, and person to *welcome a new idea and get along with it*. One of the greatest assets in our society is the ability to put to useful end the information flow. As Dr Grace Hopper aptly commented,

> We must establish a criteria for the value of information. We must learn to define the comparative value of information. In the past, the emphasis has been on the process rather than on the output . . . In most cases, information is more valuable than hardware and software. I once asked the IRS how they would depreciate information. They have not answered yet.

Typically, the bureaucrats are some light-years behind the times in which they live. Can a nation afford such backward conditions? That the answer is 'No!' is evident, and such an answer is just as valid for countries, companies and persons. Every living entity (whether physical or legal) has – or at least should have – *strategic advantages*. It should also have a *strategic market target* with precise goals to reach.

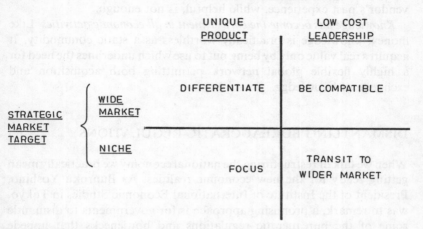

Figure 17.2   The proper top management planning would identify by product
line strategic advantages and market target. Once a product falls in
a quarter space, half the problem of elaborating valid strategies
has been solved.

Capitalising on these two issues, Figure 17.2 sets the frame of
reference for managerial decision and action. If our goal is to have a
unique product and we are in a wide market, we should differentiate. If it
is a market niche we should focus. If our goal is low-cost leadership we
should be compatible to the leader's *de facto* standard. If the initial
condition is low cost in a niche market, we should know that it is not
maintainable over a long stretch of time. Our plan should be to transit to
a wider market – and the wider market today is the world market.

A consolidation policy may also involve joining forces with other,
specialised, companies to enter product lines and markets which *our* own
firm does not have the skill to exploit. In October 1987 IBM announced
a joint venture with Nynex, the New York telephone company,
involving an integrated services digital nework (ISDN) project that will
let voice, data, and images be transmitted simultaneously over a single
phone line. The further aim of IBM in this deal is to probe the
compatibility of its proprietary data-switching solutions with ISDN
technology.

As cannot be repeated too often, the rapid evolution from industrial
society to an information society has reached a point where many of the
basic strategies and balances in key product lines have changed.
Products are rapidly evolving. The application of technological

advances has brought them to unheard levels of sophistication, where a vendor's past experience, while helpful, is not enough.

Knowledge has become the core element in all economic activities. Like money, knowledge is practically worthless as a static commodity. It acquires real value only by being put to use which underlines the need for a highly flexible global network permitting both acquisition and exchange of knowledge.

DISMANTLING BUREAUCRATIC REGULATIONS

When we talk of restructuring the national economy we practically mean getting ready for the new economic realities. As Bunroku Yoshino, President of the Institute of International Economic Studies in Tokyo, was to remark, a promising approach is for governments to dismantle some of the bureaucratic regulations and bottlenecks that impede investment. 'The fundamental problem is to deregulate and to reform our economy,' Yoshino suggested, 'But it will take a longer time.' Nils Lundgren, Chief Economist of PK Banken, one of Sweden's largest banks, says 'Deregulation, market solutions and free enterprise are the order of the day.'

Speaking for the lesser-developed countries, Arnaldo Musich warns that the debt burden is not the root cause of the region's economic problems of endemic poverty, inflation and slow growth. Many of these ills are self-inflicted by what he calls 'rigid inward policies'. This he characterises as excessive bureaucratization, protectionism, and state domination of local economies: 'With or without the debt, Latin American economies would face the necessity of removing these structural impediments.'

Everybody should be doing so. Crumbling old structures set up for the economy of yesterday and crowded with unnecessary drill whose only objective was to maintain the status quo have no place in a modern economy. The sense of survival calls for their immediate removal.

Renewal should be the order of the day, and this is what started happening in the United States in the years of the Reagan Administration. Encouraged by:

- a healthy economy,
- generous tax policies, and
- the Government's virtual *carte blanche*,

one of America's largest wave of business marriages is roaring on. In

1984 there were 2,543 corporate mergers and acquisitions with a combined value of more than $122 billion. In 1985 the merger pace quickened to about 11 every working day, and through the year it showed no sign of slackening. These mergers involved thousands of companies and millions of workers. The 100 biggest mergers of 1984 concerned firms employing 4.5 million people, or 4.3 per cent of the US workforce. If only 10 per cent of those people were affected in some manner, just 100 mergers altered the lives of 450,000 people, and as the boom continues it will touch the lives of many more.

It is not so much the number of mergers but their value which is so spectacular. Even in 1975 there were 2,297 recorded. In those days, however, only $12 billion were involved. In 1975 the megamerger, if one can use such an expression, was the acquisition by General Electric of Utah International at $1.9 billion. Nowadays mergers of this proportion tend to fall into the 'also ran' category. In the first half of 1985 no less than ten – for the most part successful – purchase offers were announced involving $2 billion plus.

The whole American economy is in the grip of a wave of mergers. One has the ever-growing impression that, following the boost in the oil sector in 1984 and the changes that have come about in the chemical, mass media, health and foodstuffs industrial sectors, there is not an area of industry or commerce that is safe from friendly or hostile takeovers. Even the banking world is going to have to get used to the idea that over the mid-term the thirty biggest institution are likely to have to expect some substantial changes. The legalisation of regional bank zones is not without effect on the financial industry.

The debate as to whether the merger wave is in the interest of the economy at large, is far from closed. The beneficial effects of some mergers are obvious. The Howard Hughes Medical Institute, which sold Hughes Aircraft to General Motors, got a $5-billion windfall, making it the largest private philanthrophic foundation in the world. Originally developed as a tax heaven by Howard Hughes, the Medical Institute will channel the billions into medical and scientific research, doubling its annual outlays.

Other mergers make lots of business sense. Allied recouped its $900-million cash investment within a year and earned nearly $200 million on Bendix operations in 1985, thanks to a booming auto-parts unit.

On the other hand, an estimated one-third of mergers in the past decade have failed, hounded by problems such as poor fit, bad management, poor timing and so on.

The board of directors must be aware of these facts and figures. While past evidence is not the only guide to a new venture, and a company can always hope to do better next time, if we do not learn from the past we are condemned to repeat the same mistakes. Dismantling bureaucratic regulations are not synonymous with a free ride on somebody else's property. The goal should be to establish laws of conduct which account for future realities rather than tying entrepreneurial hands. Only dynamic economies and fast-moving industries can survive. Let's make regulations which account for that fact.

CAN WE ESTIMATE RETURN ON INVESTMENT?

There is no conclusive evidence as to what the motives for increasing the assets might have been, but empirical investigations show that masters of the merger and acquisition business have clearly contributed to improving the performances of the managements of their *target objects*. Aggressive investors are capable of systematically pin-pointing undervalued stock and of turning companies around. As a Wall Street proverb goes: 'If a company is not the property of one majority owner – it is the property of the one who manages it.' And very often professional management gets complacent, interested more in its perks than in the shareholders who own the equity.

On that very subject of public shareholders, some research done by the Von Tobel Bank took the quoted rates of some stocks thirty days prior to announcement of the merger and compared them with the final takeover price. This proved considerable profits accruing.

● In the 1984 Texaco takeover of Getty Oil (total value $10.1 billion), the quoted rate of each share went up by 79 per cent.
● The $2.5 billion Esmark – Beatrice merger (also in 1984) produced a cut of 43.7 per cent.

More widespread research, however, whittles these record figures down to size to show an average rise of 30 per cent, which is also respectable, as the Von Tobel study documents.

Thus to conclude that every merger is a sure profit-spinner would fall far short of the truth. Many mergers leave the buyers with a tremendous debt to shoulder. In some cases the same thing is apparent where takeover offers come a cropper because of generous repurchases of the company's own outstanding shares.

If this second round of the merger game is taken into account then according to the survey carried out by McKinsey and Company, the picture is considerably less rosy. McKinsey applied two tests to 58 mergers effected between 1972 and 1983 to see whether the returns on the capital invested in the acquisitions had covered the capital costs. They found that half of the aforementioned 58 major acquisitions (1972 to 1983) failed to return the capital poured into them. But buyers, in other words, could have buried their money in the earth and ended up in better financial shape. Economist Frederick Scherer of Swarthmore College examined profits of 3,000 manufacturers. His conclusion: those acquired at premium prices produced lower profits than similar companies that remained independent.

Among the examples of mergers gone bad is Mobil Oil's acquisitions (made ten years ago) of Montgomery Ward and Company, and Container Corporation of America. Mobil sank $600 million more into Montgomery Ward. It has earned only $17 million since the purchase – and this has helped depress Mobil's stock price. Container Corporation has done little better, and earned just $1 million in 1983.

If mergers make economic sense, the share prices of the surviving company should continued to do well. But not always. Rochester economists found that a year after a merger, the bidders' stock had dropped on average by nearly 14 per cent. This contradicts some earlier statistics. For this reason, some companies have established a scrutiny policy for potential acquisitions, with return on investment rules computed in accordance with established principles. These complement other criteria such as growth potentials, compatibility, complementarity in product line, and so on.

The following is a list of principles used for calculation of rate of return of potential acquisition or of internal expansions and improvements:

- *Return* is net earnings after amortisation and/or depreciation of tangible and intangible capital assets.
- For an acquisition, 'return' is defined as demonstrable earning power less amortisation of the goodwill portion of the purchase price.

Demonstrable earning power is annual net earnings based upon reliable past performance and current net-earnings data, but adjusted for non-recurring special charges or credits, and also for added charges or credits to operations that would be normal for the future.

- For internal expansion or improvement, return is defined as incremental net earnings after amortisation and depreciation of the incremental investment.

● *Investment* is the total dollar value of total capital which must be employed to produce the return.

For an acquisition this investment is defined as the purchase price less the excess of the realisable net assets of the firm acquired over that which must be employed to produce the return – *or* plus the additional assets which must be invested to ensure production of the return.

● For an internal expansion, investment is defined as the total incremental capital which must be provided to produce the incremental net earnings.

The financing costs must be accurately enough computed. Financing a company's operations means much more than arranging a given line of credit. The rules of the game are changing. In the early years of the Financial Accounting Standards Board's history (starting in 1973), FASB seemed committed to reducing the degree to which management could control its reported financial results: greater attention was paid to the need for data to be auditable and to the necessity of avoiding dependence upon difficult, subjective judgements of the future.

In the 1980s, however, a new pattern was established, illustrated by the Board's first Statement of Financial Accounting Concepts: 'Objectives of Financial Reporting,' which underscored the Securities and Exchange Commission's (SEC) move away from its historical pattern of commitment to objectivity. Though the basic financial statements will continue to emphasise objectivity, a broadening range of financial reports will be composed of two sections:

(1) Hard numbers subject to objective verification.
(2) Softer, more future-oriented numbers, as these will be most significant in meeting the coming objective of financial reporting.

To satisfy such requirements there will be more detailed breakdowns of past-oriented data, with disaggregated information a pivotal point. In addition there wil be a growing demand for analyses of changes over time and for the presentation of data which will assist in understanding the patterns of cost and profit behaviour existing in the reporting structure.

For a dynamic company this will require a rather significant amount of detailed management- and technically oriented accounting information. At the same time, we have available today computers and communications systems which, when properly used, help meet the future-oriented challenge in an able manner. The general trend points towards continued expansion of management's responsibility to provide interpretations of the past and discuss explicitly the implications of the data for the future. This has not been the case in the past. SEC's requirement for a management analysis of business operations was the first step in this direction.

In the coming years, particular attention will be placed on the description of uncertainties, especially in those areas where historical cost is poorly correlated with economic value. Value-based data might move into financial statements, and will certainly be important to supplement statements with analytical disclosure patterns.

There might also be an increasing trend toward the provision of better descriptions of uncertainties which exist both in historical data and in future information. Superficially it may seem that this discussion has little to do with mergers, acquisitions, and consolidations. In reality the connection is much greater than it might seem. The future can act both as a stimulus and as a constraint in this process.

THE FORECAST DISCLOSURE

Today, particularly for technology-intense firms, there is developing a trend in the direction of more explicit forecast disclosure. While this might be restricted by managements, it seems *unlikely* that over the long run it will be possible to withhold, for instance, from investors the data management currently considered significant for internal decision making, and which it uses to control operations and evaluate managerial performance.

In an increasingly technology-oriented society, it is inevitable that at least the financial community will demand and get these data on a regular basis. In mid-1986 I participated in a banking meeting attended by the heads of the finance (investments, portfolio) and commerical (loans, current accounts) divisions of a leading institution. Here is a summary of the references being made:

● 'For me,' said the finance (investments) division boss; 'the prime criterion in investing is the future of the company. Our analysis is future-oriented – from management to products and markets.'
● 'From my viewpoint,' suggested the commerical (loans) division boss, 'the future prospects of the company is the number one issue

when we give a loan. The moneys which we advance are for the future, not for the past.'

These two statements should be taught in every classroom (and written in every textbook) on banking and financing. They should be the cornerstone of board decisions. From a continuing business viewpoint, a merger and acquisitions plan makes sense if it looks into the future – and strengthens the future corporate position in the process.

Once this is understood and accepted, the impact of these changes which we are discussing will be felt widely. What this essentially means is that the financial community and the well-informed investors may apply the same discipline to senior management as senior management today applies further down the line.

Another key issue is differential disclosure. The term suggests that different data are needed by different users of financial reporting and that reporting requirements should reflect these different uses. This is too tedious to do in a manual sense, but very easy and effective with computer-based systems.

The standard reporting format as we know it today should become computers and communications based. It should be interactively available, providing different data arrays for different users, including graphics, colour, exception reporting formats, and information which is summarised in certain areas and more detailed in others. Operating statements which report the balance between long-run average cash inflows and outflows at current levels of activity and taxation are desirable to supplement what is now largely cash-oriented accounting. Just as important are:

● simulators to project the future and
● expert systems to serve as investment advisors.

Furthermore, it is essential that standards for measurement (metrics) are improved, and auditing procedures not only involve the financial issues but also technology. All this will quite definitely affect the roles and responsibilities in dealing with financial reporting information – and with consolidation studies.

An acquisition's attractiveness depends on much more than:

● the cost of financing the acquisition, and
● the current and future profits of the acquired firm.

Yet both issues are very important. Certainly financial costs are now high. As a result, the potential return must also be high to justify incurring the financial cost. Otherwise, given the high cost of funds, investors are not happy with earnings potential. Well-managed companies have a capital plan that among other things specifies the desired long-term mix of debt and equity funds. However, individual acquisitions will almost always be financed with a financing mix that often differs from the target.

If equity is used and the equity/asset ratio rises above the target, debt capacity is increased, thus allowing further expansion of debt. On the other hand, the use of debt financing consumes debt capacity, thereby requiring future issues of equity.

Because funds procurement must be viewed in terms of the effect on the overall capital position of the firm, the financing of an acquisition cannot be linked in simple fashion to the acquisition itself. Dilution estimates must account for the overall effect on the capital position of the company and there are several possible ways of doing this.

This is not to say that the acquiring firm should not care whether debt or equity is used for a particular acquisition. Selling shareholders may prefer one form of compensation because of tax, liquidity and risk factors, and this preference may mean more favourable sales terms if one instrument is used rather than another. The purchasing firm may also have a preference because of different flotation costs, balance sheet effects and so on.

The point is that analysis must be in terms of overall *financial and technological* planning. Whether the acquisition is justified depends on the size of the purchase price relative to the amount and timing of future earnings, and on the technology one buys. Such technology should point to survival.

The able management of the late 1980s and of the 1990s will emphasise both effectiveness and efficiency: it must ask, does the way this company approaches technology assure fair financial results? Effectiveness will increasingly be measured by the ability to provide services and products the market would readily absorb. At the financial control side, this is consistent with the best auditor–client relationships in the past, but the implied technology will be analyses as an integral part of the reporting base.

Efficiency has different objectives. Are the products of *this* company obtained at the minimum cost technology makes possible? Is it using to the maximum the capabilities which are available? Is it ahead of competition in this sense? This kind of analysis requires some rethinking of the management approach traditionally used. It will be necessary to focus on the key technological areas which will be identified by a more systematic risk analysis, the latter being a major part of the strategic planning function.

This is the basic sense under which the board of directors should be reviewing the acquisition prospects. In an industrial era where the final product is increasingly upwards integrated, we can only gain real perspective in terms of the way in which the corporate functions effectively answer product development needs and marketing strengths by taking a long, hard look at the source.

CONSIDERING RISK, SUCCESS AND FAILURE

Looking into the 1981 to 1985 period, we can identify the ten largest mergers, consuming between them $70.4 billion. One was made in 1981, one in 1982, and one in 1983; but there were three in 1984 and four in 1985 (Table 17.1).

Table 17.1   The ten largest mergers, 1981–85

Partners	Cost (in $billion)	Year
Gulf & Chevron	13.3	1984
Getty & Texaco	10.1	1984
Conoco & DuPont	7.4	1981
Marathon Oil & US Steel	6.7	1982
Superior Oil & Mobil	5.8	1984
General Foods & Philip Morris	5.8	1985
Shell Oil & Royal Dutch/Shell	5.7	1985
Hughes Aircraft & General Motors	5.2	1985
Southern Pacific & Santa Fe	5.2	1983
Signal & Allied	5.2	1985

What will the next years look like? Predicting is perilous because there is not any definite foretelling of stock market or economic movements. There are factors that affect mergers.

In 1985 there was speculation in the United States that federal controls might be slapped on runaway merger activity. Forty-two bills were proposed in Congress to restrict hostile tender offers, but none was enacted. In 1986 Capitol Hill observers expected little, if any, move in Congress to inhibit the freedom of merger-making. Such a move did not happen in 1987 either, but if the economic and financial crisis deepens, it may happen. While the US Business Roundtable was lobbying unsuccessfully for new regulations against hostile takeovers, many of its members were completing some of the largest friendly mergers of the year. Of twenty-six transactions valued at more than $1 billion each, twelve of the buying companies were those of Roundtable members.

One of the strongest deterrents to takeovers in 1986 resulted from the Federal Reserve's proposed new restraints on the use of junk securities for more than half the financing of hostile tender offers. The Federal Reserve is concerned about possible adverse economic effects of such a heavy load of junk securities. In the first nine months of 1985, $11 billion of high-risk securities were used in merger–takeover transactions, an amount almost equal to the record in all of 1984.

Junk securities first appeared in takeover battles in 1984, but the first effective use of them came early in 1985, when Costal Corporation acquired American Natural Resources Company for $2.46 billion. Junk securities were used in six 1985 deals that were valued at more than $1 billion each. Two were hostile takeovers, including the Coastal Corporation bid. Two others involved friendly, leveraged buyouts. The use of junk securities turned around the textbook calculations about cash flow and debit financing. It also introduced a new and major element of risk, not only to the companies and the investors directly concerned with them, but to the financial markets as a whole.

A narrow view of the subject would suggest that one of the effects of mergers may be on companies themselves. They are issuing mountains of debt to finance mergers. Often this debt takes the form of low-rated or unrated (junk) bonds. Credit experts have little or no confidence that the interest on them can be paid and the principal retired, but buyers take risks on junk bonds because of their very high yields. The risk to the financial markets comes from two sources:

(1) The fact that a mounting corporate debt in junk securities superimposes itself on the nearly $1 trillion debt to lesser developed nations and to farms – which practically means to risk money.
(2) A panic which may develop out of a company's inability to repay its junk debt can easily spread to other debt markets – and it should not always be the Federal Reserve that comes to the rescue as a fire brigade.

There are other changes which come with massive mergers and slowly filter down the economic and industrial system. Honoured in the past as the basis for decision making, strict financial criteria are not today's approach. This is just as true of the acquiring company as it is of the defending one whose management is not eager to see the company absorbed by another and itself out of job. To keep raiders at bay, Champion, General Cinema, Hershey Foods and many other firms rewrite their corporate bylaws. New anti-takeover provisions are aimed at strengthening management's control. One device now in vogue allows management to issue new classes of stock with greater voting rights than those held by the shareholders. It is not one man–one vote anymore.

Harold Williams, former Chairman of the Securities and Exchange Commission said, 'The whole idea of corporate accounting to share-holders is being washed down the drain.' Understandably, stock exchanges are under pressure to ban companies with stocks that carry unequal voting rights.

Other research on the takeover front has focused on the effect of employment. Texaco, which bought Getty Oil in 1984, subsequently announced plans to trim 26 per cent of its workforce. This means some 20,000 persons. Chevron, purchaser of Gulf Oil, offered generous severance pay to 12,000 employees. In the past, labour unions merely protested over lay-offs. Now, they actively try to avert takeovers and save jobs. But nobody in his good senses would suggest that such union action is good for the economy.

There are success and failure stories. Some economists look at the wave of mergers and acquisitions characteristic of the mid-1980s as a valid way to revamp and restructure the economic system, given the unmistakable signs of stress and strain. The drop in oil prices has stunned energy-producing regions in America and hurt a wide range of industries, from real estate to banking.

Originally heralded as good news, the dislocations caused by plunging oil prices have become a drag on the entire US economy. From January to July 1986 the level of industrial production dropped 2 per cent. July 1986 brought several seismic shocks:

- the bankruptcy filing by LTV, a major steel producer;
- the failure of First National Bank of Oklahoma City, a large oil-patch bank;
- the $640 million loss reported by BankAmerica, which is saddled with numerous bad energy loans.

The First National Bank and Trust of Oklahoma City (assets: $1.6 billion) collapsed from the weight of bad energy loans. It was the second-largest bank failure in US history, after the 1974 fall of the New York-based Franklin National Bank. It was also the likely portent of another round of financial trauma in the oil patch.

Just two days later BankAmerica (assets: $117 billion), the number two banking company in the world, after New York's Citicorp, announced a second-quarter loss of $640 million. That brought the troubled bank's total deficits in the past fifteen months to $914 million and raised questions about its ability to survive as an independent institution.

But the most stunning news of July 1986 came the very next day. Dallas-based LTV, the number two US steelmaker and a major defence contractor, filed for Chapter 11 bankruptcy to keep creditors at bay while it tries to make a financial comeback. In terms of its revenues, which reached $8.2 billion in 1985, LTV is the largest US company ever to declare bankruptcy.

It is under this aspect that the wave of mergers and acquisitions should be examined. The scare of takeovers shakes out complacency. It makes company managers do a better job. Economist Jensen of Rochester argues that mergers force management 'to compete for the right to control corporate resources,' and therefore to make more prudent decisions.

Takeovers are a way to oust poor managers and install new ones – but, of course, there is no assurance that new managers will, in fact, perform better than the old ones. The only way is to keep the new management also under pressure, and that's today one of the main responsibilities of the board of directors. If the current board is unable or unwilling to do the job, somebody else will do it – somebody else who has the brains to see how essential it is to keep a dynamic economy. The acquisition entity should be careful to promote more efficient production of goods and marketing of services while holding down costs. Stock prices rise in anticipation of such benefits.

Mergers are good for the economy when well thought out, yet almost invariably traumatic for many who live through them. *They are benign and healthy when they help industries shed excess capacity and renew themselves, thereby becoming more competitive in world markets*: this means when the board of directors is properly doing its homework.

18 Government and Industry: Partnership or Conflict?

A solvent economic policy is one that balances the nation's financial, industrial, social, political and military commitments against its economic strength with a comfortable reserve of power. Seen in this light, the answer to the question posed by the title of this chapter should have been self-evident. But it is not necessarily a partnership we are talking about.

The first main obstacle to an effective government-and-industry collaboration is the entrenched bureaucracy. Bureaucracy was originally projected to manage the economy; it ended by strangling it. It is often argued in Paris that the French Revolution was not just against Louis XVI – who after all was a rather good king compared to his father Louis XV – but against the oppressive bureaucracy of the state. The king's head fell, yet the bureaucracy sprawled, and so did its defensive position.

The second main obstacle in terms of an effective collaboration between government and industry is that governments are slow to perceive the great changes taking place in our society – and their direction. A prime example is the uncoupling of the world's economies:

(1)   The primary materials (farm, forest, oil, minerals, metals) economy has become uncoupled from the post-industrial economy. This is primarily due to changing technology and way of life.
(2)   In the post-industrial economy itself, production has become uncoupled from employment. The knowledge society requires new skills for which industrial economy workers are not fit.
(3)   There is an emergence of a *logical* (symbol) economy, substituting for the physical (real) economy as number one.

The *logical economy* represents credit flows, exchange rates, capital movements. In the knowledge society, *financial assets are more important than real assets.*

These two economies will also become uncoupled – and will operate independently of one another. This new logical structure is of *world dimension*, and is *becoming the fly-wheel of the economy. Banks and electronics* – not steel, automobiles, and real estate – *are its pillars.*

GOALS OF A NATIONAL ECONOMY

The conflict between government and industry starts with a misconception: that steady economic expansion, created by business and industry, would give the government more resources to serve 'good causes'. But the time comes when the pie is not growing. This can happen for many reasons. Productivity is not advancing. The labour unions are overtaxing. Demands of government and private individuals, pressing on static supplies, are fuelling inflation. The outlook becomes one of economics of scarcity.

As we will see in the next section, even well-to-do economies can experience times of strain. This strain is more visible to some segments of the population, and we will examine why. The time comes when somebody has to pay the bill. Solutions are neither self-evident nor long lasting. Since the Second World War, modern thinking has been that we can relegate current costs to future generations. We now have full documentation that a society which attempts to protect every individual from paying economic costs ends up protecting nobody and burdening everybody – with inflation.

A second fallacy which particularly prevailed among the post-Second World War socialist governments of continental Europe is that research money is wealth hidden away from taxes by malicious company managements. Italy, for example, was taxing R & D expenditures till the mid-1960s. There is no wonder that even today Italy ranks last among the major industrial nations when it comes to investments in research.

Figure 18.1 reflects the results of a 1986 study which covered the 1969 to 1985 timeframe and focused on R & D expenditures as a percentage of gross domestic product (GDP). The US ranks first followed very closely by West Germany, Japan and Britain, in that order. France has done a very considerable effort since 1979 and may be overtaking England by the early 1990s unless the British R & D investment policy is changed. *Research money is money invested in brainpower*. It is the proper direction for a knowledge society. But there should also be tangible results from R & D. More precisely, income-earning marketable products.

Quite significantly, this is an area where government and industry can be in a partnership. *This is strategic planning*. Nevertheless, the excellent ideas advanced by the original 'plan Monnet' have been better applied by the Japanese than in its country of origin.

A joint strategic plan involves long-range forecasting and planning at the national level, to give direction and co-ordination. It also calls for partnership relations between four entities: government, industry, banking and labour. To be sustained and have a reasonable chance of

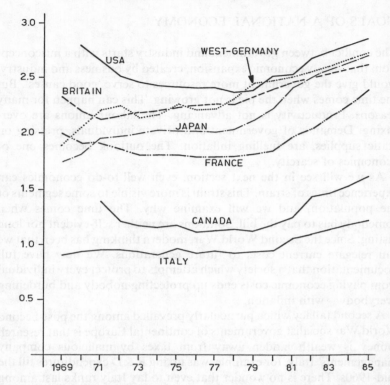

Figure 18.1 Research and development expenditures as percentages of gross domestic product. Given their export orientation, both West Germany and Japan overtake the United States in terms of R & D expenditure in gross national product percentages.

success, such a partnership should involve a worldwide strategy for export and investments, along with state-guaranteed insurance. And it should have a forward-looking orientation on the dynamic industries of the next ten to twenty years – while the 'big brown industries' are either fully revamped through robotics to become competitive, or shifted to Third World countries. The grand strategy should also include selective support to advanced industries through government-financed research projects. But it should leave the individual industries free to find their market position. The effort should be to prosper, but eventual failures are also part of the picture.

At the same time, corporate boards of directors (and their members) must understand that some of the major changes now taking place are

neither visible in a matter-of-fact manner, nor particularly well understood. One of the prime examples is the world-dimension of the world
industry. This is one of the most important developments regarding the
end of the twentieth century. As a result, the board's reference for policy
thinking needs to become the world rather than the national economy.

This is not unlike the change which took place in the post-war years
when the unit of measurement became the national rather than the local
economy in which a company is established and operates. While for a
company of large proportions the world-dimension may seem a
reasonable path, it may be tough for the board of a small 'local'
company to think in terms of the world economy. Yet this is not merely
an advisable but an absolutely necessary change. The company's
survivial depends on it.

What is more, protected markets will not only become of no use – they
will also be counterproductive. At the level of the national economy,
efforts to protect the home market are far more likely to cost jobs.
Greater unemployment will result from failure to grow in world markets
by becoming competitive in a global sense. The Japanese, the Swiss and
the Swedish seem to have understood this message. The Japanese do so
through MITI which provides a multivariant economic and social
analysis of the world's post-industrial trends. By enhancing the banking
sector, the Swiss cultivate credit flows and capital movements, effectively uncoupling the logical (or symbolic) from the real economy.

Another vital evidence of partnership between government, industry
and the most productive members of society – who also are among the
best paid – is taxation. Figure 18.2 gives some interesting statistics. Here,
Sweden fares worst of all European countries. A person making $50,000
as annual income, pays 80 per cent in taxes. The better off is the Swiss
citizen. At $300,000 yearly income, he will pay about 40 per cent in taxes.

Many governments take direct taxation as a process similar to milking
cows. Little do they understand that, like power, the money one makes is
a stimulus not only for more work but also for better work – as well as for
personal initiative.

PLANNING FOR AN ECONOMIC FUTURE

We said that a successful partnership to build the economic future and
move a nation into the twenty-first century presupposes the collaboration of many entities: the state, industry, banking, the labour unions,
and the citizen at large. Each of these partners is supposed to have

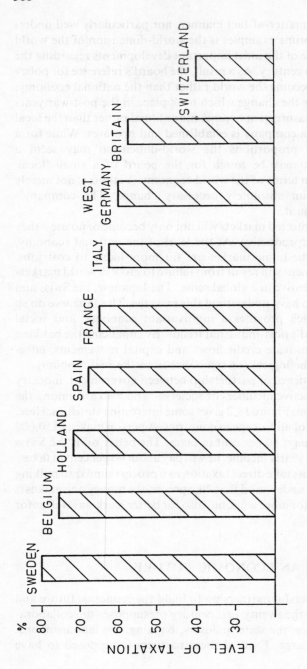

Figure 18.2 Tax rates paid by top managers in nine European countries. Not only top rates vary widely, but also the ceiling at which they are reached is very different.

control over its faculties, to be able to plan, and to critically examine its own:

● strengths
● weaknesses
● actions
● possible effect of actions.

This means a great amount of self-discipline. When there is no discipline, there is no future.

A strategic plan is not made in a vacuum. It is made against opponents. The future is technology-intense but let's never forget that technology is also available to the competition. Examples of competition catching up exist both at the business and at the national level.

In 1950 the United States accounted for 50 per cent of the world's gross world product. Its GNP per head was 350 per cent that of Western Europe and 1,350 per cent (!) that of Japan. Americans then had, on average, five to six times as many cars and telephones as Europeans had. In 1985 America's share of the world's gross world product was down to 23 per cent. Its GNP per head bettered Western Europe's by only 85 per cent and Japan's by 40 per cent. And the per capita ratio for cars and telephones between the United States and Europe was less than 2:1.

It is not that the United States stopped growing. The country is much richer and more powerful than it was a third of a century ago. Its real GNP per head has more than tripled in these years. But *the rest of the world has put on wealth and technology even faster*. In the two decades between 1965 and 1985 productivity has increased by 270 per cent in Japan; 160 per cent in Germany and England; but only 120 per cent in the United States. This has an effect on America's position in terms of industrial leadership. And the same can happen to any financial and industrial organisation.

When in the mid-1960s the then Chairman, Mr Moore, chose Walter Wriston to fill the presidency of the (then) First National City Bank of New York, he gave him some advice: 'Be brave enough to scare Chase, but not so brave to scare me.' The advice took hold. Twenty years ago, Citibank ranked third in assets among American money centre banks. It took more than a decade to overtake Chase Manhattan, and in 1983 Citibank leapfrogged the Bank of America to become the largest bank in the world, offering imaginative financial services. Figures released in early 1986 have shown that assets soared to $174 billion, up $23 billion from a year before, widening the gap from Bank of America by $55 billion. Here again, it is not that the other leading banks stop growing, but Citibank grew faster. One year's growth of $23 billion was equivalent to the size of the seventeenth largest bank.

Economics is a dynamic science. Rarely, if ever, do we step into the same conditions twice. At the same time our own well-being depends a great deal on what the other players do – or don't.

The fast-rising price of oil – a twenty-fold increase from 1973 to 1980 – forced major consumers in the industrialised countries to look for alternatives at a much faster pace than OPEC would like. Japan's entire cement industry has switched from oil to coal. Demand for oil dropped fast, with evident effects on oil-producing countries' revenues. OPEC and the other oil producers found out the hard way that the industrialised countries can move much faster towards finding alternative sources of fuel than they themselves can succeed in diversifying away from total dependence on oil exports.

And there is more bad news in store. World demand for oil from the cartel's thirteen members is projected to be lower than 12 million barrels a day by the end of the century – less than half the amount they are expected to be able to export this year. Gone are the wild forecasts of OPEC exports in the range of 40 million barrels a day, estimates that may experts were mentioning just a few years ago for the year 2000.

Mexico's plight with the 1986 sharp drop in oil prices is well known. But what about the Saudis? After a breathtaking decade, when rising oil revenues financed more than $550 billion in development programmes, Saudi Arabia is in the midst of a painful period of retrenchment, one that may last into the 1990s. After peaking in 1981, government oil revenues dropped sharply. In 1985 Saudi Arabia earned $43 billion from its oil sales, $70 billion less than it took in 1981. As a result, government spending has slipped dramatically, and the economy has been spending years in recession. Ironically, this might be good for the Saudis, who now have the chance to switch from a construction-based growth economy into a much more sober, production-based economy. This would be a transition from an economy in which government spending plays an overriding role to one placing much greater emphasis on the private sector.

Contrary to what earlier economists preached, recession and unemployment are not synonymous. The examples come from the West. The predominant type in a knowledge society is *structural unemployment*, which cannot be cured by the government's traditional pump-priming tactics of boosting spending or expanding the money supply. Admittedly, the term structural unemployment is a fuzzy concept that has no clear-cut definition. Generally, however, it refers to people out of work not as a result of a recession but because their skills do not match the available jobs. Even in an expanding economy, part of the labour force would turn out to be unemployed.

There is also the so-called *frictional unemployment*: people shifting from one job to another or changing careers; people just coming into the labour force and beginning to look for work; and persons who would rather live on unemployment benefit than do an honest day's work.

The most worrying is, of course, the mismatch between workers' skills and the skills needed by employers. Growing numbers of young people, particularly from minority groups, are joining the workforce with such poor educational backgrounds that they are ill prepared for most jobs. In the US motor manufacturing business alone, 255,000 employees, or 23 per cent of the blue-collar workforce are on indefinite lay-off. And there is the estimate that advances in microelectronic technology could cause 3 million jobs to disappear by the end of this decade. This represents 15 per cent of the manufacturing workforce.

Worst yet, governments have no comprehensive strategy for retraining workers displaced by changing technology. Instead, in the United States alone, an irrational patchwork of twenty-three programmes has grown up over the past two decades to help such diverse groups as unemployed railroad workers or lumberjacks in the redwood forests of California. Giving today's workers the skills for tomorrow's jobs will be a formidable economic challenge. But it also takes imagination and guts. No wonder that when both of them are missing, new terms must be invented like the *new poor*.

THE NEW POOR

The new poor can be people or nations. They resemble in most important respects the poor we have had always with us. The term implies recognition of the fact that the poverty born of unemployment is no longer confined to the working classes. Today's poor are drawn from portions of society which used to be immune. It can happen to people, just as it can happen to nations – if they are not careful enough about the future.

The world population explosion continues to place new demands on all economies; consumer expectations further add to the demand side for goods and services of all types; the political use of food, raw materials, technology and military hardware is even more important than before in determining world commodity prices; and there is a greater role of many governments in directing the industries of their nation either in a *state supermarket* sense or in a worldwide assault on the existing markets.

Every economy can have weaknesses. Seen at the right time, such weaknesses are subject to correction by the government, the industry, the banks, and the citizenry at large. Instead of looking always for the miracle to happen, the key players should be looking carefully at what they themselves can do to revitalise the operation of their internal economy. This is not a privilege. It is a duty.

Taking Europe as an example, the vitality, the dynamism of the European economy is not what it was in the decades immediately following the end of the Second World War. There is no doubt such vitality can be regained, but it will take more initiative on the part of governments and the business community. Like the early years of the Reagan Administration, European governments must take the difficult political step of cutting back social welfare programmes that have exploded in the past twenty years. The tax burden, which has soared to fund these programmes, must be reduced, especially for business – otherwise we will all become new poor. The tight regulatory system that makes business managers hesitate to build new plants, to move factories, to hire new workers is in need of drastic simplification.

The rigid labour market requires more flexibility. New imaginative measures are necessary to bring on the kind of economic recovery the West needs to satisfy the aspirations of its people, to bring down the rate of unemployment and to create a feeling of more hope, especially on the part of young people. The elaborate social welfare programmes of the 'state supermarket', nurtured by many European governments, have made unemployment quite attractive to individuals who lack ambition, have no spirit of enterprise, or don't put up the energy. This is not easy to change, but it can change with firm policies and courageous persistent efforts.

We cannot afford to continue doing what we have attempted to do so unsuccessfully for more than two decades, and with such disastrous results: try to keep alive yesterday and therefore miss tomorrow. Tomorrow's business is where the markets are.

In a knowledge society, the markets are shifting, and statistics have a convincing story to tell. In 1965, Japanese consumers spent 68 per cent of their income on goods, according to the Economic Planning Agency of the government. Today they spend 57 per cent of their income on services. According to the Japanese MITI, which oversees large-scale retailers, a study group on consumer behaviour has predicted that

Japanese consumers in this decade will spend even more of their money on services and distinctive, high-quality goods. This has already happened in the United States.

In a major departure from the 1950s, 1960s and 1970s, financial assets rather than real assets are the pillars of the economy. To the consumer's mind, services are more important than real goods. Coupled to the advancing technology, this trend is revolutionising our economy, our patterns of employment and our lifes. Take France as an example. According to *Le Monde*,[1] the 21.4 million people working in France could be distributed among the following classes:

- 1.6 million in agriculture, or 7.5 per cent of the total.
- 6.6 million in industry and construction, thus 30.8 per cent.
- 13.2 million in the service sector – or an impressive 61.7 per cent of the working population.

Yet, only 230 years earlier, in 1758, in their economic studies, François Quesnay and his disciples were demonstrating that agriculture was the only real source of wealth.

The more a country post-industrialises, the more its citizen become customers of other industrialised countries which are more competitive in the cost of production. The same is true for the purchasing habits of industrial firms and financial institutions. The shift in purchasing habits can have brutal effects, particularly for people, firms and nations who did not know (or did not wish to know) how to compete in the new environment. Awakening is often rude, and those who missed their *Zeitgeist* fill the ranks of the new poor.

If the world is our market – as it should be – we have to manage innovation and change. Here is where the challenge really starts. Most people, companies and states manage innovation by promise. But the successful entities rely rather on feedback and results.

Trouble is predictable. The trend is there and if we do our homework, we will see it coming sooner or later. The time to act is before trouble arrives – and the sooner we act, the better it is. Every concept, every product, every factory, ages – and eventually becomes obsolete. For the last twenty years, the pace has significantly accelerated. This is the origin of the new poor. Leadership in any nation, industry or financial institution is a matter of quality and concentration on areas of strength. What's our strength? Surely not the history of our grandfathers, no matter how glorious it might have been. We get paid only for strengths – not for weaknesses. Performance today is largely the result of the performance, or lack of it, of managements in years past. But such performance should not be gauged on a day-to-day basis; the longer term is what matters.

Change is a process embedded in the infrastructure of our knowledge society. The so-often-encountered resistance to change makes the adaptation more expensive. It does not slow down the process of change itself. If only fills the ranks of the new poor. People and organisations successful in yesterday's realities tend to be defensive. They fail to feed their opportunities and they concentrate on starving their strengths. A properly tuned strategic plan will do quite the opposite, as Figure 18.3 suggests.

This is the pace of the new society which characterises the end of this century and the beginning of the next. *Knowledge has become performance, and this means rapid change.* The rewards start from appreciating what this means, and then putting it into action.

ECONOMIC ISSUES AND INDUSTRIAL POLICY: THE JAPANESE MITI

I have often observed the preoccupation of senior governmental and industrial executives who participate in my seminars in Washington, London, Rome, Stockholm, Amsterdam and Berlin regarding the Japanese competition. The Japanese challenge to the American and West European economies is fairly complex and it involves long-term planning, modernisation, cost effectiveness, and also product quality.

On my first visit to Tokyo, in 1965, the Japanese industrialists were defensive. It was difficult to get relevant information out of them. Now the opposite is true. They give advice, as my study in Japan, of late 1986, helps document.

In recent visits to the United States, Japanese financial and industrial authorities have raised the issue that a good deal of the fundamental differences may lie in the contrast between the 'assertive spirit' of US industry, government and labour relations and the 'rather more co-operative' traditions of Japan. A Japanese industrial leader (Mr Okawara) was quoted as saying:

> I would guess that the biggest difference in the way the two economies operate is the role of the government in economic planning, or what is sometimes called industrial policy. Japanese planning is not planning

STRATEGIC PLAN

- MARKETS
- PRODUCTS
- SERVICES
- CLIENTS
- PILLARS IN LINE-
  OF-BUSINESS

C&C TECHNOLOGY

1. OPPORTUNITIES FOR NEW PRODUCTS
2. ONLINE TO CLIENTS
3. ONLINE TO SUPPLIERS
4. INFORMATION FOR KEY DECISIONS
5. HIGHER SERVICE QUALITY
6. LOWER UNIT COSTS
7. ORGANISATIONAL IMPACT

Figure 18.3   Necessary infrastructure for a valid strategic plan is state of the art implementation of computers and communications (C&C) technology. But C&C is no substitute for strategic planning nor effective organisation.

in the socialist sense. Rather it is *indicative planning*, which is in a sense the national equivalent of what every well-managed corporation does for itself.

The father of indicative planning is Jean Monnet but, as usual, the Japanese perfected the system. Between 1949 and 1955 Japan put together the institutions that were to catapult it into the economic big league. Unquestionably, the pivotal entity in this institutional structure was MITI, the Ministry of International Trade and Industry, which came into being in 1949.

The inclusion of *international trade* in the Ministry's title is indicative of the Japanese intention to guide resources toward the exploration and management of international markets. MITI is concentrating its resources on five strategic business areas:

(1) Microelectronics including PCs;
(2) Robotics and related computer products;
(3) Biotechnology, including new drugs and foods;
(4) New materials, such as ceramics and carbon fibres;
(5) Optical fibres/optical discs for communications equipment.

To promote small businesses in these four technologies, MITI guarantees up to 80 per cent of a $400,000 low-interest bank loan. MITI is also trying to create an American-style venture capital business in an effort to stimulate the Japanese economy.

As old-line industries begin to stagnate, MITI hopes to pick up the slack by nurturing high-technology start-ups with the potential to grow into big companies. 'Companies like Fujitsu, Hitachi, and Nippon Electric – which are in the forefront of technology – cannot do enough,' says Yukio Honda, Director of MITI's venture enterprise promotion office. 'We have to develop new areas of technology to replace industries of the past like oil, steel, and chemicals.'

MITI works very closely with many other governmental agencies, particularly the Ministry of Finance and the Japan Development Bank. At the core of its role lie eight separate though related goals:

(1) Establishing objectives and priorities for the Japanese economy;
(2) Developing the economic (physical) and institutional (commercial) infrastructure;
(3) Selecting target industries;
(4) Funnelling capital to target industries and specific firms;
(5) Nurturing target industries toward maturity;
(6) Developing the means to regulate all forms of competition within the Japanese economy;

(7)   Controlling the flow of foreign investment into Japan;
(8)   Managing the institutional environment.

This makes a full economic system.

Japan's industrial vision for the late 1980s and early 1990s emphasises three parallel directions:

● internationalisation of the nation's economy;
● overcoming problems of supply and the cost of natural resources and energy;
● achieving economic dynamism which will contribute to a better quality of life for all Japanese people.

Within this concept, MITI has designated a series of industries for special development and nurturing. These industries have been aided through financial, tax and technology supports and sheltered from foreign competition in the domestic market. An institutional infrastructure was erected to foster the chosen industries at home and to help them break into foreign markets. While the Japanese market itself is protected to a significant extent from foreign competitors, it is not water-tight. But it takes good planning to enter it. 'Expanding your exports to Japan will require careful planning, risk-taking and a long-term commitment to a very different and very sophisticated market,' Okawara said. 'Competition is very keen. Quality standards are very high. Language, customs and tastes are, of course, distinct from America or Western Europe.' The Japanese are noted for long-term strategic planning and careful implementation of that strategy.

Based on the premise (and forecast) that, by the end of the century nearly *two out of three jobs will depend on telecommunications*, the Japanese government pays great attention to the country's telecommunications infrastructure. This vision of telecommunications holding the employment key to the twenty-first century is so different from current employment perspectives that concrete actions must be taken today – not tomorrow – to maximise opportunities.

Japan is the only country in the world whose Integrated Network Service (INS) goes far beyond the CCITT[2] recommendation for ISDN. And besides, in Europe ISDN will take another 20 years to reach the rural areas, while INS will be available in 1990–91. Also, Japan is the only country with announced plans to integrate into the telephone exchanges an Artificial Intelligence-based simultaneous language translation. This, too, will be ready in the 1990–91 timeframe.

As Figure 18.4 suggests, Japan is making large investments in

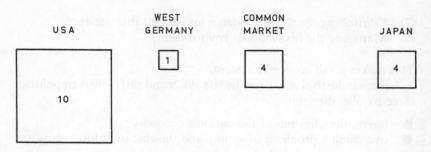

THE USA AND JAPAN ARE AND WILL REMAIN THE WORLD'S
COMMUNICATIONS MARKETS.

COUNTRY BY COUNTRY THE EUROPEAN MARKETS ARE TOO SMALL TO
SUSTAIN A HEALTHY INDUSTRY.

Figure 18.4　Relative size of communications markets in three continents.
Japan spends the same money as the whole of Western Europe in
its infrastructure. West Germany accounts for one quarter of the
European investment.

telecommunications. This creates an important internal communications market but also helps renew the installed telecommunications plant – a precondition for using networks to create employment. Japan spends on telecommunications the same amount of money as all of Western Europe, which has about three times Japan's population. In Europe the country which invests more on communications is West Germany – and it, too, spends roughly half in per capita investments as Japan.

The object of careful planning should be to provide a radically new kind of post-industrial strength, including flexibility and adaptiveness. Referring repeatedly to the effect of a fast-moving technology, the planning premises should be capable of answering projected requirements as well as adapting to unanticipated behaviour or conditions in the marketing field.

A high quality focus should be part of the flexibility. For example, instead of focusing on yarn, thread and low-quality fabrics as it used to do, Japan's textile industry is increasingly exporting high-quality woven fabric and even clothing. Where Japan is most competitive now, analysts say, is in high-quality, expensive synthetic-fibre fabrics.

The same is true with cars. The now old principle of mass production of the same (or very few) model(s) in order to swamp costs has been replaced. The new principle is flexible model design mapped all the way into manufacturing. The low cost is preserved by making use of increased store of knowhow regarding the robotics technology. At the same time, design flexibility permits the targeting of markets, tackling the sensitive cord in each.

Such a market-sensitive design and manufacturing approach should be particularly appealing to high-export countries like Switzerland and Sweden. In general, however, the whole European continent should be receptive to it. Today, Europe controls roughly one third of international commerce. This represents a major part of the GNP of every country. It is therefore easily understood that the old continent cannot afford a diminution of its part of the pie and of the whole pie itself happening at the same time.

Paring down the steel industry, as the Americans – even to some extent the Japanese – are doing, is one thing. The same is true of manufacturing less textiles. Such references are part of the change. But if these negative factors are not compensated by new activities in the upcoming growth field, then there is a decline which with time will become irreversible.

NEW FORMS OF CO-OPERATION

New forms of co-operation are necessary between industry, government, finance and labour in order to reverse a negative trend. Lack of co-ordination is damaging, and the bill is paid by everybody. In a university survey on the causes of stagflation in the United States during the mid and late 1970s:

● government actions, particularly regulations were given the most unfavourable verdict;
● tax policies were cited as the primary deterrents to innovation;
● the economic climate, characterised by inflation and shrinking markets was blamed;
● foreign competition and rising energy costs, as well as the spread of microelectronics, were credited with encouraging innovation.

The interviewed executives saw as a big boost to productivity the fact that microelectronic devices will be incorporated into traditional product lines; and that there will be increased use of computers for production, administration, design, scientific research and decision-making. The spread of the microelectronics revolution from the industries which pioneered this technology to other industries is indeed a dominant force for innovation.

One of the critiques Americans themselves made about stagflation regarded the lack of clear-cut goals and long-range national planning. 'The current national temper is that if you wish to have a gigantic goal, please demonstrate in this budget year how it will pay off in the next budget year,' said the director of NASA. 'It's a change in the national view of how to proceed into the future.'

Consistency in official policy is another issue. The average lifetime for an administrator at any high level in the federal government is eighteen months. As a senior executive suggested: 'You simply can't do a coherent, consistent program with that kind of lifetime.'

As cannot be repeated too often, one of the fundamental reasons underlining the need for long-range planning is that the infrastructure of society has changed. We have moved from an industrialised society to a new type of economy that is *based on information resources*, without appreciating the depth of the change. Yet about 60 per cent of all jobs in the United States are information-related occupations: from data processing to banking and insurance. This is $3\frac{1}{2}$ times the 17 per cent level which prevailed back in 1950. Clear-eyed executives properly underline that *the strategic issue in this kind of economy is no longer money – it's knowledge, experience, know-how.* Information is the new capital. It stands to reason that when one possesses the proper know-how he has a better chance of offering a service that is in demand.

This is precisely the premise upon which the new knowledge-intense industries are built. The result is to alter the competition of many sectors: even real estate is changing in shape and structure in a thrust of mass-marketing effort. Networks are the result. The information a national real estate network can provide to the consumer is keyed to what houses are available in a wide area of the economy, for what prices, which precise market. Networks can give a worldwide answer as to how many people might be interested in buying their own house when it's put up for sale, rather than limiting such sale to the demand existing in the property's immediate area.

The *informatisation* of such a classical industry as real estate is done in a variety of ways, depending upon the company involved, but increasingly firms utilise online terminals accessing US-wide databases. This is known as: 'resource pooling'.

'Before we can possess that which we have inherited from our fathers, we must first earn it for ourselves,' said Johann Wolfgang von Goethe – and that's what is now happening with the computers and communications intense environment into which we are moving. The recession which affected (and is still affecting) the whole industrialised West is highly related to the evolution of these new societal forms.

Ossified societies react very slowly or not at all to change, but dynamic entities live with their time and plan for the future the best they can. In January 1985 the city of Geneva worked out its plans as to what this sprawling metropolis will be in the year 2000 and beyond.

Another example is regional planning Scotland. As the steel mills, shipyards and coal mines that once befouled the Scottish air continue to decline, planners have turned to new technologies for economic salvation. They believe in Scotland's ability to match the best of US enterprise and Japanese efficiency. Heading this bid to draw new investment and promote new industries is the Scottish Development Agency. Progress is being made in what the planners call 'Silicon Glen'. Some 200 concerns in electronics-related fields cover what seems to be the full range of computer-age gadgetry, communications equipment and information systems. Among them are International Business Machines, Honeywell, Hewlett-Packard, Wang, Mitsubishi and Nippon Electric.

Statistics are convincing. The workforce in these industries is about 40,000 greater than in such older industries as shipbuilding and steel, and it is estimated that there could be 100,000 jobs in the 1990s. The Scottish Development Agency, established in the mid-1970s, is a hard-sell outfit. It offers generous financial incentives to the right business: as much as 40 per cent of the capital costs of getting started, plus training and research assistance. It is a good example of collaboration between government and industry.

In certain ways regional planning has become more aggressive than national planning. The formerly agricultural and now intense communications-technology triangle of Durham, Chapel Hill and Raleigh, in North Carolina, is a case in point.

North Carolina was one of the poorest states in America. For more than a century, Durham has been a tobacco town. But it also had Duke University. The University of North Carolina (oldest state university) is in Chapel Hill. At Raleigh, the state capital, is the North Carolina University. Between them they train 45,000 students. North Carolina has added a strong public education system that culminates in a 16-campus, state-wide university system and a network of 58 community and technical colleges. The state also operates high schools for students who excel in the arts (in Winston-Salem) and in maths and sciences (in Durham). The University of North Carolina at Chapel Hill, one of the nation's oldest public universities, was recently named as one of the country's best public undergraduate colleges and universities. Duke

University in Durham is considered by many as the best private college in the region; its Fuqua School of Business is often cited as among the nation's top ten.

The triangular area between the aforementioned three knowledge points covers some 5,400 acres. In these has now been established a high technology research, development and assembly only facility. One rule is to build on 15 per cent of the area, and keep 85 per cent green. Another is to attract know-how through the 'sunbelt pull'. For every 142 employees, there is today one PhD. Some 43 companies established themselves in the triangle, with 24,000 employees. IBM alone has 9,200 people, Northern Telecom 5,000, Burroughs 1,250. And there is no or little labour union activity – as is typically the case across the US sunbelt

Part of the reason for North Carolina's success comes from abroad, which is illustrated through the industrial investment made by Ciba-Geigy from Switzerland, Glaxo from the United Kingdom, Dynamit Nobel from West Germany, Northern Telecom from Canada, Siemens from West Germany, Kobe-Midrex from Japan, and Mitsubishi, also from Japan.

Another asset is the US banking and trucking industries centre located in Charlotte. Major banks are headquartered here, including two of the nation's 150 largest, NCNB (North Carolina National Bank) and First Union. Charlotte's banks handle a great deal of international trade, and the city is home to one of the state's four foreign-trade zones. Charlotte has grown steadily and, like the Triangle, boasts one of the lowest construction costs indexes in the country.

Apart of being the largest financial centre between Philadelphia and Dallas, Charlotte is also a large distribution centre, rating next to Chicago. And within 1,000 km from Charlotte live some 60 per cent of the US population. From the knowledge industry to finance, there are assets on which to capitalise.

Now consider the following issues:

(1) North Carolina (according to the National Planning Association, a private research group), will be among the top five states in population growth up to the year 2000.

(2) In one survey after another, North Carolina's metrópolitan areas such as Raleigh–Durham–Chapel Hill's Research Triangle, Greensboro–High Point–Winston-Salem, and Charlotte are rated among the best job markets in the country, with the Research Triangle area as one of the top ten boom towns 'you can count on'.

A 1984 *Business Week* survey of executives in 1,000 of the largest US companies rated North Carolina state as their top choice among places to locate a new plant. But North Carolina's reputation as a sunbelt star was not earned without effort.

What is true of regional planning is equally valid for industrial firms. The old structures are dying out, but adaptation to the new realities is not an evident truth. A study which has been recently conducted demonstrates that companies unable or unwilling to adapt themselves to the new computers-and-communications environment will find the greatest difficulties in the coming decade. The business failures in the 1980s, this study says, will be particularly pronounced among firms which have been unable or unwilling to use computer resources in an able manner: from client service to decision making. This should be food for thought for any and every executive: are we moving with our age or are we destined to fade away into the dust of history?

THE COMPETITIVE EDGE

We said that what is true of nations is true of firms, and vice versa. When we talk of organisations we make reference to living entities: their strategies can either be oriented to survival or to suicide. For the latter, there may be plenty of examples to cite. For the former, in the 1980s, there may be no better instance than Japan.

In the inland market, Japanese banks are willing to waive the requirement that borrowers put up collateral for a business loan. Because large companies are not demanding as much money as in the past, the banks are more prone to lend on business prospects.

There is also a loans strategy for the foreign market. Until the late 1980s Japan's foreign loans and grants were tied by agreements requiring that about 40 per cent of the funds be spent buying goods from its national industries, often at high prices. For instance, much of the aid to the Philippines until the mid-1970s had to be spent buying Japanese ships, highway-building materials and other goods. Like other recipients, the Philippines objected. Today, about 16 per cent of Japan's aid is 'tied' but the total amount of grants has grown swiftly. In 1978 the Government embarked on a campaign to double the total in three years. It did surpass that goal and spent about $3.3 billion in 1981, while US aid was diminishing and (with it) the influence which it can exercise in the world.

Japanese plans call for 40 per cent of this aid to go to five South-East Asian nations rich in natural resources which Japan needs. Several multi-million-dollar grants are earmarked to help Thailand and the Philippines develop energy sources. Japan offered each one a new technology training centre and launched two long-stalled industrialisation projects in Indonesia and Malaysia. The longer term aim of such grants is to establish a dynamic (not tied) 'buy Japanese' policy through the rich-in-response Pacific area, respectively replacing (and displacing) economic strongholds of US industry. The strategy aims the Japanese military was unable to reach during the Second World War seem to be on their way to fulfilment through an economic/industrial blitzkrieg. That's what von Neurath had suggested to Hitler before the war: 'If Imperial Germany conquered the world, the force of arms would have prevailed. But now is no more the time for the force of arms – but for industrial and economic conquest.' The Japanese follow the advice.

Confidence in an institution is created by its acts and its staying power; in fact, the one reinforces the other. The largest single factor of concern for the future is uncertainty in the industrial and financial markets. But when the acts of management demonstrate that this uncertainty is reduced through careful planning, confidence replaces the worry. Such confidence can be unsettling to competition as it destabilises the status quo. It is exactly in this sense that economic, financial and industrial reasons help explain why senior US executives (and government authorities) are so much concerned about the Japanese offensive. They are by far less impressed by the European competition.

The Japanese seem to feel the same way. Not long ago, Nobuo Matsunaga, Deputy Foreign Minister and Ambassador-designate to the United States, declared that Japan is so strong economically that the United States and Western Europe can't compete at all with its country under present tariffs. Japan, he added, received the strongest blow in the world as a result of the sharp rise in oil prices in 1973 and 1974, and has not only overcome the effects of that shock but has grown strong in the process. The logical follow-up to this statement is that the Japanese economy can cope with rather severe problems. And Mr Matsunaga added: 'The time has come for Japan to pick up the flag of free trade and take the lead in pushing for a new round of multinational trade negotiations. Our economic strength has changed dramatically. The United States and Western Europe cannot compete. That is the condition which has developed.'

Meeting strong competitors head-on poses the fundamental requirement of forcefully analysing how our image of the future can be improved. All decisions, from the most to the least vital, involve choice among alternative images of the future – and this requires information.

In sharp contrast to some European patterns, Japanese industry is in public hands. Steel, shipbuilding, electric power and much of the transportation sector are privately held. The Japanese system also contains built-in curbs on the proliferation of government bureaucracy, though they may not work to perfection. Figure 18.5 dramatises this point. For every 1,000 citizens, there are 160 (!) public servants in Sweden, 78 in the United States, 64 in West Germany, and only 34 in Japan. It takes effort to do it, and firm policies. In Japan, almost all enabling laws contain 'sunset' provisions, causing laws and institutions to go out of existence after five to seven years unless renewed by parliament.

The basic point here is that Japanese success is a powerful argument for less government rather than more. The times of turbulence in which we live demand efficient, contained, lean, market-oriented government – such government should limit itself to co-ordinating the changes required to restore and maintain competitiveness. This sort of government, with the low taxes and scope for private initiative, has been a crucial element in Japan's dynamic industrialisation and the switch which now takes place towards the post-industrial society. With its government small, Japan's burden of supporting the state has not been nearly as taxing as in other advanced nations, and resources have been freed to be used for private purposes, including industrial investment.

- Japan's effective rate of corporate taxation averages 7 per cent less than in the United States.
- There are extensive investment incentives in existence, including rapid depreciation for capital equipment.
- Personal income taxes are also low, averaging 10 per cent less than in the United States.
- Capital gains accruing from securities investments are entirely tax exempt.
- Japan combines minimal, low-budget government with a co-ordinated approach to economic management.
- Japan offers an environment able to foster economic growth.

As I have already underlined, the policy is to concentrate government support efforts on strategic sectors whose production serves a wide range of other industries. Industries such as steel, energy, shipping and semiconductors have had the bulk of government attention, oriented

386

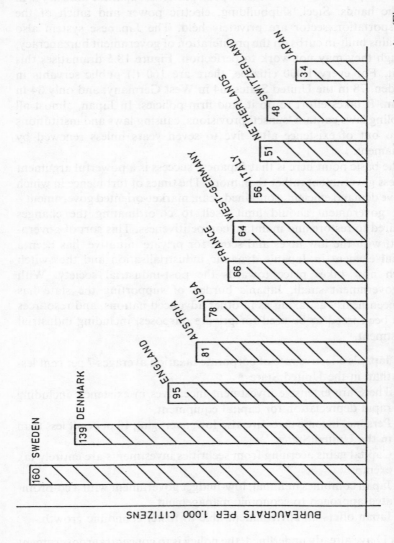

Figure 18.5   Sprawling or contained bureaucracy? This figure suggests a correlation between heavy taxation (Figure 18.2) and spending on bureaucrats the silly way. The result is an ossified environment.

BUREAUCRATS PER 1,000 CITIZENS

SWEDEN 160
DENMARK 139
ENGLAND 95
AUSTRIA 81
USA 78
FRANCE 66
WEST-GERMANY 64
ITALY 56
NETHERLANDS 51
SWITZERLAND 48
JAPAN 34

towards assuring that these sectors introduce the most efficient production facilities possible and adopt low-margin, high-volume production strategies which benefit sectors further downstream. Finished and consumer goods industries like motor vehicles and consumer electronics in most cases have received little direct government guidance or aid. The money has gone where it counts – to the industries of the twenty-first century. And there has been a valid approach to industrial policy focusing on the able use of market forces to achieve policy goals.

NOTES

1. 18 March 1987.
2. Consultative Committee, International Telephone and Telegraph.

Epilogue

The underlying message of this book is to tell the reader that rather than withdrawing from board membership he should go ahead. But he should also be prepared for it. Luck, a proverb states, is what happens when preparation meets opportunity.

In the opening chapter we examined the risks, challenges and benefits of board membership. Then we focused our attention on the need for applying imagination and clearly defining corporate objectives. This led to the reasons for strategic planning as well as the mechanics of making a strategic plan. Subsequently, the text focused on the business of the board of directors, both short range and long range. It then examined the qualifications for board membership and gave some profiles.

The Epilogue expands on this specific issue. Qualifications for board membership is the main theme. It is preceded by the concept of individual decision styles and it is followed by metrics and measurements that might be applied at the board level. While one might have put these issues immediately after Chapter 5, I chose to keep them as a conclusion. Prior to talking of needed personality traits it is proper to define the job to be done. This was the theme of Chapter 6, dedicated to the business of the board and followed by an elaboration of corporate policy and its strategic role. In terms of good business sense, this led nicely to the qualities a good director needs, and therefore the training perspectives regarding corporate directors. Subsequently the theme focused on satisfying the information needs of the board.

At a certain point in corporate life information systems dynamics become the weakest link on the work chain. In our *knowledge society* the board and its members depend so much on information that if the flow is cut, delayed or distorted they simply stop working and spend their days in a kind of idleness. Therefore the board *should be asking* tough questions about what the computers and communications department is contributing to the enterprise, and how it might contribute more. Information is vital not only to *manage our enterprise* in an able manner and keep in *steady touch with our clientele*, but also to face the savage competition for strategic products and turn our business into an international corporation. The world has become a unified marketplace. We need solid organisational perspectives to manage a multinational business successfully.

These are the themes being discussed in Chapters 11, 12 and 13, while

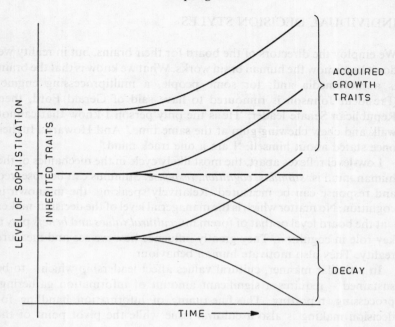

Figure E.1   Inherited traits can be manipulated through personal effort and environmental influence. The process works in three ways: growth, decay, and recovery.

Chapter 14 focuses on the big corporation's fear: litigation. It may come from dissatisfied customers, from unwarranted violation of complex and unclear government regulations, from insider trading, or from mergers, acquisitions, disinvestments.

Since our future depends on moving forward and not on hanging on to old connections, a chapter has been devoted to venture capital and the board's role in new ventures. Another major topic to which attention has been paid is that of a comprehensive consolidation policy. Finally, the vital question has been asked: 'Government and industry: partnership or conflict', and MITI was taken as an example on partnership.

Whenever we talk of strategic planning at the board level, of mergers, acquisition, disinvestment, consolidation or risk venture capital, we talk about the higher level of sophistication in the decisions reached by corporate directors. As Figure E.1 details, the hypothesis that inherited traits will continue steady as a function of time is false. *The decisions made today by the board members will see to it that tomorrow our company has acquired growth traits or, alternatively, will decay and disappear.*

INDIVIDUAL DECISION STYLES

We employ the directors of the board for their brains, but in reality we don't know how the human brain works. What we know is that the brain is a multimedia and, for some people, a multiprocessing engine. (President Johnson is rumoured to have said of Gerald Ford, then Republican Senate leader: 'He is the only person I know that cannot walk and chew chewing-gum at the same time.' And Howard Hughes once stated about himself: 'I am a one track mind.'

Low-level reflexes apart, the most likely cycle in the mechanics of the human mind is: *stimulus, cognition, response*. Stimulus can be observed and response can be measured. Relatively speaking, the unknown is cognition. No matter which is the managerial level of the decision-maker – at the board level or that of foreman – *cultural values* and *beliefs* play a key role in cognition. They greatly influence how we see and measure reality. They also motivate human behaviour.

In a similar manner, cultural values affect leadership which – to be sustained – requires a significant amount of information gathering, processing, reporting. The fine-tuning of information handling for decision making is also a cultural issue while the pivot point of the infrastructure is communications.

When it comes to decision styles, ten key variables enter into play and help decide the course of the mental process all the way to the final decision. As Alan Rowe (Professor of Organization and Management, University of Southern California. Los Angeles) aptly suggests, these are:

(1) Cognition and perception;
(2) Stimulus and response;
(3) *Culture*, values, beliefs;
(4) Motivated behaviour;
(5) Human information handling;
(6) Leadership perspectives;
(7) Interpersonal communications;
(8) Goal choosing and setting;
(9) Ability for problem solving;
(10) A factor of causality.

This factor of causality is itself a composite of other, more basic variables, the more important being the environment, opportunities, challenges, prevailing circumstances and strategic plans.

The Compaq 1987 strategy provides a good example on how these variables interact with one another. IBM has the PC-clone vendors on the defensive. In its effort to sell PS/2 models, IBM is correctly implying that in the future only companies able to share complex software with mainframes across company-wide networks would be competitive. The hinge is that if IBM persuades customers of this, it will hurt Compaq's following in large companies, whose purchases accounted for 45 per cent of this company's sales in 1986. As a result, Joseph R. Canion, the typically low-profile Compaq CEO became vocal. Canion's verbal aggressiveness is also aimed at cashing in on a golden opportunity. Since mid-1987 there have been some 10 million IBM PCs and compatibles in businesses around the world. Getting their owners to trade up to the PS/2 line may not be easy, even given IBM's marketing clout. (First, PS/2 computers use a different kind of floppy disk from the PC. Second, the new IBM machines cannot use the add-in circuit cards designed for existing PC. Third, the software that will let them use the added microprocessor power would not exist till 1988).

From cognition and perception to motivated behaviour and response, Canion's strategy is to make fresh inroads as buyers ponder PS/2. If he succeeds, he is likely to boost his market share again. Another motivation for this strategy is to slam the PS/2 now because Compaq doesn't have one to sell. Meanwhile, they will be cloning PS/2 in their laboratory.

The theoretical infrastructure in human decision making is no abstract notion or idle speculation. It highly correlates to the world in which we live. Indeed, it both derives itself from this real world and helps support it. Canion's statistics have been that since mid-1987 customers had sunk $80 billion into IBM PC, PC clones, the hardware options and software media that work with them. His perception most probably was that even IBM cannot redirect quickly enough a movement of change in standards. The business opportunity derived from this very fact. Hence the response.

The theoretical foundations of decision styles provide ample evidence that the whole process of decision making affects the person's behaviour, shapes his or her personality and greatly influences the course this person is following in future thoughts and acts. As we will see in the following sections, the analytical mind does not make snap decisions. An analytical mind needs to examine a subject or a situation in depth, using logical, deductive reasoning. Neither can he think in IF . . . THEN . . . ELSE terms. By contrast, this is the way the conceptual style is oriented for the simple reason that a conceptual mind is creative. It uses inductive reasoning based on judgement and beliefs.

QUALIFICATIONS FOR BOARD MEMBERSHIP

The most common qualifications necessary for membership of the board of directors are the representation of financial interests and professional expertise. Acting on behalf of the stockholders and other capital origin assets, like loans and investments by financial institutions, are the dominant examples of the former case.

The requirement for professional expertise is not as clearly spelled out. This is generally interpreted as the ability by board members to bring to fruition a variety of skills and experiences, including legal and consultancy expertise as well as top management functionality in other organisations. Typically, such organisations are active in similar or complementary walks of industrial and business life. While Dr Copeman *et al.* maintain that expertise in a given industry is not critical at the CEO level, my statistics and experience demonstrate that it is indeed very critical.

While there is merit in this practice, the truth of the matter is that most organisations don't take care to describe, much less define, what makes a good director. Nor can one find anywhere the answer to the question: 'What should *our* organisation expect from people qualified for board membership?'

While general traits can be misleading in a world characterised by steady and often profound changes, there is at least one common denominator which might be worth considering. This is the board member's ability to examine the critical factors that affect organisational survival, including *the capability to forecast and introduce change*. Board members must have background and experience to guess accurately the direction of events. The effectiveness of change depends on their qualifications for which no theoretical models can be developed or current instruments effectively used. But this may be changing.

Decision styles, organisation culture, the evaluation of values involved in a decision, and judgement on possible outcomes is at a premium. Though qualitative rather than quantitative decisions are the rule at board level, Alan Rowe *et al.* suggest a *decision style* tool applicable in the planning process. This tool assumes that each change agent operates according to a general decision framework. A model (shown in Figure E.2) has three axes of reference:

(1) *A perceptual and cognitive style* that deals with seeking, identifying, gathering, and processing information;
(2) An *observable effects* reference associated to problem-solving chores;

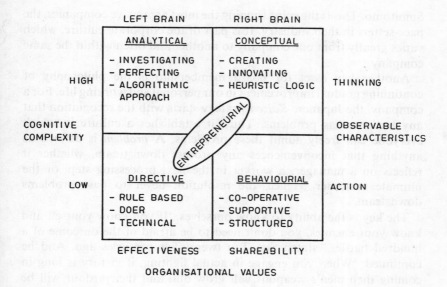

Figure E.2   Quarter spaces in managerial decision have been associated to the left and right hemisphere of the brain as well as to cognitive complexity and other observable characteristics (thinking vs action).

(3) An organisational values and *leadership style* which focuses on implementing and integrating.

Each quarter space, defined by this model, has characteristic strengths, some being more important than others for board membership. The effect of so-defined traits rests on the fact that a director interacts with various internal and external cultures relevant to decision-making situations. Even if most situations are unique, guidelines can be used which are extremely valuable in analysing a policy-making process, and in estimating the most likely outcomes of board decisions.

In a world characterised by turbulence, leadership style includes the often prized ability to make tough, unpopular decisions. 'You can't be emotionally bound to any asset,' said the Chairman of Gulf and Western. And this involves people and products. 'You need someone at the top who can change gears fast,' suggests Ichiro Isoda, Chairman of

Sumitomo. This is the spirit running the most aggressive companies, the pace-setters in their industry. It is part of the corporate culture, which varies greatly from one company to another and often within the same company.

Another key asset for board membership is the philosophy of continuing gradual improvement in our personal and working life. For a company, the Japanese *Kaizen* strategy starts with the recognition that any business has problems. Thus, it establishes a culture in which everyone can freely admit these problems. A *problem* is defined as anything that inconveniences any process downstream, whether it reflects on a manager, a worker in the next processing step, or the ultimate customer. Hence, the resolution never to pass problems downsteam.

The key is the ability to know ourselves. 'If you know yourself and know your enemies, you don't need to be afraid of the outcome of a hundred battles,' stated Sun Tzu twenty-five centuries ago. And he continued: 'When you engage in actual fighting, if victory is long in coming then men's weapons will grow dull and their ardour will be dampened. Cleverness has never been associated with long delays.'

Know ourselves and our enemies (or corporate opponents) does not necessarily mean every business move and every product proposal has a completely happy ending. There can be times when an idea would not work. In those cases the board should openly discuss the unanswered questions, – as well as the reasons for the failure. As smart investment specialists have found out, a key reason for their success is their ability to analyse the reasons for failure – and learn from them.

Creativity is nurtured only through freedom and a lack of intimidation. Enthusiasm and openness to all ideas is crucial to developing creativity within the corporate structure. Creativity starts with the recognition of good ideas. This:

● involves perception and sensitivity;
● demands total comprehension of the business;
● calls for analysis of what our competition is up to, what our manufacturing abilities allow, and, most important, what the consumer wants.

While to a very substantial measure the responsibility for these activities lies with professional management rather than board members, few can successfully argue that the board should not take an interest in them. They may mean detail, but as Mies van der Rohe, the architect, aptly stated: 'God is in the detail.'

STAYING INVOLVED: WAYS FOR RIGHT AND LEFT BRAIN PEOPLE

There is another good reason why the board should selectively focus on detail. For people at the board level, detail means staying involved. It means keeping antennae tuned in to consumer needs. Such hands-on technique keeps the responsibility for decisions about new products with the people managing the business at the top level. Above all, accomplishing most of what is laid out here requires working hard to stay entrepreneurial. The successful entrepreneur:

● understands the need for risk taking but is also continually conscious of the bottom line;
● realises the importance of building checkpoints and a tracking system into any plan to minimise losses in case of disaster;
● knows when a product is a dud and pulls out without undue delays or hesistation.

Within the perspective of this broader outline of tasks and responsibilities, the board member's job has three parts:

(1) Looking ahead, estimating, then establishing the future direction.
(2) Timing the corporate moves and seeing they are properly executed within a manageable time-frame.
(3) Maintaining standards and looking after both their observance and their improvement.

Board members should spend a good deal of their time on improvements. They must help managers develop a keen awareness of problems, learning both to qualify and quantify these problems.

In Japan, higher art is the awareness of *Warusa-kagen*, defined as things that are not yet problems but are not quite right. Both managers and workers are encouraged to report these issues to their superiors. One plant proudly reported that its workers had identified 650 'subtle abnormalities' in a single year.

Because this philosophy aims at constant revision and upgrading, it might be confused with innovation. But the two are distinct. *Innovation* focuses on rather abrupt and surely drastic changes in status, based on investments in new technology. The aim is a leap forward. Innovation is geared towards breakthroughs. The Japanese *Kaizen* is people oriented and emphasises teamwork and numerous small improvements, some achieved at no cost, but it is *not* innovation.

Kaizen trusts that if the effort is there, the result will come. So top executives will help their subordinates develop the right attitude. An underlying thought is that results-oriented criteria are a legacy of the mass-production age, and another that process-oriented criteria:

- time management,
- discipline,
- skill development,

are what is needed for the high technology and high-touch society.

But mental attitudes are *not* developed in the abstract. They are a reflection of our personal capabilities, thinking characteristics, and culture in which we live. These are factors shaping our thoughts in all spheres of endeavour, including that of corporate directors.

Notice that analytical and directive processes are associated with *left brain* (left hemisphere) functioning, but there is a major distinction. Analytical, creative and planning thinkers are able to cope with a high cognitive complexity. By contrast, the cognitive complexity of people who are best in technical, rule-based and directive roles, is rather low.

There is more that can be said on the functionalisation of the brain's two hemispheres. Spatial perception is the business of the right side of the brain and the same is true of speech recognition. Speeding is predominently the domain of the left.

This division of labour is known as brain *laterialisation* and can be found in many animals, – not only in man. In fact research results have been suggesting for some time that animal life has been lateralising long before living organisms were capable of verbalising. More recent studies have brought this subject forward by focusing on the reasoning abilities of human beings. Lateralisation is probably determined by genetics, not by the environment. But it is an environmental necessity which motivates us to interpret a stimulus correctly. This realisation goes a long way forward from what has already been known in a physical sense: that nerves are mainly contra-lateral. Right receptors connect to the left side of the brain.

Important in a social as well as in a managerial sense is the fact that the left hemisphere dominates when it comes, for instance, to responding to a distress call. In terms of decision making, a higher-up layer of reasoning adds substance to the qualification of analytical capabilities, as the preceding paragraphs have described.

The research conducted by Rowe is independent of the one reflected in Figures 1.1 and 1.2 of Chapter 1. But there is some amount of convergence and of complementarity. Bureaucrats tend to be in the directive, rule-based, mostly technical quarter space. As such, they lack perspective and are unfit for board membership. 'The trouble with American business is in the Board room and not in the assembly line,' Ross Perot was to suggest in an interview.

Cognitive complex people are able to integrate diverse sources of information, producing a meaningful representation of reality. Cognitively simple individuals process the available information differently. As such, they reach different conclusions about what has been perceived than the analytically thinking people.

What the two populations have in common is that *left brain* people look at inputs in a deductive logic, serial manner to reach conclusions, while *right brain* individuals consider the broader aspects of the inputs including visual and spacial reasoning as well as the perceived outcomes. Hence they follow a inductive approach. They generalise.

Right brain people are also divided in terms of higher and lower cognitive complexity. The former are conceptual, innovative, entrepreneurial. The latter are behavioural, supportive and prefer to live and act within a structured environment.

The point is that board membership needs both right and left brain people, but of the high cognitive complexity class. The company's directors must have the proper blend of energy and technical maturity on the one side, and intellectual breadth and business 'savvy' on the other. They must be very good at:

- evaluating situations as they change;
- keeping flexible, open to newness, and controlling the change;
- balancing innovation with stability, as the company and its products are in full evolution.

Members of the board worth their salt must be able to decide where the future lies. Having set the direction, they must have the courage to make frequent painful decisions, cutting new ground and guiding the organisation swiftly into its new environment.

'Based on a sample of two dozen Board Chairmen,' Rowe suggests, 'my data show that they tend to be typically either analytic/conceptual or directive/conceptual'. The duplication is obvious. A board member must be conceptual and forward-looking. Only then can he be of real service to the organisation he is leading.

METRICS AND MEASUREMENTS AT BOARD LEVEL

The first consistent effort to measure the results of labour was directed at the production floor. Known as time study, it started with Frederick Winslow Taylor at Bethlehem Steel just prior to the First World War. The so-called scientific management (of labour) continued with the motion study developed by the Galbraiths during the inter-war years. Time and motion approaches are not necessarily applicable to management, though the ratio delay study (of post Second World War years) might be.

Quantification is still a valid approach to labour productivity, but due to the increasing automation and robotisation of the production process its impact has greatly shrunk. Most importantly, the intellectual nature of the director's work does not lend itself to quantitative measurements of the sort of foregoing paragraphs have suggested.

● A ratio delay study would indicate whether or not a man is busy.
● It will tell nothing of the quality of his work and the imagination which he applies in his business.

There are however newer qualitative tools which can be used to advantage.

An example of a qualitative tool with applicability at the top management sphere of an enterprise is Rowe's *decision style inventory*. It bases its input on a response to twenty key questions to be answered by the executive taking the test. Two sample examples relating to persons ABC and XYZ are given in the Appendix. The derivation of personality profiles and decision styles has been assisted through a computer-based inference model.

Notice that in this inventory 300 points are allocated to a battery of behavioural and managerial decision traits. This is no intelligence quotient (IQ) test. It is a self-grading system within a well-defined environment of alternative choices. The more fair the executive is in his self-evaluation of general style and specific traits, the more accurate would be the result.

Right brain people put a premium on *shareability*. The guideline for left brain individuals is effectiveness. The intellectual capabilities of men and women in the bottom two quarter spaces (Figure E.3) are tuned to *action*. The trademark of individuals in the upper two quarter spaces is *thinking*. These are the best people for board membership.

Such references can be of significant importance to the life of a corporation. Having reached conclusions regarding the information

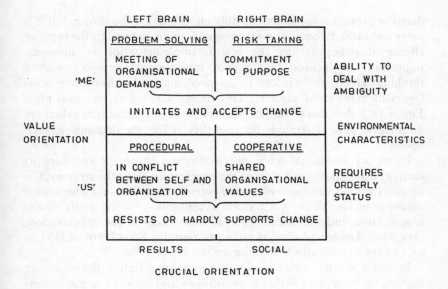

Figure E.3   Among critical factors of a value system is whether or not a person
initiates change, accepts change, or resists change. This is both
impacting and influencing the value orientation of an individual –
and of the organisation as a whole.

received, the decision-maker is able to make choices about the
alternative outcomes. Cognitive complexity and brain sidedness, Rowe
suggests, influence the manner in which choices are made. The more
simple people (bottom quarter spaces) prefer direct simple action. The
more cognitively complex individuals *want to examine many alternatives
and understand the consequences before reaching decisions.*

Board-level choices and subsequent decisions depend not only on the
information received and understood, but also – if not mainly – on the
thinking preferences of board members: action versus deliberate review
and the willingness to take risks. Choices made or to be made are often
negotiated, modified, compromised, delayed, depending on cognitive
complexity. Environmental factors affect the decision-maker.

Even after a board decision has been made about which alternative to
pursue, action has to be taken to execute the decision. This phase of the

decision process is sometimes as difficult as making the choice, but it is more technical. It focuses on a narrower domain, defined by the broader choice of policy set by the board. Implementation is, however, important. A decision that is not implemented becomes wishful thinking. Hence the wisdom of co-involving in the decision process layers of managerial support. This brings a value system into play. Figure 19.3 identifies the critical factors. In any organisation, values are an integral part of strategy because they reflect the decision-makers' beliefs.

In an organisational sense, the willingness to accept and support strategy depends on the values of the people who make the strategy, but also on the values of those who must carry it out. When and where these values coincide, there is a natural acceptability of the goals of the organisation and the commitment of individuals in the organisation, says Alan Rowe, and cites as counter-examples Ross Perot at GM as well as the culture shock shaking up the Bell system.

In other words, while qualitative and quantitative decisions are important, behaviour within organisations and between organisations depends on the match or unfitness between individual values, corporate culture, and management styles: if an organisation focuses on conformity and emphasises production and control while the individual is very self-oriented . . . the resultant behaviour is avoidance. This man or woman shows up for work but:

● At best, does as little as possible.
● At worst sabotages at every opportunity.

Just the same, when an organisation demands conformity and the individual is externally focused, the best possible result is a compromise. The person complies, meets demands, but that is all. 'Acceptance takes place when corporate values and culture is characterized by shared values,' Rowe *et al.* advise.

The critical factors of a value system can also be expressed in quarter spaces as was done in Figure 19.3. The main areas of reference are:

(1) *'Me' vs 'Us'*, in terms of value orientation;
(2) Ability to deal with *ambiguity vs* required *orderly* status – in connection with environmental characteristics;
(3) Focus on *results vs* social *aspects* in terms of a crucial orientation.

When they are at the beginning of their careers, and therefore unsure of themselves, most people start at the bottom two quarter spaces. As they reach maturity, the most willing and able graduate toward the upper layer (top two quarter spaces). The majority, however, do not make the move.

The leaders of industry and finance are found at the top layer. That's the timber the valid members of the board are made of. If they are right brain, they are planners. They have a more analytical style and are most able in determining alternatives and requirements. Both the left and the right brain references have important ingredients for board decisions. It is not enough that the chairman of the board, chief executive officer, and president, have entrepreneurial and executive styles. They must be supported by equally capable and mature board members, even if they reserve the final decision to themselves.

CONCLUSION

Together with analytically qualifiable personality traits and decision-making styles, a critical characteristic of board members should be their ability to live with their time. Computer literacy is a precise example, but it is not the only one. Equally crucial is the willingness to keep themselves and their faculties in steady evolution. In short, to remain active, be involved, look after detail.

Ours is an age characterised by technological progress. It outpaces anything we have known ever before. But technological progress is only one side of the coin. Market dynamics is the other. Every company, from the simplest to the most sophisticated, lives and operates in an environment in steady evolution. No board can successfully manage its company's business if its members permit themselves to get obsolete or distanced from steady innovation. Innovation happens in the market as it happens in the laboratory.

The personalities of the members of the board, their knowledge, information, drives, decision styles and, at the bottom line, the strategies and tactics they choose, make the corporate structure. They also affect the life cycle of an organisation, as Figure E.4 explains. In their early stages, organisations are often run by thinkers: conceptual or both analytical and conceptual individuals. During the growth phase, entrepreneurial people take over. Personalities change in the maturity phase and the thinkers move out during saturation. Whether the company will decay or survive depends on the brains of its members of the board and its senior management. If people in the two bottom quarter spaces continue to dominate, the downturn is unavoidable. For recovery, the company needs at the top the same sort of people who successfully brought it through its early stages and into growth.

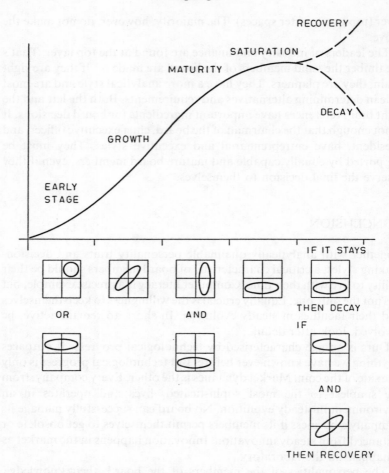

Figure E.4   Divided into phases, the life cycle of an organisation greatly
depends on the type of executives at the top of its pyramid. This
figure suggests different personalities that can lead the company
into growth, decay, or recovery.

This is a theme which preoccupied us heavily throughout the present
book. No healthy, collective decision-making body – like the board of
directors and the board of management – can live and prosper if some of
its members fall behind in a managerial, financial and technological
sense. *Good decisions are a matter of judgement. But judgement is highly
influenced by the steady upkeep of our experience and know-how as well as
by our appreciation of what a decision process is all about.*

Appendix

RESULTS OF THE
DECISION STYLE INVENTORY III
(Copyright A. J. Rowe, 1981, 1983)

Dr. ABC

PERCENTILE RANKING – BASED ON GENERAL POPULATION

PERCENTILE →	10	20	30	40	50	60	70	80	90
DIRECTIVE		—★—							
ANALYTICAL					—★—				
CONCEPTUAL								—★—	
BEHAVIORAL		—★—							

DOMINANCE →	LEAST EMPHASIS	BACK UP	DOMINANT	VERY DOMINANT

* * * * * * OVERALL CHARACTERISTICS * * * * * *

LOGICAL AND RELATIONAL

IDEAS ORIENTED

* * * * * * * * DETAILED ANALYSIS * * * * * * * *

The following analysis presents your style(s) in decreasing
order of dominance. The greater the dominance,
the more often that style is used.

* * * *DOMINANT* * * *

CONCEPTUAL – RELATIONALLY ORIENTED

HEURISTIC LOGIC:
Uses inductive reasoning.
Considers many options.

CREATIVE THINKER:
Looks for new ideas.
Is very independent, artistic, and willing to take risks. Expects recognition.

CONCEPTUAL – IDEAS ORIENTED

BROAD THINKER:
Sees many alternatives.
Is observant, able to visualize consequences, and future oriented.

IMAGINATIVE:
Finds new approaches to problems that have not been tried before.
Willing to stick neck out.

YOUR APPROACH TO PROBLEM SOLVING IS CHARACTERIZED BY:

Taking diverse cues and producing a meaningful picture, creating new ideas, considering many aspects and consequences of solutions, finding acceptable compromise rather than the best answer, and looking for multiple options.

YOUR COMMUNICATIONS STYLE IS CHARACTERIZED BY:

Considering all possible alternatives, taking a broad view which considers the consequences of actions, being able to negotiate and compromise, talking things out with others, use of visual presentations or pictures, and open discussion.

YOUR LEADERSHIP STYLE IS CHARACTERIZED BY:

Enjoying meeting with people and discussing work to be done. Compromising and sharing decisions.

* * * * BACKUP * * * *

ANALYTICAL – LOGICALLY ORIENTED

PROBLEM SOLVER:
Finds new ways of solving problems.

ANALYTICAL – IDEAS ORIENTED

INNOVATIVE THINKER:
Enjoys problem solving.

YOUR APPROACH TO PROBLEM SOLVING IS CHARACTERIZED BY:

Relying on great detail and careful analysis in finding solutions.

YOUR COMMUNICATIONS STYLE IS CHARACTERIZED BY:

Using carefully prepared material.

YOUR LEADERSHIP STYLE IS CHARACTERIZED BY:

Preferring to receive reports rather than direct interaction. Expecting others to follow up on work assigned.

* * * FLEXIBILITY IN CHANGING YOUR STYLE * * *

You are moderately able to change your outlook.

* * YOUR PREFERENCE FOR JOBS WILL TEND TO BE * * IN ONE OR MORE OF THE FOLLOWING:

Upper management, staff specialist, architect, or professions involving design.

* * * * SUMMARY * * * *

You NORMALLY use the following style:

CONCEPTUAL (RELATIONAL – IDEAS ORIENTED)

You MAY ALSO OCCASIONALLY use the following style:

ANALYTICAL (LOGICAL – IDEAS ORIENTED)

RESULTS OF THE
DECISION STYLE INVENTORY III
(Copyright A. J. Rowe, 1981, 1983)

Mrs. XYZ (Assistant to Dr ABC)

PERCENTILE RANKING – BASED ON GENERAL POPULATION

PERCENTILE →	10	20	30	40	50	60	70	80	90
DIRECTIVE					—★—				
ANALYTICAL	—★—								
CONCEPTUAL	—★—								
BEHAVIORAL							—★—		

DOMINANCE →	LEAST EMPHASIS	BACK UP	DOMINANT	VERY DOMINAN

* * * * * * OVERALL CHARACTERISTICS * * * * * *

LOGICAL AND RELATIONAL

ACTION ORIENTED

* * * * * * * DETAILED ANALYSIS * * * * * * *

The following analysis presents your style(s) in decreasing
order of dominance. The greater the dominance,
the more often that style is used.

* * * VERY DOMINANT * * *

BEHAVIORAL – RELATIONALLY ORIENTED

FEELING:
Wants to be secure.
Does not argue.
Delays making decisions, wants acceptance, is receptive to ideas, and is easily swayed.

INSTINCTIVE:
Reacts to situations and people using natural instincts.
Is sensitive.
Is receptive to ideas.

BEHAVIORAL – ACTION ORIENTED

AMIABLE:
Enjoys interacting with others.
Is concerned about the organization.
Good at negotiating. Is sensitive to the needs of others.

SUPPORTIVE:
Empathetic to the needs of others.
Cannot say 'no' to most requests.
A good listener and willing helper. Shows deep concern for humanity.

YOUR APPROACH TO PROBLEM SOLVING IS CHARACTERIZED BY:

Relying heavily on feelings and instinct, using limited information, avoiding confrontation and conflict, and looking for multiple options.

YOUR COMMUNICATIONS STYLE IS CHARACTERIZED BY:

Meeting people face to face and interacting with them, limited use of written reports, and concern about people's feelings.

YOUR LEADERSHIP STYLE IS CHARACTERIZED BY:

Wanting others to accept your ideas and suggestions. Using persuasion and explanations.

* * * BACKUP * * *

DIRECTIVE – LOGICALLY ORIENTED

Focused and results oriented.

DIRECTIVE – ACTION ORIENTED

Needs structure and clear definition. Identifies with the organization.

YOUR APPROACH TO PROBLEM SOLVING IS CHARACTERIZED BY:

Primarily considering current problems and acting quickly to find an answer.

YOUR COMMUNICATIONS STYLE IS CHARACTERIZED BY:

Oral communications.

YOUR LEADERSHIP STYLE IS CHARACTERIZED BY:

Preferring direct interaction and expecting others to perform as directed.

* * * FLEXIBILITY IN CHANGING YOUR STYLE * * *

You are moderately able to change your outlook.

* * YOUR PREFERENCE FOR JOBS WILL TEND TO BE * * IN ONE OR MORE OF THE FOLLOWING:

Professions involving sales, emergency operations, or people oriented work requiring action or results.

* * * * SUMMARY * * * *

You NORMALLY use the following style:

BEHAVIORAL (RELATIONAL – ACTION ORIENTED)

You MAY ALSO OCCASIONALLY use the following style:

DIRECTIVE (LOGICAL – ACTION ORIENTED)

Index

409